| DATE | | | |
|---|---|---|---|
| | | | |
| | | | |
| | | | |
| | | | |
| | | | |
| | | | |
| | | | |
| | | | |
| | | | |
| | | | |
| | | | |
| | | | |
| | | | |
| | | | |

# Classics In
# Child Development

# Classics In
# Child Development

*Advisory Editors*

**JUDITH KRIEGER GARDNER**
**HOWARD GARDNER**

*Editorial Board*

# STUDIES IN THE NATURE
# OF CHARACTER

I

## STUDIES IN DECEIT

BOOK ONE

GENERAL METHODS AND RESULTS

HUGH HARTSHORNE AND MARK A. MAY

ARNO PRESS

A New York Times Company

New York — 1975

Reprint Edition 1975 by Arno Press Inc.

Reprinted from a copy in
  The Clark University Library

Classics in Child Development
ISBN for complete set: 0-405-06450-0
See last pages of this volume for titles.

Manufactured in the United States of America

————◆————

Library of Congress Cataloging in Publication Data

Hartshorne, Hugh, 1885-
    Studies in deceit.

    (Classics in child development)  (Studies in the
nature of character ; 1)
    Reprint of the ed. published by Macmillan, New York.
    Includes index.
    1.  Honesty.  2.  Child study.  I.  May, Mark Arthur,
1891-    joint author.  II.  Title.  III.  Series.
IV.  Series: Columbia University.  Teachers College.
Studies in the nature of character ; 1.
BF723.H7H37 1975          155.4'18          74-21415
ISBN 0-405-06465-9

# STUDIES IN DECEIT

THE MACMILLAN COMPANY
NEW YORK · BOSTON · CHICAGO · DALLAS
ATLANTA · SAN FRANCISCO

MACMILLAN & CO., LIMITED
LONDON · BOMBAY · CALCUTTA
MELBOURNE

THE MACMILLAN CO. OF CANADA, LTD.
TORONTO

# STUDIES IN THE NATURE OF CHARACTER

BY THE

CHARACTER EDUCATION INQUIRY
TEACHERS COLLEGE, COLUMBIA UNIVERSITY

IN COÖPERATION WITH

THE INSTITUTE OF SOCIAL AND RELIGIOUS RESEARCH

## I
## STUDIES IN DECEIT

BOOK ONE
GENERAL METHODS AND RESULTS
HUGH HARTSHORNE AND MARK A. MAY

New York

THE MACMILLAN COMPANY

1928

Norwood Press
J. S. Cushing Co. — Berwick & Smith Co.
Norwood, Mass., U.S.A.

# FOREWORD

THE first definite proposal leading directly to the inauguration of the Character Education Inquiry came from the Religious Education Association. For many years the problem of how to evaluate the results of moral education objectively had been discussed at its annual meetings and definite proposals had been drawn up from time to time for the conduct of researches in this field. At the 1922 meeting the interest in these studies took the form of a resolution to attempt a careful and scientific investigation of the question, "How is religion being taught to young people and with what effect?" In following up this resolution, the late Dr. Henry F. Cope, who was then Secretary of the Association, wrote to the Institute of Social and Religious Research in May, 1922, asking for a grant for the prosecution of such a study. At the moment, however, since a statement of methods to be employed in the proposed study had not yet been prepared, the Institute decided to take no decisive step.

Meanwhile, in October, 1922, the Committee on Curriculum of the International Lessons Committee asked the Institute to provide funds for a critical study of curriculum material; and in November, 1922, the Bureau of Research Service of the International Council of Religious Education requested a grant for three successive years to carry on investigations in the field of religious education.

Confronted with these three requests touching the same general field, the Executive Secretary of the Institute of Social and Religious Research called an informal conference of representatives of the three petitioning organizations. The conference recommended that the Institute call a larger meeting, of experts, in order to discuss the entire subject of research in religious education and arrive at a judgment as to the best course to pursue.

There was therefore assembled in New York on January 6, 1923, a group of twelve specialists in religious and general education and in psychology under the chairmanship of the late President Ernest

D. Burton. After prolonged discussion recommendations in substance as follows were adopted:

1. Study the actual experiences of children which have moral and religious significance and the effects for periods of time of the moral and religious influences to which children, youth, and adults have been exposed.
2. Apply the objective methods of the laboratory to the measurement of conduct under controlled conditions.
3. Engage one or more full-time investigators and associate with them advisers and assistants.
4. Secure collaboration by various institutions and groups.
5. Make the results of the study available in both technical and popular forms.

The direction and location of the study was then made the subject of an extended inquiry by the Institute. In the spring of 1924, it secured the consent of Dr. Hugh Hartshorne, then Professor of Religious Education at the University of Southern California, and of Dr. Mark A. May, then Professor of Psychology at Syracuse University, to serve as co-directors. At the same time Teachers College, Columbia University, agreed to undertake the project as "an inquiry into character education with particular reference to religious education," and it was placed under the immediate supervision of Professor Edward L. Thorndike as director of the Division of Psychology of the Institute of Educational Research. The two investigators were thereupon appointed to the college staff.

In order to provide the investigators with effective advice and counsel, the Institute of Social and Religious Research and the College joined in the appointment of a group of advisers for the Inquiry. The original list is as follows:

| | |
|---|---|
| Ernest D. Burton | E. Morris Fergusson |
| Otis W. Caldwell | Galen M. Fisher |
| George A. Coe | Edward L. Thorndike |
| Harrison Elliott | Luther A. Weigle |
| Mary R. Ely (Mrs. E. W. Lyman) | |

Upon the death of President Ernest D. Burton, Professor Paul Monroe was asked to serve in his place.

The agreement with Teachers College called for a three-year study, to begin September 1, 1924, the entire funds being supplied by the Institute of Social and Religious Research. In June, 1926, the directors of the Institute, after reviewing the progress made to date and in accordance with the recommendation of the advisers, voted to supply funds for the continuation of the Inquiry for two additional years, making five years in all.

GALEN M. FISHER, Executive Secretary
Institute of Social and Religious Research

# ACKNOWLEDGMENTS

I⊤ would give the investigators great satisfaction to name the schools, the principals, and the teachers who have coöperated with the Inquiry. Unfortunately the nature of the material makes this undesirable, as it would enable anyone to identify the institutions where testing has been done and permit hasty comparisons and conclusions that might be not only invidious but quite unwarranted by the facts. These generous friends must therefore remain anonymous.

The advisers informally asked to coöperate with the investigators, whose names are given in the Foreword, have been astonishingly prodigal of their time in reading lengthy reports and attending meetings. And besides these official appointees there are many others to whom the investigators have turned for counsel both at Teachers College and elsewhere.

Dr. Thorndike, the administrative head of the Division of Psychology of the Institute of Educational Research, Teachers College, has always been available for the helpful criticism for which he is so justly famous, and his staff has been ready at all times to assist in field work. We are particularly indebted to Dr. Ella Woodyard, who not only read the entire set of proofs but who has also aided our work in many other ways.

The staff of the Inquiry has been unusual in its quality and faithfulness, and, as always in work of this kind, it has shouldered the bulk of the drudgery.

The manuscript of Book One was read by Mrs. W. W. Rockwell, and many changes in language and style were made as the result of her careful criticism.

This has been a coöperative enterprise with many co-workers, with all of whom the investigators are glad to share such credit as the Inquiry may deserve.

We have quoted freely from three of our published articles with the kind permission of the publications in which they have appeared:

"The Objective Measurement of Character," *Pedagogical Seminary*, March, 1925

"First Steps toward a Scale for Measuring Attitudes," *Journal of Educational Psychology*, March, 1926

"Sibling Resemblance in Deception," *Twenty-Seventh Yearbook*, National Society for the Study of Education, Public School Publishing Company

We are also under obligation to Teachers College, Columbia University, to the C. H. Stoelting Company, to the Institute for Child Guidance, and to the Public School Publishing Company for permission to quote from published material under their control.

H. H.
M. A. M.

New York,
October 1, 1927.

# CONTENTS OF BOOK ONE*

PART II

PART III

MORAL VALUES IN CONTEMPORARY EDUCATION

PART IV

GENERAL CONCLUSIONS AND PROBLEMS

# TABLES

# FIGURES

# INTRODUCTION

# STUDIES IN DECEIT

## INTRODUCTION

## THE SCOPE AND METHOD OF THE INQUIRY

The Character Education Inquiry was undertaken by Teachers College at the request of the Institute of Social and Religious Research. From the beginning there has been the most generous regard for the freedom of the investigators. Beyond defining in a general way the major field of study, no stipulation was made as to the problems to be attacked or the techniques to be used. We were asked to undertake a basic research and were left free to determine its nature and scope. Very wisely, however, a group of advisers was provided to which we could present our plans for appraisal at any stage of the enterprise.

We began in the fall of 1924 with two immediately practicable projects — a study of deception, and a beginning in the use of tests of moral knowledge and attitude. Our hope was that in executing these projects we might learn something of the possibilities of research in the highly intangible field of character study, and could mature plans for the entire period. They proved to be admirably adapted to these purposes.

In connection with these preliminary skirmishes it was necessary to make a thorough review of character testing, and a more cursory examination of other methods of studying the problems of moral and religious education. We found, as was to be expected, a disheartening lack of *method* in research, and became increasingly convinced that the best contribution we could make in the time at our disposal was precisely at this point.

This field of work may be seen in perspective as section five of the following classification of various approaches that might be made to the study of education for character:

I. Philosophical-psychological research concerning personality, society, growth, and, more specifically, the nature of character and the process of its formation

II. Historical research regarding
   A. *Theories* of character from the standpoint of modern psychology and social science
   B. Comparative study of historic *methods* of developing character
   C. Evaluation of methods of measuring character

III. Surveys, including more particularly
   A. Critical examination of current methods of moral and religious education
   B. Critical study of contemporary character in all its aspects, as exhibited in population groups distinguished by age, mental age, sex, location, standard of living, education, denomination, etc.

IV. Experimental control of specific processes of moral and religious education for the purpose of discovering and formulating improvements in method

V. Methodology. Research in the technique of research, or the creating of the tools for carrying on the above inquiries. The following research methods are being used in the study of character, but all of them need refinement and standardization as a necessary condition of thoroughly scientific work:
   A. Biography and fiction
   B. Observation
   C. Questionnaire methods
   D. Case histories
   E. Rating methods
   F. Testing and measurement
   G. Analysis
   H. Laboratory experimentation

## REASONS FOR THE APPROACH CHOSEN

We were brought to our decision to make methodology with special reference to testing and measurement our primary interest by several considerations. In the first place, circumstances imposed certain natural limitations. Originally planned for a three-year term and subsequently extended to five years, the investigation had to be confined to such problems and methods as gave promise of results within the time allotted. The historical antecedents of the research, as outlined by Mr. Fisher in the Foreword, suggested the further limitation of the study to problems which were of concern to leaders in the field of moral and religious education. In view of the fact that many researches were being carried on in the same field, we felt that it was particularly important not only to avoid duplication of effort but also to undertake a genuinely basic study. The experience of the investigators set further practical boundaries to the ground that could be covered.

In the second place, many facts pointed to testing and measurement as the most strategic point of attack. Not only is this relatively neglected approach basic to any fresh scientific research into the nature of character and its manner of growth, but studies of the relative value of current methods of moral and religious education and experiments to discover improvements in technique depend to a degree rarely appreciated on the availability of ways of *measuring results*. Theories of ethical training, furthermore, suffer from lack of data concerning the causal concomitants of specific behaviors and attitudes, and plans and programs are produced by the score which have no experimental basis and which are as likely to damage character as to improve it. Hundreds of millions of dollars are probably spent annually by churches, Sunday schools, and other organizations for children and youth with almost no check on the product — a negligence of which no modern industry would be guilty, and which the public schools have rather generally outgrown so far as routine school work is concerned. Nevertheless, although tests exist for predicting success in particular school studies, in school work in general, and in various occupations, which have real value in saving the time of individuals and the money of the school system, yet there are no tests for predicting success in living. For lack of them a vast amount of time and no one knows how much money are probably thrown away on expensive and intricate devices for moral and religious education, and on more or less futile attempts to live well in a world whose problems people are inadequately prepared to meet.

In the third place, there was available to us for measuring social behavior the experience in the building and use of achievement tests accumulated during the last twenty-five years.

We were not unaware, of course, that individual case study had been developing a distinct methodology during the same period and offered an attractive alternative to the statistical approach. Indeed, the clinical method demanded all the more serious consideration in view of the fact that, in contrast with the testing movement, it had been almost wholly absorbed in problems of personality and character.*

In spite, however, of the demonstrated value of the clinical approach, we were not deflected from the path of extensive testing and statistical interpretation. For one thing, the investigators were not trained in the field of clinical psychology and case work, whereas large numbers of highly qualified persons on ample foundations were already engaged in this type of research. Moreover, it is difficult to secure adequate contacts with normal and well-adjusted children in ordinary clinical work. In the third place, case studies, no matter how complete and informing regarding the individual, require an enormous expenditure of time and money in order to provide an adequate basis for the generalizations that must be made concerning human conduct if methods of moral education are to be developed which will be serviceable to the majority

* Churches and schools both are enormously indebted to the child guidance and mental hygiene clinics, which not only have seriously undertaken to repair the damage done to the personalities of children by life in oppressive, hostile, or degrading environments, but have also pointed the way to school, home, and community conditions which would in practice be more likely to achieve the results in character which the schools and churches have so long been proclaiming as their chief concern.

of children.   Only by building a broad foundation of statistically usable data can the science of human behavior as distinct from the art of studying and improving individuals be developed.

But clearly both approaches are needed in a well-rounded study of character, for they supplement rather than duplicate each other. The methods of statistical research might profitably be applied to case studies themselves, now that such large numbers of these have been piled up in the files of hospitals, schools, courts, and mental hygiene clinics.   And any extensive test program or educational experiment, on the other hand, will need the constant check-up of intensive work both for the validation of test procedures and the adaptation of methods to individuals.

## CLASSIFICATION OF PROBLEMS

Inasmuch as our study seeks to throw light on the nature of character by uncovering fresh empirical data rather than by reworking data already familiar, we have avoided the premature formulation of definitions.   Our only assumption concerns the location of the object of study.   We are interested in the social functioning of children.   And by this we mean that we intend to study social behavior in relation, on the one hand, to the ideas, purposes, motives, and attitudes entertained by the individual, and, on the other hand, in relation to the group life within which the observed and tested behavior takes place, including both the systems of behavior or customs of the group and its codes, ideals, and purposes.   Furthermore, we think of behavior as a function not only of the group but of the self which is becoming enlarged and organized within itself as well as integrated with its groups in the processes of social interaction which are being studied.

For convenience of reference, therefore, we may classify our work as involving the following areas of interest :

1. Mental content and skills — the so-called intellectual factors
2. Desires, opinions, attitudes, motives — the so-called dynamic factors
3. Social behavior — the performance factors

    4. Self-control — the relation of these factors to one another and to social-self-integration

The first three items are abstractions from the unitary process of social experience mentioned in item four. This is the concrete reality we hope to measure, but for practical purposes it has seemed best to approach it in a somewhat piecemeal fashion, much as a doctor examines the composition of the blood, the reflexes, skin color, and so forth to aid him in making a diagnosis of the individual as a whole, even while recognizing that blood count, taken by itself, is a relatively insignificant fact.

With methodology finally selected as our field of research, particularly as involving tests and measurements, a plan at once became necessary which would insure a practicable and rewarding development of the Inquiry. The master key to such a plan was found in the simple proposition that techniques for research should be worked out in actual service as instruments of research in order that their availability for this purpose might be continually tested in the exigencies of their application to actual problems. Since the general problems had already been classified as in the outline given on page 4, the plan of study grew very naturally into the following organization :

    I. Primary study. The development of a large body of highly standardized test material for the measurement of a wide variety of achievement in the field of morals and religion. Such test material would probably at first need to be classified as

        A. Tests of knowledge and skill

        B. Tests of attitude, opinion, and motive

        C. Tests of conduct

        D. Tests of self-control

    II. Secondary studies. These might be carried on separately or simultaneously in such combinations as circumstances might determine.

    A. The interrelations of conducts, knowledges, attitudes, and opinions among themselves — the problem of traits

    B. The biological and social concomitants of conducts, knowledges, attitudes, etc. — the problem of causes and significance

C. The results of current educational techniques purporting to develop character or certain habits and ideas — the problem of efficiency

D. Brief experiments with large populations and limited objectives and various techniques — the problem of method as applied to habit formation

E. An extended experiment with a small group for a period of years with frequent retesting — the problem of comprehensive method in character education

F. The observation of a large number of children by the most refined techniques available for discovering facts relevant to moral and religious growth, both individual and social. Such observations should be continued through not less than ten years and preferably from birth to occupational independence or even through life. It should include the social and biological background, the physiological and social history, and the results of repeated tests and measurements. The accumulation of such cases in large numbers, if properly selected, would afford a basis for statistical study of character comparable to that now available for the study of certain diseases and in general of the physical sciences. It is assumed that such individual studies would be socially conceived, and that along with the individual observations there would go a careful analysis of the experiences of the various groups to which the individual belonged, and of the individual's actual functioning in these groups.

G. Careful laboratory experiments in the field of physiological psychology to determine the laws governing the relation of ideas, bodily conditions, dispositions, and attitudes, particularly in the field of social relations. Such studies should reveal significant facts concerning the nature and function of the self, the limits of self-control and the procedures for achieving such control as is possible, and the processes of social interaction, such as discussion, dispute, study, preaching, worship. Incidentally much would be learned concerning the relation between health and mental states, which would be of first importance in a program of character education.

The work of the Inquiry has centered chiefly on the primary

study and on the first three of the secondary studies. In every case only sample studies have been possible, as the complete realization of the program outlined would require many years.

## CHOICE OF SAMPLE STUDIES

In choosing the particular conducts, knowledges, opinions, attitudes, and the like to be investigated, we have been guided largely by practical considerations. In view of the lack of scientific knowledge of the nature of character, it would have been most defensible to take random samplings of conducts, skills, ideas, and so forth, since it would be obviously out of the question to measure the entire range of social behavior. We have not selected our subject matter in this way, however. In spite of the absence of scientific treatment, the subject of morals and religion has probably received as much attention from some of the keenest minds of all generations as any other human interest, so that we are not left without any guidance at all, but have on the contrary a great wealth of careful and wise analysis of character which may be used to suggest the particular behaviors and mental contents that are of most importance.

Following the lead of recent curriculum studies, it might have seemed best to further limit our selection to *failures* in adjustment, just as a spelling lesson should focus on misspelled words and not waste time on words already known. Successes are achievements and require no further effort at learning. If the causes of failures can be ferreted out and the failures themselves be prevented, a long step forward will have been taken in moral education. One such failure with which our whole social structure is honeycombed is the practice of deceit, and it is with this that our first sample study, reported in this volume, is concerned.

But successes are also important for study, for if the causes of highly successful social behavior can be discovered, they can probably be produced at will and so be organized into a curriculum of character education. Sample studies in this direction will appear in later sections of the report.

*Studies in Deceit* includes as much as possible of the subtle inter-relations between behavior and knowledge, opinion and attitude, but is incomplete at this point in view of the practical limitations of a single volume and the need of concentrating in a subsequent section the various problems related to the organization of the self which it has been possible to study in the course of the Inquiry. The reader is asked, therefore, to remember that, while it is necessary to study deceit objectively as *behavior* which can be observed and measured, there is in this no implication that this behavior, apart from its causes, consequences, and other concomitants, has any significance. We hold no brief for absolutism in morality or psychology, which in either case tends to attribute to isolated acts some mystic meaning other than may be found in the entire train and system of experience of which the act is an inseparable part. No progress can be made, however, unless the overt act be observed and, if possible, measured without any reference, for the moment, to its motives or its rightness or wrongness. The first question to ask is, What did the subject do? Until this question is answered in quantitative terms so that what he did is clearly known, there is little use in going on to ask why he did it, and still less use in speculating whether he is to be blamed or praised.

## VALUES AND LIMITATIONS OF THE TESTS USED

The material used in the techniques developed by the Inquiry always has value for the subject quite apart from its significance as material for character testing. The situations in which the children are placed are natural and wholesome situations. It is the way they handle themselves in these situations that constitutes the test of character. An examination in arithmetic or spelling, for example, is a good thing and time well spent, in addition to what one may learn from it concerning the tendency of a child to deceive in taking it. Athletic contests and parties, works of mercy and helpfulness are in themselves significant and valuable for the children over and above what the examiner may learn about their honesty or capacity for self-denial. This fact makes possible the conscientious use of these procedures in spite of the need of keeping the subject in ignorance of those aspects of the test which make it an instrument for measuring some aspect of character as well as knowledge or skill or speed. It does not protect the tests from misuse, however, or from fatal publicity. Only the utmost precaution and restraint can insure the confidential conditions essential for successful testing.

This constitutes a serious limitation in the usefulness of character tests. It would be a fine thing if a technique could be invented which could be administered with its entire purpose known to the subject as well as to the examiner, so that the one who gave the test could say, " This is a test of honesty," or " helpfulness," or what not, without interfering with its operation ; and it is quite probable that, when an entire series of tests covering the various forms of behavior, knowledge, opinion, and attitude needed for a complete picture of character is available, it may be practicable to call it a character test without vitiating the results. Meanwhile it should be kept constantly in mind that what we have reported so far is not such a test of character as a whole, but separate tests of one type of behavior, and that at the stage of development represented by this volume these should be used only for purposes of research.

The promoters of the Inquiry have no desire to restrict the use of the materials referred to in this report. Certain of the tests described have been copyrighted, but, once published, no ideas or suggestions as to techniques could be withheld from general use. It is hoped, however, that only persons seriously interested in research and qualified by experience will attempt to apply the techniques discussed. It will of course be recognized that the conduct of any experiment requiring double testing will require the most rigorous control of the entire situation to avoid betrayal of the purpose of the tests. In this respect character testing differs widely from intelligence testing and must be handled in an appropriate way.

## THE FORM OF THE REPORT

Although the general problem of how to measure character is of widespread interest, the technical problems encountered make the preparation of a readable report exceedingly difficult. The plan adopted for this first study provides for a simple statement of our methods and main results in Book One, and the gathering of all statistical discussions and tables in Book Two. Although Book Two is large, it has not seemed wise to separate it altogether from Book One, as it is of the nature of a supplement which will require the reading of Book One to be intelligible and to which all who are interested in the technical phases of the research will wish to refer constantly.

Where statistical terms are used in the description of general methods and results, they are carefully explained so that no one need hesitate to read Book One because he feels unfamiliar with the terminology of quantitative research.* Even so, certain of the basic ideas may seem a little difficult at first, inasmuch as most of us have not been in the habit of thinking about the more subtle and inaccessible aspects of human nature, like honesty and kindness, in quantitative terms. In asking constantly how much or how often, we are not in the least belittling the spiritual significance of any kind of behavior. We are merely drawing attention to its prevalence.

Again, many may find it hard at first to substitute for classical logic the more empirical logic of scientific thought. The answer to the question, " How much? " or " How often? " is generally in terms of probability. Instead of dealing in hard and fast categories by which all cases are carefully pigeonholed in one or two or, at most, a few, clear-cut classes, such as honest, dishonest, helpful, self-controlled, we endeavor to indicate the proportion of life situations in which any individual or group would probably act honestly, dishonestly, helpfully, or with self-control. Since this proportion may fall anywhere from zero to one hundred per cent, the classification of our subjects as honest, dishonest, and the like would be quite arbitrary and of no possible service.

* The footnotes of Book One are intended for the technically trained reader.

Similarly, we avoid using such terms as " good " or " bad " or even raising any questions of this kind, since the line between good and bad is one which our tests will not automatically draw. The test records the act, but judgment of merit or demerit must be rendered on grounds which the test alone does not reveal.

Our matter-of-fact statements and records of what our subjects do are to be credited not to any lack of interest in their moral welfare but to the conviction that the solution of moral problems requires the same objectivity in the approach to facts as has been found necessary and fruitful in the study of physical events.

## GENERAL CONCLUSIONS

Our primary studies have resulted in the development of a large battery of deception tests, of which twenty-two use ordinary classroom situations, four use an athletic contest, two are in parties, and one is work done at home. There are also two lying tests and two stealing tests. These situations are intended as samples of the sort which it would be necessary to use if a complete picture of a person's tendencies to deceive were to be compiled. Similar tests can be prepared if any occasion for them should arise, but what we have are adequate for the type of research represented in the first five of the secondary studies.

This volume will report on the first four of the secondary studies, but only in so far as actual conduct was involved. The problem of the relation of conduct to knowledge and attitude will be discussed in a subsequent volume.

We find that one form of deceit or another is definitely associated with such facts as dullness, retardation, school grade, emotional instability, socio-economic handicaps, cultural limitations, certain national, racial, and religious groupings, suggestibility of a certain type, frequency of attendance at motion pictures, and poor deportment at school.

Deception runs in families in about the same way as intelligence, eye color, or height. This does not prove of course that deception is inherited, but only that certain things are found together.

Deception also goes by gangs and classrooms.   A pupil resembles his friends in his tendency to deceive.

Where relations between teachers and pupils are characterized by an atmosphere of coöperation and good will, there is less deception, and to this effect the general morale of the school and classroom also contributes.   On the other hand, attendance at Sunday school or membership in at least two organizations which aim to teach honesty does not seem to change behavior in this regard, and in some instances there is evidence that it makes children less rather than more honest.

Honesty appears to be a congeries of specialized acts which are closely tied up with particular features of the situation in which deception is a possibility, and is apparently not greatly dependent on any general ideal or trait of honesty.   Motives for cheating, lying, and stealing are highly complex, and are specialized just as are the acts of deception.   The most common extraneous motive is the desire to do well in class.

Deceit as a social problem can probably best be tackled by controlling the child's major experiences in such a way as to make deception unnecessary and by building up a series of behavior habits characterized by integrity of performance and intelligent grasp of the social significance of honor.   As an individual problem, honest conduct is just one aspect of the total character of the child and has no real significance for his moral welfare apart from its relation to his self-organization.

# BOOK ONE

## GENERAL METHODS AND RESULTS

# PART I

## THE PROBLEM OF MEASUREMENT

### CHAPTER I

### DECEIT AS AN OBJECT OF STUDY

Deception is a symptom of social friction. That it has long been a matter of interest is evidenced by the fact that Roget's *Thesaurus* prints no less than eight hundred words and phrases which are intimately related to the concept. But the practice of deception is far older than language. Enos Mills in his book *The Grizzly* describes the cleverness with which this much-hunted creature eludes his pursuers and gets the better even of his own kind. A grizzly cub was once observed chewing a ham skin. Seeing a larger bear approaching perilously near, the cub proceeded to sit on the skin and gaze with apparent absorption at something going on elsewhere. Such an instance of getting around the other fellow could be duplicated by the score from observations of animal life, both wild and domestic.

The human young are no less prone to use indirect methods of securing their ends. Being equipped with more complex brains, they are naturally more adept than their animal friends; yet one often sees in the innocent expression of a child the very same struggle to keep something dark that one finds in dogs and cats — and, if one could only believe Uncle Remus, in rabbits!

One of the most interesting episodes of the history of character is the transition from this natural state of universal deception to a social order whose very foundation is its negation. It is not our purpose to trace this history. We begin at a time when it is generally claimed in most countries that it pays to be honest. That is, life goes along more smoothly, take it by and large, if everyone can be trusted. Here and there the ideal of honesty, in theory at least, has been developed on a basis of social-minded regard for the personalities and the rights of others, though there are not so many who have actually achieved integrity of this character as there are of those who usually practice honesty because to do so is the best, that is, the safest, policy.

But how many of even these prudent ones are there?

In spite of this obeisance to the ideal of honesty, we are confronted with the extraordinary spectacle of a civilization whose institutions are founded upon the assumption that men can trust one another — a civilization whose codes of business, of personal relations, of religious experience, of military, political, and professional service everywhere lift up honesty as essential to the common weal — nevertheless exhibiting in every walk of life, in school, industry, the professions, in business, politics, religion, and private life, the most blatant use of fraud not only for ends disapproved by public ethics but even for objects which are in themselves entirely wholesome and are frequently sought by legitimate means.

This conflict between standard and performance reflects the early struggles of children with an oppressive environment. Born with budding desires which if carried out in their crude form meet the prohibitions and penalties of hostile custom, the youngster who wants his own way must use his imagination. A twenty-months-old boy greatly enjoyed playing with several forbidden objects. Although never punished for doing so, he was aware of the parental wish which contradicted his own. His first effort to circumvent the prohibition was to say, " Daddy, go 'way ! " — thus to leave him free to carry out his desire. As this did not work, he soon tried this more subtle method: " Daddy, go hide. Boy find ! " — thinking to entice his father to leave him alone for a moment. He was a perfectly good sport when he discovered that this, too, was " no go." Later he resorted to ways of getting at the forbidden object when no one was near but was so very quiet about it that the unusual silence at once gave him away and brought a suspicious parent to the door.  A further variation that developed a month or more after this method came into use was to attempt to attract attention to some other object than the one in dispute.  Having a match in one hand, this same youngster one day put this behind him as his father approached and said, " Daddy, come here," at the same time holding up for inspection an innocuous piece of paper.  This method was still being experimented with after two months of comparative failure.

This boy did not do these things because he possessed some inherent tendency to deceive, nor was he in conflict with some inborn disposition to be honest.  He was merely acting in an intelligent way to solve a new problem — the circumvention of social obstruction.  If the methods he very naturally used had succeeded and been repeated with continuing success, then he would have been achieving the behavior to which the term *deception* might properly apply, for whether it was the *end* he sought which was disapproved or the *method* he used which was frowned upon he would soon have become conscious of his method as a way of circumventing the will of another by misleading the other as to his own will.  This seems to be the essential factor in deception.  Although it is a natural, intelligent response to a thwarting social situation, it leads inevitably to a break in fellowship and the intensification of the social strain or friction out of which it arises.

That such adaptive behavior is learned very early everyone knows.  It is first learned in those situations where it constitutes the most successful solution of the problem of getting one's own way.  Frequently the easiest solution, it is at times an exceedingly arduous one.  The selective force working for its continuation and spread is simply success.

Now if deception as a mode of adaptive behavior is so readily acquired when the whole environment frowns upon the method as well as the end to be achieved, what can we say of those situations where the child's dominant group actually approves this way of gaining his ends when he is in conflict with some other group?

In many a school classroom this is precisely the situation. Honesty is bad form. It would be surprising if in such circumstances we should find anything but habitual deception wherever it proved to be the successful policy. And this is exactly what our studies tend to show.

When deception is found to be the way in which an individual usually adapts himself to a situation, we can be fairly certain, then,

1. that what he wants to get or to do is disapproved and must be concealed; or
2. that when the thing he wants is legitimate, straightforward ways of getting it are either more onerous or less adequate or have never been learned; and
3. that even if deception is disapproved by the group within which the behavior occurs, it is approved by some other group to which the individual belongs in fact or fancy; or
4. that the individual is mentally disordered and must resort to self-deception of some kind to maintain his self-respect — such as the adoption of ingenious excuses, or telling himself that it won't count this time, or finding justification in other ways.

It may be further assumed for the time being that the amount and character of the deception are primarily functions of the situation. That this assumption is borne out by the facts we shall see later; but it is stated here, along with the four propositions just given, in order to emphasize the need for studying the behavior involved in deceit. We cannot, of course, question the importance of studying also the motives and ideals, but we need first of all to establish the fact of deception and its amount and character. As these are symptoms of the social disease, they must be accurately observed if a correct diagnosis is to be reached. With the disease thus partially located, its constituent elements may then be studied and an effort made to find its causes and cures.

These figures of speech drawn from physiology will not blind us to the fact that we are dealing with areas of behavior that are more open to social and mental influence than most organs and tissues of the body. The cure will probably turn out to consist in two major processes: first, the removal of the original conflict or strain between the child and his environment and, second, the replacement of the old habit by a new one. There will doubtless be cases in which the first will be sufficient. Once a satisfactory social adjustment is secured, the dishonest habits will be abandoned. There will be other cases in which the second process will be sufficient. That is, even if the social strain is not removed, new habits of honor may be formed. Without changing the major situation itself, an educational approach can be made which will so modify the habits as to affect an adjustment to the situation as it is. The processes in each case are complex and are not to be discussed at this point. But it may be suggestive to refer briefly to types of strain that are met with.

## SITUATIONS PROVOCATIVE OF DECEPTION

In Healy's discussion of honesty,* which is an inquiry into the causes of juvenile offenses against property based on his personal observations of a large number of cases, we find helpful material for the study of deception. Concealment was inevitably involved because of the disapproval of stealing, which requires that the person taking property belonging to another work by stealth or else hide himself afterwards.

This, of course, is a modern limitation upon primitive tendencies, illustrating very well the relative success with which society has achieved the dominance among men of the ideal of trustworthy behavior, which asserts and maintains that might does not make right. But the underlying motives to concealment are the same to-day as in the past. Our primitive ancestor, to be sure, had to conceal his depredations out of fear of those physically stronger than himself, whereas modern man conceals his thieving out of fear of the forces of law and order which society has developed for its defense.

Children are more nearly on the primitive level in the matter of

* Healy, William, *Honesty*, Bobbs Merrill, 1915.

the object of fear. Direct punishment for taking things belonging to other children is apt to be meted out by the offended individual in person and at once. Even in adolescence the policeman is often looked upon as a personal enemy rather than as a social agent, and in the same class with the policeman are parents, teachers, and adults generally. From his crowd or gang the child frequently has social support and is admired for his exploits. His attacks, whether conducted in groups or alone, are sometimes the result of greed but are more often the consequence of the desire for adventure. But whatever the motive for the theft, the motive for the accompanying and essential deception is always the fear of detection. The break between the child and society is as much determined by the necessity of lying as by any material damages resulting from thefts. Ostracism by society for thefts is bad enough, to be sure, and has serious psychological consequences. But it is physical separation primarily. The offender is imprisoned, and everyone knows what for. His concealment of his acts is at an end for the time being. On the other hand, the person who is deceiving others is cut off from them psychically rather than physically and even while going about his daily occupations may be far more removed from genuine personal contact with those whom he is deceiving than the captured thief from his captors. This double life hampers the development of an organized self more than does antisocial behavior which is kept in the open.

The deceptive accompaniments of theft are not Healy's main concern. But for our purposes, his study of the motives underlying stealing are illuminating. This is particularly true in drawing attention to the fact that the situation in which the child is placed is the determining factor in his behavior. A child steals ordinarily to get something normal and worth-while with which his environment has not provided him. Poverty becomes thus a primary cause. But poverty as an effective cause is often a misfortune in well-to-do families as well as in poor ones if parents do not see to it that their children have the playthings, amusements, and clothes which not only satisfy the need for fun and self-expression but which also afford entrée to the social groups natural to the child. The practice of snobbery is doubtless learned from adults, but the resulting social ostracism of the youngster who is not equipped for the activities of his normal groups is a vigorous stimulus to get by hook or crook the things that will offer him a satisfactory social status.

There are, of course, numerous other causes of theft, such as running with a crowd and being overborne or carried away by excitement, being overtempted by the exciting opportunities of amusement parks and movies, associating with delinquents, reacting against unwholesome home conditions, being deliberately taught by adults, the example of parents careless with money, and many others. There are also abnormal conditions which, because of a vivid experience in which stealing has been in some way associated with some other malpractice, find expression in irresistible impulses to steal. From the standpoint of the Inquiry, however, thieving is a form of dishonesty in which we are interested primarily because of the inevitable deception with which it is accompanied. What methods are taken to conceal antisocial deeds? With what social groups is the break made? With whom is fellowship maintained? What social strains result from the continued necessity for concealment, artifice, and double dealing? Such questions, rather than the cause of the original antisocial behavior itself, are our more immediate concern.

A quite different approach is represented by Charters' book on the teaching of ideals.* The problem of honesty is taken up in one section to illustrate a method of teaching. Here Charters deals not so much with maladjustments accounting for dishonesty as with types of situation in which honesty is likely to be an ethical problem because the dishonest response is so safe and rewarding.

A group of thirty teachers studying how to teach ideals made a detailed classification of situations to which honesty was the ideal response, and which constituted therefore opportunities for dishonesty. These situations were concerned with: money; statements; promises; social relations; rules, directions, and orders; games; property; class recitations; examinations and tests;

* Charters, W. W., *The Teaching of Ideals*, The Macmillan Company, 1927.

and preparing lessons. Under each heading a long list of specific situations is given, such as the following, which have to do with money:

1. You borrow money.

    Someone says, " I know I owe you some money, but I have forgotten how much."

2. You find money.

    You know to whom it belongs.

    You know you will not get a reward for returning it.

There are nine of these major situations involving money, with some fifty-seven minor situations constituting the problems. The other general classes of opportunity are treated in the same way, issuing in a total of nearly two hundred fifty opportunities to deceive or be honest. This list could doubtless be amplified almost indefinitely, but it shows how complex our social situations are and how detailed our educational processes must be if they are to result in adequate control in the interest of fair dealing.

## THE PROBLEM OF CORRECTION

The illuminating work of men like Healy, who have brought to public attention the sort of situation with which dishonest behavior is associated and the frequency with which the practice of dishonesty drops out of use as soon as the social strains are released, offers us a more encouraging prospect for educational procedure than the one that looms before us when we contemplate the building of hundreds of specific habits involving the honest rather than the dishonest type of response. Yet we cannot afford to ignore the fact that the easily reformed offender who drops his bad habits had also to learn his good habits at some time. If he slips easily into good behavior, the presumption is that his bad behavior was a fall from grace, a shift from habits of honest response already learned. Certainly no one questions that the habits and skills of dishonest behavior have to be learned. Naturally, when these prove unprofitable or dangerous and the old honest ways are still available, the old are resorted to once more. They are not achieved with a miraculous suddenness. They are learned just as all other detailed habits are learned, but as is the case with other habits, they are learned far more readily and effectively when there is present an adequate motive for learning them and an adequate concept or picture of the end to be achieved and the general character of the means to be employed.

Methods of replacing old habits by new or of originating the correct, that is, the honest, types of response are age-old. Most of them are based on the assumption that honesty is not only a generic concept but a generic trait. It is supposed to be present in the child in the form of a ready-made force or mode of behavior requiring only to be evoked by precept, threat, or reward. The method is prolific of wise sayings and moral cautions, but as a means of producing universal honor among men we certainly cannot boast of its success. We need not be surprised at this, however, if the underlying assumption proves to be itself fallacious. If there be no generic trait of honesty to be evoked, then it is to be expected that the multitudinous ways of evoking it will fall short of their object. As our study proceeds evidence will be accumulated which we hope will throw some light on this fundamental problem.

# CHAPTER II

# PREVIOUS EFFORTS TO MEASURE DECEPTIVE CONDUCT

The detection of fraud has been of almost universal interest. The large rewards made possible by deception have tended to the development of a high degree of skill in the concealment of motives, intentions, and acts. With more primitive peoples it was only by the building up of a vigorous taboo that the rapacity and lust of the individual could be controlled. Furthermore, the taboo served not only to deter but also to detect, for in the ordeals imposed on the members of the tribe by the witch doctor it was the offender's consciousness of having violated the sacred code that gave him away.

Two of the modern methods of detecting deceit depend for success on the same sensitiveness of the individual about being caught. One is often called the free association method. The other makes use of various physiological tests.

A third procedure has depended on the breaking down of the barriers between the offender and those responsible for his conduct. Fear breeds deceit and raises up an almost impenetrable veil behind which the true self hides. In dealing sympathetically with young people who conceal their real motives and acts, certain juvenile court judges and social case workers have been wonderfully successful, and their general procedure is recognized as of scientific as well as human interest.

The fourth method concerns itself with the measurement rather than with merely the detection of deceptive tendencies and works without the knowledge of the subject. No barriers are erected between the subject and the examiner which require expert handling. Ordinary situations are used, and statistical methods are employed in the interpretation of the results.

In this chapter we shall review briefly what has been done with the first three methods and shall make a complete review of the fourth. A bibliography of methods one, two, and four will be found in the Appendix.

## THE FREE ASSOCIATION METHOD *

As has been suggested, this method arranges for the subject to " give himself away." A list of words is presented to him, and he is asked to give the first word that comes to his mind. Most of the list have no reference to the offense of which the subject is accused. A few " critical " words are inserted, however, which have some obvious association with what happened or with the place where the crime was committed.

If the accused is innocent, he will presumably respond as quickly to the critical words as to the rest and the words he thinks of will have no consistent reference to the deed. But if he is guilty, the presumption is that on seeing or hearing the critical words he will be startled into caution and so take time to find a word not associated with the crime, or will be taken off his guard and give a telltale response. The following list will illustrate the latter effect.

| STIMULUS WORDS | INNOCENT RESPONSE | GUILTY RESPONSE |
|---|---|---|
| many | more | more |
| weather | hot | hot |
| room | hall | hall |
| second | first | first |
| tooth | pulled | pulled |
| treat | soda | soda |
| head * | hair * | blood * |
| dress | black | black |
| knife | sharp | sharp |
| make | money | money |
| ship | sail | sail |
| ax * | handle * | head * |

* See references 16, 17, 18, 19, 28, 32, 46, 47, and 48 in the Bibliography for detailed discussions.

In this case the crime is supposed to have been committed with an ax and the critical words are starred. The same words might have resulted in a delayed response.

There seems to be good evidence that if there is emotional strain present it will affect the nature of the responses made by the subject, although experimenters have found that different persons behave in different ways, some taking less time rather than more for the critical words and still using caution enough not to give telltale responses.

The Character Education Inquiry has not used this technique as it seems to be essentially a detecting device and not a measuring device. Peculiarities of behavior during the test may be evidence of the attempt to conceal something, but unless this something is otherwise known there results no objective verification of the deceptive intent. That is, the evidence that deception has occurred either in fact or by intent is circumstantial, not direct. Furthermore, this technique does not lend itself very readily to group testing, which, as we shall see later, is a rather necessary requirement of our work.

## PHYSIOLOGICAL TESTS *

Breathing, blood pressure, and certain changes in the sweat glands have all been used to detect lying.

### A. INSPIRATION-EXPIRATION RATIO

Irregularities in breathing have long been recognized as accompaniments of emotional condition. The significant fact seems to be the relation of the time it takes to breathe in to the time it takes to breathe out. The average ratio before telling a lie is less than the average ratio after telling a lie. The average ratio before telling the truth is greater than the average ratio after telling the truth.

### B. THE SYSTOLIC BLOOD PRESSURE

Here again we have an effort to discover some constant relation between well-known physiological changes and specific stimuli.

* See references 1, 3, 4, 5, 6, 11, 12, 14, 15, 21, 22, 23, 24, 25, 29, 30, 31, 33, 34, 35, and 36 in the Bibliography for details.

In this case, as before, the stimulus we are concerned with is the consciousness of deception.   It is supposed that when an individual deliberately lies his blood pressure shows a characteristic fluctuation, rising above the point to which fear or anger alone would send it, just before the lie is told, and dropping again as soon as the lie is out.  The result, when recorded on a revolving drum, gives what is known as the " lying curve."

Obviously the curve does not indicate the objective truth or falsity of a statement but merely the conscious attitude of deception.   A person may in all good faith make a statement which does not correspond with the facts.  Such a statement would not show as a lie on the drum.  On the other hand, a person might state a fact when he thought he was telling a carefully prepared lie.  In such a case the record would appear as a lie.

### C.   The Psycho-galvanic Reflex

Certain electrical changes take place in the human body which can be measured by delicate instruments such as the galvanometer. The electrical conditions recorded on the instrument alter with other observable conditions in such a way as to suggest the possibility of using the first as an indication of the second when the second are not otherwise known.   Thus, emotional excitement is supposed to accompany deception.  This excitement may be concealed from the observer by a well-controlled and experienced deceiver.   But the electrical changes which accompany the bodily disturbances associated with consciously felt emotion go on just the same and can be detected by the instrument.  This is the theory that is back of the use of the galvanometer as a lie detector, but the practical results are not yet encouraging on account of the complexity of the electrical changes that are registered by the instrument.

### D.   Combinations of Methods

Of the techniques described the three best are association reaction, breathing ratios, and blood pressure.  These have been tried out two at a time and all three at one time.  The results vary.

Some of the records agree, and on some there is a conflict between the results of the separate techniques. That is, one may indicate that the subject lied, while the other may indicate the opposite.

## CLINICAL CASE STUDIES

The case-study procedure is not primarily concerned with detection or measurement and is referred to here only because it frequently makes use of measuring devices as supplements and takes the needed time to become acquainted with associated series of facts about the subject which are quite inaccessible to present methods of testing. It treats the case as a human being living in a complex environment all details of which are significant for a true understanding of his behavior. It spares no pains to discover relevant data about the child's physical and mental condition, his daily regimen at home, his school placement and adjustment, his opportunities for play and self-expression, his relations with members of his family and with his companions.

In its earlier applications the case method (which is really not a method but a principle or spirit) was primarily interested in individuals who had come to public attention because of delinquency of some kind. The most common occasions for arrest or reference to social agencies were lying, stealing, fighting, and sex offenses. It was quite expected that deception would be a factor to be contended with in the handling of individuals, and although no technique was developed for eliminating this obstruction to diagnosis, experienced case workers and judges became extremely skillful in winning the confidence of youthful offenders and so breaking down the barriers of deceit with which they had sought to protect themselves from a too hostile environment.

In more recent years, attention has been increasingly given to that much larger class of children known as potential delinquents. These children have not as yet come to public attention, but they show symptoms of maladjustments which when long continued are found to lead eventually to some open break with society, such as truancy, adventurous thieving, running away from home, abnormal sex activity, or even more dangerous efforts to escape the restrictions of home or school. Mental hygiene and child-guidance clinics have been springing up in numbers of communities, whose purpose it is to get in touch with such cases before they grow to the point of delinquency and by intelligent study of the causes of unrest and by suitable treatment, physical, mental, and social, to effect readjustments much more readily than is possible when antisocial habits have become firmly established.*

Although the study and treatment of children by the case-study procedure is highly developed, its techniques are largely those of medicine and psychology and are applied by specialists in these fields. The "case worker," or field worker, needs to know human nature both in the abstract and concrete and to have a way of getting along with people which makes it natural for them to confide in her. Her work is largely scouting, digging up facts, securing the coöperation of teachers, parents, employers, and club leaders in a program of readjustment which must be well organized to be effective. Such methods as these workers develop to win the confidence of their cases are largely individual in character and conform to no standardized scheme comparable to a test. This does not make them less useful but merely places them in a different category.†

* In this connection the work of the Joint Committee for the Prevention of Juvenile Delinquency was of great importance in organizing and stimulating work of this character. Its publications may be secured from the Commonwealth Fund, 578 Madison Ave., New York.

† The oath taken by witnesses in court may be mentioned as a device associated with deception, but its purpose is not to detect falsehood but to prevent its occurrence. Cross-examination, on the other hand, while not conforming to any standardized procedure, is in part intended for the purpose of demonstrating the truth or falsehood of the statements made by the accused or by the witnesses to the case. Such cross-examination even in court sometimes approaches the brutality of the "third degree," which is an under-cover method of extracting confessions by wearing down the resistance of the accused. All such procedures are of course condemned by enlightened people as crude, barbaric, insecure, and bungling substitutes for real skill.

## CONDUCT TESTS OF DECEPTION

We come now to the type of work most closely related to our own study. It is not our purpose to assign historical credit for such tests as have been devised nor to offer any extended criticism of work already accomplished by Voelker, Cady, Raubenheimer, and others. The numbers attached to the names of investigators refer to the studies listed in the Bibliography printed in the Appendix.

Voelker's work (44) is of interest because of its pioneer character. He attempted by a series of conduct tests to demonstrate that the effort of the Boy Scouts to teach ideals could be made effective in changes in conduct. Undertaken in coöperation with the Indiana Survey of Religious Education and developed as a doctor's dissertation at Teachers College, Columbia University, Voelker's study has received considerable publicity in popular magazines and is probably familiar to hundreds of thousands of their readers. It has been attended by more critical attention* than has the work of subsequent students, who have succeeded in building better statistical foundations under the structure of character testing, but who have all been indebted to this work for suggestive ideas.

Cady's study (8) was for the purpose of finding out " to what extent it is possible by means of the test method, supplemented by character ratings, observational data, and other aids, to identify in advance of overt delinquency children of abnormal moral tendency." Working on a grant from the U. S. Interdepartmental Social Hygiene Board to Stanford University and under the joint supervision of the University and the California Bureau of Research, Cady limited his investigation to factors involved in incorrigibility, using as his criterion of the existence of this tendency both the ratings of teachers and the presence of children in corrective schools.

Raubenheimer (41) was concerned with the discovery of a method for distinguishing potential delinquents before the stage of actual delinquency. He limited his purpose to group discriminations,

---

* See the discussions carried on by Watson, Athearn, and Voelker in *Religious Education*, issues of June, 1925, and February, 1926.

feeling that it was too much to hope for the immediate development of ways of measuring individuals which would offer a basis for accurate diagnosis and prognosis.  He used public school groups of two types, one the upper twenty-five per cent and the other the lower twenty-five per cent in reliability, stability, and healthy-mindedness, fifty boys from two parental schools for delinquents, and thirty-six boys from a reform school.

In his study of the character and personality traits of one thousand gifted children, Terman (43) took over certain tests developed by Voelker, Cady, and Raubenheimer, three of which are tests of deceptiveness.  These tests were administered both to the selected gifted children and to an unselected control group in order to find whether superiority in character accompanies superiority in other particulars.

We are interested in this review in a detailed study of the *techniques* that have been so far developed and regard it as of scientific interest to summarize and evaluate them before proceeding to discuss our own.

### A. THE OVERSTATEMENT TECHNIQUE

This consists essentially in first asking the subject a question about his ability in some respect or about his knowledge of certain facts, and getting him to make a statement about what he knows or can do.  This statement is recorded.  A little later he is given an actual test to see if he overestimated his knowledge or ability.

Voelker first used it by asking a single question concerning the subject's school marks: " Did you receive 95 in arithmetic (or some other subject) in your last examination? "  The check-up was to ask the question only for some subject in which the grade was below 95.  In his second set of tests he used a series of questions concerning abilities and knowledge.  The check on the statements about knowledge of facts was made by a retest asking for specific information.  For example, one of the questions on the preliminary test is this : " Do you know the names of all the oceans and the continents? "  Then on the retest comes this question :

"Name all the oceans." The deception score is the number of failures to make good.

In 1922 Knight and Franzen (20) reported a study which included an effort to measure the tendency of students to over- or under-estimate their qualities. Ratings were used for this purpose. The subject's rating of himself was compared with others' ratings of him and with his rating of others.

Cady used Voelker's technique and some of the same questions on more subjects than Voelker had. Raubenheimer followed with a still longer test.* The procedure finally appearing in the Raubenheimer paper is as follows:

First, there was a short practice exercise to establish an appropriate attitude and to familiarize the subjects with the technique.

Second, two sets of forty questions each were asked, the subject marking his knowledge 2, 1, or 0.

Third, two sets of check questions were administered, the answers to which displayed the extent to which the pupils had overstated their knowledge on the original test.

**Results of the Overstatement Technique.** Cady found that children who overestimate their ability to do things incline also to overstate their knowledge.† Further, as shown by Raubenheimer, a child who overestimates his knowledge in one test will do it again when another test of the same sort is presented. But at least 120 questions would have to be asked, as against Raubenheimer's eighty, before one could be sure of the percentage of exaggeration one could expect on subsequent trials.‡

We can see therefore that this sort of test may be so constructed as to test *something* very well. But just what is it that it tests? Voelker uses it as a measure of trustworthiness. Cady regards it as

---

* "Developed," he says, "in conjunction with Dr. G. M. Ruch."

† Cady reports a correlation of .505 between the scores on estimates of ability and scores showing overstatement in regard to knowledge, using ten questions for each. Raubenheimer secures an $r$ of .76 between two sets of forty questions each.

‡ Spearman's formula yields a predicted $r$ of .86 with another set of eighty and of .90 when the test is tripled, or between one set of 120 and another set of 120.

a test of deception because the dominating motive seems to be to " put something over." But Knight and Franzen found a general tendency to overrate oneself even when no deception was involved. That there is some relation between this behavior and that complex of conditions called incorrigibility is shown by the fact that the mean score on this test achieved by Cady's group of corrigible or normal boys is significantly.lower than that achieved by incorrigibles. The corrigible group made good in 54% of their statements (low enough, in all conscience !) and the incorrigibles made good in 42%.

Raubenheimer reports that this test will not distinguish between the highest fourth of a school population and the lowest fourth, highest and lowest meaning the most and least reliable as rated by teachers. But it will distinguish the most reliable 25% of either a privileged or more usual community from a group of reform school boys.

This capacity to distinguish groups makes this a useful test but does not establish the fact of its being a test of deception. Doubtless deception is often, perhaps usually, present. But there is also a large factor of intelligence in the scores.*

Summarizing what we know of this technique : Whatever it measures it will do it well provided there are over 120 items used. It distinguishes a group of delinquents from two groups of nondelinquents, but with only eighty elements it will not distinguish the 25% most reliable from the 25% least reliable in either a normal or privileged group, nor will it distinguish individuals. But whether it tests deception or something like " cocksureness " or tendency to overestimate (though honestly) is not known.

### B. Books-Read Technique

This is a variation on the overstatement technique and is reported by Terman to have been suggested by Knight. It consists in submitting to the subject a list of book titles with the instruction that he check the titles of the books he has read. In-

---

* Raubenheimer reports an $r$ of .64 with National Intelligence Test scores, which becomes .75 when corrected for attenuation. See his monograph, p. 82.

serted in the list are several titles of books that do not exist. The question is: How many of these faked titles will the subject check as having read?

Franzen (13) embodied the idea in a test for teacher efficiency and reports that in a typical school somewhere in the Middle West one-third of the teachers showed unmistakable signs of dishonesty.*

Raubenheimer " in conjunction with Dr. G. M. Ruch " developed it further and Raubenheimer made it one of his battery of tests. He had two forms of 25 items each, each form containing ten fake titles. The score is the number of such titles checked.

**Results of the Books-Read Technique.** Raubenheimer's results show that this procedure does not give quite as consistent (reliable) results as the overstatement test, but this is doubtless due to the fact that there are fewer items. It does, however, distinguish the best fourth of a privileged group from the children in the parental school.

On a priori grounds this technique is open to serious criticism. The directions say that the subject is to check every title he has read, no matter how long ago he read it. Nothing is said about degrees of recognition. All psychological experiments in recognition show how large the errors of honest recognition are. Suppose, for example, the reader were faced with a list of book titles but did not know that the list was constructed in this way. How many would he recognize? In short the strictly honest person is likely to mark many fake titles simply because he mistakes them for actual titles. On the other hand, a dishonest or careless person who is merely guessing has in each list fifteen chances of marking a real title and ten chances of marking a fake one.

### C. The Paraffin-Paper Technique

This ingenious technique was used by Voelker and Cady. Voelker's first procedure made use of a four-page folder, on the third page of which was a tracing test, which required that the subject make a tracing of an irregular figure showing through a waxed paper. The folder was then turned so that page 1 was on top of

* See Raubenheimer's paper, p. 17.

page 3 directly beneath it. On page 1 was an opposites test. In writing in the words an exact copy was made on the wax paper attached to page 3. As soon as the opposites test was completed, the examiner removed the second half of the folder (pages 3 and 4) and the wax paper containing now the impression of the words as well as the tracing of the figure, ostensibly to score the tracing test, and then someone read to the pupils the correct opposites in order that they might score their own papers. Any changes of course were detected by comparison with the wax impression.

Voelker's second method involved the concealment of a waxed surface on page 3 of a folder which had a completion test on page 1 and the answers on page 4. When the test was taken, the booklet was folded so that the wax took the impression. Then the booklet was opened with pages 1 and 4 exposed, and page 3, with the wax coating, now under page 4, which contained the answers used by the pupils in correcting their work. Cady followed this second procedure, using more sentences and grading them in difficulty so that no one could honestly complete the test.

**The Results of the Paraffin-Paper Technique.** Unfortunately Voelker does not report the results of his separate tests. Cady found that with fifteen sentences the test had a satisfactory reliability — that is, it measured well whatever it measured.*

But as a measure of incorrigibility the technique is not so good, although it does discriminate between two groups fairly well. Twenty-five per cent of the corrigibles cheated as against 41% of the incorrigibles in the school groups and 39% of the reform school boys. The teachers, however, could not seem to estimate the presence of this tendency at all accurately as there was almost no relation between their individual ratings and the deception scores made by those rated.

---

* He found a correlation of .578 on alternate items. If he had used thirty elements, the $r$ would have been around .75. The $r$ between this test and the circles and squares described later was .56. The $r$ with the criterion of incorrigibility as determined by teacher ratings was .188 and the $r$ with an "honesty" criterion only slightly higher even in 150 cases selected because of certainty of judgment by the raters.

In the form in which Cady used the test certain practical difficulties arose from the necessity of using hard pencils and thin paper,
which caused some annoyance and possibly suspicion.    The presence of the paraffin may also have been observed.

On the other hand the scores are unequivocal.    There is no
doubt of the fact if a pupil does make any change in his paper,
though of course his understanding of the directions is not so easily
assumed.    If we can assume that he knows he should not change
his paper, this method gives an indubitable score of deception.

### D. The Peeping Technique

Like many others, this technique was first used in an extensive
way by Voelker.    Cady also adopted it with modifications and it
has since been used by Murdoch (38) and Terman.

It consists in giving the subject a task to do with his eyes closed.
The success with which the subject does the task will indicate
whether he peeped or not.    It is known beforehand just what
results may be expected if the subject does the task honestly; if
his score exceeds this normal
expectation, the inference is
that he peeped.

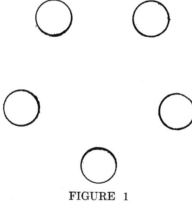

Here again the materials
used vary.    Voelker used two
kinds, objects, and pencil and
paper.    The objects consisted
of a form of the Pintner profile
test which requires the subject
to arrange certain blocks of
painted wood so that they will
form a profile.    The chances
of getting the blocks in correct
order in one trial with the eyes
closed are reported by Voelker
to be 1 in 16; of getting them

FIGURE 1

Voelker's Cardboard Test (Original 12″ × 12″)

correct twice in succession, 1 in 256; three times in succession,
1 in 4096.    Thus if a subject gets them right three times in suc-

cession, the inference of peeping is very strong.  The paper and pencil test consisted of a series of identical circles arranged at the angles of an imaginary pentagon on a paper twelve inches square. A facsimile is shown in Figure 1.  The subject, with eyes closed, places a pencil mark in each circle.  Five trials are given and the subject records his own success or failure.  Cady used circles of different sizes so as to make partial success possible.  He added

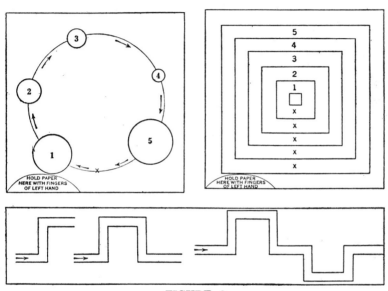

FIGURE 2

CADY'S TRUSTWORTHINESS TESTS (GREATLY REDUCED)

a series of concentric squares and a series of mazes.  In the squares test the subject runs his pencil around the alley formed by having one square inside another.  There are five of these alleys.  His maze test is something like it except that the mazes are rather complicated.  It is hard enough to do the maze with eyes open, making success almost impossible with eyes closed.  These tests were presented as " scientific experiments in measuring distances with the eyes closed."  Illustrations are given in Figure 2.

In order to get at the degree of success that chance and other factors would provide, Cady submitted his circles, squares, and mazes to several presumably honest adults. He thereby established a kind of limit of possible honest achievement. Several methods of scoring have been suggested. Cady first scored his tests either zero or one depending on the evidence of peeping. Later he introduced an intermediate score and ran his scores zero for an apparently honest performance, one for a performance which showed occasional peeping, three for a performance that showed gross and continued peeping. The Terman study adopted Cady's circles and squares tests, but used graded scores according to the relative success of the performance. Thus the score for the circles was:

> Number of crosses in circle 2 multiplied by 3
> Number of crosses in circle 3 multiplied by 4
> Number of crosses in circle 4 multiplied by 5

Circles 1 and 5 could be honestly checked and so were not included in the scoring. In the case of the squares the procedure was to ignore the smallest square and " . . . score 1 for each *corner* (except the first) where the line drawn is within the boundary lines. In addition give 1 if the entire line is within the boundaries (does not actually cross the line). This makes a possible unweighted score of 4 for each square. These scores are then weighted in the following manner:

> Score on square 2 is to be multiplied by 2
> Score on square 3 is to be multiplied by 3
> Score on square 4 is to be multiplied by 4
> Score on square 5 is to be multiplied by 6 "

As we shall see later, such scores are useful for purposes of statistical comparison even though no exact score is set in excess of which one can be certain that deception took place in the case of an individual.

**Results of the Peeping Technique.** Cady reports remarkably consistent results among his three pencil and paper peeping tests, which indicates that if enough are used one can predict from one occasion to another how the subject will behave.*

With a test of the length given he can give no assurance of exactly what it is that is measured by this test.†

He finds, however, that these techniques will distinguish his delinquent and non-delinquent groups very well. On the whole, Cady seems well pleased with this technique and believes it a good measure of deception.

Terman and his students in their work with gifted children found that these peeping tests did not distinguish the brilliant group from the control group as well as some of the other tests used by them. But as this technique correlates lower with intelligence than some of the others, this failure to discriminate these groups is not remarkable.

This technique seems on the whole very satisfactory. Cady points out as a possible objection that the pupils find it difficult to inhibit the " look habit." Working with eyes closed is a new experience to many of them, and once in a while some pupil will perhaps " forget " and open his eyes without intending to deceive. There is certainly a strong resistance here to be overcome in this matter of the vision habit. It is really hard not to peep. But this makes it all the more satisfactory as a test because a more or less constant resistance is supplied. The test is simple to give and easy to score. The results must be interpreted in terms of probabilities but this is characteristic of most deception tests.

* He reports an $r$ of .744 between the circles and squares on a population of 150. With 44 cases his $r$'s run

| | |
|---|---|
| Circles and squares | .59 |
| Circles and mazes | .51 |
| Squares and mazes | .63 |

† Correlations with his rating criterion run .318 for circles, .297 for squares, and .398 for squares and circles combined for the larger population of 150. With the smaller group of 44 he gets for circles, squares, and mazes .526, .324, and .524 respectively.

Dr. Murdock used a modified form of the circles test in a study of race differences and found an $r$ of .53 between this test and a weighted average of the six character traits estimated by means of a questionnaire.

## E. OTHER TECHNIQUES FOR TESTING DECEPTION

Voelker reports other techniques used in his study, but since he has not given evaluations of individual tests all we can do is to describe them.

**1. The Over-Change Test.** The subject is sent on a purchasing errand. It is prearranged with the merchant to give him a certain amount of over-change. The test is what he will do with it.

**2. The Let-me-help-you Test.** The subject is given a difficult task such as a puzzle, which he promises to do without receiving help. A confederate of the examiner incidentally offers help. If the subject refuses it, he is scored plus; if he accepts, the score is minus. A variation of this is to give the pupil a simple arithmetic test, telling him not to look on the back page. On this page is printed a series of answers, some of which are right and some wrong. If he disobeys and copies from the back sheet, he is likely to copy some of the wrong answers and thereby get caught.

**3. The Reliability Test.** The subject agrees to deliver a letter to his parents and see that a reply is mailed within twenty-four hours. He further agrees not to read the letter. The letter is left unsealed. It is a letter to the parent about the bearer, asking for ratings on certain character traits. If no reply is received or if the reply appears to have been written by the bearer, he is scored as deceptive (untrustworthy).

**4. The Missent Letter.** The subject receives a letter from a business firm enclosing twenty-five cents. The letter says that this amount is sent to balance his account with the firm, and requests that the receipt be sent back in the addressed and stamped envelope which is enclosed.

**5. Other Tests.** Gundlach (15) has reported a method used to detect amounts of cheating in tests or examinations. Students taking a true-false examination were seated by pairs at tables. Half the class or half the number of pairs were given the same questions; in the case of the other half one member of a pair got a different set of questions from the other. The next week the process was reversed. A pair getting different questions the first week got identical questions the second week and *vice versa*. When collusion is possible (that is, when each member of a pair had the same questions) the number of errors is reduced ten per cent and the number of identical errors is increased eighteen to twenty per cent. This technique of course tells nothing about how many individuals copied, much less which individuals did. It is only a method of finding out how much actually went on.

Persing (40) systematically graded certain students' papers too high or too low over a period of years. Papers were returned to the students to be checked. Ninety-seven per cent reported the fact when the grades given were too low, and 9.5% when the grades given were too high. Chambers (10) observed students by means of a mirror, while he stood concealed, to see if they copied from one another or turned the page to get answers to questions. The results were checked by repeating the test without any answers available. Bird (2) used objective examinations of the multiple choice type and noted the number of identical errors in the papers of students suspected of copying from one another. By finding the probable number of identical errors due to chance alone, he was able to prove when copying took place.

## CONCLUSIONS

We have now reviewed the various methods of detecting and measuring deception that had been devised by others. With ingenious efforts such as these to stimulate us and at the same time to warn us against engaging in projects doomed to failure in advance, we were able to move ahead into this little known field with some confidence of our direction if not of the outcome of our expedition.

The association and physiological techniques we can wisely let alone. Their concern is with lying only, but deceptive behavior is vastly broader and more complex than this. Furthermore, the interest of these techniques is in the detection and circumvention of deceit rather than in its measurement. Finally, the procedures used depend too much for success upon an actual rupture of relations between the examiner (as representing society) and the subject, with all the emotional accompaniments of such a break. On these accounts these techniques are ill adapted to the testing of normal populations of children for the purpose of measuring their tendency to deceive in normal situations, when there is no breach between tested and tester and no thought of accusation or defense.

We are not unmindful of the need and value of the studies of the more subtle and minute changes which it is the purpose of physiological tests to detect and record and would not be understood as standing for anything but the vigorous extension of such experiments as have been reported here into other fields and still more refined techniques.

Case studies come much nearer our present need and certain uses of this more broad and concrete approach will be reported on as we proceed. Their interest, however, has only incidentally involved deception, and no standard techniques have been developed which we could have taken over for our work even though this type of approach had seemed adapted to the needs of exact measurement.

We have steered our course therefore between the Scylla of high abstraction in laboratory methods and the Charybdis of confusing concreteness of detail in case studies, trusting rather to the indications of the advancing science of human behavior as it seeks to establish itself on foundations of adequate data concerning the overt behavior of suitably selected populations of such sizes as to afford the basis of assured statistical conclusions.

We turn then to the consideration of the conduct tests utilized by the Inquiry.

# CHAPTER III

# METHODS USED BY THE INQUIRY FOR MEASURING DECEPTION

In Chapter II we reviewed briefly previous efforts to detect and measure deceptive behavior. Most of these methods, however, for one reason or another proved unsuited to our purpose and we have therefore devised other techniques as needed. Since the value of our studies of deception hangs upon the nature of our tests and the meaning of the test scores, we shall present at once a description of the techniques we have used and our method of scoring. We have been faced with many difficult problems of interpretation which have involved technical matters of no interest to the average reader but which were absolutely fundamental to our whole procedure. This technical material will be found, as referred to, in Book Two.

In setting up our techniques we tried to satisfy as many as possible of the requirements which should be met by tests of this type. We have formulated these in ten criteria which it would be well for all readers to examine carefully.

1. The test situation should be as far as possible a natural situation. It should also be a controlled situation. The response should as far as possible be natural even when directed.

2. The test situation and the response should be of such a nature as to allow all subjects equal opportunity to exhibit the behavior which is being tested. That is, there should be nothing about the test itself which would prevent anyone who desired to deceive from so doing; on the other hand, there should be nothing about it to trick an honest subject into an act he would repudiate if he were aware of its import.

3. No test should subject the child to any moral strain beyond

that to which he is subjected in the natural course of his actual life situations.

4. The test should not put the subject and the examiner in false social relations to one another. The examiner should guard against being deceptive himself in order to test the subject.

5. The test should have " low visibility " ; that is, it should be of such a nature as not to arouse the suspicions of the subject. This is one of the fundamental difficulties in all such testing since the entire purpose of the test cannot be announced in advance. This criterion is all the more difficult to meet when coupled with criterion number four, for the examiner must keep secret one aspect of his purpose and at the same time be honest with the subjects.

6. The activity demanded of the subject in taking the test should have real values for him whether he is aware of these values or not.

7. The test should be of such a nature as not to be spoiled by publicity.

8. If tests are to be used in statistical studies they should be group tests. They should also be easy to administer and should be mechanically scored. They should be short enough to be given in single school periods.

9. The test results should be clear and unambiguous. It should be obvious from the results whether the subject did or did not exhibit the behavior in question. The evidence should be such as would be accepted in a court of law.

10. The scores should be quantitative, showing the amount as well as the fact of deception. Each test therefore should be flexible enough to include within its scope wide ranges of deceptive tendency.

These requirements are quite rigid and no technique has yet been devised which will meet all of them. Only one previously used method came sufficiently within the standard set to warrant our adopting it. This was the peeping type of test, which we took over with certain modifications.

We shall present our own techniques in accordance with the following outline :

I. Methods for measuring the cheating type of deceptive behavior
   A. As exhibited in classroom situations
      1. The copying technique
      2. The duplicating technique
      3. The improbable achievement technique
         *a.* Puzzle performance tests
         *b.* Paper and pencil tests
      4. The double testing technique
         *a.* IER achievement tests
         *b.* Speed tests
   B. As exhibited in work done at home
   C. As exhibited in athletic contests
   D. As exhibited in parlor games
II. Methods for measuring the stealing type of deception
   A. In party or play situations
   B. In classroom situations
III. Methods for measuring the lying type of deception
   A. To escape disapproval
   B. To gain approval

Perhaps with this little map to aid him the reader will be able to find his way about more readily among the descriptions contained in this chapter.

## METHODS FOR MEASURING THE CHEATING TYPE OF DECEPTIVE BEHAVIOR

### A. As Exhibited in Classroom Situations

**1. The Copying Technique.** Copying from another pupil is supposed to be one of the most common types of cheating. One of the first methods we devised was intended to cover such cases. It consists in using two different forms of some short-answer school test which look alike but have slight, imperceptible, but important differences. The two sets are distributed alternately and " staggered " so that no two pupils side by side or back and front will have the same set. Then if a pupil attempts to copy answers from the pupil at either side of him or in front or back, he will copy the wrong answers. Unless he is a very close reader, the papers of his neighbors will appear to be exactly the same as his. This procedure may be worked with an arithmetic test, a true-false test, or any multiple answer test in which the choices are numbered and the pupils write the number of the correct answer in the margin rather than underline it.

We tried it with an " opposites " test. The task is to find the word which has an opposite meaning to the word in capitals and write its number on the dotted line at the right.

### Form A

1. GIVE......1 present..2 accept..3 take..4 wish..5 absent.. (....) 1
2. FRIEND ..1 soldier..2 true..3 false..4 enemy..5 fight.. (....) 2
3. HELP .....1 hinder..2 assist..3 someone..4 need..5 chantey (....) 3
4. BORROW..1 steal..2 return..3 book..4 loan..5 debt.. (....) 4
5. KIND .....1 sweet..2 cruel..3 sort..4 sympathy..5 always.. (....) 5

### Form B

1. GIVE......1 present..2 accept..3 wish..4 take..5 absent.. (....) 1
2. FRIEND ..1 soldier..2 false..3 true..4 enemy..5 fight.. (....) 2
3. HELP .....1 hinder..2 need..3 someone..4 assist..5 chantey (....) 3
4. BORROW..1 steal..2 book..3 return..4 loan..5 debt.. (....) 4
5. KIND .....1 sweet..2 sort..3 cruel..4 sympathy..5 always.. (....) 5

Here, both forms contain the same words, the only difference being a slight rearrangement so that the correct answer to item number one on form A is word number three, and on form B is word number four, but the same word as number three in A. If pupil B copies from pupil A, the answers on the dotted lines will be the same; if A's answers are correct, B's will be incorrect.

We tried these opposites tests on a small group of children in the sixth grade. On two larger groups of university students we used the same method with different material. The results in both cases were so ambiguous and hard to interpret that we abandoned the method entirely. Even with a knowledge of the seating of the pupils on the examination and even by comparing the papers pair by pair according to the seating arrangement, it is very difficult

to be sure whether cheating took place.   The difficulty is this.
Suppose that the test has, say, ten elements or items.

| ELEMENTS | 1 | 2 | 3 | 4 | 5 | 6 | 7 | 8 | 9 | 10 |
|---|---|---|---|---|---|---|---|---|---|---|
| Form A | 3 | 3 | 5 | 4 | 1 | 2 | 2 | 5 | 4 | 1 |
| Form B | 2 | 1 | 4 | 3 | 2 | 3 | 1 | 4 | 2 | 2 |

Suppose also that the correct words to each multiple choice are as
given above.   Now a pupil taking form B may mark " 3 " instead
of " 2 " as the correct response for No. 1, and make an honest mistake.   But if *all* his answers to B are wrong and are at the same
time the correct responses for A, then we may be sure that he
cheated.   But this rarely happens, for B will know some answers,
will guess at or think he knows others, and may copy some from A.
The net result is that one cannot tell from his paper whether he
copied from A or whether he simply made mistakes, unless of course
there is a great number of these mistakes that match the correct
responses of the other form.*

Not only are the results ambiguous but such a technique does
not give equal opportunity to all who may desire to copy.   Pupils
know the relative abilities of their classmates.   A very dishonest
pupil may show up honest on the test only because there is no one
near enough from whose paper he would care to copy.   Since this
test failed to meet requirements numbers two and nine, we dis-
continued its use after the preliminary trials.

2. **The Duplicating Technique.**   Another rather common form
of classroom deceptiveness occurs when the pupil makes illegitimate
use of a key or answer sheet either in doing his work or in the scoring of his own test paper.   This is one type of behavior which we
have been most successful in testing.   We have two ways of handling this situation.   The first we call the duplicating technique,
which affords the same results as the paraffin test described in the
previous chapter.   The second we shall discuss presently when
dealing with the IER tests.

Any sort of test is given, preferably the short answer type.   The
papers are collected and taken to the office, where a duplicate is

* See article by Bird, Bibliography (2).

made of each paper.  Great care is taken to be certain that an exact record is made of what the pupil actually did on the test. At a later session of the class the papers are returned and each child is given a key, or answer sheet, and is asked to score his own paper.  The self-scored papers are then compared with the duplicates and all changes are recorded.  Deception consists in illegitimately increasing one's score by copying answers from the key.

The following test materials were used for this purpose:

(a) *The Information Test.**  This consists of twenty-eight items.  Instead of underlining the correct answer, the pupil in this case is required to encircle it in ink.  He is not allowed to hand in his paper until he has at least attempted every question.  In order to cheat on this test a child has to erase the circle drawn in ink and make another, when he is asked to score his paper.†

Sample items are:

1. Bombay is a city in   China      France      Japan      India
2. Pongee is a    dance      food      fabric      drink
3. Hannibal is the name of a    general      king      prize fighter river
4. One horse-power equals   746 watts      1000 watts      $16\frac{2}{3}$ watts      2.45 watts
5. Brahmaputra is the name of a    flower      goddess      language river

(b) *The Sentence Completion Test.**  Cheating here consists in either adding on more words, that is, doing more items, or in changing words previously written in pencil by erasing and rewriting. Fifty-five sentences such as these were used:

1. Men _____ older than boys.
2. The poor little _____ has _____ nothing to _____ ; he is hungry.

* Tests *a, b, c,* and *d* were supplied by the Institute of Educational Research through the courtesy of Professor Thorndike.

† These tests were devised in order to measure the amount of resistance an individual could overcome or of trouble he would take in order to cheat.  This phase of the experiment is discussed fully in Chapter XXI of Book One and Chapter XII of Book Two.

3. No ———————— what happens wrong is ————————
   right.
4. He believed in ———————— hard things ————————
   because ———————— ———————— hard.
5. He must ———————— further assistance from us.   We
   cannot give it.

(c) *The Word Knowledge Test.** This is arranged as a multiple
choice test.   The response words are numbered from one to five.
When the correct response word is located, its number is written
on the dotted line at the margin.   Cheating consists in either erasing this number and entering the correct one or in writing down
more numbers.   There were 120 items in all, such as these :

1. boyish   1 naughty. .2 male. .3 impudent. .
              4 like a boy. .5 informal. .                      . . . .1.
2. blunt    1 dull. .2 drowsy. .3 deaf. .4 doubtful. .
              5 ugly. .                                          . . . .2.
3. default   1 defeat. .2 blame. .3 failure. .4 libel. .
              5 displace. .                                      . . . .3.
4. allusion  1 aria. .2 illusion. .3 eulogy. .4 dream. .
              5 reference. .                                     . . . .4.
5. astute    1 rigorous. .2 shrewd. .3 unsound. .
              4 bony. .5 astonished. .                          . . . .5.

(d) *The Arithmetic Test.** Here also the answers are written
at the margin and changes are made as in the case of the previous
test.   The original test had fifty examples of which the following
are illustrations :

1. When sugar costs 10 cents a pound, how much
   will 5 pounds cost?   .   .   .   .   .   .   .   Answer ( . . . )
2. How many eggs are needed to make 3 cakes if
   you use 2 eggs for one cake? .   .   .   .   .   .   Answer ( . . . )
3. $\frac{1}{8} \times 22$ equals   .   .   .   .   .   .   .   .   .   .   Answer ( . . . )
4. 18 equals ——% of 40?   .   .   .   .   .   .   .   Answer ( . . . )

* Tests *a, b, c,* and *d* were supplied by the Institute of Educational Research
through the courtesy of Professor Thorndike.

5. A push-cart man buys eggs at 15¢ per dozen and
   sells them at 15 for 25¢. How many eggs
   must he sell to gain $1.80? . . . . . . Answer ( ... )

(e) *The Thorndike-McCall Reading Scale.* This test consists of short paragraphs to be read by the subject. Then follow a few questions the correct answers to which can be given in a single word or short phrase. Cheating consists in changing one or two words or sometimes a whole phrase, or in filling in more answers.

(f) *An Original Disarranged Sentence Test.* In this test the task is to straighten out mixed-up words so they will make a sentence. If the child finds any problem too difficult he is required to draw a line through the blank space, to indicate that he has omitted it. Cheating can be accomplished therefore only by erasing a line or sentence and substituting something else. There were fifteen word groups such as these :

1. houses people live in _____

2. teacher to I paper my correct asked my _____
   _____

3. pies Will feel sick and eskimo could not eat five _____
   _____

4. aggravate miseries pleasure present recall past to is but to our
   _____

5. to to to is is be be good good noble, how teach but others nobler —
   and less trouble _____
   _____

(g) *An Original Spelling Test.* The test is made up of ninety words some of which are misspelled. The task is to check misspelled words. To cheat, one had only to add more check marks or erase those previously made.

1. —— ache          6. —— genuine
2. —— beleive        7. —— niece
3. —— laid           8. —— sacreligious
4. —— hybred         9 —— chauffeur
5. —— rythm          10. —— parlimentary

It was necessary to have each test steeply graded in difficulty and to give less time than even the most competent would require to complete the test, so that when the papers were scored there would be abundant opportunity to make use of the keys if any were disposed to do so.    Thus for the Thorndike-McCall Reading Test we allowed only fifteen minutes although the standard time is thirty.

The directions for handling the duplicating technique will be found in Appendix B.

*Scoring.*    In all these tests, two kinds of scores are used, the *amount score* and the *fact score*.    The *amount score* is the total score when the test is given under conditions permitting dishonesty.    It ordinarily contains an element of honest performance for which allowance is properly made as will be explained later. In the case of the duplicating technique, each change counted as one point.    If the pupil made only one change in his paper and this did not affect his score it was counted as zero.    Two or more changes were counted whether they affected the score or not.*    The amount score is simply the number of changes made.    The total amount score for all the tests was obtained by summing up all the changes after they had been reduced to a common denominator.†    The *fact score* ‡ is a record of the fact of honesty or deception.    It is simply a " c " (cheating) whenever two or more changes are made or when one change affects the score.

This technique meets most of the requirements very well.    It would seem at first sight to have rather " high visibility " and not be applicable to older groups.    We have evidence, however, that it has been successfully used with a group of college sophomores. We have not employed it extensively, however, because it is too expensive and time-consuming.

**3. The Improbable Achievement Technique.**    This consists in giving a test under conditions such that achievement above a certain level will indicate deception.    An example is the circles

---

* Pupils sometimes make changes in spelling or wording which do not affect the answer.

† Each score was divided by the standard deviation of its distribution.

‡ In most cases this " fact " represents a *probability* of 999 chances in 1000.

test described in Chapter II. It will be recalled that the pupil is given a sheet of paper with a number of small circles placed on it. The pupil is instructed to close his eyes and make a pencil mark of some sort in each circle. Even chance alone will provide a certain amount of success. But achievement beyond a certain point is evidence of deception by peeping.

We have used this technique with two kinds of tests, one requiring the use of paper and pencil and the other the use of objects like puzzles or games. As the puzzle tests are the simpler we will describe these first.

(a) *Puzzle Performance Tests.* There are certain kinds of mechanical puzzles which may be effectively used. The puzzle must appear simple but be in reality very difficult. It must require genuine skill rather than the knowledge of a secret trick or principle. It must be of such a nature that the dishonest pupil can fake a solution or appear to have solved it when he really did not. After considerable preliminary searching and experimenting we settled on three puzzles.

(1) *The Puzzle Peg (or Peg Solitaire).* This is a game of solitaire which may be bought in the toy stores. It consists of a circular board about six inches in diameter with thirty-three holes arranged as in the diagram. Each hole has a peg in it except the center one. When two pegs are adjacent with a vacant hole next in line, one peg may jump the other and land in the vacant hole. The peg " jumped " is removed. The problem is to jump all the pegs off the board except one and leave this one in the center hole. Anyone who has tried this knows how very difficult it is. The time allowed was five minutes for the first trial and three for the second. Cheating consists in faking a solution by pulling out all the pegs but one and placing it in the middle hole without playing the game at all. Or the solution may be partly faked by pulling out some pegs and jumping some.

In administering the puzzle tests a score sheet was used of which a portion is shown below. It should be noted that in all the puzzle tests we have only the record made by the child on his score sheet. We do not know of course whether the deceptive child falsified his performance but made a true record of it, or whether he did not falsify his performance but made a false record of it. In one puzzle for one group this matter was checked and we found that in over ninety per cent of the deceptive cases the peg boards and score sheets agreed.

PUZZLE TESTS SCORE SHEET

Name................................................................................ Grade........................................................................

School.............................................................................. Date..........................................................................

The following spaces are for recording your scores. Do not make any entries until told what to do.

*Pill Boxes:* Weight discrimination.

In the spaces below copy the numbers from the bottoms of the boxes to show the order in which you had them at the end of each trial.

1st trial  ☐ ☐ ☐ ☐ ☐ ☐ ☐

2nd trial  ☐ ☐ ☐ ☐ ☐ ☐ ☐

*Puzzle Blocks* "Sixteen"

Copy the numbers off the blocks into the squares at the right to show the order they were in at the end of the test.

*Peg Board*

a. Write in the space at the right the number of pegs left on the board at the end of the first trial................................................................................ (.......................)

b. Write in the space at the right the number of pegs left on the board at the end of the second trial.................................................................. (.......................)

c. Write "yes" in the space at the right if you had only one peg left on either trial and it in the middle............................................................... (.......................)

We have found no one yet who, without considerable previous experience with this game, could solve it in five minutes. Consequently any child who claims to have solved it in the time allowed is cheating or else he is one of those very rare persons who by many hours of previous practice has learned the game so well as to do it in five minutes. It is only slightly less difficult to leave one or two pegs standing anywhere on the board.

The amount score was the number of pegs left on the board at the end of the second period, or the smallest number achieved during the period.

For the fact score, the pupil was scored as having cheated if only one or two pegs were left in any holes on either trial.

(2) *The Fifteen Puzzle.* This puzzle had a certain advantage over the peg board in that it could not be bought in the toy shops in New York during our testing although a modified form was issued as advertising material by a commercial company. We did find three sets in a small store that deals exclusively in magicians' trick materials. Every dealer professed to have known it years ago but informed us that it was now out of style and off the market.* It consists simply of a small box four inches square with sixteen blocks each one inch square and numbered zero to fifteen. The small squares are made of wood. We arranged them in a standardized chance order which was as follows : †

$$10 \quad 8 \quad 5 \quad 13$$
$$15 \quad 6 \quad 2 \quad 3$$
$$9 \quad 11 \quad 12 \quad 0$$
$$14 \quad 1 \quad 7 \quad 4$$

The problem is to remove the one marked 0 and then by sliding the others around get them in this order :

$$1 \quad 2 \quad 3 \quad 4$$
$$5 \quad 6 \quad 7 \quad 8$$
$$9 \quad 10 \quad 11 \quad 12$$
$$13 \quad 14 \quad 15$$

It is strictly forbidden to remove any block from the board. The puzzle must be solved by sliding the blocks around. Five to eight minutes were allowed. Here cheating consists in taking the blocks out and placing them in the correct order without playing the game.

* It has since reappeared in the toy stores.

† For future work we have adopted a different arrangement, only partially solvable.

As these puzzles were not available, we had to manufacture them ourselves.

In the spaces provided on the score sheet the child makes a record of the numbers on the squares as they appeared when time was called.

To obtain the amount score, the rows across the square were taken as units and weighted thus:

|  |  |
|---|---|
| 1st row correct, 1   2   3   4 . . . . . | 1 credit |
| 2d row correct, 5   6   7   8 . . . . . | 2 credits |
| 3d row correct, 9   10   11   12 . . . . | 3 credits |
| 4th row correct, 13   14   15   . . . . | 4 credits |
| Maximum score . . . . . . . . . | 10 credits |

Before a pupil was marked " c " or negative, he must have scored the maximum.

(3) *The Weight Discrimination Test.* This was really not a puzzle, but a modification of the weight discrimination test used in the Binet intelligence test and in routine experiments in psychological laboratories. It consisted of seven small pill boxes. The boxes were filled in our office with cotton batting and buck shot so that in each set of seven no two weighed the same. They were numbered on the bottom from one to seven, in order of weight. The difference in weight between any adjoining boxes of the set, as one and two or three and four, was too slight to be detected,* so that no one could arrange the boxes in order of weight without looking at the numbers, except by chance.

The instructions were to turn the numbers down and arrange the boxes in the order of their weight. After the first trial the pupils were told to look at the numbers on the bottom and copy these numbers off on the score sheet to show how they had been arranged. They were then told that the correct arrangement was the serial order 1, 2, 3, 4, 5, 6, 7 and were asked to turn the numbers down again and not look at them during the second trial. Three min-

---

* The weights averaged in grams (1) 3.6, (2) 3.7, (3) 3.8, (4) 3.9, (5) 4.0, (6) 4.1, (7) 4.2, with variations always checked so as to secure real differences in any one set.

utes were given for each trial. Cheating consists in peeping at the numbers.

The weights were arranged twice and a record made each time on the score sheet. These records were scored as follows: First, a position score was given each trial by giving one point credit for each weight in its correct position. Thus all weights in correct order scored seven. Any weight in its correct position regardless of the others was scored one credit. For example, an arrangement like this: 2 1 3 5 7 6 4 was scored one, because weight number three was in position number three. This scheme gave two position scores, one for each trial. But since on the second trial the pupils were told that the numbers indicated the correct order, more significance was attached to the second trial.

The two position scores were combined and " weighted " according to the likelihood of dishonesty.* That is, the combinations that were least likely to occur by chance were given correspondingly larger cheating scores and *vice versa*.

Any combination was rated " c " which contained a position

* To get the amount score, the following table of arbitrary weights was constructed. The first column represents the first trial and the second column the second trial. "W" means the weighted total score assigned to the raw score values shown in the first two columns.

| 1st | 2d | W | 1st | 2d | W | 1st | 2d | W | 1st | 2d | W | 1st | 2d | W |
|-----|----|----|-----|----|----|-----|----|----|-----|----|----|-----|-----|---|
| 7 | 7 | 11 | 4 | 5 | 6 | 4 | 7 | 4 | 4 | 3 | 3 | 3 | 2 | 1 |
| 5 | 7 | 10 | 3 | 5 | 6 | 3 | 7 | 4 | 4 | 2 | 3 | 2 | 2 | 1 |
| 4 | 7 | 10 | 7 | 4 | 6 | 2 | 7 | 4 | 4 | 1 | 3 | 1 | 2 | 1 |
| 3 | 7 | 9 | 5 | 4 | 6 | 1 | 7 | 4 | 4 | 0 | 3 | 3 | 1–0 | 0 |
| 2 | 7 | 9 | 2 | 5 | 5 | 0 | 7 | 4 | 3 | 2 | 3 | 2 | 1–0 | 0 |
| 7 | 5 | 8 | 1 | 5 | 5 | 5 | 3 | 4 | 2 | 2 | 3 | 1 | 1–0 | 0 |
| 5 | 5 | 8 | 0 | 5 | 5 | 2 | 4 | 1 | 1 | 3 | 2 | 0 | 1–0 | 0 |
| 1 | 7 | 7 | 7 | 0 | 5 | 5 | 1 | 4 | 0 | 3 | 2 | | | |
| 0 | 7 | 7 | 7 | 1 | 5 | 5 | 0 | 4 | | | | | | |
| | | | 7 | 2 | 5 | | | | | | | | | |

Any amount score of 7, 8, 9, 10, or 11 was scored "c." See Book Two for further explanations.

score of 7 on the second trial, or of 5 on the second trial provided the 5 was preceded by a 5 or 7 on the first trial.

(b) *Paper and Pencil Tests.*    Three tests were used, namely, a Squares test, as devised by Cady, a Circles test, similar to Voelker's

## SQUARES PUZZLE

Put your pencil point on the cross in Square No. 1.    When the signal is given, shut your eyes and move the pencil in the direction of the arrow around the center and back to the cross, without touching the sides of the lane.    Wait for the signal for each trial.

After each trial if you succeeded in doing that square correctly, put a check mark on the line after the number of the square you have just tried.    If you touched the side once you lose the square, and get no score for it.    After the last trial enter the total score using the table at the right for finding the score. The maximum score is 100.

Record of Trials

Square 1............................

Square 2............................

Square 3............................

Square 4............................

Square 5............................

Total Score............

Score Values Table

Any one right is............ 5

Any two right is............ 15

Any three right is........ 30

Any four right is........... 60

Any five right is..........100

## CIRCLES PUZZLE

Wait for the signal for each trial. Put the point of your pencil on the cross at the foot of the oval. Then when the signal is given shut your eyes and put the figure 1 in each circle, taking them in order. For the second trial, put the figure 2 in each circle. For the third trial, the figure 3, etc. After each trial put a check mark in the score box under the number of each circle you succeeded in striking, count the checks and enter the total in the column headed T at the right of the score box. After the last trial add up Column T. This is your score. The maximum score is 50.

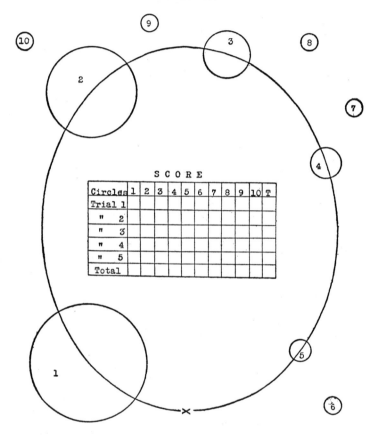

SCORE

| Circles | 1 | 2 | 3 | 4 | 5 | 6 | 7 | 8 | 9 | 10 | T |
|---|---|---|---|---|---|---|---|---|---|---|---|
| Trial 1 | | | | | | | | | | | |
| " 2 | | | | | | | | | | | |
| " 3 | | | | | | | | | | | |
| " 4 | | | | | | | | | | | |
| " 5 | | | | | | | | | | | |
| Total | | | | | | | | | | | |

and Cady's, and a Mazes test suggested by Cady's. These we have called " coördination " tests inasmuch as the function involved seems to be that of muscular coördination. The facsimiles will

make these clear.   Full directions for giving them will be found
in section C of the Appendix.   The pupils were told frequently to

## MAZES PUZZLE

Wait for signal for each maze.  Each time put the point of your pencil on the cross.  Then when the
signal is given shut your eyes and move the pencil through the maze without touching the sides.  After
each effort enter the score value on the dotted line at the left after the maze number.  The score value of
the maze is given in the right hand column.  When through, add your scores.  The maximum score is 100.

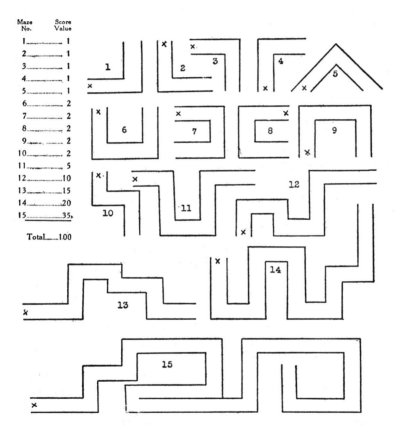

| Maze No. | Score Value |
|---|---|
| 1 | 1 |
| 2 | 1 |
| 3 | 1 |
| 4 | 1 |
| 5 | 1 |
| 6 | 2 |
| 7 | 2 |
| 8 | 2 |
| 9 | 2 |
| 10 | 2 |
| 11 | 5 |
| 12 | 10 |
| 13 | 15 |
| 14 | 20 |
| 15 | 35 |

Total......100

keep their eyes shut while making their marks on the papers.
Cheating consists in opening the eyes to improve one's score.

Both Voelker and Cady made some effort to find out the limit of honest ability on tests of this sort, but only by using themselves or adults as subjects. The children were then scored " yes " or " no " according to whether they exceeded these limits when their eyes were supposed to be shut. As we wanted a score that would show the amount as well as the fact of cheating, we used a control population of 275 children in grades five to eight of a public school under conditions which precluded the use of the eyes. We tested only half the pupils in a classroom at one time. One row would sit at the desks ready to take the test and the other would stand beside the first row, each pupil with a cardboard in his hand. When all the directions had been given and the seated pupils were ready to shut their eyes, the standing pupils placed the cardboards in front of the eyes of those who were seated at their desks so that the entire test paper was concealed from the subject taking the test. No change in posture was needed. From these " honest " results we found the limits of probable achievement and the relative amount of achievement to be expected on the three tasks.

When the tests were first given we had the pupils score their own papers. We felt that this put too much strain on the honest pupils and so later abandoned all scoring by pupils. Only three trials were used for the Circles test, instead of five. The final scoring methods may be summarized as follows :

1. Squares. Amount score equals number of corners turned correctly. Fact score allows 13 corners ; 14 or more is called a " c."

2. Circles. Amount score equals total number of figures in all ten circles in the three trials. Fact score allows 13 marks in the circles and calls 14 or more a " c."

3. Mazes. Amount score equals total number of corners turned correctly. Fact score allows 31 corners and calls 32 or more a " c."

4. Total score on Coördination tests. In adding these scores together allowance is made for the extra length of the Mazes test, which is twice as long as the others. The total amount score thus

equals the sum of the Squares and Circles plus half the Mazes score.*

*Value of the Improbable Achievement Technique.*    On the whole the improbable achievement technique is satisfactory.    Its chief weakness lies in the difficulty of discovering just what level of achievement is probable or improbable for individuals or groups. The Puzzle tests are rather cumbersome to handle as group tests, due to the fact that thirty or forty boxes of the size used are somewhat unwieldy.    And of course in testing several groups it is a saving of time to have enough for two or three groups to use simultaneously.    But this is a minor difficulty.

**4. The Double Testing Technique.†**    When this method is used the pupils are tested twice.    On one occasion there is strict supervision and no opportunity to deceive is given.    On the other occasion the conditions are such as to permit deception : the barriers are let down, and the only resistance to the tendency to cheat is

---

* The scores are weighted by their respective SD's.    The means and SD's of honest performance are as follows :

|  | MEAN | SD | ALLOWANCE |
|---|---|---|---|
| Squares  .  .  .  . | 5.26 | 2.71 | 13 |
| Circles  .  .  .  . | 5.71 | 2.55 | 13 |
| Mazes  .  .  .  . | 14.17 | 5.66 | 31 |

The allowance is the honest mean plus three times the honest SD.

The method of getting what we call the Xi score, which is in terms of the ratio of deviation from the honest mean to the honest SD, is discussed in connection with the IER material and defended at length in Book Two.

† The overstatement test described in Chapter II is an illustration of this technique.    Voelker suggested a test of this nature also, although he did not use it.    He proposed that the subjects be asked to memorize a poem and then try to write it without referring to the copy which they retained.    When the pupils are writing off the poem the examiner is supposed to leave the room. At the next meeting the poem is returned to them and they are asked to read it through.    It is then collected and they are again instructed to write it from memory and the examiner remains in the room.    Score is obtained by dividing the percentage of words correctly written in the second test by the percentage correctly written in the first test.

in the individual's own habits and attitudes. The difference between the scores made on the two occasions is roughly a measure of the tendency to deceive. Cheating consists in either copying answers from the key or in changing answers to match the key.

Any sort of test material may be used for this method. It may be intelligence tests or educational achievement tests (such as arithmetic, spelling, or reading) or it may be any sort of traditional psychological test. The chief requirements of the material are that it be available in two equivalent forms and that these forms all have the same degree of difficulty at all levels.* To illustrate, suppose we have two sets of arithmetic problems. Each set is arranged in order of difficulty from the easiest to the hardest. Further, suppose that every problem in form A is matched with a similar and equally difficult (but not exactly identical) problem in form B. Now the assumption is that if a pupil scores twenty in form A he will also score twenty or thereabouts in form B. Suppose that form A is given on Monday and each pupil is given an answer sheet and told to correct his own paper but to keep the answer sheet out of sight until he is ready to score ; then on Tuesday form B is given but now no answer sheets are passed out. If a pupil scores thirty on Monday with the key and twenty on Tuesday without the key, then the presumption is that he made illegitimate use of the key on Monday.†

We have used the double testing technique with two kinds of material. The first kind was intelligence testing material developed by the Institute of Educational Research in connection with a series of studies made on levels of intelligence. This material was placed at our disposal through the courtesy of Professor Thorndike. We shall refer to it as the IER tests. The second kind of material was developed by us out of the stock varieties of

---

* The two forms must also have reasonable reliability, as will be discussed later.

† The technical problems involved in the scoring, standardization, and interpretation of this material are all discussed at length in Book Two, the statistical supplement.

psychological speed tests.    We shall describe these tests presently
and refer to them as Speed tests.

(a)  *The IER Achievement Tests.*    From Professor Thorndike's
intelligence level materials we selected five kinds:

1. Arithmetic problems
2. Mutilated sentences for sentence completion tests
3. Information test elements
4. Word knowledge or vocabulary test elements
5. Selections for reading tests *

Samples of the first four were given in connection with the discussion of the duplicating technique on pages 51 ff.    These were particularly adapted to our needs.    In the first place, the material had
already been carefully validated as intelligence testing material
so that the total score obtained under supervised conditions gave
an excellent measure of the pupils' intelligence.    In the second
place, the difficulty of each test element had been experimentally
determined.    Two parallel sets or forms of each test were built
by taking two or three elements from each level of difficulty.
Tests thus constructed were easy enough for fifth-grade children
at the lower end and hard enough for eighth-grade pupils at the
upper end.    In fact, all pupils tested were able to do something
with each test, and no pupil was able to make a perfect score when
the tests were given under supervision.    This gave even the bright-
est pupils room to use the key if they wanted to.    Thus by using
such tests we measured both intelligence and deception.

We have just observed that the two forms were built so as to be
approximately parallel and equal in difficulty.    This meant that
if a pupil reached a given level under supervision he would be
expected to go no higher under conditions permitting the use of an
answer sheet.    But even when no deception is present there will
be variations in scores from day to day on tests that are as nearly
alike as it is now possible to make them.    In other words, the best
arithmetic test made will not measure arithmetical ability as accurately as a yardstick will measure the length of a table.    It was

* Omitted after  preliminary experimentation as it was found unsuited for
this use.

necessary, therefore, to make allowance for normal fluctuations in scores and not credit to deception any differences that might be due to imperfections in the tests or to variations in the interest and ability of the pupils.

We can best illustrate how we made this allowance by taking some actual cases. Table I gives a list of scores on the Arithmetic test on two occasions when no chance to deceive was permitted, and on two other occasions when on the first day an answer sheet was at hand and on the second day no answer sheet was given.

TABLE I

COMPARISON OF CHANGES FROM DAY TO DAY IN TEST SCORES OF SIXTEEN PUPILS (I) WHEN NO CHANCE TO CHEAT WAS GIVEN AND (II) WHEN THERE WAS A CHANCE TO CHEAT ON ONE OCCASION BUT NOT ON THE OTHER

| | (I) | | | | (II) | | |
|---|---|---|---|---|---|---|---|
| | No CHEATING | | | | CHANCE TO CHEAT ON FIRST DAY | | |
| PUPIL | 1st Day Score | 2d Day Score | Difference | PUPIL | Key 1st Day Score | No Key 2d Day Score | Difference |
| A | 32 | 32 | 0 | M | 36 | 22 | − 14 |
| B | 31 | 30 | − 1 | N | 39 | 7 | − 32 |
| C | 29 | 24 | − 5 | O | 47 | 10 | − 37 |
| D | 27 | 28 | + 1 | P | 39 | 13 | − 26 |
| E | 24 | 26 | + 2 | Q | 51 | 21 | − 30 |
| F | 29 | 34 | + 5 | R | 40 | 15 | − 25 |
| G | 29 | 29 | 0 | S | 32 | 26 | − 6 |
| H | 38 | 39 | + 1 | T | 20 | 17 | − 3 |
| Average . . . . . . | | | + .37 | Average . . . . . . | | | − 21.6 |

To make the evidence of the use of answer sheets rather obvious we have taken for illustration under (II) of Table I a group from an extremely deceptive population. Here, it will be noticed, the differences between the scores of the two days are enormous. The average difference of the honest scores is a gain of .37 examples and the average difference of the dishonest scores is a loss of 21.6 examples. That is, the presence of the key made possible an average score 21.6 points bigger than was possible when the answer sheet was not present.    In the case of one of the pairs of honest scores (I), however, there was a loss of five points even though no answer sheet was involved at all.    On this basis we could say that the two last cases under (II) probably did not cheat and that the rest probably did.

Of course to be sure of our judgment we had to use a large number of cases in order to find the most extreme differences that are

TABLE II

TYPICAL GAINS AND LOSSES IN ARITHMETIC BETWEEN THE FIRST AND SECOND DAY WHEN NO CHEATING WENT ON

| GAIN OR LOSS | FREQUENCY |
|:---:|:---:|
| + 11 | 2 |
| + 10 | 1 |
| + 9 | 3 |
| + 8 | 2 |
| + 7 | 2 |
| + 6 | 14 |
| + 5 | 20 |
| + 4 | 19 |
| + 3 | 57 |
| + 2 | 31 |
| + 1 | 57 |
| 0 | 45 |
| − 1 | 30 |
| − 2 | 20 |
| − 3 | 28 |
| − 4 | 6 |
| − 5 | 9 |
| − 6 | 2 |
| − 7 | 2 |
| − 8 | 2 |
| N or total  .  .  .  . | 352 |

Average or mean $= + 1.06$
Standard deviation $= 3.10$
This table reads: 2 pupils gained 11 points, 1 pupil gained 10 points, 3 pupils gained 9 points; also 2 pupils *lost* 8 points, 2 lost 7 points, etc.

likely to occur when no answer sheets are available. The details of this process of standardization will be found in Book Two. It is sufficient for the guidance of the general reader to know that we must allow a difference of eight arithmetic problems before assuming that cheating took place.

Some confidence in the trustworthiness of this procedure may be gained by picturing what we actually find in large populations. Table II shows the gains and losses actually noted in 352 children of grades five, six, seven, and eight. The figures represent the same thing as those in the " Difference " column under (I) of Table I. They are differences between the first and second day when no answer sheets are available and no cheating is permitted. The amount of gain or loss is shown in the column at the left and the number of pupils having this amount of gain or loss is given in the second column. This way of presenting a set of scores is called a " distribution " or " frequency distribution."

When these figures are graphically portrayed they make Figure 3. Along the base line the amount of gain or loss is laid out in equal steps. The number of cases showing each amount is indicated by the height of the column rising above each step on the base line. It will be seen that about as many gain as lose. The average, in fact, is a gain of 1.06 examples.

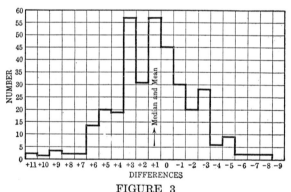

FIGURE 3

HISTOGRAM SHOWING GRAPHICALLY THE DISTRIBUTION OF HONEST DIFFERENCES IN ARITHMETIC SCORES ON TWO OCCASIONS

Now look at Figure 4. This shows the gain and loss when on the first day the children have an answer sheet with which to score their papers but are instructed to keep it out of sight until time to use

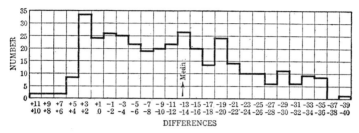

DIFFERENCES

FIGURE 4

HISTOGRAM SHOWING GRAPHICALLY THE DISTRIBUTION OF DIFFERENCES BETWEEN HONEST AND DISHONEST ARITHMETIC SCORES

it for scoring. Note the position of the two means in relation to zero gain or loss.

Smoothing these curves as they would appear if we had still more cases and putting them on the same graph, we have Figure 5, in which the solid line is the honest difference and the dotted line the dishonest difference.

In nearly all our scores we use as a unit of measure the amount an individual, under conditions permitting dishonesty, deviates from what might be expected of him when dishonesty is impossible. This involves a common statistical concept which we should like to make clear to the non-technical reader in a brief digression.

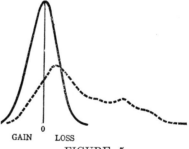

GAIN 0 LOSS

FIGURE 5

COMPARING TEST RESULTS WHEN NO ANSWER SHEET IS USED ON EITHER DAY WITH RESULTS WHEN ANSWER SHEETS ARE AVAILABLE ON THE FIRST DAY

(1) *Explanation of Statistical Terms.* In the first place, all measurements require at least two things: first, a unit for measuring,

such as the inch, the yard, the dollar; second, a point of reference from which measurements are taken, such as sea level for altitudes, the freezing point of water for centigrade temperatures. In statistics it is customary to use as the point of reference some central tendency of the set of facts in question, such as the mean (average) or median. The unit is some measure of the variability or the fluctuation of these measures around this point of reference. In this particular problem and in fact always throughout this investigation the point of reference from which measures are taken is the mean or average. Thus in Table II let us now think of these differences as deviations from the average, which is 1.06. A *loss* of 8 points on the Arithmetic test now becomes a deviation of 8 plus 1.06 or −9.06 from the average; a *gain* of 3 points is a deviation of 3 *minus* 1.06 or +1.94, and so on for all the rest. Thus even a zero difference becomes, in accordance with this plan, a deviation of −1.06.

It will make it easier to understand these terms if the reader will refer to Figure 3, which visualizes the figures of Table II. Along the line at the bottom are counted the gains or losses in units of one. The number of individuals making each gain or loss is shown by the height of the column over each step on the base line. These numbers are called "frequencies," and the space inclosed by the curve and base line is called a "surface of frequency." The vertical line at the center shows the position of the mean, or arithmetical average, which is simply the sum of all the measures divided by their number. It happens also in this one case to be the median. The median is found by counting in from either end to the point on each side of which one-half the cases fall when the series of measures is arranged in a distribution as in Table II. Thus for the figures of this table, the sum of the frequencies is 352, *i.e.*, there are 352 individuals. One-half of this figure is 176. So counting in 176 from either end we come to plus one as the mid-point. This is the median of the distribution.*

We shall state most of our scores, then, as deviations from the

* Strictly, of course, the median is $\frac{32}{17}$ beyond .5 or 1.06, since the figures are differences, not original scores.

mean or median of the corresponding distribution of an "honest" population such as is shown in Table II, *i.e.*, which had no chance to cheat. A loss of four on the Arithmetic test is scored $4 + 1.06$ or 5.06 instead of 4.

This takes care of the point of reference, but we still lack a common unit of measurement. In this work we have used for the most part the "mean square deviation," or what is often called the "standard deviation" (SD), commonly referred to as "sigma" ($\sigma$). This also requires a word of explanation. Suppose we take all the deviations from the average of the arithmetic differences in Table II and square them. One reason for squaring them is to get rid of the signs, as some deviate upwards ($+$) and some downwards ($-$) from the average, but the squares are all $+$. The average, of course, deviates zero from itself. After these deviations are all squared, the average of these squares is found. This figure tells what the average squared distance is from the mean. Then to get this figure back in terms of the deviations with which we started we extract its square root. This is the *standard deviation*. We do this for every distribution of measures such as given in Table II and use it for the unit. Now we can express such deviations as are shown in Figure 4 in terms of this unit. To do this we simply divide each by it. In the case of the Arithmetic test the SD is found to be 3.1. Thus a loss of eight points is a deviation of $8 + 1.06$, or 9.06, which, when divided by 3.1, becomes 2.92 SD's.

We now have a common point of reference for all our tests and can measure all differences in a common unit, the SD or $\sigma$ of "honest" differences. From now on instead of talking about a loss of eight points or twenty points, we shall talk about a deviation of $-2.92$ SD, etc., and shall call this for short the Xi score or amount score.

The practical advantages of this scheme are at once apparent. For instance in the Word Knowledge test the mean difference when no keys are available is $+3.31$ and the SD is 8.48. Consequently in this test a loss of eight points is a deviate of $8 + 3.31$ or 11.31, but when this is divided by 8.48 it becomes only 1.33 SD's from the point of reference. Thus a loss of eight points on the

Arithmetic is as much more significant of deception than a loss of eight points on the Word Knowledge test as 2.92 is greater than 1.33.

Another very marked advantage of using the SD is that we can state all scores in terms of probabilities. If a distribution of measures is fairly symmetrical, that is, high in the middle and tapering off at each end, as is the case with the distributions in Table II, we can state the chances of occurrence of any given deviations. To make this clear let us picture the facts. The diagram of Figure 6 is a " normal " curve, which in addition to being perfectly symmetrical has certain mathematical properties that belong to curves representing chance distributions of facts. Such a curve

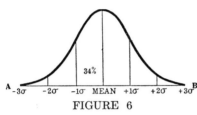

FIGURE 6

PROPERTIES OF THE NORMAL CURVE

would result from tossing, say, ten coins a large number of times and recording each time the number of heads that come up. This curve affords a picture of the statistical concepts used here. The mean and median are the same here, being at the mid-point of the base line. The SD is a *distance* along the base line from the mean to a point on either side of it which includes 34.13% of the cases, or 34.13% of the area inclosed by the curve, base line, and two perpendiculars. Distances along the base line to the left are usually marked minus and those to the right plus. The curve, theoretically, never really touches the base line but approaches it. For practica purposes it is regarded as touching it at a distance of three times the SD from the mean. Between the mean and $-3$ SD there are 49.865% of the cases. Thus between the limits of $+3$ SD and $-3$ SD there are 99.73% of the cases. Between the limits of $-4$ SD and $+4$ SD there are 99.994% of the cases.

Tables have been prepared which give for each value of SD (or $\sigma$) the proportion of the entire surface falling on each side of the line projected from the SD to the curve, and which will therefore show the probability that any given measure will occur. These are known as tables of the values of the normal probability integral. Suppose we have a case that deviates $-1\sigma$ from the mean. The table shows that there are 34.134% of the cases between the mean and $-1\sigma$. By subtracting this from 50% we find what per cent lie between $-1\sigma$ and the left-hand limits of the curve, since this entire area includes 50% of the cases. In this instance the figure is 15.866%. By adding 50% we get the per cent lying between $-1\sigma$ and the right-hand limit of the curve. These figures can be expressed directly as probabilities. The chances of a deviate of greater than $-1\sigma$ occurring are 15.866 in 100, or 158.66 in 1000, or 1586.6 in 10,000, etc. Conversely the chances of a deviate of less than $-1.0$ SD or some positive SD occurring are 84.134 in 100, or 841.34 in 1000, etc. Thus any SD score can be translated into terms of the probability that cheating did or did not take place.

(2) *Application of Terms to the IER Material.*  With this explanation of terms in mind, we can now see why we drew the line of honest difference at eight points on the Arithmetic test. We found that this score was 2.92 times the Arithmetic $\sigma$. The table shows that two cases in a thousand will fall beyond this point, or have a loss of more than eight points from one test to the next. But the next possible difference is nine points, and this is a deviation of 10.06, which is 3.24 times the standard deviation of the honest arithmetic difference, and the table of probabilities shows that this would occur only six times in 10,000. In other words, if we give a cheating score " c " to an individual who does nine fewer problems on the second test, when there is no answer sheet, than he does on the first day, when there is an answer sheet, we shall be wrong in six cases out of every 10,000. This perhaps would compare favorably with the best courts of justice throughout the world.*

---

* As a matter of fact, we do not actually do injustice to anyone by this procedure, for we make no use of the results in a personal way, and deal for the most part with groups rather than with individuals. All our relations are worked out on paper for the purpose of discovering facts about human nature. They are not used as a means of "catching" the individual and then confronting him with the "crime." Praise and blame we leave to other occasions.

Similarly we have determined the limits of honest difference on each * of the three other IER tests and in each case have called cheating a difference which is three or more times the standard deviation of that found under "honesty" conditions.   The limits for the tests are as follows :

1. Arithmetic          8
2. Completions        10
3. Information          9
4. Word Knowledge  22

The fact score is thus found by giving a " c " to any difference bigger than those just listed.   The amount score is simply the Xi deviation, or the actual deviation from the honest mean divided by the standard deviation of the honest differences.

(b) *The Speed Tests.*  While the IER material has the great advantage of being at once an intelligence test, a set of achievement tests in certain subjects, and a set of honesty tests, it has at the same time certain disadvantages.   First, the IER tests used by us usually require a total of about four school hours to give both forms, two hours the first day and two hours the second.   Second, they are expensive both to print and to score.   Third, they are not adapted, in their present form at least, to pupils below the fifth grade.   For these reasons it seemed likely that this material could not be used widely for honesty tests.

In the hope of developing something that could be used by school principals and others to measure the tendency to deceive, at least until spoiled by publicity, we turned to some of the older psychological speed tests for material.   Short tests with high reliability, easily scored and applicable to all ages and grade levels, were needed.   After some preliminary experimenting we selected six tests :

1.  A simple test of addition requiring the rapid addition of one or two digit combinations, such as 4 and 5, 6 and 2
2.  A number checking test similar to the one in Army Beta

---

* The method of deriving the probability of deception when all tests are taken and none shows a loss of $3\sigma$ is given in the statistical supplement.

3. Cancellation of A's
4. The digit symbol substitution test
5. Making dots in small squares
6. Cancellation of single digit as in the Woodworth and Wells
   series

These will be adequately illustrated by the following samples:

### TEST 1

Add each pair as fast as you can, moving across the page from left to right.

| 3 | 4 | 2 | 8 | 5 | 2 | 4 | 2 | 3 | 5 | 4 | 2 | 2 | 2 |
|---|---|---|---|---|---|---|---|---|---|---|---|---|---|
| 8 | 5 | 3 | 9 | 9 | 6 | 8 | 5 | 9 | 7 | 9 | 8 | 7 | 9 |

| 4 | 5 | 3 | 6 | 3 | 5 | 2 | 7 | 6 | 3 | 2 | 3 | 7 | 4 |
|---|---|---|---|---|---|---|---|---|---|---|---|---|---|
| 7 | 6 | 7 | 8 | 4 | 8 | 7 | 8 | 9 | 6 | 4 | 5 | 9 | 6 |

| 8 | 5 | 7 | 8 | 5 | 9 | 6 | 9 | 3 | 7 | 7 | 6 | 9 | 9 |
|---|---|---|---|---|---|---|---|---|---|---|---|---|---|
| 3 | 2 | 4 | 7 | 4 | 3 | 5 | 6 | 2 | 5 | 3 | 3 | 8 | 4 |

| 8 | 4 | 9 | 8 | 4 | 5 | 6 | 7 | 8 | 9 | 8 | 9 | 7 | 6 |
|---|---|---|---|---|---|---|---|---|---|---|---|---|---|
| 6 | 2 | 5 | 2 | 3 | 3 | 2 | 6 | 5 | 7 | 4 | 2 | 2 | 4 |

### TEST 2

Look at each pair of numbers: Make a cross after every pair where the two numbers are not alike (as shown here):

| 907328 | 907329× | 760023 | 760023 |
|--------|---------|--------|--------|
| 216540 | 216540  | 297500 | 297600× |
| 856728 | 847628× | 107910 | 107910 |
| 700035 | 70035×  | 864271 | 864271 |
| 380270 | 380270  | 915823 | 715823× |

| 286090 | 289060 | 329865 | 329865 | 702645 | 702645 | 908701 | 908701 |
|--------|--------|--------|--------|--------|--------|--------|--------|
| 976534 | 976534 | 574052 | 574052 | 610124 | 611124 | 116872 | 116872 |
| 821004 | 821004 | 738216 | 783216 | 503763 | 503763 | 805794 | 805794 |
| 598362 | 598362 | 895422' | 895422 | 921821 | 921821 | 248067 | 248067 |
| 774819 | 747189 | 635767 | 635767 | 869030 | 863090 | 753915 | 753915. |
| 612345 | 612345 | 942424 | 942424 | 274502 | 274502 | 310283 | 210283 |

### TEST 3

Draw a line under every A (as shown here: M̲A̲G̲N̲O̲A̲A̲R̲C̲A̲S̲).

GWBTBVKIKSCSAUEBCIWVABZSMDUBKLWHKHYCGYGK

NANNCBVBSAKOIUPEKCXVGSTVRIWYBYGKHAZLPBYO

XAPYEXXHUFSBVDYDIAZLRSATZAZVFCOFSAIPTDOK

BBISKAKHXDYIUZRHVRZYSCIGECPOFKBICBMGFSDG

YHSRMVBLYICKZBMXFVBBIKUCBZLOGLVKGFMOATUN

TEST 4

Work across the page from left to right beginning at the top. Do each figure as you come to it.

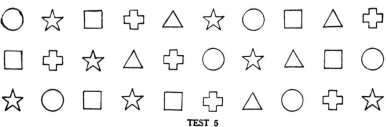

TEST 5

Put a dot in each square beginning at the top and working from left to right. Work as fast as you can. **Speed counts.**

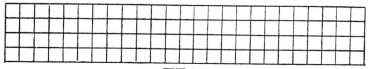

TEST 6

Draw a line under every 4 on this page (as shown here: **264137　　956378　　419356**)

| | | | | | | |
|---|---|---|---|---|---|---|
| 983642 | 168379 | 694517 | 253914 | 745682 | 158923 | 729648 |
| 426357 | 372159 | 754936 | 297835 | 627519 | 786531 | 731469 |
| 654173 | 947386 | 589761 | 134852 | 146237 | 194526 | 936425 |
| 837162 | 691324 | 814536 | 326175 | 368792 | 549826 | 672194 |
| 458671 | 971648 | 479612 | 495683 | 784295 | 817243 | 916328 |

*Test 4 copyrighted 1921, C. H. Stoelting Company.　Used by permission.*

The essential feature in the administration * is that each child takes each test three times and is allowed one minute for each trial on each test. The first two are given under " honesty " conditions. After these are completed they are called " practice "

* The directions for administration are in Appendix F.

trials. On the third trial the pupils are allowed to score their own papers. Time is allowed for those who are inclined to be dishonest to add on more to their papers and thereby increase their scores unfairly. So this is really a triple testing technique using the same material each time.

It will be noted that this is a quite different kind of deception from that exhibited on the IER tests. There the dishonest pupil copies from a key or makes illegitimate use of it. Here he improves his score by adding on more marks after time has been called. When the tests are administered the pupils are given distinctly to understand that when time is called they must stop work, and that when the examiner gives instructions to score that means to score the work already done.

Tests using this material and technique have the following advantages: They are quick to administer. The entire time for the three trials on all the tests, together with time for directions, self-scoring, etc., is one school period of forty minutes. They do not require that the examiner return for a retest as the IER material does. They apply from the third grade up. There is so much material on every test that no one can do it all in one minute.

It has also this other advantage. It is test material that in no way resembles ordinary school examinations. Consequently dishonesty on these tests is less likely to be motivated by a suspicion that the scores will count in the pupils' grades. We should thus expect less cheating on these tests than on the IER tests. But what shows up here may turn out to be symptomatic of tendencies to cheat under a greater variety of conditions.

These tests are not, however, without certain disadvantages. First, considerable skill is required to give them. It is essential that all pupils work exactly sixty seconds on each of the first two trials. This means that the starting and stopping signals must be given on the dot, and that every pupil must start on the signal and stop on it. To achieve this result requires skill on the part of the examiner. Second, the scores are somewhat more difficult to interpret than the IER scores. This is a statistical matter which is given detailed consideration in Book Two.

*Scoring the Speed Tests.* The Speed tests were standardized just as were the IER tests. When the speed material was used for measuring deceptiveness the last trial was the one scored by the pupils, so that whatever falsification took place was roughly measured by the difference between the second and last trials. This we called Difference Two, or D2. Hence, in order to know how much to allow before regarding a given difference as an instance of cheating, it was necessary to determine the normal range of D2's between two tests when there was no scoring by the pupils. This is analogous to what we did in the case of the IER tests when we found what differences could normally be expected between two occasions on neither of which the pupils scored their own papers. A large number of children were given the tests without any opportunity to score their own papers, so that they had no chance to add on more answers after time was called. We thus found how much variation from one trial to the next was to be expected from children of the ages to be tested.

As before, our allowance was three times the standard deviation of the honest difference beyond the honest mean gain. This kept the probability that a " c " thus figured was a genuine case of cheating up to about 999 in 1000. For the fact score we were able to allow the following differences between the second and third trials without scoring the test a " c." A " c " was given for any differences greater than these :

1. Additions                13
2. Number checking   12
3. Underlining A's       14
4. Digit symbols          24
5. Dots                         45
6. Underlining digits   18

For an amount score we used only the sum of the differences* and did not find an Xi score for the separate tests. The total Xi score, however, was found by the same method as that described for the IER tests, *i.e.*, we first reduced the differences to a com-

* Weighted according to their SD's.

mon denominator by weighting each according to the standard deviation of the honest differences; then we allowed a certain amount as a total honest or normal gain; third, we divided the remainder, or the deviation from the normal gain, by the SD of the sum of the honest D2's.

Illustrations from the records of one or two pupils will make this procedure clear:

CASE 1, AGE 10 YEARS, 8 MONTHS

| TESTS | TRIALS | | | D2 | WEIGHTED D2 | | C's * | | | |
|---|---|---|---|---|---|---|---|---|---|---|
| | 1 | 2 | 3 | | | | | | | |
| 1 | 49 | 57 | 86 | 29 | × 1 | 29 | 1 | | Gain | 107 |
| 2 | 9 | 14 | 24 | 10 | × 2 | 20 | 0 | | Honest gain | |
| 3 | 11 | 10 | 10 | 0 | × 2 | 0 | 0 | | for age | 26 |
| 4 | 36 | 39 | 59 | 20 | × 1 | 20 | 0 | | | 81 |
| 5 | 50 | 124 | 200 | 76 | × ¼ | 19 | 1 | | SD of honest | |
| 6 | 23 | 32 | 51 | 19 | × 1 | 19 | 1 | | gain | 17.52 |
| Totals | . | . | . | . . . . . . | | 107 | 3 | | Speed Xi | 4.6 |

CASE 2, AGE 10 YEARS, 11 MONTHS

| TESTS | TRIALS | | | D2 | WEIGHTED D2 | | C's * | | | |
|---|---|---|---|---|---|---|---|---|---|---|
| | 1 | 2 | 3 | | | | | | | |
| 1 | 33 | 34 | 41 | 7 | × 1 | 7 | 0 | | Gain | 82 |
| 2 | 16 | 10 | 21 | 11 | × 2 | 22 | 0 | | Honest gain | |
| 3 | 13 | 14 | 18 | 4 | × 2 | 8 | 0 | | for age | 26 |
| 4 | 33 | 31 | 51 | 20 | × 1 | 20 | 0 | | | 56 |
| 5 | 62 | 100 | 126 | 26 | × ¼ | 7 | 0 | | SD of honest | |
| 6 | 28 | 28 | 46 | 18 | × 1 | 18 | 0 | | gain | 17.52 |
| Totals | . | . | . | . . . . . . | | 82 | 0 | | Speed Xi | 3.2 |

* Based on the D2, not the weighted D2. The limits are shown above.

## B. As Exhibited in Work Done at Home

For this purpose we used the IER Word Knowledge test, already described. One form was handed to the pupils at the close of the first testing period with instructions for them to take the test at home and bring it back the next day.   They were told twice not to get any help on the test either from a dictionary or from a person.   When the second testing period came, the equivalent form of this test was given along with the other three, with no answer sheet available.   Cheating, of course, consists in getting the forbidden help.

### C. As Exhibited in Athletic Contests

In addition to the ten general requirements for conduct tests which were outlined at the beginning of this chapter, there are three more which apply especially to efforts to measure deceptive behavior in athletics.   These are as follows:

1.   They should be approximately real contest situations.   That is, the child should be placed in a genuine contest of some sort. Further, the contest should be social.   If the pupil cheats he must be cheating a rival contestant rather than the teacher and must be conscious of this.

2.   The factor of *social inhibition* should be eliminated as far as possible.   Many contestants desiring to play unfairly will not do so because their opponents won't let them.   Hence in the test situation the opponent must either be absent or else the situation must be such that he cannot readily detect the dishonesty.   But if he cannot detect it neither can the experimenter.   The only alternative is that the opponent shall be absent.   Thus we must use individual test situations.

3.   The behavior in question must be simple and easily recorded in quantitative terms.   This means that games involving complex responses should be avoided.

**1.   The Methods Used.**   In selecting the tests for this part of the work we had two things in mind:   first, meeting the above requirements; and second, securing at the same time a measure of physical ability in the same fashion in which IER tests give a measure of intelligence.   Looking over the attempts to measure general physical ability, we found that Rogers* has done the most

* Rogers, F. R., "Physical Capacity Tests in the Administration of Physical Education," *Teachers College Contributions to Education*, No. 173, 1925.

serviceable piece of work.   We selected certain tests that he had used and adapted them to our purposes :

1. The dynamometer test.   This is a little machine* for measuring the strength of one's hand grip.
2. The spirometer test.   This is a measure of lung capacity.*
3. The pull-up or chinning test
4. The standing broad jump

These tests were administered in such a way as to meet the above requirements.

1. They constituted a real athletic contest.   When the pupil entered the examining room he was told that the pupils of his school were having a " physical ability contest," that certain handicaps had been arranged so that all might have a chance to win a badge.   Twelve badges were to be given, three for each of the four events.   The three grades in each event were to be the usual light weight, middle weight, and heavy weight.   These grades were determined by the customary procedure in the particular school tested.   The badges were attractively designed.   The boys' badges consisted of a metal bar and a ribbon ; the girls' badges consisted of a ribbon only.   Here are samples of the wording of the boys' badges.

| GRIP CHAMPION | LUNG CAPACITY | PULL-UP CHAMPION | BROAD JUMP |
|---|---|---|---|
| Light Weight P.S. 000 1926 | First Place Middle Weight P.S. 000 1926 | Heavy Weight P.S. 000 1926 | First Prize Light Weight P.S. 000 1926 |

These badges were on display in the examining room where the pupils could see them while taking the dynamometer and spirometer tests.

2. The factor of social inhibition was eliminated by making the

* We used Smedley's hand dynamometer and the Simplex dry spirometer with washable mouthpieces.

tests entirely individual. They were more than individual: they were private. That is, the pupil was first shown by the examiner how to read the instruments and how to record his performance and then left *entirely alone*.

3. The general procedure for administering these tests was as follows: First, a small table was provided which was out of sight of the examiner's table. The chinning bar and the broad jump mat were also out of view. The pupil was brought into the examining room and told that he was to take part in a physical ability contest. Its nature was explained and the badges exhibited. Then certain physical data were recorded on a four by six card. If the height and weight were not previously known from school records, they were taken. A sample of this record card is given here:

TESTS OF PHYSICAL ABILITY

Name ＿＿＿＿＿＿＿＿＿＿＿＿＿＿＿ Age ＿＿＿＿＿ Grade ＿＿＿＿＿

Height ＿＿＿ Weight ＿＿＿ Date ＿＿＿＿ School ＿＿＿＿＿＿

1. Dynamometer: 1st trial ＿＿＿ 2d ＿＿＿ 3d ＿＿＿ 4th ＿＿＿

 5th ＿＿＿ 6th ＿＿＿ 7th ＿＿＿ 8th ＿＿＿ 9th ＿＿＿ 10th ＿＿＿

2. Spirometer: 1st trial ＿＿＿ 2d ＿＿＿ 3d ＿＿＿ 4th ＿＿＿

3. Chinning: 1st trial ＿＿＿ 2d ＿＿＿ 3d ＿＿＿ 4th ＿＿＿

4. Standing Broad Jump: 1st trial ＿＿＿＿ 2d ＿＿＿＿

 3d ＿＿＿＿ 4th ＿＿＿＿＿

The full directions for giving the physical ability tests are in the Appendix. In the case of the hand dynamometer the examiner demonstrated the way to proceed, and then had the subject try himself, showing him very carefully how to use the instrument, read the dial, and make his record on the card, at the same time urging him to do his very best. The examiner took mental note of the highest of the three trials made in his presence and recorded it later. He then said: "Do you understand how to do it? While I start the next boy, you go and try five times and record each trial on your card. Your best score is the one that counts.

Go over there now and do your best.   Use the same hand (right or left) and work fast.   As soon as you are through, come back and I'll show you the next test."   The examiner then recorded the highest score made in his presence.

The spirometer directions were similar, except that there were only two preliminary trials and three final trials.

The pull-up test came next.   Here the subject was tried out only once as the fatigue effect was considerable.   The examiner made mental note of the number of times the subject chinned himself and recorded it later.   In one school the bar was adjusted so that the subject could just reach the floor and thus give himself a boost contrary to the rules, but in the others it was stationary.   After showing the subject what to do, the examiner said :  " Now while I attend to the next boy, you go ahead and see how many times you can chin.   You may have two trials.   Remember what you did on each trial.   The best record counts."

In the broad jump there were two preliminary trials with careful directions in jumping and measuring and each boy had four private trials, making his own record.

**2.  Scoring Methods.**   (a)  *The Amount Score.*   In all these tests the amount score was the difference between the highest of the practice trials and the highest of the self-recorded trials.*   The use of this difference as a measure of the amount of deception requires some analysis.

In the case of the dynamometer test, previous work indicates that after three trials under coaching and urging it is not at all likely that anyone can improve in five succeeding trials, all with the same hand and following in rapid succession.   There is a great fatigue effect.   Hence a higher record on one or more of the five self-recorded trials than the highest practice trial, as noted by the examiner and recorded privately when the subject was not present, is evidence that deception has taken place.   The amount of

---

* Of course the examiner did not know in the case of the dynamometer or spirometer whether the pupil pushed the dial forward with his finger and recorded the false score or just simply lied on his score card about his record. In either case it was deception and this is what we were trying to measure.

this difference includes both the factor of deception and the factor of errors of measurement, just as in the classroom tests.

The three other tests are scored by the same technique. The fatigue effect, however, is not so great in the spirometer and broad jump as in the dynamometer and chinning tests.

(b) *The Fact Score.** Only honest scores were used in giving the prizes. In order to find the borderline between honest and dishonest performance, we followed a method very similar to those already described. The mean honest loss or gain between certain trials with each machine and in the pull-up and broad jump was allowed and the largest amount of honest difference in addition. The limits beyond which any difference was called a " c " are as follows:

| | |
|---|---|
| Dynamometer | 3 kilograms |
| Spirometer | 25 cubic inches |
| Chinning | 3 times |
| Broad jump | 7 inches |

### D. As Exhibited in Parlor Games

As in the case of contests, it was necessary to establish natural conditions. There would have been little advantage in merely repeating the " test " situation of the classroom type in either the contests or the parties, as behavior under such conditions had already been measured with a large variety of opportunities. What we were after here was a measure of the extent to which cheating was a function of total situations of a quite different character, where, in the case of the contests, serious individual competition entered into the motivation and, in the other, the atmosphere was just " fun," with the customary trivial prizes given at children's parties.

To secure this party atmosphere it was essential to have the children in groups rather than singly, as the chief part of the fun is the social character of the games. This placed a rather strict limit on the number of opportunities to deceive that could be offered in any single party.

* For details see Book Two, Chapter III.

Certain requirements for these opportunities needed constant emphasis :

1. The deceptive aspect of the behavior must be a matter of objective record, and not a matter of judgment on the part of an observer.

2. Each child must have the same opportunity to deceive as every other child.

3. The opportunities must be in games or stunts where the interest is high.

4. The deceptive aspect of the behavior must have low visibility so that, if one child cheats, the rest will not notice it and protest.

**The Techniques Used.** With the assistance of a professional recreational leader, a large number of parties were first conducted in order to standardize the procedure. A great many games and stunts were tried out, which it is not necessary to describe here. It was found that in the course of an hour and a half from thirty to fifty children could all be tested in four different games or stunts as follows :

(a) *A Peeping Stunt.* The coördination material previously described we had prepared either for classroom testing or for games.* As all the children tested with the party technique had already taken these tests in the classroom, we did not use them in any of the actual test parties.

(b) *Pinning the Tail on the Donkey or the Arrow on the Target.* Each child is blindfolded by a standardized bandage so adjusted that there is room to see the floor under the bandage. The technique here is of the " improbable achievement " type. The likelihood that a child will be able to get the tail or the arrow in the exact spot without peeping is remote. But if he uses his eyes and follows the lines on the floor boards and looks at the donkey or target when he gets to it, he can place the tail or arrow very accurately.

As each tail is pinned on it is removed again before the next child approaches, so he cannot guide his hand by feeling for the

---

* It would be desirable to duplicate these tests in the two types of situation as a measure of the effect of the total situation on the behavior.

tails already pinned on.　Each child is rotated three times before he starts for the donkey, to decrease the chance of honest success. As children are apt to question all correct performances and accuse one another of peeking, it is desirable to have this test in a room apart and to have only such children present as are actually engaging in the test.　With at least two games going at once, four or five children can be present without interfering with one another.

The cheating score is a " c " if the child pins the tail or arrow correctly.　The same score is used in choosing the winner for the game, except that approximations to the center are discriminated among those getting the tail or arrow near the proper point.

(c) *Bean Relay.*　This is a modified potato race, using beans instead of potatoes, which we developed for this purpose after considerable experimentation.　Each row has four boxes, the first empty, the second and third with three beans each, and the fourth with ten or more.　If possible, five rows are run at once to give the atmosphere of contest.　Each heat is thirty seconds, which is time enough for eight or more runs, that is, for eight or more chances to cheat.　The rule is to pick up one bean at a time, and each runner has an observer who has a counter and records his runs.　At the end of each heat the beans in each child's home box are counted and the sum is his score for the game.　Obviously, since he is supposed to take only one bean at a time, the number of beans in the home box should correspond with the number of runs, which has been checked by the observer.　If a child is found to have more beans than runs, this is evidence of deception and he is given a " c."

As in the tail-pinning game, the bean relay should be run in a separate room or a corner of the room in order that there may be no children present but those who are engaging in the heat, as observers would tend to inhibit the tendency to cheat or to direct attention to cheating if it occurred.

(d) *The Mystery Man.*　This may be regarded as either a cheating test or a stealing test.　The children are in a circle facing in. The Mystery Man passes around in back and places in each child's hand an object which the child is to identify without looking at it. When he thinks he knows what it is he goes to one of the helpers and reports.   The helper then looks at the object, shows it to the child, and records whether or not he guessed right.   The child is then told to take the object to a box in another room where all the objects are being collected to be used again.

Every alternate child is given a ten-cent piece, and the other children certain small objects.   The procedure is of course repeated so that each child has the dime once.   The objects may be either attractive and desirable or merely neutral in value, but somewhat hard to identify.   In the former case there is the temptation to keep the object as well as the dime.   In the latter case, only the dime is likely to be a temptation, which simplifies the test. In some cases it has been found practicable to give each child both a dime and an object at the same time.   This avoids the necessity of repeating the performance, and also allows more freedom in disposing of either the dime or the object otherwise than by placing it in the receptacle.

As the box is in another room, it is perfectly possible for a child not to show up with the objects at all, but to start for the room and when out of sight slip the coin or object or both into his pocket or dress.   But some will not do this, and so the box is so arranged that, even if one comes to it, provided he has two objects to deposit, there is no apparent way by which anyone will know whether he drops in both or only one.   The box is solid toward the child with only a small slit through which he is to pass the objects.   A helper sits near the box, with a sheet of paper on which he checks or records the number or name of each child as he comes to the box. But the box is open on the side toward the helper so he can see what is dropped in and make a cryptic note of it on his paper opposite the child's name or number.

The cheating or stealing score is " c " if the dime or object or both are not returned.

The complete plan for the standard party is printed in the Appendix together with such modifications as were found necessary under the restricted conditions met with in our actual testing.

## METHODS FOR MEASURING THE STEALING TYPE OF DECEPTION

Here again it was necessary to conform to certain requirements in addition to the ten general criteria cited at the beginning of the chapter. These are as follows:

1. It must be a group situation.

2. Money must be used in a natural way or appear as a natural part of the situation.

3. There must be an opportunity to take all or some known part of the money apparently without being detected in the act.

4. The subject must feel that he is not merely being clever in getting away with the money but that he is actually stealing it from a particular person or institution.

5. It must be possible to check exactly what the subject does.

We used the stealing tests in two situations — party and classroom.

### A. STEALING EXHIBITED AT PARTIES

The Mystery Man test has already been described under the cheating type of deception and needs only to be listed at this point.

### B. STEALING EXHIBITED IN CLASSROOMS

**1. The Planted Dime Test.** In connection with the administration of the Puzzle tests in one school a little box was given to each pupil containing several puzzles not all of which were used. In each box was a dime ostensibly belonging to another puzzle, which the examiner showed to the pupils but did not ask them to solve. This other puzzle required the use of a dime, but no mention was made by the examiner of the dimes in the boxes.

Each pupil returned his own box to a large receptacle at the front of the room. Check on what each pupil did was arranged for by numbering and distributing the boxes according to the seating plan of the class. The purpose of this test was to see which children would take the dime before returning the box.

**2. The Magic Square Test.** This is a puzzle and was given along with the other Puzzle tests already described. In this case, however, there was no possibility of faking a solution to the puzzle. The only deception involved was in not returning any or all of the coins that make up the puzzle.

The test material consisted of a handkerchief box six inches square, on the bottom of which we had drawn the design shown below, which is the bottom part of the Puzzle score sheet shown on page 57. There were in the box seventeen coins: 1 quarter, 4 dimes, 4 nickels, 4 pennies, and 4 Chinese coins, making a cash value of 89 cents. The Chinese coins were used because some coin of zero value was required for the solution of the puzzle.

Full directions are included in the Appendix along with the other Puzzle directions, but the essentials are as follows: After

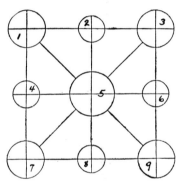

SCORE

If each of the six rows (1-2-3, 4-5-6, 7-8-9, 1-4-7, 2-5-8, 3-6-9) and the two diagonals (7-5-3, 1-5-9) adds to the same total, your score is 100.

If each of the six rows and one diagonal adds to the same total your score is 75.

If each of any four rows and one diagonal adds to the same total, your score is 50.

Any other arrangement is zero.

describing the puzzle, the examiner said: " You will see as you open the box that it contains a lot of coins. Take the coins all out and put them beside the box or keep them in your hand. On the bottom of the box you will see some circles around a square, three circles in each direction, making a place for nine coins in all. You have *more* than nine coins, unless there has been some mistake, so there will be more than enough to have one in each circle. But there is only one way to place them correctly in the circles; and this is to place them so that each row will add up to exactly the same amount as every other row, and to exactly the same amount as each diagonal, or cornerwise, row. I am not going to tell you what this amount is, nor just what coins will make it work. The penny is called 1, the nickel 5, the dime 10, the quarter 25, and the Chinese coin 0. At the bottom of the score sheet at the left you will see the directions and can refer to them at any time. Now let's see who is bright enough to get this puzzle."

After from two to seven minutes had elapsed the examiner said: " Now you have probably done at least one of the three things described on the score sheet, so write carefully on the score sheet the value of the coins as you now have them placed in the box. As soon as you have done that pass in your score sheet."

Examiner then collected score sheets, thus apparently breaking all connection between the boxes and the pupils.

" Now put all the money back in the box, put the band around it, and we will collect it. Pass the boxes to the center aisle."

These directions were modified in various ways. In one situation, where only boys were being tested, the examiner said, " If you think it would be easier to solve this puzzle if you had more coins to work with, you are at perfect liberty to use any coins you may have in your pocket. The coins in the box are sufficient for one solution, but there are other possibilities. Only if you use your own money, write down carefully what you put in so you will leave in the box exactly what is there now." This provided a legitimate excuse for putting their hands in their pockets, but as it added one more source of error we did not try it again.

In another situation the pupils were brought from their class-rooms to a vacant room for the Puzzle tests. The coin test came last. They were told to hand in their score sheets, take the coin box to the principal's office, and leave it there. This gave the pupils a chance to take the box of coins out of the examining room, and since, on finishing the test, they left either alone or in groups of two or three, they could easily have made off with the boxes, money and all. In order that they might know that they were unobserved, the attendant in the office was instructed to pay no attention whatever to those who came in to deposit their boxes.

Another modification, not changing the character of the test materially, adapted it for younger, but bright, pupils by offering for solution one of the easier puzzles adapted to the magic square, but involving the same coins.

*Scoring the Magic Square Test.* The fact score was simply whether or not any money was missing. The amount score was the total amount of money missing, not the number of coins.

In order to check each pupil's behavior it was necessary to identify the persons using the boxes and to count the money returned by each. Identification was effected by the use of a key number combination placed in the magic square design on the score sheet (see page 91).*

**3. The Coin Counting Test.** As the Magic Square test was too complicated for some of the younger children, a simpler plan was evolved. Each child was given a sheet of paper on which were printed some arithmetic problems involving the counting of money. Here is a sample:

What three (3) coins add up to forty (40) cents?

(   ) quarters (   ) dimes (   ) nickels (   ) pennies

What three (3) coins add up to twelve (12) cents?

(   ) quarters (   ) dimes (   ) nickels (   ) pennies

What three (3) coins add up to thirty-one (31) cents?

(   ) quarters (   ) dimes (   ) nickels (   ) pennies

What three (3) coins add up to twenty-seven (27) cents?

(   ) quarters (   ) dimes (   ) nickels (   ) pennies

Each box contained just the same coins as the Magic Square box,

* Each child wrote his name on his score sheet. On the design for the magic square were placed certain figures numbering the circles to correspond to the directions at the left of the design, but placed on the circles in accordance with a definite scheme as follows: Each circle is divided into four parts by the lines drawn through them. Figures placed above the horizontal line are significant. Of these one is always to the left of the vertical line. This is the first figure of the identifying number. The central circle is not used for this purpose, so this first figure might be anything from one to nine except five. At the right, above the horizontal line, might be placed either one or two of the figures numbering the circles. If one, this is the second figure of the identifying number. If two, the smallest is read first, giving an identifying number of

except for the omission of the Chinese coins. The pupils were told that it was a money counting test and that, in order to make it a real test, the coins were to be used to count with instead of writing on the paper.

In this case, identification was effected by the following device: The arithmetic problems were mimeographed. A blur in one of the problems was purposely left so that it had to be filled in with pencil. These figures were made to correspond to figures placed on the bottoms of the boxes. The numbers on the boxes had a ¢ mark after them, furnishing thus a red herring for the child who wanted to speculate concerning this number. As the child placed his name on the sheet he identified his box at the same time and they could then be collected separately.

## METHODS FOR MEASURING THE LYING TYPE OF DECEPTION

### A. LYING TO ESCAPE DISAPPROVAL

If lying is defined as misstatement of fact with intent to deceive, it becomes at once very difficult to test, because intentions are not directly known. But if lying is regarded only as making a false statement instead of a true statement when the truth is known to the one making the statement, it is not so difficult to measure. Some of the techniques already described have this element in them. The overstatement test is in a sense a lying test. Or, in the case of the Puzzles tests, if the pupil does not fake the solution to the puzzle but gives himself credit on the score sheet for having solved it, he is really lying rather than cheating.*

three figures. Using this plan, the number of the box corresponding to the design on page 91 is 234.

As the figures on each box were placed to correspond to the figures on its accompanying score sheet, and as no two were numbered alike, each box became identified with a child as soon as his name was written on the score sheet. The score sheets of course were assembled with the boxes and they were passed out together. But they were collected separately.

* There is a sense in which lying is basic to all deception except stealing and it is ordinarily an accompaniment of this form of dishonesty also.

The first method which we used to detect lying was employed in connection with the IER tests.  A week or more after these tests were given in any group an examiner returned with a set of general questions of a more or less personal nature.  This was called the Pupil Data Sheet.  Toward the end of the sheet the following questions were asked:

33.  Did you ever cheat on any sort of test?

34.  Have you cheated on such tests more than once?

41.  Did you actually do this test all alone without getting help on it?

42.  If you did get help, was it from some person?

43.  Or was it from a book or dictionary?

44.  Did you understand at the time that you were not to get help in doing the test?

45.  On some of these tests you had a key to correct your paper by.  Did you copy any answer from the keys?

46.  Do you think that to do so is really cheating?

47.  On any of these same tests did you copy answers from other pupils' papers?

48.  Do you think that to do that is really cheating?

56.  If you did copy on any of these tests that you took a little while ago, or received any help you should not have received, just why did you do so?

57.  Have you answered all the questions honestly and truthfully?

It will be noted that questions 33, 34, 56, and 57 have only a general significance, whereas questions 41, 42, 43, 45, and 47 are entirely specific.  Questions 44, 46, and 48 serve as a check on the other answers, but in this connection no other use was made of the answers to 46 and 48.

There were two ways of handling the results of these questions.  First we recorded the admissions of those who said that they cheated on the IER tests.  Then each pupil was given an honesty score or a truthfulness index.

The second way of handling the answers was to secure the lie index or dishonesty score.  As this is based on the cheating tests,

it is no more reliable than they.   Furthermore, only the cheaters
are included, as the others had nothing to lie about.   But the
facts as given are objective.   The method of scoring is illustrated
by the samples shown below.   In this table the signs + and −
represent the answers " Yes " and " No " respectively to the questions referred to by the numbers at the tops of the columns.   A
blank means that the question was not answered.

| Cases | Sex | Questions | | | | | | | | | | C's School | C Home | Lie Index | |
|---|---|---|---|---|---|---|---|---|---|---|---|---|---|---|---|
| | | 33 | 34 | 41 | 42 | 43 | 44 | 45 | 46 | 56 | 57 | | | School | Home |
| 1 | M | − | − | + | − | − | + | − | + | | + | 0 | 0 | 0 | 0 |
| 2 | M | − | − | + | − | − | + | − | − | | + | 2 | 1 | + 4 | + 4 |
| 3 | F | + | + | + | − | − | + | + | + | + | + | 3 | 0 | − 4 | 0 |
| 4 | F | + | + | − | + | + | + | − | − | − | + | 2 | 1 | + 1 | − 1 |
| 5 | M | − | − | + | − | − | + | − | + | + | | 1 | 0 | + 2 | + 1 |

The column marked " C School " gives the fact score or number of times the subject cheated on the first three opportunities,
which were offered in school.   " C Home " refers to the test which
was taken home.

Case 1 shows an unequivocal record.   No cheating was discovered and none was admitted.   Case 2 consistently denied cheating
although the record shows he cheated twice in school and once at
home.

For purposes of scoring, questions 33 and 34 are treated as one.
Questions 41, 42, and 43, which refer to the home opportunity, are
treated as one.   In question 57 an opportunity is given for stating
whether the previous answers have been given honestly.   If they
have not been honest answers, as shown by the record, then
any affirmative answer to this question is one more lie.   No
answer at all is regarded as a lack of frankness equivalent to
an affirmative.

Question 56 asks for a motive.   If a motive is given, this constitutes an admission and a truthfulness credit is given for it.
Frequently the pupil simply says, " I did not do it," which con-

stitutes another denial. "45" is simply a statement of fact as to whether the keys were used improperly or not.

Thus one can tell three general truths and make an admission with reference to both the school cheating and the home cheating, or he may tell three general lies and make two specific denials, one for school and one for home. The handling of the school and home separately gives, therefore, a maximum lie index of plus four and a maximum truth index of minus four.

Case 1 is neutral, as already seen, and so has a neutral lie index. Case 2 denies everything, and omits 56, which means the maximum lie index of plus four on each of the two situations. Case 3 cheats only on the school situations and admits it both specifically and generally, saying that she has cheated, has cheated more than once, denies any cheating at home, admits copying from keys at school (45), regarding this as cheating (46), gives the reason for doing it (56), and says she has answered truly (57) as she apparently has. So she has on the school opportunity the maximum truth score of − 4, and the neutral score on the home opportunity.

Case 4 admits cheating in general and specifically so far as the home opportunity is concerned, but denies cheating at school although she was caught at it on two tests. She also says she did not cheat, on question 56, and says she is telling the truth on 57. This is therefore a mixed score. For the home opportunity, 33 and 34 count − 1; 41, 42, and 43 count − 1; 56 counts +1; 57 is not counted as it is partly true and partly false since the girl is partly truthful and partly lying. These add to −1. For the school situation we have the −1 on 33 and 34, and +1 on 56, 0 on 57, and a +1 on 45 because this is a denial. This makes a school lie index of +1.

Case 5 denies cheating in general, which is of course an untruth and equals +1, denies it on 45, which is also a lie and equals +1, admits it on 56, which is −1, and does not answer 57, which is +1. Hence the school lie index is +2. He does not cheat on the home test, which would leave his home lie index 0, but for the fact that 57 is left blank, which gives him a +1 for the home lie index.

## B. Lying to Win Approval

The second method is like the first in that it consists of a series of rather personal questions. There are many specific acts of conduct which on the whole have rather widespread social approval, but which at the same time are rarely done. The questions revolve around situations of this sort.

The test is in two forms. Each form contains 36 questions.

### CEI ATTITUDES SA

#### Form One

Name_____ Date_____

School_____ Grade_____

Answer the following questions by underlining YES or NO. If your answer is YES, draw a line under YES. If your answer is NO, draw a line under NO. Please answer every question.

1. Did you ever accept the credit or honor for anything when you knew the credit or honor belonged to someone else? . . . . . . . . . YES <u>NO</u>   1.
2. Did you ever act greedily by taking more than your share of anything? . . . . . . . . . YES <u>NO</u>   2.
3. Did you ever blame another for something you had done when you knew all the time it was your fault? . . . . . . . . . . . . . . . YES <u>NO</u>   3.
4. Do you usually report the number of a car you see speeding? . . . . . . . . . . . . . <u>YES</u> NO   4.
5. Do you always preserve order when the teacher is out of the room? . . . . . . . . . . . <u>YES</u> NO   5.
6. Do you report other pupils whom you see cheating? <u>YES</u> NO   6.
7. Did you ever pretend to understand a thing when you really did not understand it? . . . . . YES <u>NO</u>   7.
8. Have you ever disobeyed any law of your country or rule of your school? . . . . . . . . . YES <u>NO</u>   8.
9. Do you speak to all the people you are acquainted with, even the ones you do not like? . . . . <u>YES</u> NO   9.
10. Do you usually call the attention of people to the fact that you have on new shoes or a new suit or dress? . . . . . . . . . . . . . . . YES <u>NO</u>   10.

11. Are you always on time at school or for other appointments? . . . . . . . . . . . . YES NO 11.
12. Do you always smile when things go wrong? . . YES NO 12.
13. Do you usually pick up broken glass in the street? YES NO 13.
14. Do you stick with your gang even when they go wrong?. . . . . . . . . . . . . . . . YES NO 14.
15. Do you usually sneeze whenever you feel like it? YES NO 15.
16. Did you ever take anything (even a pin or button) that belonged to someone else? . . . . . . YES NO 16.
17. When you see other children fighting, do you stop them? . . . . . . . . . . . . . . . YES NO 17.
18. Do you always accept the decisions of the umpire without question? . . . . . . . . . . . YES NO 18.
19. Do you always obey your parents cheerfully and promptly? . . . . . . . . . . . . . . YES NO 19.
20. Even when others will not play your way, do you keep on playing anyway? . . . . . . . . YES NO 20.
21. Do you try to take an interest in some things you do not like? . . . . . . . . . . . . YES NO 21.
22. Did you ever say anything about your teacher that you would be unwilling to say to her face? . . YES NO 22.
23. Did you ever feel that you would like to "get even" with another person for something he had done? . . . . . . . . . . . . . . . YES NO 23.
24. Do you often give away anything which is very dear to you or which you have obtained at a sacrifice? . . . . . . . . . . . . . . YES NO 24.
25. Did you ever pretend that you did not hear when someone was calling you? . . . . . . . . YES NO 25.
26. Did you ever hurt or cause pain to a dog, cat, or other animal? . . . . . . . . . . . . YES NO 26.
27. Do you go to church and Sunday school every Sunday? . . . . . . . . . . . . . . YES NO 27.
28. Do you keep a diary regularly? . . . . . . . YES NO 28.
29. Do you read the Bible every day? . . . . . . YES NO 29.
30. Were you ever rude or saucy to your parents or teacher? . . . . . . . . . . . . . . YES NO 30.
31. Do you usually pick up papers and trash that others have thrown on the schoolroom floor? . YES NO 31.

32. Do you usually correct other children when you hear them using bad language? . . . . . . YES NO 32.
33. Did you ever do any work on Sunday or go to the movies or a baseball game on Sunday? . . . YES NO 33.
34. Did you ever break, destroy, or lose anything belonging to someone else? . . . . . . . . YES NO 34.
35. Did you ever tell on another child for something wrong he had done? . . . . . . . . . . YES NO 35.
36. Do you always do to-day things that you could put off until to-morrow? . . . . . . . . . . YES NO 36.

## CEI ATTITUDES SA

### FORM TWO

Name_____ Date_____

School_____ Grade_____

Answer the following questions by underlining YES or NO. If your answer is YES, draw a line under YES. If your answer is NO, draw a line under NO. Please answer every question.

1. Do you always apologize when you have been rude or discourteous? . . . . . . . . . . . YES NO 1.
2. Did you ever accept the credit or honor for anything when you knew the credit or honor belonged to someone else? . . . . . . . . . . . . YES NO 2.
3. Do you always care for the property of others even though it has not been placed in your care? . . YES NO 3.
4. Did you ever act greedily by taking more than your share of anything? . . . . . . . . . YES NO 4.
5. Did you ever blame another for something you had done when you knew all the time it was your fault? . . . . . . . . . . . . . . . YES NO 5.
6. Do you throw waste paper on the floor when there is no waste paper basket handy? . . . . . . YES NO 6.
7. Have you ever disobeyed any law of your country or rule of your school? . . . . . . . . . YES NO 7.
8. Are you always on time at school or for other appointments? . . . . . . . . . . . . YES NO 8.
9. Do you always congratulate your opponents? . . YES NO 9.

10. Do you usually "give in" when others are against you? . . . . . . . . . . . . . . .  YES NO 10.

11. Did you ever carve your name on your desk? . .  YES NO 11.

12. Did you ever write your name in the books you use which belong to school or library? . . . . .  YES NO 12.

13. Do you always sing when others are singing? . .  YES NO 13.

14. Do you usually pick up broken glass in the street?  YES NO 14.

15. Do you usually report to the police the numbers of cars you see speeding in the city streets? . . .  YES NO 15.

16. Do you always finish your work before you play? .  YES NO 16.

17. Did you ever take anything (even a pin or button) that belonged to someone else? . . . . . .  YES NO 17.

18. Did you ever say anything about your teacher that you would be unwilling to say to her face? . .  YES NO 18.

19. Do you always keep every secret that you promise to keep? . . . . . . . . . . . . . .  YES NO 19.

20. Do you keep quiet when older persons are talking?  YES NO 20.

21. Do you always leave the table hungry? . . . .  YES NO 21.

22. Did you ever feel that you would like to "get even" with another person for something he had done?  YES NO 22.

23. Did you ever pretend that you did not hear when someone was calling you? . . . . . . . .  YES NO 23.

24. Did you ever hurt or cause pain to a dog, cat, or other animal? . . . . . . . . . . . .  YES NO 24.

25. Do you give something to every beggar who asks?  YES NO 25.

26. Do you usually correct another pupil when you hear him using bad grammar? . . . . . .  YES NO 26.

27. Do you spend some time each day acquiring a liking or taste for good music, fine art, and good literature? . . . . . . . . . . . . .  YES NO 27.

28. Do you pray at least once a day? . . . . . .  YES NO 28.

29. Do you ask others to join your Sunday school? .  YES NO 29.

30. Were you ever rude or saucy to your parents or teacher? . . . . . . . . . . . . . .  YES NO 30.

31. Do you usually pick up papers and trash that others have thrown on the schoolroom floor? .  YES NO 31.

32. Do you usually correct other children when you hear them using bad words? . . . . . . . .  YES NO 32.

33. Did you ever do any work on Sunday or go to the
movies or a baseball game on Sunday?    . . .   YES   NO   33.
34. Did you ever break, destroy, or lose anything belonging to someone else? . . . . . . . . .   YES   NO   34.
35. Did you ever tell on another child for something
wrong he had done? . . . . . . . . . .   YES   NO   35.
36. Do you always do to-day things that you could
put off until to-morrow?   . . . . . . . .   YES   NO   36.

There are, no doubt, many children who could answer some of
these questions quite truthfully as scored above.   But the child
who could answer thirty-six truthfully would be a pious fraud.
The test is scored in such a way as to give one point credit for each
question answered in the approved way.   For example, affirmative answers of questions 4, 5, 6, and 9, and negative of 1, 2, 3, 7, 8,
and 10 on form one are all scored as receiving one point each.
This gives the highest score to the greatest amount of falsification.
The question is, How big a score should any pupil have before he is
accredited with having lied?   This again is a matter of probabilities.

In order to find the limit of honest answers, we gave the test to
several classes in a school where we had found almost no deception,
explaining to the children that we really wanted to know what
children like themselves did in the situations listed in the test.
No names were written on the blanks.   In spite of (or perhaps
because of) these precautions, this supposedly honest population
as a matter of fact reported scores higher than those found in some
of our most dishonest populations.   We therefore gave up the
hope of getting straight answers from children and turned for help
to a graduate class in educational psychology, the members of
which were interested in the moral aspects of education.   We
asked these men and women to think back over their early adoles-
cent and pre-adolescent years and answer the questions in such a
way as to represent what was probably true of their own childhood.
The number claiming a perfect childhood was so small that it did
not need to prevent our determining a workable limit of honest
performance.   Just as for the tests already described, we placed

this at three times the standard deviation of the " honest " group, beyond the mean of the honest group.  Thus for form one, any child scoring 24 was given a " c," and on form two a " c " was recorded for any pupil reaching a total score of 28.

The amount score used was either the total number of " right " or conventional answers given, or an Xi score found as usual by dividing the subject's deviation from the honest mean by the standard deviation of the honest scores.

---

So much for the various methods used by the Inquiry to measure the tendency to deceive in the ordinary life situations of normal children.  We shall next sketch rather briefly the application of these tests to real situations and the general results secured from the use of each technique.

# CHAPTER IV

# APPLICATION OF TECHNIQUES AND GENERAL RESULTS

One of the principles on which these studies in deception are built is that they shall be centered on age groups as young as possible. As has previously been suggested, it would be highly desirable to begin such studies with infancy and investigate the processes leading later to various kinds of social conduct. But this has been out of the question here because of limitation in time. Moreover, since this research is largely on a statistical rather than a clinical basis we have developed techniques to be applied to children when found in groups.

The most accessible groups are school classes. Here attendance is required, and regular, and the population is less selected than is the case with clubs and Sunday schools. Consequently we cut our tests to fit general school situations or situations connected with schools. All our techniques are applicable in grades five to eight inclusive. Some of them may be used in grades as low as the third, and some will work up through high school and even in the college ages. But as we shall presently see, most of our work has been done in grades five to eight.

In selecting school populations for trying out these techniques and collecting data on deception, we have endeavored to use representative samples of the following social groups:

1. Various social, economic, and cultural levels
2. Various intelligence levels within grades three to twelve
3. Various types of community
4. Various degrees of socialization or levels of character (delinquents excepted)
5. Various national or racial groups
6. Various occupational groups
7. Various religious groups
8. Both sexes

We have also tried without uniform success to crisscross these groups so that each one will offer samples well distributed through each of the others.   In discovering possible national differences, for example, it is essential that the national groups shall each represent the same social, economic, cultural, and religious types. Our total population has been too small to accomplish cross-sampling as adequately as must be done before certain important questions relating to the comparison of social groups can be answered.

## DESCRIPTION OF SCHOOL POPULATIONS STUDIED

Letters A to O refer to public schools.    P to S are private schools. T to W are schools used only for standardization purposes.

A. A suburban community of 10,000 population with about 1000 children in the public school grades five to eight.   This community is composed socially of the ultra-wealthy on the one hand and the very lowest in the economic scale on the other, with a fair representation of the middle classes.   Furthermore, there are many nationalities and religions.   There are five elementary schools, grades one to six, one intermediate school, grades seven to eight, and one high school.

B. In a mid-western city of 200,000 about 1000 children in grades five to ten were tested.   The fifth- and sixth-grade children were in two elementary schools in two different geographic sections of the city.   The other grades were in one large junior high school which draws from a general district covering about half the total population of the city.

C. A public school serving a metropolitan population which on the whole is above the average in social and economic conditions.   Above grade four this school was almost entirely restricted to boys at the time we did our work there.   The average intelligence quotient is above normal, varying from 110 to 120.

D. Another group of public school children who because of broken homes are situated in an institution for such children located in a suburban community.   This is a rather unique group in that they represent the low end of the scale in the way of home background and economic level. The average intelligence of this group is less than normal.

E. A vocational high school in a fine section of a large suburban city.

F. A public school in a congested metropolitan area, recent immigration stock, mostly Russian Jews, girls only, grades four to eight.

G. A public school in the vicinity of F, mixed, grades four to six only.

H. As above, but boys only, grades four to six.

I. As above, but girls only, grades four to eight.

J. As above, boys and girls, grades four to six, and girls only, grades seven and eight.

K. An orphanage, from which a selected group of brothers and sisters was used.

L. An experimental public school associated with a normal school in a suburban community, grades four to seven.

M. A regular village school in the same community as L, grades four to seven.

N. Certain classes in a university junior high school in a mid-western city.

O. Some two hundred children in a large mid-western city contrasted with two hundred in surrounding rural districts.

P. A private school, grades one to six, having mixed sexes, and grades seven and eight, only girls, located in a large city and drawing from the upper social levels. The average intelligence quotient is well above 100.

Q. Another city private school of very much the same level as P but with smaller classes and mixed sexes running all the way through.

R. A boys' private school located in a suburban community. The grades run from the fourth up through high school. The social level is high and the intelligence is high.

S. Three small private schools in Pennsylvania.

T. A metropolitan school of the better type in a residential section.

U. A metropolitan public school drawing from a foreign and negro population. The average intelligence and the social and economic status of the homes are below the normal level.

V.  A metropolitan elementary school.

W.  A metropolitan junior high school.

Table III shows how many pupils were tested with each type or battery of test in the various school populations.   The more accessible and more unselected groups received most of our attention, and some groups were tested for standardization purposes only.

TABLE III.  (A) PUBLIC SCHOOLS

APPROXIMATE NUMBER OF PUPILS IN EACH SCHOOL OR SYSTEM SUBJECTED TO THE DECEPTION TESTS

| TEST | TOTAL | A | B | C | D | E | F–J | K | L–M | N | O |
|------|------|------|------|------|------|------|------|------|------|------|------|
| IER | | | | | | | | | | | |
| 1–4 tests | 6675 | 1000 | 940 | 800* | | 900 | 2185 | 200 | 250 | | 400 |
| Duplicating | | | | | | | | | | | |
| 7 tests used twice | 295 | | | 30 | 265 | | | | | | |
| Speed | | | | | | | | | | | |
| 8–12 tests, 2 forms each | 6295 | 1300 | | 285 | 275 | 900 | 2610 | | 350 | 175‡ | 400 |
| Coördination | | | | | | | | | | | |
| Squares | 3940 | | | 165 | 265 | 900 | 2610† | | | | |
| Circles | 3775 | | | | 265 | 900 | 2610† | | | | |
| Mazes | 4300 | | | | 265 | 900 | 2610† | | 350 | 175‡ | |
| Puzzles | | | | | | | | | | | |
| Pegs | 245 | | | | 245 | | | | | | |
| Fifteen | 220 | | | | 220 | | | | | | |
| Weights | 380 | | | 160 | 220 | | | | | | |
| Contests | | | | | | | | | | | |
| Grip | 615 | 135 | | 235 | 245 | | | | | | |
| Lungs | 615 | 135 | | 235 | 245 | | | | | | |
| Pull-up | 335 | 15 | | 170 | 150 | | | | | | |
| Jump | 615 | 135 | | 235 | 245 | | | | | | |
| Parties | | | | | | | | | | | |
| 3 tests | 490 | | | 215 | 275 | | | | | | |
| Money | | | | | | | | | | | |
| Planted Dime | 265 | | | | 265 | | | | | | |
| Coin Counting | 75 | | | | 75 | | | | | | |
| Magic Squares | 355 | | | 165 | 190 | | | | | | |
| Lying | | | | | | | | | | | |
| Pupil Data | 2570 | 900 | 940 | 730 | | | | | | | |
| SA test | 1315 | 840 | | 285 | 190 | | | | | | |
| Total population | 8150 | 1500 | 940 | 800* | 275 | 900 | 2610† | 200 | 350 | 175‡ | 400 |

* 240 tested twice.              † 300 tested twice.              ‡ Tested twice.

TABLE III.   (*B*) PRIVATE AND STANDARDIZING SCHOOLS

| Test | Total | P | Q | R | S | T | U | V | W | E |
|---|---|---|---|---|---|---|---|---|---|---|
| IER | | | | | | | | | | |
|   1–4 tests | 1540 | 250* | 170 | 175 | 305 | 640 | | | | |
| Speed | | | | | | | | | | |
|   12 tests, 2 forms | | | | | | | | | | |
|     each | 1595 | 345 | | 170 | | | 315† | 350 | 230 | 185† |
| Puzzles | | | | | | | | | | |
|   3 tests | 165 | | | 165 | | | | | | |
| Money | | | | | | | | | | |
|   Magic Squares | 160 | | | 160 | | | | | | |
| Lying | | | | | | | | | | |
|   Pupil Data | 300 | | | | 300 | | | | | |
|   SA tests | 250 | 250 | | | | | | | | |
| Total population | 2715 | 345* | 170 | 175 | 305 | 640 | 315† | 350 | 230 | 185† |

      * 120 tested twice.       † Tested twice.

    Table IV gives the same facts by grades in terms of separate tests administered rather than pupils tested. These figures indicate our concentration on grades five to eight.

TABLE IV

APPROXIMATE NUMBER OF DECEPTION TESTS ADMINISTERED, BY GRADES

| Test | Total | III | IV | V | VI | VII | VIII | IX | X | XI | XII |
|---|---|---|---|---|---|---|---|---|---|---|---|
| IER, 1–4 tests | 45,092 | | 210 | 10,116 | 9932 | 9808 | 9426 | 3436 | 1630 | 396 | 138 |
| Duplicating, 7 tests | | | | | | | | | | | |
|   used twice | 2072 | | 154 | 595 | 399 | 476 | 322 | 77 | 49 | | |
| Speed | | | | | | | | | | | |
|   8–12 tests, 2 | | | | | | | | | | | |
|   forms each | 99,276 | 6552 | 12,468 | 16,500 | 17,652 | 20,672 | 17,740 | 6612 | 636 | 168 | 276 |
| Coördination | | | | | | | | | | | |
|   1–3 tests | 15,618 | | 1911 | 2796 | 2804 | 3875 | 3029 | 1182 | 21 | | |
| Puzzles | | | | | | | | | | | |
|   1–3 tests | 1378 | | 93 | 274 | 247 | 287 | 215 | 65 | 92 | 42 | 63 |
| Contests | | | | | | | | | | | |
|   3–4 tests | 2175 | | 33 | 99 | 527 | 614 | 715 | 159 | 28 | | |
| Parties | | | | | | | | | | | |
|   3 tests | 489 | | | 43 | 150 | 123 | 119 | 40 | 14 | | |
| Money | | | | | | | | | | | |
|   1 or 2 of 3 tests | 851 | | 29 | 162 | 217 | 182 | 149 | 35 | 43 | 13 | 21 |
| Lying | | | | | | | | | | | |
|   1–2 tests | 4643 | | 1120 | 980 | 973 | 955 | 385 | 191 | 39 | | |
| Total tests | 171,594 | 6552 | 16,018 | 31,565 | 32,901 | 36,992 | 32,100 | 11,797 | 2552 | 619 | 498 |

Our data are derived from a population of some 10,865 pupils, who gave an average of four hours apiece to this part of our test program.

As our work involved many separate tests, some printed, some mimeographed, some requiring the use of objects, and some needing no material, data on these points may also be of interest. Table V shows these facts by types of material used.

TABLE V

TYPES OF TEST USED TO MEASURE DECEPTION

| PRINTED TESTS | Folders | Pages | | MIMEOGRAPHED TESTS | Folders | Pages |
|---|---|---|---|---|---|---|
| IER | 45,186 | 134,382 | | Coördination | 1000 | 1000 |
| Speed | 17,158 | 167,725 | | Duplicating | 600 | 900 |
| Duplicating | 1,180 | 3,540 | | Coin Counting | 100 | 100 |
| Pupil Data | 3,000 | 12,000 | | Lying | 1800 | 3600 |
| Score Sheets | 750 | 750 | | Total | 3500 | 5600 |
| Coördination | 14,661 | 14,661 | | | | |
| Total | 81,935 | 333,058 | | | | |

| MANUFACTURED TESTS | | | PURCHASED TESTS | | | APPARATUS |
|---|---|---|---|---|---|---|
| Fifteen | 75 | | Reading | 375 | | Dynamometer |
| Weights | 70 | | Peg Boards | 75 | | Spirometer |
| Magic Squares | 200 | | Total | 450 | | Mat |
| Total | 345 | | | | | Horizontal bar |

## APPLICATION AND RESULTS

So much for the scope of the testing. It remains now to show in somewhat greater detail how these various methods worked out in practice. This will require that we refer to each technique once more, but this repetition will not be a net loss for the reader inasmuch as his understanding of the entire report will depend in large part on his grasp of the methods employed.

We shall now take up our methods chronologically, beginning with our first technique, which involved the use of Thorndike's IER material for measuring levels of intelligence.

## A. The IER Tests

**1. Preliminary Experimental Testing.** It is one of the elementary principles of good testing to keep the test situations as much alike for all subjects as possible. In the case of intelligence tests, the primary factor in the situation is the problem to be solved, although the children are doubtless influenced also by the extent to which the ambition to make a good score is aroused, by their confidence in their own ability, by the heat of the room, and by their physical condition. When testing the tendency to deceive, these secondary influences loom larger in the total situation, and may indeed be primary factors. To the list already given we should add the pupil's attitude toward the teacher and the examiner, and for the problem to be solved we should substitute the kind of opportunity to deceive which the test offers. To keep all these matters constant from pupil to pupil would be too much to expect, but we felt we could keep them relatively constant from room to room.

In order to try out and standardize our method of administration, we set up a preliminary experiment. The variables we consciously attempted to control were the teacher, the examiner, the behavior of the examiner in the room, the opportunity offered to be dishonest, the motive under which the pupil was operating, and the type of test material used. School system A was used for this preliminary work.

(a) *The Teacher.* We saw no way to make classroom teachers alike, and therefore excused them from the room during the testing. It is generally supposed that the amount of cheating that takes place in a room is partly a function of the teacher's personality, and there is no doubt that the effect of this influence continues when the teacher is not present. This factor, therefore, we could not entirely control. The best we could do was to have the examiner take sole charge on the occasions when deception was possible.

(b) *The Examiner.* As we were obliged to use many examiners at one time, and could not therefore keep this factor absolutely constant, we used trained examiners and coached them carefully in the procedure. The factor of strangeness was kept constant by using different examiners for the two or more occasions on which a group was tested.

Such differences in the personalities of the testers as might affect the amount of cheating we could not eliminate, but a rough check on what took place in our experimental testing revealed no significant differences for groups. What differences among individual pupils were due to the personality of the examiner we have no means of knowing.

When expert examiners were not available, we used trained teachers, coaching them for the particular work on hand.

(c) *The Behavior of the Examiner.* Mimeographed directions were provided, and these were discussed in advance of the testing. In addition, suggestions were made as to manner, the amount of freedom to give the pupils when they were scoring their own papers, and the like. The examiners reported their experiences in the first efforts and the results were incorporated in the revised directions subsequently adopted.

(d) *Opportunity, Motive, and Test Material.* It will be recalled that the IER tests use four different kinds of material: an arithmetic test, the answers to be written at the margin; a sentence completion test, the answers to be written in on blank lines; an information test, the answers to be underlined; and a word knowledge test, the answers to be indicated by numerals placed in the margin. It was necessary to associate with each of these different types of material the various opportunities to deceive offered in school situations, and the various motives under which children ordinarily do their school work. Also each opportunity had to be associated with each motive.

In the suburban system used for this preliminary work there were five elementary schools scattered about the town, and one intermediate school consisting of grades seven and eight. Realizing the possibility that age and community background might affect the amount of deception, we endeavored to subject each grade and each type of school to all the different combinations of opportunity with which we were experimenting.

The opportunities presented to each child were as follows:

Opportunity 1. An answer sheet or key, giving all the answers to the questions on the test, was passed out after the test had been taken. As the sheets were handed out the examiner said: " Now I am going to pass out a key or answer sheet to each of you which gives the correct answer for each question and you are to correct your own papers. Put a C after each answer that is correct and a cross (X) after each answer you get wrong. Pay no attention to the ones you skipped. Count the number of C's. This is your grade. Put this number at the upper right corner of the front page of the test."

Opportunity 2. A key or answer sheet was passed out with the test. When the test and the key to it were passed out the examiner said: " Now I am going to pass out a key or answer sheet with each test so you can correct your own papers. The key is on the typewritten sheets. Keep it under your paper until you have finished. Is that clear? "

Opportunity 3. Copying from one another. No keys were passed out at all, but during the test the examiner either left the room or busied himself with a newspaper or desk work, paying no attention to the pupils except to preserve quiet.

Opportunity 4. Securing illegitimate help at home. This opportunity was always attached to the Word Knowledge test which was taken home. This test was chosen because help could be secured from the dictionary or another person. It was thought that this would offer more equal chance for cheating than any of the other tests. The time was so arranged that this test came just as school was closing. After the directions for doing the test were fully explained the examiner said: " Time is passing rapidly, so we shall take this test home and do it there. Do the test all by yourself, and don't get any help from anyone, or even from the dictionary. Do it to-day and bring it back to-morrow. Is that all clear? Do it to-day and bring it back to-morrow, and don't get any help on it."

The motives we attempted to arouse were those in constant operation in the child's everyday experience : (1) personal achievement, (2) individual competition, (3) group competition, (4) helpfulness. To have a check on these we tested several groups with no attempt at motivation, but with a standardized routine procedure.

The personal achievement motive was given as follows: Just before the first test was passed out the examiner said : " We are going to have some tests to-day which will enable you to see for yourself just how well you are getting on. No one in the class but yourself will know what you make on these tests, but you will be told how your own mark compares with the class average on each test." The essentials of this formula were repeated just before each of the four tests was passed out.

The formula for the individual competition motive was : " We are going to have some tests to-day to find out which pupils are doing the best in this class and in other classes. As soon as possible I will report to you in order the names of those who get the ten highest scores on each test. If you can't be at the head on one test, perhaps you can on another. Work hard and get on one of the honor lists." The essentials were repeated each time just before the test was passed out.

The formula for group competition was : " We are going to have some tests to-day to see how this grade compares with others of the same grade in other schools and in this school. Is this a pretty good class? Do you think you could make a better score than any other class of your age? When I report your class average I'll give you also the averages for some other classes of this same grade so you can see just how you stand. No individual scores will be reported." (Repetition as before.)

The formula for helpfulness was : " To-day we want you to help us make some tests. All tests of this sort are made with the help of the children. You can help us a great deal by showing what you can do on the tests. When they are perfected they will be given to hundreds of children. The scores will not be reported to you, but you may write what you think of each test as you finish it. We want you to do the best you can." (Repeated in substance with each test.)

The formula when no motivation was attempted was: "We are going to have some tests to-day. When the papers are passed out they will be fully explained."

Thus we had four tests, four motives, and four opportunities. Our problem was to rotate these among the twenty-three classrooms of school system A so as to get a fair picture of the relative influence of each on the practice of deception. For all but two groups we kept the motive constant for all four tests. In all cases we associated the vocabulary test with opportunity 4. In the case of the three other tests we associated each with each of the three other opportunities, getting five out of the six possible combinations as follows:

OPPORTUNITIES AND TESTS

| Test: | 1 | 2 | 3 |
|---|---|---|---|
| Opportunity 1 . . . . . . . . . | 1 | 2 | 3 |
| Opportunity 2 . . . . . . . . . | 2 | 1 | 3 |
| Opportunity 3 . . . . . . . . . | 2 | 3 | 1 |
| Opportunity 4 . . . . . . . . . | 3 | 1 | 2 |
| Opportunity 5 . . . . . . . . . | 1 | 3 | 2 |

Full details of this preliminary work will be found in Book Two.*
The main results are as follows:

(1) *Effect of Motive on Cheating.* The attempt to control the amount of deception by varying the motive was not successful. We do not mean to say that motives make no difference. But statements such as those we quoted from the experimental directions did not induce significant differences in the average amount of deception exhibited. The children used the answer sheets in order to boost their scores quite as much under the influence of

* Chapter III.

what we called the helpfulness motive as under what we called the individual competition motive. As we shall have occasion to point out later, this is an illustration of the enormous strength of the school drive, or interest in grades, which swallows up or discounts anything anyone can say to the children when the test is being administered.

(2) *Effect of Opportunity on Cheating.* The next question is whether the kind of opportunity offered makes any difference in the amount of cheating. The opportunities were : (1) having an answer sheet at hand after the test was taken ; (2) having an answer sheet at hand during the test ; (3) having no answer sheets but with conditions so arranged that copying from another pupil was possible ; and (4) using the dictionary or otherwise getting help at home.

In the first place the pupils evidently did not copy much from one another. If they did, it did not materially improve their scores over what they would have been without such copying. There are several possible explanations of this. If they did not copy, it may have been because they had been taught specifically not to do so. There is probably no corresponding drill in refraining from the use of other aids. Again a pupil will not copy from someone in whose ability he has no confidence, or if the person whose paper he wants to use keeps his answers covered. If any did copy, the results need not have benefited those who did to such an extent that the average score of the whole class was raised by it on the first day. The number of attempts at copying might have been estimated by comparing the number of identical errors on the day when copying was possible with the number of identical errors when copying was not possible. Since the scores were not affected, we did not trouble to do this and definitely abandoned copying as a useful opportunity in measuring deception by the double testing technique.

The two opportunities of which the pupils made most use were 1 and 4, having the key at hand during the test, and having access to help at home. The second, having the key at hand after the test was taken, comes in between.

(3) *Effect of Test Material on Cheating.* No matter what opportunity is offered, there is a constant relation between the amount of deception and the type of material used. In order of amount Arithmetic comes first, Word Knowledge second, Completion third, and Information fourth, although the difference between the last two is slight. In the case of the Completion test, cheating is somewhat troublesome, requiring the writing of several words to an answer. In contrast, the Arithmetic or Word Knowledge test requires the writing of only one or two digits as an answer. On the Information test the answer is given by underlining a word or phrase, but the test is very short and so offers less room to deceive. It is quite possible also that Arithmetic, being very common school material, has been the occasion of deception before, and is more closely associated with school marks. Certain habits of practice and motive may therefore be attached to this material but not to the more unusual information or completion type of test.

**2. The General Procedure as Revised.** Profiting by our first experience, we revised our testing technique. In the first place, we omitted all attempts to motivate cheating by repeating a formula. A colorless routine statement was adopted: " We are going to have some tests to-day. When the papers are passed out they will be fully explained. Be sure you have a sharpened pencil." In the second place, we attached the most favorable opportunity for cheating to the tests on which cheating was easiest. Thus we associated opportunity 2 (key passed with test) with Arithmetic. This allowed for one extreme. The other extreme was also provided for in attaching the hardest opportunity to the test on which there is least likelihood of cheating. Thus we put opportunity 1 (key passed out after test is taken) with Completions. Then between these two we put Information with opportunity 2, and left the Word Knowledge test as it was. The scheme then appears as follows:

Arithmetic :  Key passed out with tests (with the request that it be concealed until needed for scoring)

Completion :  Key passed out after test was taken

Information :          Key passed out after test was taken
Word Knowledge : No key but the test taken home and done
                 there

The revised directions are printed in full in the Appendix.* From this scheme we expected that Arithmetic and Word Knowledge would yield the heaviest cheating, Information next, and Completion next. Having the difficulty of cheating in school scaled in this way gives us a better insight into the child's character. If the child has only slight inclination to cheat, he may cheat on Arithmetic because it requires very little effort or temptation to do so. It takes more effort to cheat on Information. Finally it requires considerable effort to cheat very much on Completion when the key is passed out after the test is given.

Certain other essential features of the original procedure were retained in the revised directions, namely :

1. The answer sheets and cheating opportunities were always given on the first day of testing. The first day the tests were given in an afternoon school session, so that the Word Knowledge test directions could be given just before time for the close of school for the day.

2. At least one day and two nights elapsed between the first and second day's testing.

3. The tests were given in the same order always : Arithmetic, Completion, Information, Word Knowledge.

4. On the first day the teacher was always absent from the room. On the second day all tests were given in class and closely supervised ; the teacher and the examiner were both present.

**3. Typical Results of the IER Technique.** Complete tables showing the statistical returns by populations and groups are given in Book Two. We present here simply one illustration to show the nature of the material. We take two classes, one that averaged very high and one that averaged very low in honesty. Figure 7 shows the facts as to the per cents cheating. Figure 8 shows the facts as to the amount scores or Xi scores.†

* We adhered to these directions in all subsequent use of the IER material.
† See discussions in Chapter III.

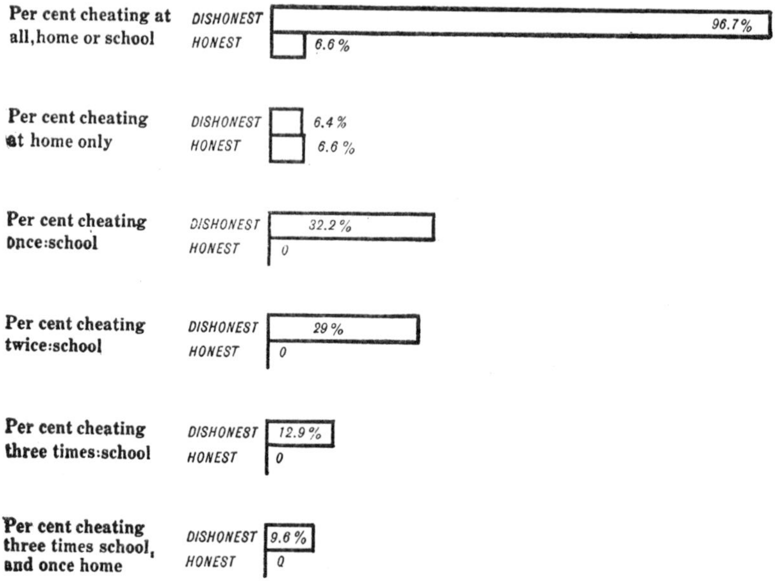

| Per cent cheating at all, home or school | DISHONEST | | 96.7% |
| | HONEST | | 6.6% |

| Per cent cheating at home only | DISHONEST | | 6.4% |
| | HONEST | | 6.6% |

| Per cent cheating once:school | DISHONEST | | 32.2% |
| | HONEST | | 0 |

| Per cent cheating twice:school | DISHONEST | | 29% |
| | HONEST | | 0 |

| Per cent cheating three times:school | DISHONEST | | 12.9% |
| | HONEST | | 0 |

| Per cent cheating three times school, and once home | DISHONEST | | 9.6% |
| | HONEST | | 0 |

FIGURE 7

PER CENT CHEATING ON IER TESTS IN TWO TYPICAL GROUPS, ONE
ESPECIALLY DISHONEST AND ONE ESPECIALLY HONEST

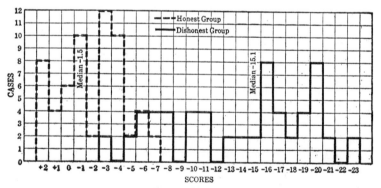

FIGURE 8

GRAPHIC DISTRIBUTION OF TYPICAL AMOUNT SCORES ON IER TESTS

## B. THE SPEED TESTS

The double testing idea was used also with the speed material described in Chapter III. These tests were administered in schools to children in grades three to twelve with the identical technique, except that the third-grade children omitted two of the six tests and the fourth-grade children one. The complete directions are printed in the Appendix.

As the six tests could be given three times and the last one self-scored all in forty minutes, it was a simple matter to maintain uniform conditions, for the same four or five examiners could handle practically all the groups; and in the case of population A, where thirty-three groups had to be tested in one day, ten examiners sufficed for the entire program.

The tests were printed in two folders. The first folder contained two sets of the six tests and the second folder one set. As the examiner entered the room to test a class the teacher left, so that there was always the uniform condition of a stranger administering the test. The first folder was passed without comment save this introductory statement: " To-day we are to have some tests which will show how fast and accurately you can do certain kinds of work. Tests like this were used in the army and are now used in civil service examinations. In taking these tests it is necessary to do exactly what the examiner says. Do nothing to the papers until you are told what to do."

As the success of the procedure depended on accurately starting and stopping each test, the examiners had to be trained to watch their time and to give the pupils the snap and vim required for carrying the thing through. Everything during the period was consequently handled in a brisk and businesslike way. Practice in starting and stopping was given even in writing name, grade, age, etc., and the first minute for each test afforded further familiarization with the procedure before the last two trials were attempted, which were used for measuring deception.

The directions for each test were as follows: Say to the pupils: " Look at Test 1 at the bottom of the page. This is an additions test. When I say ' Go,' begin at the upper left corner and add as many of these examples as you can. Work across the page from left to right. Write the answers under the lines. Work fast. Ready? Go." In one minute say: " Stop. Pencils up. Turn the page with your free hand. We will try this again. When I say ' Go,' add as many of these examples on page 2 as you can. Ready? Go."

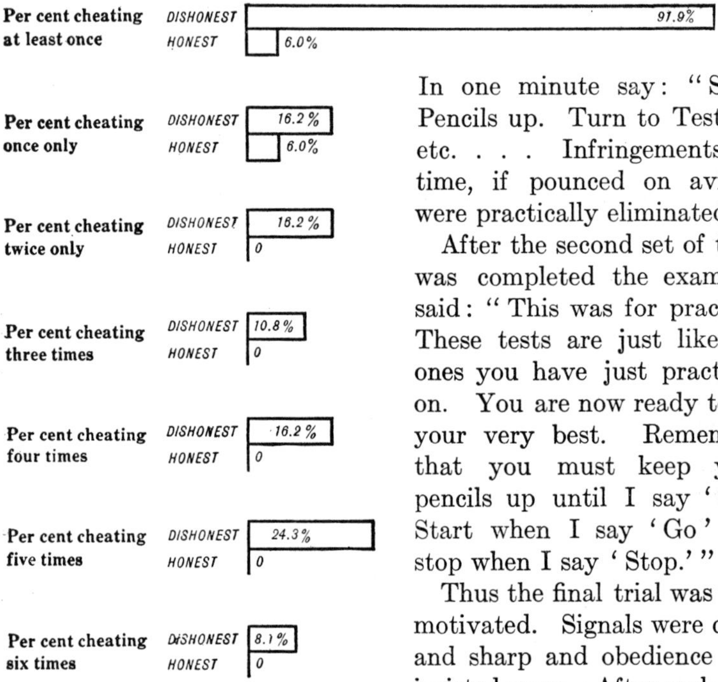

| | | |
|---|---|---|
| Per cent cheating at least once | DISHONEST | 91.9% |
| | HONEST | 6.0% |
| Per cent cheating once only | DISHONEST | 16.2% |
| | HONEST | 6.0% |
| Per cent cheating twice only | DISHONEST | 18.2% |
| | HONEST | 0 |
| Per cent cheating three times | DISHONEST | 10.8% |
| | HONEST | 0 |
| Per cent cheating four times | DISHONEST | 16.2% |
| | HONEST | 0 |
| Per cent cheating five times | DISHONEST | 24.3% |
| | HONEST | 0 |
| Per cent cheating six times | DISHONEST | 8.1% |
| | HONEST | 0 |

FIGURE 9

PER CENT CHEATING ON SPEED TESTS IN TYPICAL GROUPS, ONE ESPECIALLY DISHONEST AND ONE ESPECIALLY HONEST

In one minute say: " Stop. Pencils up. Turn to Test 2," etc. . . . Infringements on time, if pounced on avidly, were practically eliminated.

After the second set of tests was completed the examiner said: " This was for practice. These tests are just like the ones you have just practiced on. You are now ready to do your very best. Remember that you must keep your pencils up until I say ' Go.' Start when I say ' Go ' and stop when I say ' Stop.' "

Thus the final trial was well motivated. Signals were clear and sharp and obedience was insisted upon. After each test was completed the pupils were asked to score their own papers as follows: " Stop. Pencils up. When I say ' Go,' count the examples you got right. You can easily tell the right answer. Your score on this test is the number you got right. Put this number in the lower right corner where it says 'Score.' Ready? Go." In two minutes or less, say: " Stop. Pencils up. Turn to Test 2," etc. . . .

It is at this point that pupils so disposed had the opportunity of adding on more examples, crossing out more A's, underlining more 4's, etc., beyond the point at which they left the test when time was called. While they were counting, it was almost impossible for anyone to see that additions were being made and of course it was not clear to the pupils that there would be any way of finding out about it. They wanted a good record and did not realize that they had already done as well as they were likely to do on the preceding trials which had been collected.

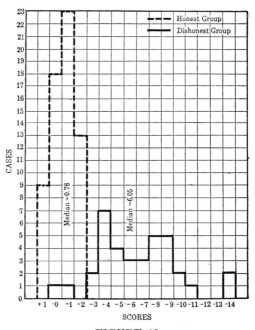

FIGURE 10

GRAPHIC DISTRIBUTION OF TYPICAL AMOUNT SCORES ON SPEED TESTS

Pupils almost always enjoyed taking these speed tests. They are good practice for them and a pleasant relief from school routine. There is a kind of excitement in the intensity of a mechanical speed test, especially when everyone in the room is also working as fast as he can. The tests also constitute an excellent measure of this sort of ability.

The detailed results of the application of the Speed tests are given in Book Two.

Typical examples are shown graphically in Figures 9 and 10. These correspond to Figures 7 and 8 except that the percentage figures here refer only to school tests as none of the Speed tests were taken at home.  There were six chances to cheat on the speed material and the per cent cheating once, twice, three times, etc., is shown for an extremely dishonest room and an extremely honest room.

There is noticeably less cheating on the Speed tests than on the IER tests of the arithmetic type, where an answer sheet is available all through the test.  The one who deceives must want to badly enough to go to some trouble and add on a few more answers. If he does this for some time after the rest have stopped he becomes conspicuous.

### C. The Coördination and Puzzle Tests

**1. Coördination Tests.**  The Coördination tests are printed in Chapter III.  The procedure in administering them is given fully in the Appendix.  The essential feature is to secure the coöperation of the pupils in the task as a serious undertaking rather than as a stunt or game.  Here again the manner and skill of the tester is taxed to the utmost in many groups.

The visibility of these tests is not low enough to warrant our attempting to use them above the eighth or ninth grades, and even here the atmosphere was sometimes unfavorable on account of the apparent childishness of the requirement that the eyes be closed.  To an intelligent boy of fifteen the Circles test would be obviously impossible of complete accomplishment.  A simpler form such as used by Cady would be better adapted to children of twelve or over.

The Coördination tests require thirty minutes to administer. Amount scores and cheating scores as described in Chapter III are reported fully in Book Two.

The significant thing about this technique is that a very large proportion of all children will open their eyes to guide their pencils, being apparently unable to resist the tendency even when to yield to it is unfair.  As it is easy to squint without being noticed, this test offers little external resistance to deception.

**2. Puzzle Tests.**  It was felt to be important to give the pupils an opportunity to deceive with objects or in connection with the use of objects as well as with pencil and paper. It was fortunate that we decided to do this; for we found, as will be discussed later, that the tendency to cheat is intimately tied up with the particular kind of opportunity presented. What will stimulate one child will leave another child untouched. A pupil may feel quite free to falsify his arithmetic paper, who will not fake a solution to a puzzle.

Puzzles were chosen as objects because of the high interest of most children in reaching solutions and the widespread impatience children usually exhibit in the process of manipulation and search. Large numbers of puzzles were studied and tried out, resulting in the selection of the three described in Chapter III.

Here even more than in the case of the Coördination tests, it was necessary to have most careful testing done on account of the tendency of the pupils to go wild over the puzzles. The investigators consequently administered all these tests themselves and often had an assistant in the room to help care for the bulky material. The Magic Square money test, which was intended to test honesty in handling money, was usually given at the same time, so that a single score sheet sufficed for recording everything. A facsimile of the sheet used is printed part on page 57 and part on page 91.

It is clear that a pupil might falsify by faking a solution or by merely claiming a solution on the score sheet. In either case deception has occurred.

When these tests were first administered it was thought necessary to use buffer puzzles easy of solution so as not to allow the pupils to be discouraged by the difficulty of the tasks but rather to establish the mental set: " These puzzles can be solved." The buffer puzzles could be explained by the tester so all could see how easy they were. We found, however, that the pupils became too excited over so many interesting toys. On first opening the little box containing a selection of puzzles the children would fairly shout with joy. Since no problem of discouragement arose in actual practice, the buffer puzzles were later omitted.

The order in which the puzzles were given varied from group to group as it was not practical to make enough for more than two or three groups to use at the same time and consequently rotation was resorted to. To what extent this affected the results is not known.

In the case of the Peg Board and Fifteen puzzle, large models were used * to facilitate explanation of the procedure. The proper way to handle the pegs and blocks was demonstrated on the models so that the element of misunderstanding was reduced to a minimum.

Both the amount and the fact scores as described in Chapter III are shown in Book Two. A glance at the tables will reveal that this test also is effective in differentiating both individuals and groups.

## D. THE ATHLETIC CONTESTS

After the general method to be followed had been planned, two experienced men† were selected to administer the contests. Beginning with a small group at school C these men worked the procedure down to certain standardized essentials which could then be adapted to different situations. These are fully described in Chapter III.

Each test had to be given to one pupil at a time with an allowance of about twenty minutes per pupil. The examiners could keep two or three going at once as there were four tests in all, and while one pupil was working on the machines, another could be jumping or using the bar.

Such difficulties as arose were not due to any lack of interest on the part of the pupils, although in a few cases there was evidently no desire to compete or to display physical prowess. No other pressure was brought to bear on the pupils to do their best, as it was the contest situation that was being measured as a stimulus to deception.

It was soon found that in most cases the girls could not chin even once, so this test was usually omitted in their case.

In situations of this sort, which are intended to be, and are, very serious from the standpoint of the pupils, great care needs to be exercised to fulfill all promises made and to enter with entire

* Made for us at school D by the teacher of manual arts.
† A. G. Truxal and G. S. Sheppard.

sympathy into the program from the pupils' standpoint. In awarding the medals in one school, for example, it was found that two boys tied for a lung capacity prize. We followed our rule and awarded the prize to the smaller of the two boys, both of whom of course belonged in the same weight class. Later one of the pupils told the principal that the other boy was somewhat crippled. Note of this fact should have been made on our records, but with the information now in our possession we could do no less than have a duplicate medal made for this boy. He was of course greatly pleased to receive it as medals for physical ability had not often come his way.

For similar reasons we found it necessary to test *all* the pupils in comparable groups even though for our purposes we needed the records for only a few. Otherwise the idea of a school contest could not be carried out. In testing these additional cases we kept all under close supervision as our interest here was in the discovery of ability rather than the measurement of deception; and in awarding prizes only the " honest " scores of the pupils tested for deception were utilized.

The tests proved quite satisfactory both in administration and results. Amount and fact scores are given in Book Two.

## E. The Party Tests

The administration of the test party is described fully in Chapter III and in the Appendix. All the parties were conducted by a professional recreational leader * with the assistance of her pupils and sometimes of members of our own staff. The play atmosphere made it difficult to maintain the conditions required for objective testing and doubtless there was occasional laxity in substituting opinion for recorded fact in the case of pinning the tail on the donkey. As the tests proceeded, however, the technique was improved and simplified so that it turned out fairly well.

Deception in a game is generally recognized to be quite a distinct sort of behavior frequently engaged in just for fun as a part

* Madeline L. Stevens, Director, The School of Play and Recreation, New York City.

of the spirit of the occasion. This bantering type of deception, however, is not the real article, for in most cases part of the fun is to be found out. With children, parties are usually more serious affairs and cheating is frowned upon even when it is not actually prevented as it is in the case of contests.

The party thus stands midway between the classroom, where prevention of deception by pupils is rare, and the athletic contest, where deception is prohibited, if discovered, by public opinion.

It would have been better if our parties could have been conducted entirely away from the schools. It did not prove possible, however, to secure the attendance of the children at any other place. Social periods in the case of school C were utilized, and at school D, a twenty-four hour institution, the children's Friday evening social hour in their cottages was turned over to our party. The modifications in the party made necessary by this limitation on space and time are noted in the Appendix.

Only fact scores are available for the party tests. Each child had two opportunities to cheat and one to steal. The tests worked well. The results appear in Book Two.

### F. The Tests for Measuring the Stealing Type of Deception

**1. Classroom Situations.** The classroom does not often afford opportunities to steal money. Consequently our tests suffer somewhat by their abstraction from real life situations. This may in part account for the infrequency with which money was actually taken on these classroom tests.

On the other hand, it may be argued that the essence of the situation was having access to money that could be taken apparently without detection. But again such situations usually arise or are arranged for in solitude. Theft is not usually a gregarious offense. The group, consequently, although possibly either unaware of what was going on or, if aware, unsympathetic* with the culprit, furnished a subtle inhibition not easily to be overcome.

---

* The class group is not often a gang which includes petty larceny among its approved activities.

The classroom money tests were given along with the Puzzles. In the case of the Planted Dime, which was simply placed in each box of puzzles as part of a puzzle which was not used at that time, only five dimes in a population of 260 in school D were removed.

The Coin Counting for younger children was not given as a puzzle but as a test.

The Magic Squares was itself a puzzle the solution of which could not be faked. The puzzle was made up in part of actual coins which could easily be slipped into one's pocket or dress before the puzzle was returned. The results of the money tests for two populations are given in Book Two.

**2. Out-of-classroom Situations.** In addition to the classroom situation, the more natural atmosphere of the party was chosen for another stealing test called the Mystery Man, described in Chapter III. This was certainly not open to the criticism of artificiality made above on the classroom test.

In the case of the Mystery Man, as was noted in Chapter III, those taking the money did not for the most part go near the box to deposit their " object " but kept both coin and article — where both were used at the same time. In this respect the act was typical of an act of theft, the thief keeping out of sight as much as possible. The results are given in Book Two.

### G. The Tests for Measuring Lying

**1. Lying to Escape Disapproval.** As was pointed out on page 95 of Chapter III, there are two ways of handling the answers to the pupil-data questions which give the pupil a chance to admit or deny having cheated if he has done so. One is to consider only admissions. Before reporting typical admission figures it would be well to repeat the questions utilized for the measurement of lying:

33. Did you ever cheat on any sort of test?
34. Have you cheated on such tests more than once?
41. Did you actually do this test all alone without getting help on it?

42. If you did get help, was it from some person?
43. Or was it from a book or dictionary?
44. Did you understand at the time that you were not to get help in doing the test?
45. On some of these tests you had a key to correct your paper by. Did you copy any answer from the keys?
46. Do you think that to do so is really cheating?
47. On any of these same tests did you copy answers from other pupils' papers?
48. Do you think that to do that is really cheating?
56. If you did copy on any of these tests that you took a little while ago or received any help you should not have received, just why did you do so?
57. Have you answered all the questions honestly and truthfully?

It will be remembered that questions 33, 34, 56, and 57 have only a general significance, whereas questions 41, 42, 43, 45, and 47 are entirely specific. Questions 44, 46, and 48 serve as a check on the other answers.

A few records of the replies* to these questions will make it easier to understand how they were used. The following are taken from the records of schools A and B:

| QUESTIONS: | 33 | 34 | 41 | 42 | 43 | 44 | 45 | 46 | 56 | 57 | CS | CH |
|---|---|---|---|---|---|---|---|---|---|---|---|---|
| | − | − | + | − | − | + | − | + | | + | 1 | 1 |
| | − | − | + | − | − | + | − | + | | + | 1 | 0 |
| | + | + | − | + | + | − | + | − | + | + | 1 | X |
| | − | − | + | + | − | − | − | − | − | + | 2 | 0 |
| | − | − | + | − | + | | − | + | − | + | 1 | 0 |

CS = School cheating
CH = Home cheating
X = No test returned

* As noted in Chapter III, the sign + means " Yes," −, " No," and a blank, no answer.

Characteristic differences are seen between those who do not
and those who do cheat, the more honest group having a typical
" truth profile " as follows:

| Questions: | 33 | 34 | 41 | 42 | 43 | 44 | 45 | 46 | 47 | 48 | 56 | 57 |
|---|---|---|---|---|---|---|---|---|---|---|---|---|
| | − | − | + | − | − | + | − | + | − | + | − | + |

This typical response stands out clearly when the zero C's or
non-cheaters are grouped as from the following class:

| Questions: | 33 | 34 | 41 | 42 | 43 | 44 | 45 | 46 | 47 | 48 | 56 | 57 |
|---|---|---|---|---|---|---|---|---|---|---|---|---|
| 1 . . . . . | − | − | + | − | − | + | − | + | − | + | | + |
| 2 . . . . . | − | − | + | − | − | + | − | + | − | + | − | + |
| 3 . . . . . | − | − | + | − | − | + | − | + | − | + | | + |
| 4 . . . . . | − | − | + | − | − | + | − | + | − | + | − | + |
| 5 . . . . . | + | − | + | − | − | + | − | + | − | + | − | + |

Contrasted with this is the record of those who cheated twice
in the same class:

| Questions: | 33 | 34 | 41 | 42 | 43 | 44 | 45 | 46 | 47 | 48 | 56 | 57 |
|---|---|---|---|---|---|---|---|---|---|---|---|---|
| 6 . . . . . | + | − | + | − | − | + | − | + | − | + | − | + |
| 7 . . . . . | + | − | + | − | − | + | − | + | − | + | | + |
| 8 . . . . . | + | − | + | − | − | + | + | + | − | + | | + |
| 9 . . . . . | + | − | + | − | − | + | − | + | − | + | − | + |
| 10 . . . . . | − | − | + | − | − | + | − | + | − | + | − | + |

Some clearly deny the fact of having cheated, as in case ten;
others tell some truths and some falsehoods, as in case eight;
while others own up completely.

From these records it was possible to secure a corrected list of
cheaters, adding to the list of those actually caught by our technique those who did not cheat enough to reach the limit of 3 Xi but
who nevertheless admitted using the key or getting help at home.

On the school tests fewer admitted getting help than on the home tests.   In one system (B) the average per cent admitting cheating in school was sixteen, whereas the average per cent admitting getting help unfairly at home was sixty-one.

Chapter III tells how the lie index was secured, and the necessary tables are printed in Book Two.

This technique grew out of our own situations and is of course unstandardized.   Any further applications would need to be adapted to the local conditions and circumstances of the testing.

**2. Lying to Win Approval.**   The SA lying tests were administered along with a number of others just as an ordinary test. The two forms are printed in full in Chapter III, and the results appear in Book Two.   There is some doubt as to what is tested here, but the administration of these tests offered no particular problems and the scoring was quite simple.

# CHAPTER V

## THE VALUE OF THE TECHNIQUES FOR MEASURING DECEPTION

Nothing has so far been said to establish the truth of the statement that these tests we have been discussing really measure deception, or that they measure it consistently. What reason is there to suppose that differences among individuals and groups are not due to some feature of the test procedure? And can we be sure that if we go back and measure these same individuals again with these same tests or their equivalents the results will be at all comparable to what we have found? Before entering upon any extended interpretation of the data gathered it is essential that these questions be answered. Stated formally they are: (1) How accurately do these tests measure what they claim to measure? (2) How consistently do they measure anything? Stated technically, (1) What is the validity of the tests? and (2) What is their reliability?

In the measurement of physical conditions, changes, and objects, we are accustomed to the use of devices which appear to be absolutely valid and reliable. A good thermometer, for example, measures temperature accurately. The degrees we read are so closely related to changes in temperature that any given change in the latter is accompanied by a given change in the former. The thermometer does not measure partly temperature and partly barometer pressure and partly the direction of the wind. It is a valid instrument.

But even with a thermometer we know that inaccuracies do occur. No two bath thermometers we buy in a store are likely to read exactly the same. It is exceedingly difficult to make them accurate — perfect devices for measuring temperature. They are never *absolutely* valid. Clinical thermometers, for example, are often accompanied by a slip òf paper showing the amount of correction to be made in the readings at different levels in order to approximate the exact temperature.

Furthermore, these physical instruments are so nearly unchangeable that we feel no hesitation in asserting that they always measure the same thing in the same way. A pound of sugar weighed to-day on one pair of scales will weigh a pound to-morrow on the same scales. Our foot rule always measures a foot. Our gas meter always lets through exactly the same amount of gas for every quarter we put in. If it does not (and of course no one doubts that it does!) it is not reliable. As a matter of fact it probably does not. Nor is your foot rule exactly the same length to-day as it was yesterday. Only by the most carefully guarded conditions does the " standard " length, kept in the museum of the Bureau of Standards, remain relatively unaffected by general changes in atmospheric conditions. Our measuring devices are only approximately reliable. In the conduct of experiments involving exactingly minute weights or sizes this is sometimes a source of great error in computations.

Let us take up first the problem of the reliability or constancy of the instrument.

## RELIABILITY

Before any mental tests were made, one who wanted to measure any sort of mental work was in precisely the position that we should be in if we wanted to measure the length of a pile of wood and had no standard units in terms of which to state the results. We might get around the difficulty by picking up a stick and counting the number of times it would be necessary to lay it down in order to cover the length of the pile. The results could not be stated in units other than the stick itself, which would have to be produced if we wanted to communicate to anyone else any idea of the length of the pile.

To make sure of the results we secured the first time, we might lay the stick down along the pile several times. Sometimes it would come out exactly even, sometimes a little short, sometimes a little long.  Our results would contain errors.  Is the difference due to some change in the pile, or in the stick, or to the fact that we are careless and do not lay it in a straight line, introducing therefore elements of height as well as length?  To settle the matter we might first exercise greater care in keeping the stick horizontal and in a vertical plane, so that it would measure only length and not height or breadth.  Doing this we might find that we actually could repeat exactly the number of stick lengths required to compass the pile.  We could conclude therefore that

1.  the pile does not change in length ;
2.  the stick does not change in length ;
3.  the stick is a reliable instrument for measuring the pile.

The procedure in mental testing has been of this empirical character.  It was discovered by repeated experiments that in the case of intelligence tests certain specific stimuli would secure approximately the same responses in the same individual if the interval between two applications of the stimuli were not too great.  This fact furnished scientific evidence for the common observation that intelligence is a relatively fixed trait.  But in establishing this as a usable working hypothesis the uniformity of results with these tests also gave evidence of the capacity of the particular stimuli used to secure uniform results on separate occasions.  To revert to our analogy : The pile (intelligence) does not change ; and the stick (the test) does not change in its power to measure the pile.  Since in the case of testing, the subject is a highly complex organism making active response to a highly complex situation, the analogy of the pile and the stick cannot be pressed very far.  The possibility of variation in the general test situation is very great.  In the long run and for large groups these variations tend to balance one another, but it has so far proved impossible to make two measuring instruments in the field of psychology as identical as two thermometers recording exactly the same temperature.  As in the case of the imperfect measures of the pile of wood, the results of mental tests contain " errors of measurement."

The errors or fluctuations to which most attention is given in testing are due to such facts as these. First, taking a test leaves a certain practice effect so that on repetition of the test the behavior of the subject is changed from what it otherwise would have been. Second, such factors as the mood of the examiner, the mood of the subject — his health, ambition, etc. — the quality of the atmosphere are never twice alike. Third, if two tests are used, one for one day and the other for the repetition, these are not capable of eliciting from each individual at each point exactly the same response as was secured from the previous test. However, when the responses for a whole group are lumped together, the two tests may be found to be, for the group, identical, since for each subject who does a little better there is one who does a little worse.

In the case of intelligence and most forms of school achievement there does not seem to be much change in the subjects over short intervals, but in the case of character tendencies, common observation asserts that there is greater variation in performance from time to time, even over very short intervals. Apparently one's emotional set materially influences what one does in adjusting himself to other persons and consequently in what one utters as his opinion or reveals as his attitude, whereas the same emotional condition has much less power to affect one's behavior on an intelligence test. It would appear to be much more difficult in the nature of the case, then, to establish the reliability of methods for testing character, since the chance alterations in the mood and attitude of the subject loom up so large in their effect on the results.*

We are consequently obliged to recognize in our test results several types of error: (1) practice effect and errors of measurement involved in the material that is used, such as arithmetic test material; (2) variability in the trait that this material is supposed to measure, e.g., arithmetical ability; (3) variability in the tendency of the individual to change his response because of the extrane-

---

* Of course, if a technique for measuring emotional set could be produced, this could be employed to ascertain whether this fact remained the same on the two or more occasions of testing.

ous stimulus we have introduced, as the presence of a key to get answers from; and (4) practice effect and errors involved in the measurement of this tendency.

The duplicating technique was used for the purpose of eliminating one of these sources of error, namely, that due to incapacity of the material to measure its correlative ability with absolute accuracy. This, as will be remembered, was accomplished by the simple expedient of making a copy of the papers of the pupils and then counting the changes made in them when they were scored with a key. In the case of the IER tests and Speed tests it was necessary to measure the practice effect and chance errors of measurement involved before it was possible to tell how much of a pupil's score was due to the several types of error we have just named. This procedure is discussed in detail in Book Two.

For present purposes it is necessary only to summarize these results rather briefly. The problem is: To what extent are our deception tests vitiated by errors of measurement of the sort discussed? In general and test for test, we are able to measure deception almost as consistently and with almost as little error as we are able to measure intelligence. Just as one test is an insufficient and unreliable measure in the case of intelligence, so one test of deception is quite incapable of measuring a subject's tendency to deceive. That is, we cannot predict from what a pupil does on one test what he will do on another. If we use ten tests of classroom deception, however, we can safely predict what a subject will do on the average whenever ten similar situations are presented.*

But even if we use fewer than ten such tests, this does not mean at all that our results are valueless. Fortunately, there are statistical devices for getting rid of the errors of measurement already referred to. These devices do not apply to individual scores, but only to computations based on large numbers of such scores. For such researches, therefore, as are reported subsequently in this volume, for which the score of no particular individual is of im-

* Ten tests of the IER type would yield a reliability coefficient or self-correlation of .90.

portance but only the general trends of large groups, it is possible to satisfy all statistical requirements although using a much smaller number of tests than would be necessary for predicting the behavior of an individual.*

## VALIDITY

Let us turn now to the second of the two problems with which this chapter deals, namely, How completely do these tests measure what they claim to measure? The water meter claims to measure the cubic feet of water used by a household. It does not claim to measure the flow of an electric current. It is a valid instrument to the extent that it accurately measures the amount of water used. But how do we know that the dial records on the water meter actually represent cubic feet of water used? The meter has been tested against some other way of measuring the water. Possibly the meter is attached to a tank the volume of which is computed from its dimensions. This is filled with water and the meter adjusted so that the readings on the dial will tally exactly with the *known* amount of water in the tank.

If we apply this same procedure to tests, we have to find some

---

* The following table may assist the reader familiar with statistical terms without making it necessary for him to turn to the elaborate treatment of this problem in Book Two. All the *r*'s except the last are predictions from the intercorrelation of the separate tests rather than self-correlations of the same tests repeated.

RELIABILITIES OF TECHNIQUES USED FOR MEASURING DECEPTION

1. Copying from a key or answer sheet (3 tests) . . . . . . . . . .871
2. Copying from a key or answer sheet; duplicating technique (7 tests) .825
3. Adding on more scores (6 Speed tests) . . . . . . . . . . . .825
4. Peeping when eyes should be shut (3 Coördination tests) . . . . .721
5. Faking a solution to a puzzle (3 tests) . . . . . . . . . . .750
    2 tests, Pegs and Fifteen puzzle . . . . . . . . . . .620
6. Faking a score in a physical ability contest (4 tests) . . . . . . .772
7. Lying to win approval [1] . . . . . . . . . . . . . . . .836
8. Getting help from a dictionary or from some person on one test done
    at home . . . . . . . . . . . . . . . . . . . . . .240

[1] The reliability of this test is doubtless affected by the fact that part of the items are common to both forms.

other way of measuring the variable which the test claims to measure, and check the test against this independent result. The test corresponds to the meter and what we need now is the tank. In test making this independent measure of the thing which the test is supposed to measure is called the " criterion." Our own tests purport to measure various types of conduct commonly called dishonesty, deceit, unfairness, and the like. To determine how well this is accomplished we also must have a criterion or some quantitative description of this conduct in the children whom we have tested.

As criteria of this sort psychologists have sometimes used the judgments or ratings of persons who know the subjects who are being tested. In building the army intelligence tests, for example, officers were asked to rate or rank their men in the order of their intelligence. These ratings or rankings, representing the opinions of the officers, constituted one criterion against which the tests were checked. A test which would give high rating to those rated high by the officers and a low rating to those rated low was a good test.

It is very difficult to build up a trustworthy empirical criterion for character tests. In our particular case what we want to know is the honesty, or dishonesty, or tendencies to deceive, of the pupils whom we have measured. How are we going to find this out apart from the tests? There are two or three things we can do.

First, we can get the opinions of teachers, parents, and other children concerning the dishonesty or deceitfulness of this or that child. If a child is definitely known to be deceitful, or dishonest, by teachers, parents, and other children always and on all occasions, then we should expect him to cheat on our tests; conversely if a child is known to be honest always, everywhere, by everyone, then we should expect him to be honest on the tests. But in actual practice we get into trouble right away. Children are deceptive on some occasions and not on others; they are honest in certain situations and not in others. Neither the ratings nor the tests take *all possible* situations into account. It would seem to be necessary, then, to have the subjects judged or rated for the specific types of honesty or dishonesty which the tests measure.

A second thing that might be done is to gather conduct records on the children tested. In some schools and some institutions careful conduct records are kept. These might be used as a criterion, or as one component of a more complex criterion. We have not found actual records in our schools which include data on deceptiveness, but in one case the children were regularly graded in honesty.

In the third place, we might ask the children themselves what they thought about it. Do they think that getting help from a dictionary is cheating when they were told not to get such help? Do they think that using an answer sheet for improving their scores is cheating?

We have done something with each of these methods and will now present the results.

### A. Validation by Ratings

We found it very easy to get the opinions of teachers with regard to the honesty of their pupils. It was not so easy, however, to find teachers whose opinions were either consistent from week to week or in agreement with the opinions of other teachers. In other words the reliability and validity of our proposed criterion were not such as to justify our placing much confidence in it.* From the results of three tests we could predict more accurately than most of the eighteen teachers concerned whether their pupils would cheat or not in the next test.

One of the most common difficulties encountered in rating pupils for honesty was general unwillingness to " mark a pupil down." On an eleven-point scale, for example, 32% of the cases were rated above five on the scale in intelligence, and 32% in word knowledge ; but 73% were rated above five in general honesty, and 72% above five in tendency to cheat on examinations.†

---

* Average reliability of eighteen teachers' ratings, .50. Average correlation between independent ratings of twenty teachers on 600 pupils, .54. For full details see Book Two.

† Someone has suggested that this inhibition against placing a pupil low on a character scale would be automatically overcome if a scale ranging from 90

Allowing for these limitations, we find that our tests agree almost as well with teachers' ratings of honesty as the results of tests of intelligence do with their ratings for intelligence as measured by the CAVI tests.*

## B. Validation by Records

In one of the private schools tested provision is made for recording from time to time whether a child is above or below average with respect to various forms of desirable conduct. Among the list of acts is the practice of honesty. In a population of 146 only seven received a notation of below average in this particular during several school terms. Of these seven there were three who cheated on the IER tests and four who did not. Of the 139 who were marked above average or else not marked at all 18% cheated.

## C. Validation by Confession

As reported in Chapters III and IV, we took occasion to ask the first population tested whether or not they used the answer sheets wrongly or got help at home and whether they regarded this as cheating. We have usable returns on 2141 cases. The following facts are of interest regarding the question as to whether the children thought that copying answers from the keys was " really cheating."

Over 91% answered this question. Of those who answered it, 88% did so in the affirmative, that is, 88% said they thought that to copy answers from keys was cheating.

If we take only such cases as in all probability actually did use the keys, the proportions are a little different. 44% of the 2141 pupils apparently did copy from the keys. 89% of these answered the question about using answer sheets and of these 82% said they thought that to copy from the keys was cheating.

Of course, many of the 56% not caught at cheating probably did

to 100 instead of from 0 to 10 were used, as 90 seems good enough for anyone and so even the worst child may be placed properly lower than the average without any embarrassment to the teacher.

* See Book Two, Chapter VII.

use the keys somewhat, but 93% of them answered the question about it and of these more honest children 93% said they thought that to copy from the keys would be cheating.

We do not know, of course, whether those who cheated are giving us a straight answer as to their real opinion. Probably many of them are anxious to appear honest. Only a few of them, at all events, admitted using the keys. Let us assume that a true picture of pupil opinion is about what is presented by the whole population, including cheaters and non-cheaters. If this assumption is correct, then in about 90% of the subjects measured, the scores represent not only the fact of deception or falsification but also the attitude of deception or the feeling that the act is a genuine case of cheating.

A personal interview with each pupil would have been desirable and will later be included in some of our studies; but lacking this mode of discovering the real attitudes of those tested, these results constitute as complete a validation of the technique as is likely to be secured.

## THEORETICAL VALIDITY

So far we have been discussing what might be called the empirical validity of the tests as measures of deception. Following the general practice in psychological testing we have depended on an independent measure of the function represented in the test. In doing so we have been tacitly assuming that the tests used to measure the conduct we are studying were indirect, abstract, laboratory methods of gaining evidence. In Chapter I of Book Two this extreme type of test is contrasted with others in which the situation and response both more nearly approximate real life situations. Free and spontaneous responses to uncontrolled life situations as they occur would not be a test but would constitute natural conduct in the raw state — the ultimate fact of which the more selected and controlled behavior of the test is supposed to give us a short-cut knowledge without the more tedious procedure of observation. To revert to our analogy of the tank and the meter, we can observe the daily use of the water, count the pitcherfuls and bucketfuls that are removed from the tank, and so ultimately find out how much water is consumed. Or we can substitute the meter, which provides an element of control. But here again it would be tedious to wait for the water to be exhausted from the tank or for the meter to run for a month to know how much is consumed; and so we might limit the time during which we shall let the meter run, or even take a bucket and let it be filled through the meter and so shift to a more experimental type of situation. If all the buckets used in practice are of one size and if we know the rate at which buckets are drawn, we can tell from one bucket how much water is consumed, for we have in the test a *measured sample* of the daily behavior.

Now the tests we have been discussing differ from many sorts of test by being of the performance type. When a child deceives in a test he does so in a natural though controlled situation, making a natural though directed response. Consequently there is literally the conduct itself, observed under carefully controlled conditions. It is a measured *sample* of behaviors of similar type.

At this point we stumble against the problem of what we are really trying to measure after all. If the true object to be attained by the test is knowledge of a unified trait manifesting itself in the test response, then we are still in the abstract laboratory situation in our conduct samplings in relation to this supposed concrete reality, the trait. We are reduced in this case to finding our criterion in ratings or some procedure which, as we have seen, is independent of the test. But if the concrete reality is not a generic trait but an accumulation of loosely connected habits, our criterion becomes, in the nature of the case, a series of records of responses in an adequate sampling of all situations which are alike in their capacity to elicit the response under consideration.

This brief statement of this alternative way of conceiving the reality that is being measured will have to suffice until we reach Chapter XXII, which will present in some detail our reasons for favoring the view that we are dealing fundamentally with specific learned habits and not with generic traits.

The adequacy of the selection of situations in a criterion is a matter of convenience. The customary standard of adequacy is the competence of the sample to represent the entire range of situations which elicit the response in question in human life. As no complete measures of any behavior are in existence, reliance is usually placed on common sense to determine the adequacy of the criterion, but the claim of specificity to which we have just referred requires that the standard of common sense be applied to the capacity of the criterion to represent $n$ (an indefinite number of) *behaviors* rather than to its capacity to represent some hypothetical unified trait. As we approach complete specificity of behavior, $n$ approaches infinity. A perfect measure would be the record of an infinite number of instances. This is of course a theoretical measure. We shall call it the " hypothetical criterion."

### Applying the Hypothetical Criterion

In performance tests, the score is a record of a specific mode of response in a specific situation. That is, the test is a single sample or small collection of samples of the behavior in question. As such a sample it does not *ipso facto* measure anything else whatever. But if it can be shown to be reliable, then it is *ipso facto* a valid measure of the particular behavior in question in the particular types of situation embodied in the test.* Whenever, for example, it is established that a pupil copied from the answer sheet and thus actually claimed a higher score for himself than he was capable of making, this fact score is a *record* and is inherently valid as far as this situation goes. If he does the same thing again in the same way when he is tested on another occasion, the test procedure acquires reliability and becomes valid for like situations as they may occur. Behavior on a test of this sort is a reliable basis for predicting similar behavior.

By accumulating the results of a series of individually reliable performance tests, then, we can *build up* a true empirical criterion. The number of such samples needed to make this empirical criterion adequate would be simply the number that would give results practically identical with the hypothetical criterion or an

* Its validity is the square root of its reliability. See Book Two for the statistical background of this whole discussion.

infinite number of similar records.   This number can be statistically determined.*

Let us apply this principle to our own material.   Our tests provide records of dishonest or honest behavior in a certain number of very specific situations.   Suppose a child has taken twenty of these tests.   We now know what he did in twenty situations.   What does this knowledge tell us about what he will do in the next twenty situations, or the next ten, or the next forty, or any number?   Now we have already seen in the section on reliability that if a child copies from answer sheets on one occasion he is quite likely to repeat the performance on a second occasion.   This is what we mean by the reliability of the test and the constancy of the behavior.   Provided the situation remains the same, the test is valid.

But what does copying from a key tell us about the likelihood of his stealing money from his mother's purse, or lying about his age, or similar behaviors?

A test may be highly valid as a measure of the specific situations with which it deals and yet have low validity as a measure of dishonesty in general or rather of dishonesty in a wide variety of situations.   Thus the validity of a test must be determined always from the point of view of what the test *claims* to measure.   If the IER tests claim to measure only the copying-from-a-key type of deception, they have a satisfactory validity,† but as measures of deception of various sorts their validity is much lower.

By way of analogy suppose we had as a problem that of determining the customary behavior of an individual in a ten-room house.   The observer is limited to 100 minutes of observation.   Now the observer may put his subject in one room and observe him there for 100 minutes.   This would undoubtedly give a better notion of his customary behavior in that room than would ten minutes' observation ; but it would give a very inadequate idea of his behavior in the other rooms.   Suppose, then, the observer puts his subject in each of the ten rooms, ten minutes to the room.   Now his observations will more adequately represent the total

* See Book Two.         † About .90.

house-behavior, but less adequately any given room-behavior. Ideally he should leave him in each room long enough to get a good picture of his behavior in that room ; then the total would be valid for the whole house. Now if the rooms represent the various situations or types of deception and the tests represent samples of each type, what we have done is to sample the behavior in a few rooms of a rather large house. For the room representing " copying-from-a-key-in-a-classroom " we have taken three samples (Arithmetic, Completion, Information). These three samples are reasonably adequate for this room. They tell us about what would happen if we had an infinite number of similar tests. In the " adding-on-more-scores-after-time-is-called " room we have taken six samples (six tests), which is also reasonably adequate, having high validity * as a measure of this type of deception. The question now is, How adequately have we sampled the whole house? †

Readers are referred to Book Two for the technical discussion of this complex problem. Following our illustration of the house, we find that while we have measured a few rooms fairly well with our seven different test situations involving some twenty-five different tests, in order to get a fair picture of the whole house or of the whole range of deceptive possibility, we should need thirty-one different test situations instead of seven, including a total of possibly a hundred different tests. What then is the practical value of the tests we already have?

## PRACTICAL VALUE OF THE DECEPTION TESTS

### A. The Tests as Instruments for Diagnosis

That the tests reveal a state of affairs of some consequence to moral education there can be no question. The situations used in

* About .93.

† There is no reason to suppose that any small sample of situations will ever adequately represent the entire range of situations of which it is a part, that is, that it will have a high validity. If it should be found to have a high "validity," this, indeed, would be evidence of the existence of a general trait. In distinction from the trait theory, the claim of specificity makes the selection of situations for a valid test primarily a problem of probability.

the tests, however, are not varied enough nor numerous enough to give a complete picture of all deceptive tendencies that may exist. The picture that is given, however, is important whether one is thinking of individual tendencies or the characteristic attitudes of groups or classrooms.   In either case the fact of deception is both an instance of unfortunate maladjustment and a symptom of underlying conditions needing attention and remedy.

### B. The Tests as Instruments of Social Study

The maladjustment of deception and its fundamental causes may well be studied by our techniques as they stand.   We shall illustrate in Part II how statistical methods may be employed to reveal facts associated with dishonesty, such as age, intelligence, sex, race, family, economic background, and school placement.

As tendencies to deceive vary enormously from school to school, we may also use the tests described to discover factors in school method which promote honest relations between teacher and pupils and among pupils.   Part III will give sample studies of this sort.

Furthermore, sundry devices for teaching honesty are being used to-day with vast numbers of children.   Our techniques enable us to evaluate such devices in terms of their actual effects on the children.   Certain of these procedures have been studied and are reported in Part III.

### C. The Tests as Instruments of Prediction

Within the situations utilized in our tests, we may safely predict the behavior of a group.   We can tell in advance approximately what proportion of the pupils will cheat, and what the average amount of cheating will be.   If it were necessary to predict what an individual pupil would do, we should require six instead of three IER tests of classroom deception, where an answer sheet is used, and twelve instead of six Speed tests, where deception consists in adding on answers while scoring one's paper.   Similarly, for each of the other types of deception, the number of sample situations would need to be greatly increased.

Even doubling the number of tests would not be adequate if we wanted to be able to predict conduct on a broader scale. To tell whether a child would be honest in *just any* situation would take a vast amount of work. A slight extension of the kind of situations used in our tests, however, would greatly augment their predictive value. In particular, more samples are needed of playground situations and occasions involving the use of money and property.

We can be fairly certain, however, that within the limits of the type of situation and behavior represented in our techniques anyone having taken twenty tests is practically measured. That is, if a pupil cheats ten times in twenty tests, the chances are that he will cheat approximately once in every two chances in all similar situations until something happens to change his conduct.

## D. The Tests as Measures of Character

In the Introduction we warned the reader against assuming that when we have tested conduct even in a large number of situations we have thereby tested character. We have not. Our tests of deception are not, as they stand, tests of character. All we have is a series of records of specific acts. Even when these records are highly prophetic of future acts of the same sort they are not to be taken as quantitative descriptions of character. We shall leave to a later volume the discussion of what is involved in testing character as a whole.

## SUMMARY

We have rehearsed the less obvious values and disadvantages of the various techniques used. A few of the facts are brought together in Table VI, which may be used as a convenient reference for keeping in mind the characteristic features of all the tests.

## TABLE VI

CHARACTERISTIC FEATURES OF CEI TECHNIQUES FOR MEASURING DECEIT

| TEST | TYPE | MODE OF DECEIT | ADMINISTRATION | | SCORING |
| --- | --- | --- | --- | --- | --- |
| | | | Time per group | Difficulty | Time per child † |
| IER | Double testing | Copying | 4–5 hr. | Easy | 20 min. |
| Speed | Double testing | Adding on | 40 min. | Hard | 15 min. |
| Coördination | Improbable achievement | Peeping | 35 min. | Easy | 8 min. |
| Puzzles | Improbable achievement | Faking Stealing | 40 min. | Hard | 2 min. |
| Parties | Improbable achievement | Faking Stealing Peeping | 45 min. | Hard | 2 min. |
| Contests | Improbable achievement | Faking | 20 min.* | Hard | 3 min. |
| SA lying | Improbable achievement | Misrepresenting | 15 min. | Easy | 2 min. |

\* Per individual.          † Including checking.

# PART II

FACTORS ASSOCIATED WITH DECEIT

## CHAPTER VI

## METHODS EMPLOYED IN STUDYING THE CAUSES AND SIGNIFICANCE OF DECEIT

Specializing as we did on tests and measurements, we have been dependent on statistical methods of handling our data, both in the building of tests and in the interpretation of results. We have been able so far to outline our general approach to the problems of measurement without introducing much technical material. But before attempting to report our findings as to the causes, significance, and control of deceit, it will be necessary to explain certain elementary statistical devices on the use of which our knowledge of the facts depends. Elaborate details would not be appropriate here, but in Book Two we discuss extensively the more difficult mathematical problems associated with the adaptation of statistical procedures to our study.

The statistical devices employed in this book are those commonly used in describing and comparing quantitative data and in finding relations between them. If we attempted to keep in mind each separate fact about each child, such as his score on each of fifteen deception tests, his intelligence rating, his age, and a dozen other important things about him, we should be hopelessly confused by the mass of detail. It is necessary to summarize our data. But to summarize facts, they must be expressed quantitatively rather than qualitatively.

Here is a classroom of forty children. Each child is different from every other in appearance, ability, talents, and character. A complete picture of all the facts is to be found only by sitting in the classroom and studying each child. John has red hair, white, regular teeth, and small feet; he answered all his arithmetic problems and failed in geography; he smiles a great deal; his blue eyes twinkle at every funny remark; and so on. We could fill volumes with such descriptions before child number forty was reached at all, and no one could profit much by the record. It can readily be seen, therefore, that if any use is to be made of these facts, some sort of classification is essential. We have already begun to classify when we have used words about John. For instance, we classed his hair as red and his teeth as white. But these facts are worth more if we can say also that only John has red hair and he is one of four children whose teeth are regular. But if we are to grasp the whole classroom, our picture is still too detailed. We shall have to let John be swallowed up in a statement about all the children or we shall never be able to comprehend the class as a whole. So we count the number having hair of each color and find that there are one red head, fourteen brown heads, six black, etc.; that two children did all their arithmetic problems, five did all but two, ten did six problems, etc. That is, we have begun to summarize. We can summarize the facts about the arithmetic problems more readily than the facts about the hair color simply because in the one case we are thinking about the amount or quantity of something having only one quality (arithmetic), whereas in the other case we have several different qualities to deal with. If all the hair had been brown, we could have summarized the facts by stating how much brownness each child's hair showed, placing it on a scale ranging from just no brownness at all, through one degree brown, two degrees brown, and so on.

This illustration gives an idea, in simple form, of how, in summarizing facts, we have to free ourselves from bondage to the concrete thing and begin to be abstract or to use ideas about the thing or about a number of things at once. The way of making these summaries and of stating how one set of facts is related to another set of facts is called statistics. It enables one to grasp many facts at once and thus to comprehend relations that would otherwise be obscure.   It does not do violence to the facts nor change them in any way.

Usually the first thing to do with a set of facts is to " distribute " them, or make a frequency distribution such as the one described on page 70.   This, it will be recalled, is simply a table or a chart showing how individuals differ in a given respect.   The following is a table of intelligence test scores of the eleven-year-old boys of population C.

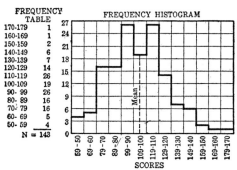

Here the scores are grouped in tens or in " class intervals " of ten.   Any convenient grouping might be used.   The table reads, " 2 pupils scored between 150–159, 6 between 140–149," etc.   This table and its accompanying graphic diagram, or histogram, present the facts in the most useful way for statistical purposes.   But it is not always convenient to present data in such detail, and further it is difficult to describe in words these total distributions.

Certain outstanding features of a distribution may be shown without presenting all the data.   The features usually given are :

1. The range, or the highest and lowest scores
2. The median, or the point on the scale of scores on each side of which just 50% of the cases fall
3. The 25 percentile and 75 percentile, or the score reached by 75% of the group and by 25% of them.   Any other percentile may be similarly used.

4. The average (arithmetical mean), or the sum of all the scores divided by the number of pupils
5. The semi-interquartile range, which is the distance between the 25 percentile and the 75 percentile. This simply states the range of the scale covered by the middle 50% of the group. It is called Q and also the probable error (PE).
6. The standard deviation (sigma). Another measure of spread or dispersion, which defines the limits of the scale covered by about the middle $\frac{2}{3}$ of the cases

Now instead of presenting the entire distribution of a set of facts we can give a verbal description by using the terms just defined. To refer to our illustration, we can say that we tested 143 eleven-year-old boys with the IER intelligence tests and found that the scores range* from 53 to 176, that the median or 50 percentile score is 102.4, that the 25 percentile is 86.7, the 75 percentile is 118.2, that the average or mean score is 103.3, that the Q (or semi-interquartile range) is 15.75, that the SD (standard deviation, or sigma) is 23.4. We might go on and state many other so-called statistical constants, thus describing the distribution in greater detail. Such a verbal description has advantages other than those of mere statistical shorthand, for by the use of these terms comparisons may be made and relationships, associations, and concomitants found.

## HOW COMPARISONS BETWEEN DISTRIBUTIONS ARE MADE

The only complete way to make a comparison between two or more groups is to give all distributions in one table, or to plot all the data in histograms or curves on the same base lines. For example, let us compare the intelligence test scores of the eleven-year-olds with the twelve-year-olds of population C. The frequency distributions are as follows:

* Found by referring to the original scores.

| Scores | Frequencies | |
| --- | --- | --- |
| | 11-Year-Olds | 12-Year-Olds |
| 170–179 | 1 | 2 |
| 160–169 | 1 | 4 |
| 150–159 | 2 | 5 |
| 140–149 | 6 | 10 |
| 130–139 | 7 | 13 |
| 120–129 | 14 | 24 |
| 110–119 | 26 | 24 |
| 100–109 | 19 | 18 |
| 90–99 | 26 | 15 |
| 80–89 | 16 | 9 |
| 70–79 | 16 | 10 |
| 60–69 | 5 | 6 |
| 50–59 | 4 | 3 |
| | 143 | 143 |

It happens here that we have the same number of cases in each distribution, so that we can plot them without computing the per cent each frequency is of its total. The two curves are as follows:

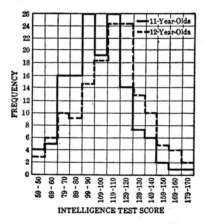

It will be seen at a glance that the dotted line tends to bear to the right of the solid line (or up scale), indicating that the twelve-

year-olds tend to score higher.   Using statistical language, the
difference between these two groups may be described as follows :

| Comparison in Respect to Intelligence Test Scores | 11-Year-Olds | 12-Year-Olds |
|---|---|---|
| Range * . . . . . . . . . . | 53–176 | 52–179 |
| Median . . . . . . . . . . | 102.4 | 114.4 |
| 25 percentile . . . . . . . . | 86.7 | 95.2 |
| 75 percentile . . . . . . . | 118.2 | 129.3 |
| Mean . . . . . . . . . . | 103.3 | 112.8 |
| SD . . . . . . . . . . . | 23.4 | 26.4 |
| Q . . . . . . . . . . . . | 15.75 | 17.05 |

* Found from the original scores.

Another useful way of describing the difference between two
groups is to state the percentage of the one group that reaches or
exceeds the median or mean of the other group.   In this case the
median of the twelve-year-olds is 114.4 points.   Only 32% of the
eleven-year-olds succeeded in getting a score as high as or higher
than this.

## HOW INDIVIDUAL COMPARISONS ARE MADE

In the foregoing discussion we assumed for the sake of simplicity
that the two groups had the same test.   Suppose now that the
same group has two *different* tests.   How may the scores of the
members of the group be compared?   Clearly they must first be
expressed in comparable terms.   To be in comparable terms they
must have the same point of reference and be in the same units.
Suppose John Doe scores 160 on an intelligence test and 60 on an
arithmetic test.   Which represents the greater achievement?
There is no way to find out except to compare these scores with
those made by other pupils of his age, grade, and general status
in both tests.   Suppose John is twelve years old and in the seventh
grade, and that the mean scores of a large group of twelve-year-old
seventh-grade pupils for the two tests are respectively 150 and 50.
In both tests John is ten points above the mean.   But a point in

one test does not equal a point in the other.    Comparable points
are needed.    The usual way around this difficulty is to take some
measure of the spread of each distribution as the unit.    The most
common unit, as was pointed out on page 73, is the SD (standard
deviation).    The facts we need to know, then, to compare John's
score on one test with his score on the other are the mean and
standard deviation of the twelve-year-old seventh-grade scores on
each test, which may be assumed to be as follows:

| INTELLIGENCE TEST | | ARITHMETIC TEST | |
| --- | --- | --- | --- |
| TEST 1 | | TEST 2 | |
| Mean | SD | Mean | SD |
| 150 | 25 | 50 | 5 |

In the intelligence test the point of reference is 150 and the unit is
25; in the arithmetic test the point of reference is 50 and the unit
is 5.    The rest is simple.    John's two comparable scores are now,
for the intelligence test, $\dfrac{160 - 150}{25} = \dfrac{10}{25} = +.4$, and for the arithmetic test, $\dfrac{60 - 50}{5} = \dfrac{10}{5} = +2.0$.    Thus John really scored very
much higher in arithmetic than in intelligence, even though his
gross score on the intelligence test was 160 and on the arithmetic
test, 60, and even though he deviated 10 points above the group
mean on both.

This is one of the most important determinations in all statistics.
It is fundamental to all mental and social measurements.    It constitutes the basis of measurement not only of the facts themselves
but also of their relations.    But before discussing how to state
relations between facts let us consider briefly the question of the
influence of chance errors on group means.

In comparing one group with another or what a group does one
day with what it does at another time, one often wishes to know
how great the difference between the two means or medians should

be in order to have real significance. Obviously slight differences may occur by chance. The problem is to determine whether a given difference might be a chance difference. There is a way of figuring the unreliability of a difference between two means, of determining, that is, how great any difference should be to have more than a chance significance; but the mathematics of this procedure is too complex for treatment here. It is enough to say that this unreliability of the difference between two means depends on the unreliability of the two means themselves. In measuring anything, one cannot safely generalize from what is found to be true of one small group to what may be true of other groups or of the population as a whole. A mean or average has only limited significance. Statistically, this limitation is expressed in terms of the range within which a large number of similar means would fall if other similar groups were measured, or if the same group were measured several times. This range is, as usual, expressed in terms of the SD of a distribution — in this case a distribution of a series of such means. The amount of fluctuation in a series of such means depends on the number of cases included in each group measured and on the spread of the scores up and down the scale. Obviously, the more cases there are in any single group, the more likely will the mean of the group represent the mean of all possible cases. On the other hand, the wider the spread or range of scores, the less representative the mean is of them. On page 157, for example, are two sets of scores having almost the same means. One distribution is scattered and the other is condensed.

The range or amount of spread is indicated by the size of the standard deviation (SD), which in the case of A is 2.14 and of B is 3.14. A's mean is a much more stable and secure measure than B's mean.

When the SD and the number of cases are known, the unreliability of a mean can be determined and is stated in terms of the range within which a series of similarly determined means would fall by chance, or, in other words, in terms of the SD of a distribution of the means of a large number of similar groups. The more reliable each of two means is, the more reliable will be the difference between them.

| Scores | A | B |
|---|---|---|
| 140–149 | | 5 |
| 130–139 | | 5 |
| 120–129 | | 10 |
| 110–119 | 2 | 10 |
| 100–109 | 10 | 15 |
| 90–99 | 25 | 15 |
| 80–89 | 45 | 20 |
| 70–79 | 45 | 25 |
| 60–69 | 20 | 15 |
| 50–59 | 10 | 15 |
| 40–49 | 5 | 10 |
| 30–39 | 3 | 10 |
| 20–29 | | 5 |
| 10–19 | | 5 |
| | 165 | 165 |

$$M = 79.8 \qquad M = 80$$
$$SD = 2.14 \qquad SD = 3.14$$

The formula for expressing the unreliability or standard deviation or standard error of a mean is $\dfrac{SD}{\sqrt{N}}$ when SD is the standard deviation of the distribution in question and N is the number of cases. The unreliability of the difference between two means, called the SD of the difference or the standard error (SE) of the difference, is expressed as $\sqrt{\dfrac{SD_1^2}{N_1} + \dfrac{SD_2^2}{N_2}}$ or $\sqrt{SE_1^2 + SE_2^2}$ where $SD_1$ and $N_1$ refer to one distribution and $SD_2$ and $N_2$ to the other.* This figure shows what the standard deviation of a distribution of differences between the mean of one group and the means of a large number of similar groups would be if these other means were

* The statistician will recognize the absence from this formula of the term $(-2r_{M_1M_2} \cdot SD_1SD_2)$, which has been omitted to simplify the statement, and which usually equals zero under the assumptions of our study.

actually found. As was noted in our discussion of the meaning of the standard deviation, 999 cases out of 1000 fall within the limits of plus and minus 3 SD. Consequently if the difference between two means is three times its standard error, it is regarded as statistically significant or beyond the limits of mere chance difference.

It should be borne in mind that the obtained mean measure or the difference between means, even though very unreliable, is more likely to be the truth than any other one measure or difference; and also that the truth is just as likely to vary from the obtained mean measure in one direction as in the other. Results with small reliabilities may thus be results of very great value.

## THE MEASUREMENT OF RELATIONSHIP

Science seeks facts and relations among them with a view to determining causes and predicting effects. The facts we are dealing with are such things as test scores, ages, school status, and social and economic status. These facts are usually expressed quantitatively and recorded in frequency distributions. Relations, associations, concomitants, and the like between facts may be described in various ways. The manner and the language of the descriptions are usually suited to the nature of the facts and to the purpose or aim in view.

The most commonly used statistical device for stating relationship between two sets of facts is known as the coefficient of correlation, or $r$. The facts to be compared or related are called variables. The two facts about each individual may be such things as two arithmetic scores, or size of hands and size of feet, or a deception score and age, or the sum of several deception scores and the length of time in a particular school. Perfect resemblance or complete association between two series of facts or variables is expressed as $+1.00$, complete absence of association by $0$, and completely inverse association by $-1.00$. Thus the correlation between any two variables may result in such figures as $+.90$ or $-.60$ or $-.07$ or $+.01$ or anything from $-1.00$ to $+1.00$. The important thing is to become so familiar with the concept that a correlation of +.90 or +.40 or +.10 or −.30 or what not will have a fairly definite meaning. A correlation of +1.00 means that the very highest scores in one variable are associated with the very highest in the other variable, that the second highest scores in one are associated with the second highest in the other, and so on down to the lowest. For example, the correlation between the height of a column of water in a pipe and the pressure it exerts at the bottom is +1.00 or at least +.999. On the other hand, the correlation between the distance above the sea level and barometric pressure is −1.00 because the greater the altitude, the less the pressure. But the correlation of daily records of barometric pressure and temperature at a given spot is close to zero.

When applied to mental and social measurements, the concept of correlation is closely allied with that of comparable scores. It will be recalled that the scores in two tests are made comparable by taking each as a deviation from its mean and dividing it by the SD of the distribution. This is called an SD deviation. The correlation between two tests is +1.00 when these SD deviations of the individual scores on the two tests exactly match. This $r$ of +1.00 may be illustrated as follows:

| | Test 1 | | | Test 2 | |
|---|---|---|---|---|---|
| Pupils | Score | SD Deviate | | Score | SD Deviate |
| A | 10 | − 1.50 | | 118 | − 1.50 |
| B | 11 | − .75 | | 121 | − .75 |
| C | 11 | − .75 | | 121 | − .75 |
| D | 12 | 0 | | 124 | 0 |
| E | 12 | 0 | | 124 | 0 |
| F | 12 | 0 | | 124 | 0 |
| G | 13 | + .75 | | 127 | + .75 |
| H | 13 | + .75 | | 127 | + .75 |
| I | 14 | + 1.50 | | 130 | + 1.50 |

If they exactly match but are reversed, so that plus deviates on one variable are associated with minus deviates on the other variable, the correlation is −1.00. Any kind of divergence from this per-

fect matching of comparable scores will tend to reduce the correlation. When they are paired in a mere chance order the correlation is zero or nearly zero.

A helpful way of picturing relations between two sets of facts is
to plot them on what is sometimes called a scattergram. One set
of scores or facts is laid off on a scale along a line. Small sections
of the line represent a single score or group of scores. Let us
plot our two sets of scores to illustrate the meaning of a scattergram.

The scores on the first test run from 10 to 14, or, as SD deviates,
from $+1.50$ to $-1.50$, so we make a scale like this:

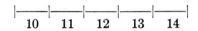

$$|\text{—}|\text{—}|\text{—}|\text{—}|\text{—}|$$
$$10 \quad 11 \quad 12 \quad 13 \quad 14$$

or like this:

$$|\text{———}|\text{———}|\text{———}|\text{———}|\text{———}|$$
$$+1.50 \quad +.75 \quad 0 \quad -.75 \quad -1.50$$

The other set of scores runs from 118 to 130, or, as SD deviates, from
$+1.50$ to $-1.50$. This time the scale is placed at right angles to
the first like this:

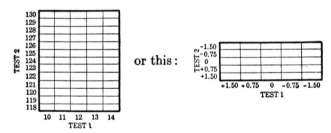

or this:

If we draw lines in each direction so as to block off the sections
of the scale, the result gives us a surface of rectangles called
cells, each of which is above one section of the bottom scale and
opposite one section of the vertical scale. Now we can say two
things at once about each pupil by finding the cell that is above his
first score and at the right of his second score, and putting a mark

in this cell to stand for both scores.   The next diagrams show the
scores of our two tests for pupils A, B, C, etc., thus entered:

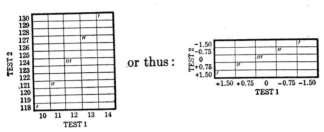

or thus:

The marks are seen to fall symmetrically on a diagonal.   This,
therefore, is what a correlation of +1.00 looks like.

The scattergram will illustrate how the coefficient of correlation
may be thought of in terms of the prediction of one variable from
the other.   Although the coefficient never shows which variable
is causing the other or whether both are dependent on a third factor, it does tell to what extent one set of facts can be predicted from
the other set.   If the two tests correlate +1.00, as in the illustration just given, the score on either test can be predicted from the
score on the other, for all the entries opposite any section of either
scale are opposite just one section of the other scale.   All who scored
12 on test 1 scored 124 on test 2, etc.   Prediction is just as certain
in the following scattergram when the correlation is −1.00.

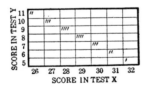

Figures 11, 12, and 13 are correlation scattergrams illustrating
correlations of .93, .49, and .21.   Figure 11 shows that all those
who scored at a certain point on test Y scored around the same
point on test X.   For example, those who scored either 18 or 19
on Y scored between 18 and 23 on test X.   Their mean X score is

the mean of that row or slice of the table.   It is clear that the more
scattered the dots are across and up and down, the less reliable is
the prediction.   In Figure 13, where the coefficient (*r*) is .21, one

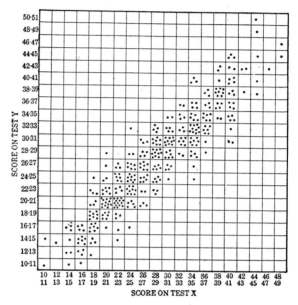

FIGURE 11

ILLUSTRATING A CORRELATION OF +.93

Scattergram of the two forms of the Arithmetic test used for the IER
deception testing.   Here the two forms were given with no chance to deceive.
The scattergram therefore shows the equivalence of the two tests and the
amount of *honest* variability to be expected when these same tests are used to
measure deception by having an answer sheet available on one of the two
days but not on the other.   The likeness between the two tests is called their
reliability.   In this case the coefficient of correlation, or *r*, is .925.   Each dot
stands for the two scores of a single pupil.   The scores are grouped in twos.

can predict one set of scores from the other almost as well by guessing as by consulting the scattergram.

Although small correlations have low predictive value, they
may express genuine relationship.   There is a real relation between

test 1 and test 2 in Figure 13.    If the number of cases is large enough to make the coefficient genuinely reliable, it represents what organic relation there is between the tests.    The only difficulty with small $r$'s is that when the number of cases is small (less than 100) they may be merely chance happenings.    The unreliability or " probable error " (PE) of a coefficient of correlation is given by the formula $.6745 \left( \dfrac{1-r^2}{\sqrt{N}} \right)$.    The co-efficient should be at least four times its probable error, or PE, to have very much importance.*

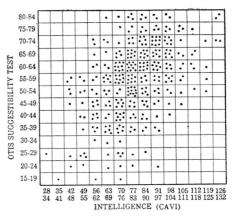

FIGURE 12

ILLUSTRATING A CORRELATION OF $+ .49$

Scattergram showing the relation between scores on the Otis Suggestibility Test and scores on an intelligence test.    Here the $r$ is .488, showing that intelligence goes with greater resistance to suggestion; but the relationship is not close, since those receiving about the same intelligence rating, e.g., 84–90, vary all the way up and down the suggestibility scale.

## PARTIAL CORRELATIONS

As has been noted, the coefficient of correlation between two sets of measures does not indicate which is the causal or independent variable and which is the dependent.    Indeed, they may be correlated because they are each associated with some third or fourth variable.    For example, there is a correlation between the

---

* The non-technical reader is referred here to any text on elementary statistics.    The probable error of a distribution is a distance which, when laid off in each direction from the mean, includes 50% of the cases.    Four times the PE in each direction includes about all the cases.    The chances are negligible that an $r$ would vary beyond four times its PE if a long series of similar $r$'s were computed on equivalent data.

intelligence of children and the size of shoes they wear; but no one would suppose that the size of foot is caused by the intellect nor intellect by size of foot. They are correlated because each is associated with age. If we consider only children of a given age, or

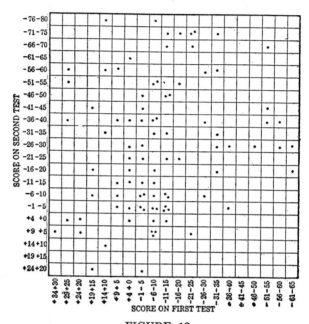

FIGURE 13

ILLUSTRATING A CORRELATION OF +.21

Scattergram showing relation between amounts of home cheating on two separate occasions six months apart. Here the r is only + .2126. Evidently one cannot predict from one test only what a pupil will do six months later.

keep age constant, as we say, then the correlation between size of foot and intelligence is zero or nearly zero. Taking another illustration from our own data, we find a certain small but positive correlation between moral knowledge and conduct. Now these two may be associated because each is connected with intelligence. That is, intelligence may be the link that binds them together.

To find out, we keep intelligence constant, or find the correlation between conduct and knowledge for different groups having approximately the same intelligence ratings. There may be several such groups. The average of the resulting correlations is the equivalent of the partial. In actual practice we apply a short cut by finding out the intercorrelation between each of the three variables and substituting these in a formula.

In case we wish to keep constant two variables such as age and intelligence, the procedure is the same. Take groups of the same age and the same intelligence, find the correlation between knowledge and conduct with each subgroup, average these correlations, and the result is the partial. When we talk about " partialing out " a variable, all we mean is that we have held it constant.

# CHAPTER VII

## AGE, SEX, INTELLIGENCE, AND PHYSICAL AND EMOTIONAL CONDITION

When the facts which combine in an event are few and simple, it is comparatively easy to arrange them in a causal sequence. For example, a boiling radiator and an overheated engine are associated. Here we are dealing with straightforward facts the meaning of which is clear. There is a direct and simple relation between the temperature of the engine and the temperature of the water. Since one is hotter than the other, the heat tends to pass from the hotter to the cooler. But if we say that boys cheat more than girls or girls more than boys, while it is perfectly clear that cheating is not the cause of any fundamental physiological differences, it is by no means clear whether or not the physiological differences to which the word " sex " refers have anything to do with the relative tendency of the two sexes to cheat. Boyhood is not a simple fact in direct relation to other facts. It is a symbol for a highly complex set of facts, some of which, like size, strength, depth of voice, are causally related to primary sex differences, and others of which, like occupations, interests, codes, and clothing, are accidents of circumstance and culture associated now with one sex and again with the other.

The same is true of chronological age. On the one hand it means or symbolizes physiological changes which take place primarily through the operation of biological forces, and on the other it means the accumulation of experiences which vary greatly from family to family, from nation to nation, and from generation to generation.

Consequently it must not be supposed that, when we point out the extent to which deception is associated with sex or age, or with

166

the still more complicated factors of intelligence, race, and home background, we are attributing to any of these congeries of fact some mystic potency to cause an individual to cheat.  We shall do what we can to pick out the invariable and necessary antecedents of the tendency to deceive, but these are so intermingled in a matrix of irrelevant data that they cannot for the most part be completely isolated from one another.

Social facts differ from physical facts not only in their complexity but also in another respect, which still further increases the difficulty of isolating and measuring them.  If one wishes to know the constituents of a rock, he has no hesitation in crushing it, dissolving it, or subjecting it to any other experimental procedures in the course of which it is disintegrated.  When dealing with a human being, however, or with a social group, there is not the same freedom of method.  Such analysis of social objects as is made must proceed without disturbing the objects themselves.  It is here that the statistical devices described in the last chapter come to our rescue.  Our laboratory is our coördination paper and our calculating machine, and for test tubes we substitute tables and graphs, correlation coefficients, means, and medians.  Instead of taking one child and dissecting him physically and spiritually, we take a large number of children, find out a large number of facts about each, and then recombine these facts in such a way as to show how they are related to one another in the individual.  Let us turn then to the statistical analysis of our data in the hope of reaching a little better understanding of the factors which combine in an act of deception and of their relations to one another.

The facts which will be dealt with in Part II are in most cases a mixture of social and biological ingredients which we make only a slight attempt to disentangle.  The complete list is as follows :

| | |
|---|---|
| Age | Occupation |
| Sex | Cultural background |
| Intelligence | Family |
| Physical condition | Race and nationality |
| Emotional condition | Religion |

School grade                    Suggestibility
Retardation                     Attendance at motion pictures
Attendance                      Work and play
School achievement              Deportment
Association of friends          Motives
Sociability

## SEX AND AGE

We shall consider age and sex together.  Many tests which measure the individual's response to his physical environment show large age differences and small sex differences, whereas most tests which measure the individual's response to his social environment show large sex differences and small age differences.  In the case of deception, however, we find no such consistent differences that can be attributed to either the group of facts called " age " or the group of facts called " sex."  In some populations, the older children cheat more and in other populations they cheat less.  On some tests the girls are the more dishonest, whereas on others the boys show the greater tendency to deceive.

In view of the fact that different tests were given to different ranges of ages and to different populations, it is not possible to combine all our data in one age-sex comparison, but we shall make such summary graphs and statements as the data will permit.  In Figures 14 to 23, the prevalence of deception is expressed by the percentage of those cheating on the different tests and for both sexes.  The r's given in the accompanying tables are the correlations between age and the " amount " scores for each type of deception test.

### A. AGE-SEX DIFFERENCES IN IER SCHOOL CHEATING

**1. Sex Differences.**  Figure 14 shows the situation in schools A, B, and P–Q.  Although the girls appear more deceptive in B and P–Q, the reverse is the case in A and for certain age levels in B and P–Q.  When all the boys are combined, as in Figure 15,

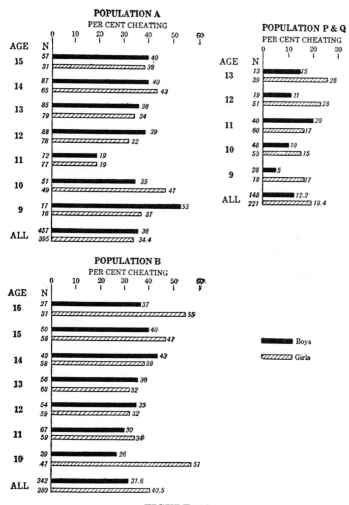

FIGURE 14

Age-Sex Differences on IER School Tests in Terms of
Per Cent Cheating at Each Age Level

they appear more deceptive than the girls; but this is due to

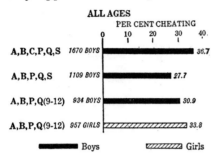

**ALL AGES**
PER CENT CHEATING

the inclusion of school C, which is all boys and rather more deceptive than the average. Leaving out C, the per cent of cheating among the boys drops to 27.7, which is 6% lower than the girls; and even when the two sexes are exactly matched for ages and schools, the boys still have the advantage by 3%.

**2. Age Differences.** When all populations and both sexes are combined, as in Figure 15, a slight tendency for deception of this type to increase with age is observable. The amount of this tendency is statistically expressed in the correlation coefficients given in Table

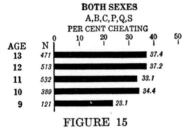

**BOTH SEXES**
A,B,C,P,Q,S
PER CENT CHEATING

FIGURE 15

SUMMARY OF AGE-SEX DIFFERENCES ON
IER SCHOOL TESTS FOR POPULATIONS
A, B, C, P, Q, AND S

VII, which, while small, are mostly positive.

TABLE VII

AGE-DECEPTION CORRELATIONS FOR IER SCHOOL Xi SCORES

| POPULATION | COEFFICIENT ($r$) |
|:---:|:---:|
| A | − .025 |
| B | + .079 |
| C | + .219 |
| P, Q, S | + .289 |
| A, B, C, P, Q, S | + .140 |

## B. Age-Sex Differences on the Speed Tests

**1. Sex Differences.**   In the Speed tests the boys cheat slightly more than the girls, as shown in Figure 16, which summarizes the facts available.   The same chart, however, indicates that at the

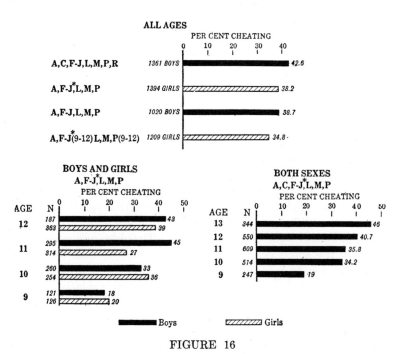

FIGURE 16

Summary of Age-Sex Differences on Speed Tests for
Populations A, C, F-J, L, M, P, and R

lower age levels the girls exceed the boys.   The differences in either case are not large enough to be beyond the limits of chance, however, and so we may conclude that there are no general sex differences on these tests.

* To equalize the groups, there were taken of the F-J girls $\frac{2}{5}$ of the 9-, 10-, and 11-year-olds, $\frac{1}{2}$ the 12-year-olds, and $\frac{1}{4}$ the 13-, 14-, and 15-year olds.

TABLE VIII

AGE-DECEPTION CORRELATIONS FOR THE SPEED Xi SCORE

| POPULATION | COEFFICIENT ($r$) |
|:---:|:---:|
| A | + .123 |
| C | + .217 |
| D | + .004 |
| J | + .320 |
| F to J | + .211 |
| L and M | + .219 |
| P | + .246 |
| R | + .245 |

**2. Age Differences.** Except for the ages from ten to eleven there is a rather conspicuous tendency for deception on these tests to increase with age. The correlations of Table VIII are considerably higher than those previously reported. In Chapter VIII of Book Two, however, it is explained that this age difference is due not to a difference in the *tendency* to cheat but rather in the *ability* to cheat by the means provided. The older pupils can work faster on the speed type of test than the younger ones so that, if they do choose to take advantage of the opportunity to add scores when scoring their own papers, they can add on relatively more than the younger ones. When allowance is made for this difference in ability, the $r$'s reported in Table VIII all drop to zero or nearly zero. That is, genuine age differences on the Speed tests are not apparent. The older pupils cheat no more and no less than the younger ones.

### C. THE COÖRDINATION, PUZZLE, ATHLETIC, PARTY, AND LYING TESTS

Figure 17 shows no sex or age differences on the Coördination tests. The tendency to open the eyes while doing the test is almost irresistible to both girls and boys. The Puzzle tests (Figure 18), used only in schools D and R, show no distinctive age differences;

but in school D, the girls consistently cheat a little more than the boys at each age level except fourteen.    In the Athletic Contests (Figure 19), the girls cheat a little more than the boys, but the age differences are slight and irregular.

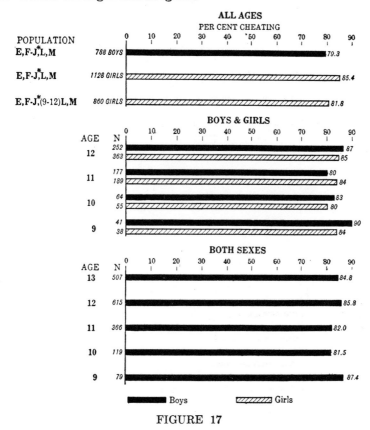

FIGURE 17

SUMMARY OF AGE-SEX DIFFERENCES ON COÖRDINATION TESTS
FOR POPULATIONS E, F–J, L, AND M

\* To equalize groups, we have taken of population F–J, girls, ⅛ of ages 9 and 10, ⅓ of 11, ½ of 12 and 13, and ⅓ of 14 and 15; boys, ⅕ of ages 9 and 10, ½ of 11, and 1½ of 12.

Figure 20 shows a distinct sex difference in population D in the cheating at parties. The other population in which the party tests were given was mostly boys, and no sex comparison is possible. When populations C and D are combined no consistent age differences appear. The biserial coefficient between cheating and age is −.084.

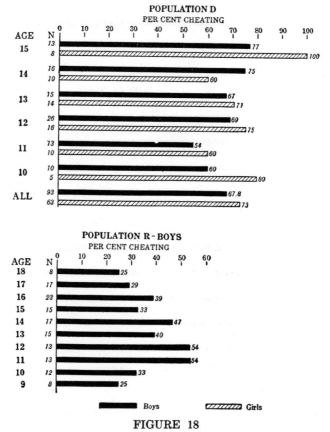

FIGURE 18

AGE-SEX DIFFERENCES ON PUZZLE TESTS FOR POPULATIONS
D AND R

Age-Deception $r$, Populations D and R, + .147

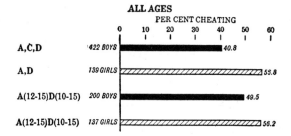

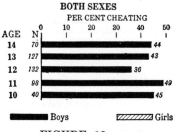

FIGURE 19

SUMMARY OF AGE-SEX DIFFERENCES ON ATHLETIC CONTESTS
FOR POPULATIONS A, C, AND D

TABLE IX

AGE-DECEPTION CORRELATIONS FOR THE COÖRDINATION Xi SCORES

| POPULATION | COEFFICIENT ($r$) |
|:---:|:---:|
| E | + .050 |
| F to J | + .140 |
| L and M | + .184 |

TABLE X

AGE-DECEPTION CORRELATIONS FOR THE ATHLETIC CONTEST SCORES

| POPULATION | COEFFICIENT ($r$) |
|:---:|:---:|
| A | + .283 |
| C | + .233 |
| D | + .218 |

Figure 21 reveals no age differences in the tendency to lie except at age ten for boys and ages ten and eleven for girls, but the girls

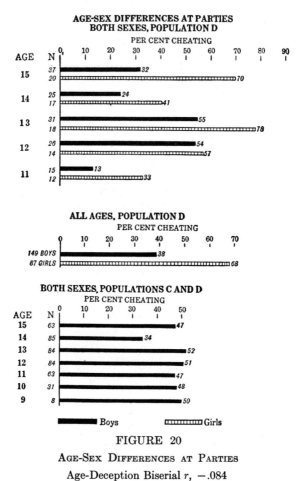

FIGURE 20

Age-Sex Differences at Parties

Age-Deception Biserial $r$, $-.084$

as a whole and for each age level are conspicuous for their large scores. It will be recalled, however, that the SA test of lying consists of a series of questions concerning conventionally approved

acts, such as not talking back, picking up paper, and the like.    The
standard on which we based our computation of the point at which
to draw the line between truth and falsehood on this test was a
mixed standard, and it is quite possible that girls can truthfully

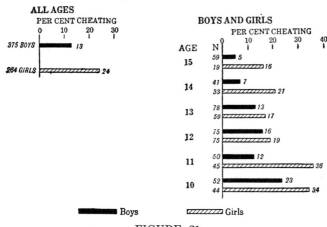

FIGURE 21

SUMMARY OF AGE-SEX DIFFERENCES ON THE SA LYING TEST
FOR POPULATIONS A AND D

Age-Sex $r$, Population A, $+ .134$; Age-Sex $r$, Population D, $- .012$

claim a more complete observance of conventional requirements
than boys can.    If this should be the case, the differences between
boys and girls on this test would be in part, if not wholly, accounted
for by a difference in conventionality rather than in deceptiveness.
The fair sex may take its choice of the alternatives.

### D. AGE-SEX DIFFERENCES IN IER HOME CHEATING

**1. Sex Differences.**    Figure 22 shows the almost uniform tendency for girls to cheat more than boys on the test taken home.
Where all ages are combined and the sexes are matched so as to be
drawn from the same ages and schools, the difference between boys
and girls is found to be five times its unreliability.    The interpretation of this difference is very likely to be found not in the greater sus-

ceptibility of girls to the temptation to get away with something which will prosper their interests but rather to their greater desire to make good in school.   The relative indifference of boys to the formal requirements of the school has often been commented on; and as it takes considerable effort to look up words in a dictionary in order to find their meanings, the lack of motive would be a suf-

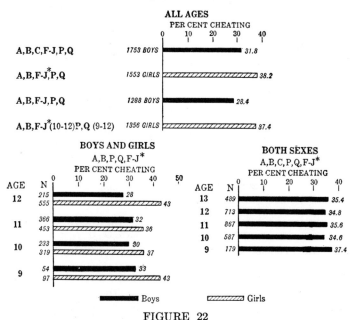

FIGURE  22

SUMMARY OF AGE-SEX DIFFERENCES ON IER HOME TEST FOR POPULATIONS A, B, C, F–J, P, AND Q

ficient explanation of the failure to do even as well on the test taken home as on the one done in school.   In schools P and Q, where motive is probably much more evenly distributed between the sexes, it is the boys who take the greater advantage of the situation to deceive rather than the girls.

* To equalize the groups there were taken of the F–J girls ⅔ of the 9-, 10-, and 11-year-olds, ½ the 12-year-olds, and ¼ the 13-, 14-, and 15-year-olds.

**2. Age Differences.** In some populations, deception on the home test increases with age and in others it decreases with age. In other words, other influences are determining the change rather than mere chronological age. When all populations and both sexes are combined, as in Figure 22, age differences disappear.

TABLE XI

AGE-DECEPTION CORRELATIONS FOR IER HOME Xi SCORES

| POPULATION | COEFFICIENT (r) |
|---|---|
| A | − .222 |
| B | − .144 |
| C | − .042 |
| F to J | + .088 |
| P, Q, S | − .026 |

E. AGE-SEX DIFFERENCES ON THE CT RATIO

Figure 23 is a summary of factual scores on a series of classroom tests and represents the percentage of times the subject cheated.

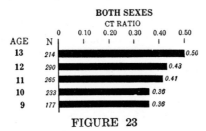

FIGURE 23

AGE DIFFERENCES IN CT RATIOS FOR POPULATIONS C, D, F–J,* L, AND M

The age differences in this CT ratio (per cent of C's to chances to cheat) are apparent only when the populations are lumped together. When treated separately, as in Table XII, the r's are low and average zero.

* One-third of population F–J to equalize groups.

TABLE XII

AGE-DECEPTION CORRELATIONS FOR CT RATIO

| POPULATION | COEFFICIENT (r) |
|---|---|
| C | − .092 |
| D | − .153 |
| F–J | + .246 |
| L and M | + .123 |
| Average | + .031 |

## F. CONCLUSIONS CONCERNING THE RELATION OF AGE AND SEX TO DECEPTION

The age summaries of Figures 14 to 23 and of Tables VII to XII indicate that within the age limits of our data there is only a slight association between age and the tendency to deceive. How or when cheating in school begins we do not know. Recent discussions of the situation in colleges and professional schools do not suggest that as pupils get older there is any strong tendency for the practice to be dropped. On the contrary, since the less intelligent children are gradually eliminated from the school system, the fact that honesty correlates positively with intelligence would lead one to conclude that our low correlations with age really represent a spreading of the tendency to deceive, new cheaters being recruited to take the place of the cheaters who drop out, thus keeping the average constant.

Statistically significant differences between the sexes occur only in the case of the test taken home, the Party tests, and the Lie test, although the girls are also considerably more deceptive than the boys on the Puzzle tests and in the Athletic Contest. In the case of the parties and the last two types of deception, the cases are too few and highly selected to warrant drawing any generalization, and we have already pointed out the ambiguity of sex differences on the SA test of the tendency to lie in order to gain approval. There remains, then, only the home test; and even on this, as we have suggested, there is strong probability that the cause of the difference is to be found in the superior motivation of the girls rather than in an inferior sense of honor.

## INTELLIGENCE AND CHEATING

Wherever a school record of the ages of the pupils was available we used it, and elsewhere we depended on the statement of the children themselves. Even so the facts as to age were far less subject to error than the miscellaneous intelligence scores we could secure. Here again we used the school records, but as four or five different tests were used by the schools the intelligence scores were not exactly comparable. In the case of populations tested with IER material we had of course the bona fide scores on the second day's testing as a satisfactory measure of intelligence,* and for populations F, G, H, I, J, and K we were fortunate in being able to have the Pintner Non-Language Tests administered to all our groups by the Department of Psychology of Teachers College. The complete list of intelligence tests used or found is as follows:

| POPULATION | TESTS USED OR GIVEN |
|---|---|
| A | IER |
| B | IER |
| C | IER and National Intelligence, Scale A |
| D | Stanford-Binet |
| E | Otis Advanced |
| F to J | Pintner Non-Language |
| K | Stanford-Binet |
| L and M | McCall Multi-mental |
| N | Terman Group Test |
| O | |
| P | IER and Stanford-Binet |
| Q | IER and Stanford-Binet |
| R | Stanford-Binet |
| S | IER |

* See Chapter III, pages 52–53. These tests are fully described by Dr. Thorndike, to whom we are indebted for their use, in his *Measurement of Intelligence*, Teachers College Bureau of Publications, 1927. Following his nomenclature, we shall hereafter refer to these as the CAVI measure of intelligence, the initials standing for the four types of material used in the tests.

These scores were expressed in some cases as mental ages and in some cases as point scores. In some instances an intelligence quotient was either available or calculable and in other cases it was not. Since intelligence increases with age and we did not wish the relation between intelligence and deception to be mixed up with even the slight relation found between age and deception, it was necessary to express our intelligence scores in such a way as would relieve them of dependence on chronological age, somewhat as the IQ does by dividing mental age by chronological age. These two problems — to make our scores comparable and to keep them free of the age factor — we solved in the following manner. First we expressed each child's intelligence score as a deviation from the mean score of his age and in terms of the SD for that age distribution, thus transmuting all scores into comparable units. Next we adopted a letter rating scheme similar to that used with the Army tests.

> The upper 5% were rated A.
> The next 10% were rated B.
> The next 20% were rated C+.
> The next 30% were rated C.
> The next 20% were rated C−.
> The next 10% were rated D.
> The lower 5% were rated E.

By this scheme, the letter A is applied to the 5% whose test scores deviate upward the most from the mean scores of their respective ages. As the means, SD's, and percentages are based on some 3000 cases they are reasonably satisfactory.*

* Those accustomed to thinking in terms of IQ may wish to refer to the following approximate IQ equivalents:

| | |
|---|---|
| A | IQ, 140 and up |
| B | IQ, 120 to 139 |
| C + | IQ, 110 to 119 |
| C | IQ, 90 to 109 |
| C − | IQ, 80 to 89 |
| D | IQ, 60 to 79 |
| E | IQ, below 60 |

As usual, the discussion of more technical problems may be found in the parallel chapter of Book Two (Chapter VIII).   We follow here the plan used in presenting the facts regarding age, sex, and deception, printing only graphic summaries and tables of correlations.

Even a cursory glance at Figures 24 to 33 and Tables XIII to XVIII will make clear the association of honesty and intelligence.

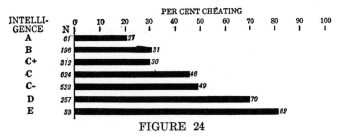

FIGURE 24

<small>Per Cent Cheating on IER School Tests at Each Level of Intelligence (CAVI), Populations A, B, C, K, and Q</small>

Except in the case of puzzles, cheating at parties, and stealing, there is a strong tendency for cheating to increase as the level of intelligence decreases.   The $r$'s reported with Figures 27 and 28 show the amount of association between the type of deception involved and the A, B, C intelligence rating which we have just now described.   Since these intelligence scores are sigma deviations from

TABLE XIII

<small>Correlations between IER School Cheating and Intelligence Level (CAVI)</small>

| Population | Coefficient ($r$) |
|---|---|
| A | − .492 |
| B and C | − .331 |
| K and Q | − .489 |
| All cases * | − .493 |

\* See Book Two, Chapter VIII.

age norms, the factor of age is in effect eliminated, and the $r$'s give the relation between intelligence and deception, with age constant.

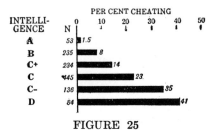

FIGURE 25

Per Cent Cheating on Speed Tests at Each Level of Intelligence (IQ), Populations C, E, D, and P

TABLE XIV

Correlations between Speed Tests and Intelligence Level (IQ)

| Population | Coefficient ($r$) |
|---|---|
| C | − .385 |
| E | − .410 |
| D and P | − .469 |
| L and M | − .302 |
| All (N = 1514) | − .410 |

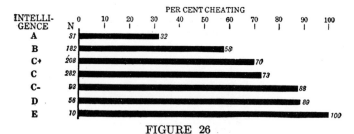

FIGURE 26

Per Cent Cheating on Coördination Tests at Each Level of Intelligence (IQ)

## TABLE XV

CORRELATIONS BETWEEN COÖRDINATION TESTS AND INTELLIGENCE LEVEL

| POPULATION | COEFFICIENT (r) |
|------------|-----------------|
| E | − .475 |
| L and M | − .242 |
| E, L, M | − .445 |

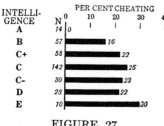

FIGURE 27

PER CENT CHEATING ON PUZZLE
TESTS AT EACH LEVEL OF
INTELLIGENCE (IQ), POPU-
LATIONS D AND R

r between Puzzles and IQ, − .183

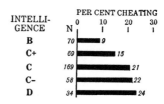

FIGURE 28

PER CENT CHEATING ON ATHLETIC
CONTESTS AT EACH LEVEL OF
INTELLIGENCE (IQ), POPU-
LATIONS C AND D

r between Cheating in Contests and
IQ, − .235

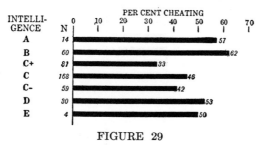

FIGURE 29

PER CENT CHEATING AT PARTIES AT EACH LEVEL OF INTELLIGENCE,
POPULATIONS C AND D

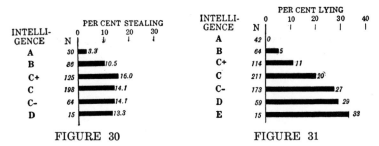

FIGURE 30

PER CENT STEALING AT EACH
LEVEL OF INTELLIGENCE, POP-
ULATIONS C, D, AND R

FIGURE 31

PER CENT LYING (SA) AT EACH
LEVEL OF INTELLIGENCE

TABLE XVI

CORRELATIONS BETWEEN LYING (SA) AND INTELLIGENCE LEVEL

| POPULATION | COEFFICIENT ($r$) |
|---|---|
| A | — .333 |
| D | — .399 |
| P | — .327 |
| Average | — .353 |

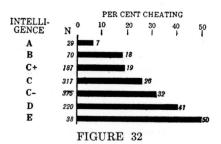

FIGURE 32

PER CENT CHEATING ON IER HOME TEST AT EACH LEVEL OF
INTELLIGENCE (CAVI), POPULATIONS A, B, P, AND Q

TABLE XVII

CORRELATIONS BETWEEN IER HOME CHEATING AND INTELLIGENCE
LEVEL (CAVI)

| POPULATION | COEFFICIENT ($r$) |
|---|---|
| A | — .258 |
| B | — .238 |
| C | — .248 |
| P | — .345 |
| Q | — .350 |
| All cases * | — .255 |

*See Book Two, Chapter VIII.

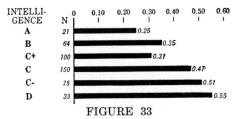

FIGURE 33

MEDIAN CT RATIO AT EACH LEVEL OF INTELLIGENCE,
POPULATIONS C AND D

TABLE XVIII

CORRELATIONS BETWEEN CT RATIO AND INTELLIGENCE LEVEL

| POPULATION | COEFFICENT ($r$) |
|---|---|
| C and D | — .278 |
| L and M | — .247 |

From a perusal of the tables it may be seen that the $r$'s for the
IER school tests, the Speed tests, and the Coördination tests are
all around — .40.    Inasmuch as the test taken home and the Lying

test consisted of only one test each, their respective $r$'s of $-.255$ and $-.353$ are really equivalent or even proportionately higher. Just why the $r$'s for the Puzzle tests and the Parties, Athletic Contests, and Stealing tests should be so much lower is not clear. Possibly the more intelligent, feeling no such sense of mastery in these situations as in the others, are more anxious about their achievement when pitted against their opponents, as in the Parties and Contests, or when confronted with a strange task, as in the Puzzles, and are therefore more strongly tempted to cheat than on school tests. The money test is in a class by itself, as here the stealing had nothing whatever to do with achievement in the test. The money was there to be taken or left. It is rather significant, therefore, that in this kind of situation the relation between intelligence and honesty should be so slight. It is difficult to see, moreover, why the more intelligent should have any feeling of confidence regarding their superior ability on the Coördination and Speed tests, for as a matter of fact ability on these tests does not correlate with intelligence.

Another way in which greater intelligence might indirectly influence the $r$'s might be through the association of greater intelligence with greater caution. The brighter pupils may be wary of getting into a false situation, and this would make them appear less deceptive quite apart from their genuine motives or ethical standards.*

Finally, there is a well recognized relation between intelligence and higher cultural levels, and as we shall see later, cultural level is definitely associated with honesty. Are the correlations between honesty and intelligence due, then, to this factor of culture? Not

---

* A similar capacity associated with intelligence is what is often called resistance to suggestion. As we shall point out in Chapter XIII, the correlation between one measure of suggestibility and the IER school tests is $-.60$. Keeping this factor constant, we find that the $r$ between intelligence and school cheating drops from $-.423$ to $-.193$. Too much weight should not be placed on this partial, however, for reasons we shall present later, but suggestibility probably plays a large part in the association of intelligence and honesty of the classroom type. This would not account at all for the association of cheating and intelligence on the home test, however, for here suggestion plays almost no part at all.

in the case of the test taken home, for Table XVII shows that populations P and Q, which since they are private schools represent a very narrow range of cultural background, have the higher $r$'s between home cheating and intelligence.  If the cultural factor were primarily responsible, the reverse would be the case.  We have also the following partial $r$'s between various deception tests and intelligence, with home background, as measured by methods to be reported later, kept constant:

TABLE XIX

PARTIAL $r$'S BETWEEN INTELLIGENCE AND DECEPTION, HOME BACKGROUND CONSTANT

| TEST | POPULATION | N | OBSERVED $r$ | PARTIAL $r$ | $r$, HOME BACKGROUND INTELLIGENCE | $r$, HOME BACKGROUND CHEATING |
|------|-----------|---|-----------|-----------|----------|----------|
| School Xi | C + P | 282 | $-.503$ | $-.397$ | .362 | $-.504$ |
| Home Xi | C + P | 244 | $-.305$ | $-.240$ | .362 | $-.242$ |
| Speed | C + P | 304 | $-.450$ | $-.361$ | .362 | $-.385$ |

The column headed " Partial $r$ " shows the correlation between intelligence and deception with home background constant.  That is, if all the children had come from homes of the same general social-economic level, the more intelligent would still have been the more honest.

It is quite possible, of course, that there are other factors bound up with intelligence, such as general biological superiority, which might still further lower the $r$'s we have reported between intelligence and deception.  If all such factors are for the moment taken for granted and intelligence is regarded as standing for a highly complex social and biological phenomenon, we may summarize the facts for all the various deception tests by stating, as our best estimate of the relation between intelligence and a theoretical combination of *all* our deception tests, a correlation of $-.50$ to $-.60$.*

* See Book Two, Chapter VIII.

## PHYSICAL CONDITION AND CHEATING

A child whose school work is made difficult by some physical handicap such as defective eyesight or hearing, undue lassitude, emotional disturbances, or pain is subjected to a greater temptation to cheat than the normal child, in order to compensate for his handicap in any way that presents itself. Whether deception is a characteristic method of compensation or whether the need for compensation expresses itself in an atrophied sense of honor is an important question for moral education. We are not in a position at present to offer an answer inasmuch as the necessary data were not available and the medical skill required for gathering them was not within the reach of our budget.

Although we were not able to determine the relation of physical condition to deception in the classroom, we were not thus limited in the case of deception in athletic contests, for the " events " of our Contests, it will be recalled, were themselves measures of the strength or physical ability required for success in the contest. In this respect these tests are analogous to the IER and Speed tests, which also measure the ability required for success in each. This is accomplished by means of the " double testing " procedure which is outlined in Chapter III. In the case of the physical ability tests, the examiner tried out the subject before allowing him to do the test by himself, and kept a record of the subject's " honest " ability. There were three such preliminary trials with the hand dynamometer, two with the spirometer, one with the pull-up, and two with the broad jump.

We selected these particular tests not only because they would give us reliable measures of the particular abilities involved but also because in combination they would yield a good measure of general strength or ability, which presumably helps to determine the attitude of an individual toward any physical contest. For evidence as to the validity of these tests we have depended on Rogers * and have followed his method of scoring and weighting them so as to secure a total physical ability score.

* *Loc. cit.*

The significance of physical ability, however, both as a factor in determining success in a contest and as a factor in influencing attitude toward a contest, lies not merely in its gross amount, but chiefly in the relation of the gross amount to what may be expected of a child of a certain age and weight.  Of two children who have the same total physical ability score, the younger and lighter is obviously in better *physical condition*.  Thus *ability* is analogous to mental age and *condition* to IQ.  In competing with his peers it is condition rather than mere ability that provides the handicap which makes for confidence and success or trepidation and failure. We therefore found the physical ability norm for each age and weight and divided the individual's total score by this norm for his own age and weight.*

Having calculated our physical condition scores or ratios, we were now in a position to determine whether this factor was asso-

---

* Rogers used the first three of these tests in his battery of physical fitness tests.  He used the standing broad jump as a measure of athletic ability. But we found it quite satisfactory as a test of physical ability.  Following Rogers, we gave the following weights to the scores of these four tests:

> Dynamometer in kilograms — times 2
> Spirometer in cubic inches — times $\frac{1}{2}$
> Broad jump in inches — times 1
> Pull-up (chinning) — times chinned
> multiplied by $\frac{1}{10}$ weight in pounds
> plus (height in inches −48)

Some of our subjects could not pull up even once.  In some instances we omitted this test because of lack of apparatus.  In these cases we predicted the most probable chinning or pull-up score from the scores on the other tests.

Physical ability is a function of age and weight.  Rogers found that height is not an important factor.  To get a measure of *physical condition* corresponding to IQ, we followed the procedure of Rogers and determined first the norms for each age and weight.  This was accomplished by plotting weight against the physical-fitness total score for each age.  Ages 8, 9, and 10 were thrown into one plot; then separate plots were made for ages 11, 12, 13, 14, 15, and 16.  In each plot we found first the line of relation, using medians for origins and Q's (semi-interquartile ranges) as units.  The reasons for not using the regression of physical ability score on weights are given by Rogers on page 59.  The normal physical ability score for each weight was read off the line in each age plot.  This gave different physical ability expectations

ciated with the practice of deception in the contests which we had set up. The facts are reported in Table XX, which gives the coefficients of correlation between physical condition and deception for both the athletic contests and the classroom tests, and for all deception tests combined.

TABLE XX

CORRELATION OF PHYSICAL CONDITION AND DECEPTION

| r BETWEEN PHYSICAL CONDITION AND | POPULATION C | POPULATION D |
|---|---|---|
| Cheating in classroom . . . . | + .157 | − .126 |
| Cheating in athletic contests . . | − .018 | − .122 |
| All deception tests . . . . . . | + .202 | − .186 |

One would hardly expect the type of physical condition thus measured to be associated with classroom deception, but it seems a little surprising that it is as little associated with the tendency to deceive in the very tests by which the ability and condition is measured. There is no evidence here that the oversized but under-strengthened children compensate for their defect by resorting to falsification. Whatever deception takes place cannot be accounted for by physical limitations.

## EMOTIONAL CONDITION AND CHEATING

It may be recalled that in populations A, B, and C a question-naire which we called the Pupil Data Sheet was given to the pupils

for varying weights in the different age levels. Finally a physical condition score was obtained by dividing the pupil's actual score by the norm for his age and weight.

Rogers got reliabilities of over .90 with the first three of our tests. He does not report a reliability on the standing broad jump. We have estimated reliabilities on the basis of *honest scores*, using the highest of the first two with the highest last two in the case of the dynamometer, spirometer, and broad jump, and the first trial with the second in the case of chinning. These yield self-r's of well over .90, confirming Rogers' results. The reliability of the whole battery is at least .95.

after the IER tests had been given.   Among the questions asked, all of which are printed in Appendix I, are the following:

17.  What are you most afraid of?_____

20.  Which teachers have you disliked or not got along with?

21.  Why have you liked or disliked certain teachers?_____

26.  Are you ever punished for doing something you know you ought not to have done?_____  About how often?_____ By whom?_____ What kinds of punishment do you the most good?_____ What kinds of punishment do not do you any good?_____

We also used several questions from the Woodworth-Mathews list for measuring neurotic tendencies.   From these two sets of questions we computed a neurotic index or index of maladjustment by counting one point for each abnormal answer to the Woodworth questions, one point for each two questions not answered in this list, one point for each object of fear named, one for each teacher disliked, and as many more points as there were punishments received weekly.   We had no means of validating this index, but we did find, as will be shown later, that a small group of children who admitted having cheated had a significantly higher index than the most honest children.

In a normal population such as school B, we found the slight emotional disturbances and maladjustments registered in our neurotic index were also slightly related to the tendency to deceive. In this population the mean maladjustment score for the cheaters was 5.1 and of the non-cheaters, 4.6.   The chances are 94 in 100 that this difference is not due to chance.

# CHAPTER VIII

## METHODS OF MEASURING THE CULTURAL BACKGROUND

At the very beginning of the Inquiry it became apparent that for our causal studies we should require some objective measure of the cultural influence of the home. For one thing, it is a commonplace of current psychiatry that many conditioning causes of social maladjustment are to be found in abnormal situations in the home through which certain personal relations among the members of the family become distorted. For another thing, we were ourselves discovering that something closely tied up with occupation, such as socio-economic level, was intermingled with intelligence, race, religion, and emotional condition in the association of these factors with deceit. These miscellaneous influences, which we have gathered under the general term " cultural background," we have attempted to study in two main ways. In the first place, we have dealt directly with the cultural factors themselves, either by observation of the homes or by getting from the children certain significant facts about their homes which experience proved they could report reliably. In the second place, we have dealt with the *effects* of these influences on the children, in so far as they were registered in measurable information, ideas, attitudes, emotions, and habits. These several methods will now be described.

## THE SIMS SCORE CARD

The Sims Score Card is a standardized questionnaire which attempts to get at the facts about the home background by asking questions of the children. We were attracted to the possibilities of this method by an article * in which the late Dr. Chapman and Dr. V. M. Sims, then one of his students, supported the proposition that a score card could be produced which would reliably measure the socio-economic level of the home.    As Dr. Sims was interested in following up this work as a research for the doctorate and as we were convinced that the instrument was worth the final expense involved in refining and standardizing it, we made an arrangement with him to press the work rapidly to a conclusion with the aid of such clerical help and other coöperation as we were able to supply.    This work is described in a monograph† and the revised score card with directions for its administration and scoring are now available.

When Sims completed his score card no similar instrument had made its appearance, though various studies had been reported showing the relative significance of single facts, such as occupation, the possession of a telephone, number of books in the home library, and the like, as measures of economic status.    Feeling that no single item could be an adequate index of the general level of the home, Sims combined a large number of items into a general socio-economic index, which we refer to in this book as the " Sims score." It will be of assistance in understanding just what is meant by this score if the way in which the score card was constructed is understood.    We quote here from Sims's dissertation :

" The problem arose out of an attempt to determine some of the selective factors operating in the participation in extra-curricular activities by high school students.    The conclusion was soon reached that one of the most significant factors determining participation in these activities was the social level from which these students came.    But there was no simple method of determining this level.    Consequently, it was decided to attempt the construction of such an instrument.    A preliminary study was

* Chapman, J. C., and Sims, V. M., " The Quantitative Measurement of Certain Aspects of Socio-economic Status," *Journal of Experimental Psychology*, Vol. XVI, No. 6, pp. 380–390.

† Dr. Sims's monograph has been printed by the Public School Publishing Company, under the title *The Measurement of Socio-Economic Status*.

made based upon material which had been previously collected in connection with the above mentioned study. These data were in the form of an elaborate questionnaire which had been given to the entire population of the New Haven High School. From this questionnaire those questions that were considered significant of the level of the home from which the child came were selected. The relative value of each question was determined on the basis of two criteria:

1. The correlation with the total of the others

2. The degree of intercorrelation between the test questions. The questions selected were each weighted and combined into a total.

" The procedure used in this study is similar. The chief differences are (1) a more complete and reliable list of questions was used, and (2) they were subjected to far more careful testing before they were finally retained. The elaborations and refinements employed and the greater security of the statistical procedures, demanded in part because of the larger number of cases used, make the instrument here presented vastly superior for practical use to the tentative measure presented in the preliminary study."

### Securing the Data from Which the Scale Is Built

The points considered in selecting the questions for the scale were the following:

1. Each question must be indicative of the economic or the cultural level of the home or of both.

2. The questions must cover as many aspects of the home background as possible.

3. The questions must be so stated that the child can understand them.

4. The questions must ask for information which the child is willing to furnish.

5. The questions must ask for information which the child can furnish.

6. The questions must be stated in such a manner that there will be a minimum chance of error.

7. The questions must allow answers that are comparable.

With these points in mind, fifty-six questions were worked out by Sims. He continues:

> " In selecting the questions the attempt was made as adequately as possible to cover aspects of the home and of the family life of the child. Starting with the questions which had been found significant in the original study, each new question considered was judged not only by the seven criteria listed above but also by an eighth: ' Has this special phase been covered by one of the other questions? ' "

The preliminary list was tried out in a sixth grade, revised to meet the difficulties presented in wording, etc., and then printed for extensive use. In this form it was given to children in six New Haven schools which were rated by the superintendent as selecting children respectively from five levels of home background. Six hundred eighty-six blanks were filled out.

The following criteria were applied in selecting the twenty-three questions for the second revision made in coöperation with the Character Education Inquiry.

> " I. Ability of the children to furnish the information
>
> II. The internal consistency as a part of the total series, measured by:
>
> > A. Relatively high correlation with the total of all other questions
> >
> > B. Relatively low degree of association with the other questions
>
> III. The reliability, as measured by per cent of unlike answers for paired siblings (children of the same parents)
>
> IV. The per cent of the population studied who possess the items called for in the questions
>
> " These questions, scored on the basis of the degree to which they approached these criteria, were totaled and averaged. This average is the measure of the socio-economic status.

" The result, then, is a score card, with a manual of directions for giving and scoring, which expresses in a single figure (as opposed to the usual lengthy description) a rough measure of the cultural and economic level of the home. This score card may be administered to large groups in a period of twenty minutes.

" The instrument is found to have a coefficient of reliability of .94, as measured by the correlation between the scores of two hundred paired siblings."

Typical questions on the score card are:

1. Have you a telephone in your home? . . . . YES NO
2. Do you have a bathroom that is used by your family alone? . . . . . . . . . . . YES NO
15. Did your father go to college? . . . . . . YES NO
22. About how many books are in your home? (Be very careful in answering this one. A row of books three feet long would not have more than twenty-five books in it.)

25 or less   26–125   126–225   226–525   526–1000   more than 1000

## THE GOOD-MANNERS TEST

Our first effort to evaluate home background by measuring its *effects* on the children grew out of the feeling that " manners " might afford a key to refinement of a sort that would be symptomatic of careful family training. In this preliminary skirmish we had the coöperation of a graduate student,* and the test, samples of which follow, was largely her own product.

The statements below are true or false. If true, draw a line under the word *True* in front of the statement. If false, draw a line under the word *False*.

(True False)   If soup or any liquid is too hot, blow on it slightly to cool it.

* Miss Cora Orr.

(True False)    In helping yourself to sugar always use your own
                spoon.
(True False)    It is in good form to show general courtesies of
                " Please " and " Thank you " to waitresses and
                maids.
(True False)    It is more important to be neat at school than at
                home.
(True False)    If a boy meets his mother or sister on the street, he
                is not expected to tip his hat.
(True False)    A boy should not detain a girl to talk on the side-
                walk.
(True False)    When yawning, make no attempt to suppress it by
                covering the mouth.

In the following, put a cross before the answer which you consider the best:

When not in use the teaspoon should be
    1. Left in the teacup
    2. Placed on the table
    3. Placed on the saucer
Approval of a program may be shown by
    1. Stamping feet
    2. Clapping
    3. Whistling

Answer the following questions.    If the answer is " Yes," underline the word *Yes*.    If " No," underline the word *No*.

Should a man tip his hat to a strange lady when
    picking up an article which she has dropped?    .    YES    NO
If the door is closed, is it necessary to knock before
    entering a friend's room?    .    .    .    .    .    .    .    YES    NO
Is it considered ill mannered to turn and look at a
    person who has passed in the street?    .    .    .    .    YES    NO
Jane introduces her roommates to her mother as
    follows: " Mother, may I introduce Miss Brown
    and Miss Thompson? "    Is this correct?    .    .    YES    NO

The test was scored in accordance with the judgment of presumably cultivated people and has interesting qualities.\* We have evidence to indicate that whatever leads to knowledge of what to do in moral situations leads also to knowledge of what to do in "social" situations, using "social" in the narrower sense. We have no data to tell us just what the Good-Manners test measures, but the lead it offered seemed worth following up. This was done by another graduate student, whose work will be described after we consider a third procedure, on the results of which she depended for the validation of her test.

## THE DIRECT STUDY OF HOMES

Our third effort to measure cultural influence took the form of an intensive study of homes by an experienced " school visitor."† Through the courtesy of the superintendent of schools and the board of education, we were able to secure her appointment as visitor in one of our communities while she was serving at the same time as a member of our staff. She was able to give us only a half year instead of the year we had planned for this work, but even so she visited one hundred fifty homes and succeeded in making fairly complete reports on over a hundred of them.

As a school visitor acts as an intermediary between school and home, it was helpful to have our representative introduced to the community by a leading article in the local paper as well as by

---

\* Vocabulary was measured by a test devised by Miss Gladys Schwesinger and reported in her monograph "The Social-Ethical Significance of Vocabulary," *Teachers College Contributions to Education*, No. 211, 1926. Scores on the Good-Manners test correlate with intelligence .583, with chronological age .533, with the Schwesinger social-ethical vocabulary .720, and with the sum of seven moral knowledge tests .560. Even with intelligence constant the partial $r$ between moral knowledge and good manners as thus measured is .426.

The moral knowledge tests referred to are described in the monograph "Testing the Knowledge of Right and Wrong," Religious Education Association, 1927, and are a product of the Character Education Inquiry.

† Miss Mabel Huschka.

official communications from the school to the parents and teachers. It was explained that she was coöperating with Teachers College in a research project, and that she was to visit representative homes in all sections of the town, not just a few homes selected because they furnished " problem children " to the schools. Nevertheless, although not asked to study them specifically, she came upon forty-four cases of maladjustment and was able to be of material assistance in several instances. The following quotation from her report to the school board will show briefly her method and results :

" In the case of each child whose social background was to be studied, the school visitor first interviewed the principal of the school which the child attended, in order to secure the data which he already possessed and to get the latest news regarding the child's school progress so that it could be reported directly to the parent. Next she consulted the school nurse, who proved to be exceedingly helpful. Then she consulted the secretary of the Social Service Federation, and if the family happened to be known to any branch of that organization, she was granted the privilege of reading the case record for the family, it being understood of course that she was to regard the information as highly confidential. These records were a very valuable source of information, for often the Federation had known the family under study over a long period of years. If the case were one which was still receiving assistance from the Federation, the visiting teacher interviewed the worker most closely in touch with the family in order to get any personal slants and opinions regarding the child's background which may not have appeared in the record. Having made these preliminary inquiries, she then proceeded with her visit to the home itself.

" The number of homes studied was 150. This obviously included a much larger number of school children, for in many of the families there were several children enrolled in school. Geographically the homes were well distributed throughout the entire city, and concomitantly they were equally well distributed throughout the various ' social classes,' as we sometimes express it.

" The data secured for each child in question was briefly as
follows: economic status; home conditions; constructive and
destructive influences in the neighborhood; education, occupation, health, and character of parents; and lastly, parent-child
relationships including among other things the parent's ideals
and 'expectancies' for his child, parental insight, and method of
discipline.

" That was the aim.    Data on all points were not secured in
every case, for the visiting teacher's method was not that of
question and answer.    What she did was to establish friendly
feeling, direct the conversation to the subject of education in its
broader sense, and then sympathetically listen to what the
mother or father wished to say.    In no case did she press for
information upon a point surrounding which there was any suggestion of sensitiveness.

" Of the 150 homes studied, in only one did the visiting teacher
fail to receive a cordial invitation to come in and sit down, and
that was in the case of a skeptical young mother who, as she
put it, had 'been fooled so many times by book agents' that
she could not be convinced that the visiting teacher's mission
was of another kind.    Not only were the parents cordial: they
were earnest, and often in discussing the problems they had
encountered in the perplexing field of child training, they spoke
of matters and experiences which were of a very intimate
nature."

As we were concerned to have all facts stated quantitatively, the
problem of how to translate the usual qualitative descriptions of
case studies into numerical scores was a serious one.    We felt that
the most reliable procedure would be to have the visitor state her
facts in two ways, descriptively and quantitatively, and we therefore drew up a graphic rating scale on which each observation of
the family status could be numerically expressed.    The complete
scale, as enlarged and modified by Miss Huschka, is printed in the
Appendix, but the following samples will illustrate its general
nature:

I. FAMILY
  A. Father
    2. Education

| 0 | | | | 100 |
|---|---|---|---|---|
| Illiterate | Literate but little formal education | Finished grades | Finished high school | Finished college |

    3. Physical health

| 0 | | | | 100 |
|---|---|---|---|---|
| Always sick | Usually sick | Occasionally sick | Fair health | Exuberant health |

    6. Church relationship
      a. Attendance

| 0 | | | 100 |
|---|---|---|---|
| No attendance | Occasional attendance | Irregular attendance | Regular attendance |

      b. Interest and activity

| 0 | | | 100 |
|---|---|---|---|
| No religious interests | Routine religious observances | Occasional religious interests | Well-established religious convictions |

II. ECONOMIC STATUS
  A. Income

| 0 | | | | 100 |
|---|---|---|---|---|
| Insufficient. Relief necessary all or part of time | Occasional relief necessary | Sufficient | Sufficient for comfortable standards of living | More than sufficient |

  C. Furnishings

| 0 | | | | 100 |
|---|---|---|---|---|
| Inadequate. Less than bare necessities | Inadequate. Bare necessities | Fairly adequate. All necessities but in poor condition | Adequate and comfortable | Luxurious |

III. HOME LIFE
  H. Mutual adjustment of parents

| 0 | | | 100 |
|---|---|---|---|
| Completely antagonistic. Abuse. Infidelity | Domination of one by the other. Suspicion of either's fidelity | Occasional quarreling of inconsequential sort | Supremely happy |

  I. General atmosphere of household

| 0 | | 100 |
|---|---|---|
| Constant friction and bickering | Members get along together | Gracious coöperation |

  J. Attitude of mother toward child
    1. Personal relationship

| 0 | | | 100 |
|---|---|---|---|
| Grudging, antagonistic. Willing to exploit | Selfish affection varying in degree or dependability | Generous, sympathetic, but fostering infantilism. Tendency to repress | Generous. High degree of insight. Tries to develop child's affection and independence |

  K. Discipline

| 0 | | | 100 |
|---|---|---|---|
| No attempt at supervision. Discipline unintelligent and abusive | Inadequate. Divided authority | Kind and intelligent but left to one parent. Intelligent but variable | Kind and intelligent. Good example. Parents in agreement |

General factual material about the family, such as address, names of members, nationality, occupation, relatives, were placed

on a Face Sheet, also printed in the Appendix, and the visits themselves were recorded sometimes chronologically and sometimes in
classified notes on the basis of the following outline, the details of
which were borrowed in part from the Westchester County
Schedule and are printed in full in the Appendix.

I. Family
   A. Father
      1. Intelligence
      2. Education
      3. Physical health
      4. Physical defects
      5. Mental health
      6. Church relationship
      7. Personality habits and behavior
      8. Interests: civic and cultural
   B. Mother
      1–8, as for father

II. Economic status
   A. Income
   B. Shelter
      1. Ownership
      2. Size
      3. Other physical aspects
   C. Furnishings

III. Home life
   A. Housekeeping
   B. Meals
      1. Sufficiency
      2. Quality
      3. Palatability
      4. Regularity
      5. Mood
   C. Sleeping conditions
   D. Language spoken in home
   E. Employment of mother
   F. Integrity of family life

G. Marital status
H. Mutual adjustment of parents
I. General atmosphere of household
J. Attitude of parents toward child
   1. Personal relationship
   2. Ideals and expectancies
      *a.* Degree of ambition
      *b.* Occupation desired for him
      *c.* Cultural aspirations
K. Parental discipline
L. Recreation and amusements taken together

We were not able to check our visitor's ratings by the judgments of another case worker, but we had her repeat her own ratings on each family and check her own judgments in this way. Whatever errors she may have been temperamentally inclined to make will thus appear in all her records; and as her judgments were based on intensive study of actual facts which were selected for attention because of their observability as well as because of their importance, we feel that our procedure yields a fairly exact distribution of our cases. By comparing her case histories with her quantitative ratings we were able to make a further estimate of the reliability of her findings, as will be reported presently in connection with the Burdick Apperception test, which will now be described.

## THE BURDICK APPERCEPTION TEST

Following out the principle embodied in the Good-Manners test, the Apperception test seeks to measure the cultural factors in the home by their influence upon the children. The four major problems faced in the production of an instrument of this kind were, first, the selection of the social factors which should be included; second, the discovery of the ways in which these factors influenced the children; third, the building of a test instrument with which to measure these effects; and fourth, the validation of the scores on such a test by reference to some direct study of the cultural factors themselves as these were to be found among the families of the children.

In view of the fact that we were securing quantitative records of the cultural background of some of our cases, as just now described, we felt that serious effort to produce a test of culture would be worth while and were glad to encourage one of our research students* to undertake the work. She says of her problem:

" The present study makes an effort to develop a method of determining with a minimum of time and expense the home background of groups of children. Whereas intelligence tests seek to measure innate ability by questioning the child concerning those things which every child should know regardless of social and cultural opportunities, the test here described seeks to question him concerning those things he will know only if he has been subjected to certain sorts of environment, or the questions asked have been designed to stimulate answers significant of the environment in which he lives.

" The first step in the preparation of the test was to make a survey of the elements in home environment commonly supposed to be contributing causes of character formation or of delinquency. In the vast amount of literature on the subject there are few case studies of children of superior character. Facts about good boys and girls are not given to the public, unless, after the passage of years, they appear in the form of biographies. On the other hand, there are a great many case histories of young delinquents and a number of carefully made studies of the home factors believed to be partly responsible for their deviation from socially acceptable conduct. The following analysis was finally made :

I. Economic factors
   A. Income
   B. Living conditions
   C. Members of the family working
   D. Occupational level
   E. Division of labor in the home
   F. Recreational facilities for the child

* Miss Edith M. Burdick.

II. Cultural factors
   A. Familiarity with music
   B. Familiarity with literature
   C. Familiarity with nature
   D. Familiarity with art
   E. Manner of spending leisure time
   F. Knowledge of etiquette
   G. Breadth of view and freedom from prejudice
III. Ethical factors
   A. Affiliations with religious bodies
   B. Religious formulae observed in the home
   C. Character of the adult members of the family
   D. Nature and degree of parental supervision
   E. Attitude of members of the family toward one
      another

" As was to be expected, but nevertheless unfortunately, it is most difficult to test the very elements upon which students of character place the most emphasis, namely, character of the adult members of the family, nature and degree of the parental supervision, and the attitude of members of the family toward one another. It was decided to omit any reference to distinctly religious matters. With the exception of G under II and A and B under III, some measure of all the items which appear in the analysis has been included in the test."

Several hundred items are included in the test, of which the following are samples, selected from its various sections.

1. Gets at the character of the house furnishings. The directions read: How good are you at guessing things? Do you know the game called " Twenty Guesses "? Somebody thinks of an object in the room and the other people may have twenty guesses as to what it is. This time an object belonging in a living room has been selected. Each pupil may have twenty guesses as to what it is. The teacher will tell the class later what the object is.

2. Indicates type of literary contacts. This is a completion test. The directions read: Each of the words given below has

another word (or words) which is usually used with it. Fill in the blank spaces.

Examples are:

| MAGAZINES | BOOKS | MUSICIANS |
|---|---|---|
| Snappy ——— | Dr. ——— | Josef ——— |
| American ——— | Thunder on the —— —— | John ——— |
| Woman's ——— ——— | The White ——— | Galli ——— |
| National ——— | Encyclopedia ——— | Irving ——— |
| Yale ——— | | |
| Boy's ——— | | |

3. Concerns the child's preferences for companions. It is in the form of a completion test. Examples are:

When I go to the movies I prefer to have ——— go with me.

When I go to church I prefer to have ——— with me.

In the evening I prefer to have ——— with me.

4. General cultural information. A multiple choice test, requiring the pupil to check the right answer. Examples are:

What is a second girl?

( ) A servant      ( ) Next to the top in her studies

( ) A little sister      ( ) The next to the oldest

What are the Psalms?

( ) Tall trees      ( ) Games

( ) A book in the Bible      ( ) A race of people

5. Further general information. The directions are: Underline the right word.

Examples: Beethoven was famous as a — poet — musician — painter — writer.

Hooch means — bricks — goblins — liquor — hoodlum.

6. Attempts to reveal family practices. The directions read: Some of these things tell about things which are usual or which happen often, and some of them tell about things which are not usual or which do not happen often. If what a sentence says is usual, draw a line under the word *Usual*. If what a sentence says is not usual, draw a line under the words *Not usual*.

Examples :
Each child in the family has a separate bed.    Usual    Not usual
The man beats his wife and children.    Usual    Not usual
The mother slaps the children and screams
    at them to make them mind.    Usual    Not usual

7. Refers to personal relations within the family. The directions read : Find the one word in each line which most nearly describes the first word in the line. When you have found this word, draw a line under it.

Examples : Father — strict, good, cruel, stingy, friendly
             Mother — lazy, lovely, mean, kind, cranky

With these words referring to members of the family are a number of words intended to camouflage the real purpose of the test, but which also may have some diagnostic significance.

8. Concerns the household régime. Gives a list of duties which must be performed for nearly every household. The child is asked to indicate in each case the person or persons whose regular task it is to do the thing named.

Examples : To earn the family income _____
           To teach the children how to behave _____
           To serve the meals _____

9. States situations which have actually happened to children. The pupil is asked to write his best guess as to what happened next.

Examples : It was a cold winter's night and a snowstorm was raging. It was a whole hour before bedtime. The children said, " Mother, what shall we do next ? " What did their mother say ?

Edward's father had told him to come home immediately after school each night. One day Edward went for an automobile ride with a chum and did not get home until eight o'clock. What happened when he reached home ?

10. A completion test, concerned with pertinent information.

Examples : Milk costs _____ cents a quart.
           Most men I know go to work at _____ o'clock.
           A boy's best friend is _____.

A rough method of scoring the test was worked out by comparing answers of populations which differed widely in social background. In the case of questions whose answers must be definitely correct or incorrect, right or wrong, only those were retained which distinguished the higher from the lower level. Other items which admit of a wide variety of answers were scored according to common sense and the combined ratings of judges. Reliability was found by correlating the scores on two forms of the test as scored by this first method.*

The validity of the instrument was assured in advance by the method of scoring, but only so far as it would distinguish between widely different groups. Its validity as an instrument to measure accurately the cultural background of individuals was found by correlating the test scores of the children whose homes were studied and rated by Miss Huschka with her home background scores.

But before doing this it was felt that Miss Huschka's ratings should be more carefully scrutinized. Accordingly we secured the services of another young woman† who had just been making a study of homes in relation to school achievement, and had her go over Miss Huschka's original descriptive data and classify the homes in some seventeen or eighteen social levels without reference to the quantitative ratings. Meanwhile Miss Burdick took the headings of the Huschka study and asked eighteen experienced students of family life to weight the various factors listed in accordance with their contribution to an all-around family. This request was worded as follows:

" Consider that the following eight factors jointly create the qualities of a home capable of performing all its proper functions.

* The r between form I and form II (144 cases, — 36 each from grades 5, 6, 7, 8, population T) was .621.

The r between form I and form II (221 cases, — grades 5 and 6, population U, and grades 5, 6, 7, 8, population T) was .708.

The r between form I and form II (48 cases, — all the twelve-year-olds in the population U and population T groups) was .741.

The r between scale A and scale B (168 cases, — 28 each from grades 6, 7, 8, population C and population P) was .766.

† Miss Marian B. Nicholson.

How would you suggest that 100 points be distributed so that each of the eight factors be given its due weight? If you think that they contribute equally, give each 12½ points. If you consider some more important than others, give to those a greater proportion of points, provided each item be rated more than zero and less than 100.

1. Intelligence of parents. By intelligence we mean good planning and reasoning ability.
2. Education of parents. This refers to formal education, a parent being well educated if he has completed college.
3. Physical health of parents. This includes the presence or absence of serious sensory, motor, organic, or endocrine defects.
4. Interest of parents in church, civic, and cultural affairs
5. Personality and behavior of parents. By personality and behavior we mean social adjustment, responsibility in meeting obligations, mental health, degree of integration and of emotional stability.
6. Economic status as indicated by the family income, the nature of the shelter, the adequacy of the furnishings
7. Home life. By this broad term is meant the housekeeping, the meals, the sleeping conditions, the language spoken in the home, the mother's employment, whether there are outsiders in the home, the adjustment of the parents one to the other, the general atmosphere whether of friction or of coöperation.
8. Attitude of parents toward children. This means the personal relationship to the children, whether cold and antagonistic, selfish or generous and intelligently sympathetic, the ideals and expectancies of the parent for the child, the cultural aspiration."

From these ratings the score value or weight representing the combined opinion of the judges was found for each section of the rating scale, and each family's score for each section was multiplied by its weight or importance. When these weighted scores were added together they constituted the total background score for the family. These scores and Miss Nicholson's classification of the original case records gave almost the same results. Indeed they correlated $+.90$, which was rather high in view of the variety of ways in which the material was handled, and was felt to be a sufficient estimate of the reliability of the quantitative home background ratings made by Miss Huschka.

The next step was to correlate the first rough method of scoring the Apperception tests with the Huschka home background score. The final score assigned to each home was obtained by multiplying by two the score obtained from the weighted Huschka ratings and averaging it with the Nicholson rating. This was used as a criterion against which to validate the Apperception test. Of the pupils whose homes had been rated one hundred and twenty-three also took the test. The $r$ between the test and the criterion was .659.*

The reliability was further tested by finding the $r$ between the scores of 250 siblings. This is .499. The $r$ between age and the Apperception test scores in this group is .186. With age of one sibling constant, the $r$ between siblings is raised to .562. But the range of homes of the 123 cases was somewhat restricted. When allowance for this is made, the reliability coefficient becomes .60. This $r$, it will be observed, is lower than any of those obtained by correlating the scores on two forms of the same test. Even were the intelligence of the siblings the same, probably the same home can never *mean* exactly the same environment to two different children.

———

We now have before us four of the more elaborate methods we have used to discover and express in quantitative terms the cultural differences among the homes of our subjects, and are ready to point out such relations as we have found between these differences and the tendency to deceive.

———

* By weighting the scores the raw $r$ goes up to .669; by correction for restricted range, to .695; and by correction for attenuation, to .95.

# CHAPTER IX

# ECONOMIC AND CULTURAL FACTORS ASSOCIATED WITH THE TENDENCY TO DECEIVE

We have used each of the four methods of measuring cultural level described in Chapter VIII for the purpose of discovering the relation of home background to deception.  Although these measures are quite diverse and independent of one another, they show comparable amounts of association between culture and honesty. We shall venture later in the chapter a prediction of the correlation between several modes of deceptive behavior and a combination of certain of our methods of evaluating the social background, but we may well anticipate our discussion by reporting at once that the *average* of the $r$'s between all our home background ratings and our various classroom tests on all our populations is $-.369$.

## THE SIMS SCORE AND DECEPTIVENESS

The measure we have used most extensively is the Sims score. We described in the previous chapter how this was based on a large number of facts about the parents and the home conditions, presenting a comprehensive picture of the economic and social status. The Sims card was used with schools C, E, F, G, H, I, J, L, M, and P.  To illustrate the large differences among these populations both in the mean Sims score and in the range of scores, we print in Table XXI the distributions for five schools, ranging from a very low socio-economic level of 6 to a very high level of 17.

Many of our school groups are thus seen to represent restricted ranges of socio-economic status.  In order to approximate the facts for the whole school population, we have therefore made such

213

combinations of schools as would yield a set of scores spread well up and down the scale.*

TABLE XXI

SAMPLE DISTRIBUTIONS OF SIMS SCORES

| SCORES | SCHOOL P | SCHOOLS L AND M | SCHOOL C | SCHOOL J | SCHOOL F |
|---|---|---|---|---|---|
| 17 | 7 | | | | |
| 16 | 44 | 12 | 12 | 1 | |
| 15 | 85 | 26 | 19 | 3 | |
| 14 | 45 | 50 | 26 | 7 | |
| 13 | 14 | 45 | 26 | 7 | 2 |
| 12 | 4 | 39 | 22 | 16 | 9 |
| 11 | 2 | 29 | 29 | 30 | 27 |
| 10 | 2 | 19 | 37 | 68 | 52 |
| 9 | | 17 | 20 | 132 | 91 |
| 8 | | 7 | 17 | 178 | 117 |
| 7 | | 2 | 5 | 133 | 69 |
| 6 | | | | 9 | 11 |
| Number | 203 | 246 | 213 | 584 | 378 |
| Mean | 15.3 | 13.0 | 12.2 | 9.1 | 9.1 |
| SD | 1.18 | 1.89 | 2.41 | 1.61 | 1.37 |

Since the Sims scores range from 6 to 17, we now have at least nine clear socio-economic levels. The per cent of cheaters in the IER tests, both school and home, and in the Speed tests † are charted for each of these nine levels in Figures 34 to 36.

The association of socio-economic level with deception, which is so clearly evident from the diagrams of Figures 34 to 36, is less apparent in the case of the Coördination tests, the Athletic Contests, the Parties, or the general CT ratio or number of cheatings

* In view of the fact that these combinations were possible, this procedure seemed wiser than to depend on correction of correlations for restricted range. As an illustration of how selection affects correlation, it might be noted that the $r$ between Sims score and school Xi is *positive* in school P and only slightly negative in school C, yet when the two schools are combined in one plot the $r$ becomes −.490.

† Detailed tables are printed in Book Two, Chapter IX.

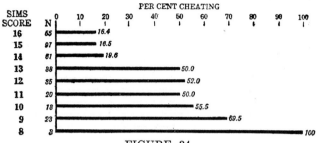

FIGURE 34

SIMS SOCIO-ECONOMIC LEVELS AND IER SCHOOL CHEATING,
POPULATIONS C AND P

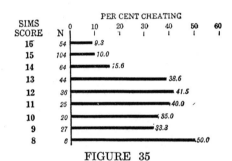

FIGURE 35

SIMS SOCIO-ECONOMIC LEVELS AND IER SPEED TESTS,
POPULATIONS C AND P

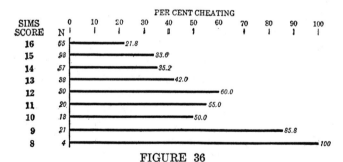

FIGURE 36

SIMS SOCIO-ECONOMIC LEVELS AND HOME CHEATING,
POPULATIONS C AND P

in ten chances.   The facts for all the techniques are summed up in terms of correlation coefficients between Sims score and decep-

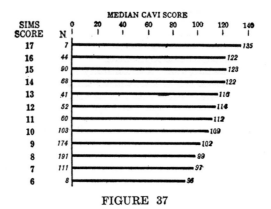

FIGURE 37

tion in Table XXII.   The first column is the observed $r$, and the second column is the partial $r$ with intelligence constant, showing what the relation between Sims score and deception is when the factor of intelligence does not enter to affect the matter.

The extent to which the observed relation between socio-economic level and deception, as expressed by the $r$'s of the first column of Table XXII, is a function of intelligence or of some factor or factors of which intelligence is also a function is shown by the partial $r$'s of the second column.   The IER tests show the closest relationship.   If all the children had had the same intelligence, those coming from the higher social levels would still have cheated less on the IER tests than those coming from lower social levels. The IER tests, it will be remembered, are like regular school examinations or tests and involve the use of answer sheets and dictionary.   They are therefore more probably connected in the children's experience with the teaching of honesty and with established habits of honesty than are the less usual peeping tests and speed tests.

The question of honesty at parties may never have arisen in the experience of the children of any social level, but it might well be supposed that in the case of the homes of higher social level some attention had been given to the question of cheating on school tests

TABLE XXII

CORRELATION OF SIMS SCORE WITH DIFFERENT TYPES OF DECEPTION

| SCHOOL | TEST | OBSERVED $r$ | PARTIAL $r$, INTELLIGENCE CONSTANT |
|---|---|---|---|
| Schools C and P | IER school Xi | — .490 | — .399 |
| Schools C and P | IER home Xi | — .307 | — .156 |
| Schools C and P | Speed Xi | — .294 | — .165 |
| Schools C, P, L, M, F to J | Speed Xi | — .293 | — .207 |
| Schools L, M, F to J | Coördination Xi | — .100 | — .055 |
| School C | Contest | — .100 | — .078 |
| School C | Parties | — .210 | — .172 |
| Schools C, L, M, J | CT ratio | — .130 | — .104 |

or of getting unauthorized help. By the same token, however, one would expect that athletic contests as well as school cheating would be a matter of home discussion or discipline, yet no difference in the behavior of the various social levels in the contest is apparent. It is quite possible, of course, that the factors favorable for the development of honor which we have just now attributed to the higher socio-economic levels may relate so exclusively to routine schoolroom practices and home practices as to have slight bearing on more unusual situations or on situations somewhat removed from family supervision. Certain it is that, in the Speed, Coördination, Athletic, and Party tests and in the combined deception tendencies measured by the CT ratio, to come from more favorably situated homes carries with it very little presumption of superior honesty.

## THE GOOD–MANNERS AND APPERCEPTION TESTS IN RELATION TO DECEPTION

In these tests, which were described in the previous chapter, we are dealing not directly with the home or with facts about the home, but with the effects of the home that may be registered in the ideas, information, and attitudes of the children. The association of knowledge of good manners with deception can be reported only for 200 cases in school C. Here the $r$ between the scores on this test and the IER school Xi is $-.376$, and the home Xi, $-.03$. With intelligence constant, the $r$ with school cheating drops to $-.25$, but even this suggests a slight tendency for knowledge of etiquette and honest conduct in school to go together.

One form of the Burdick Apperception test was administered to schools C and P; and a much longer edition, made up of the best of three forms, was given to several hundred pupils of population A, including the cases selected for special study by our school visitor. Table XXIII gives the correlations between the Burdick scores and intelligence, age, and the Sims scores. For the intelligence scores we used the CAVI achievement scores obtained from these pupils some months previously.

### TABLE XXIII

CORRELATION OF BURDICK SCORES WITH AGE, INTELLIGENCE, AND SIMS SCORES

| SCHOOL | AGE | | INTELLIGENCE | | SIMS | |
|---|---|---|---|---|---|---|
| | N | $r$ | N | $r$ | N | $r$ |
| A | 455 | .079 | 219 | .529 | | |
| C and P | 339 | $-.263$ | 278 | .409 | 311 | .510 |

Table XXIV gives the correlations between the Burdick scores and two types of deception, together with the partial correlations when intelligence is kept constant.

TABLE XXIV

CORRELATION OF BURDICK SCORES WITH DECEPTION

| SCHOOL | IER SCHOOL Xi | | | SPEED SCORES | | |
|---|---|---|---|---|---|---|
| | N | r* | Partial | N | r* | Partial |
| A | 208 | − .463 | − .285 | 449 | − .450 | − .415 |
| C and P | 282 | − .385 | − .319 | 304 | − .375 | − .233 |
| A special | 94 | − .536 | | | | |

\* The r's reported in Table XXIV have been corrected for errors of type I. See Book Two, Chapter VI.

Comparison of Tables XXII and XXIV will show that the Burdick test is more closely associated with intelligence than the Sims score card and, except for the Speed scores, less closely associated with honesty. The rather high $r$ of −.536 for the special group is due to the fact that these cases represent the two extremes of honesty and dishonesty. The $r$ of .510 between the Sims score and the Burdick score indicates that the two devices do not measure the same thing in the home background, yet whatever each measures is somewhat associated with deception. We may therefore profitably combine the two scores in a single home background score and correlate this with the three forms of deception reported for the Burdick scores on schools C and P. The results appear in Table XXV.

TABLE XXV

CORRELATION OF BURDICK-SIMS TOTAL SCORE WITH DECEPTION, POPULATIONS C AND P

| IER SCHOOL Xi | | | SPEED | | |
|---|---|---|---|---|---|
| N | r | Partial | N | r | Partial |
| 282 | − .504 | − .374 | 304 | − .385 | − .236 |

Thus in these tests, when intelligence is held constant, we have significant partials between home background, as measured by Sims and Burdick combined, and deception.

## QUANTITATIVE HOME BACKGROUND SCORES AS COMPARED WITH DECEPTION SCORES

The results of our direct study of homes will be given in detail in Chapter XIV, but it is appropriate to report here the correlations between the ratings assigned to the homes by our school visitor and the deceptiveness of the children from these homes. The cases we selected for study consisted of three groups, the most honest, the most dishonest, and a small group who admitted they had cheated when asked about it on the Pupil Data Sheets. Thus the two extremes of the population are represented rather than the population as a whole, and the r's are somewhat spurious in consequence. We will nevertheless report them for what they are worth.

In the case of cheating on the test taken home, the r between deception and the home background score is zero. That is, the children from the best homes cheated as much and as little as the children from the worst homes. This relation is due, however, not so much to the fact that there were children from good homes who cheated as to the fact that there were so many from poor homes who did not. That this may be in part accounted for by the lack of opportunity in the poorer homes to get the correct meanings of words on the Word Knowledge test is suggested by the fact that the r between home background scores and cheating in school is −.40.

Owing to the fact that home background is positively correlated with intelligence and cheating negatively correlated with intelligence, the relation between home background and deception would appear considerably reduced if the factor of intelligence could be kept constant. Unfortunately, the data do not permit the use of the partial correlation technique, but from other considerations we estimate that, if intelligence were constant, the r between deception and the home background scores of our visitor for an unselected population would be about −.30.

## OCCUPATION IN RELATION TO DECEPTION

The quantitative ratings, the Burdick tests, and the Sims card all yield scores which are a composite of many factors constituting the cultural background of the home. It is rather surprising, therefore, that a single item like occupational level should prove to be as closely associated with honest behavior as any of these other more complex pictures of home background. Yet such is the case, as the charts which are to follow will show.

The facts concerning occupations were secured as follows: In populations A and B we distributed slips of paper and asked the pupils to give their father's occupation. To populations C, F, G, H, I, J, L, M, and P we gave the Sims Score Card, which asks four questions * about occupation from which it is possible to make a very satisfactory classification into four socio-economic levels. The classifications of schools A and B, being based on less information are less accurate but are nevertheless made in accordance with the plan† used by the Sims card, which is as follows:

Group I. Professional, large business, managerial service, commercial service. Illustrations are accountant, architect, banker, broker, inspector, officials of various sorts, physician, teacher.

Group II. Artisan proprietors. Owners of small business, foremen, highly skilled laborers

Group III. Skilled laborers, such as plumbers, electricians, plasterers, mechanics

Group IV. Unskilled workers, day laborers

After we had classified the occupations of the fathers into these four groups, we took one school at a time, and for each occupa-

---

* The questions relate to name of occupation, ownership, title or position, and number of employees, if any.

† See the Taussig Scale.

tional group we made separate distributions of the different kinds of deception scores. Complete tables showing the median amount of cheating and the per cent of cheating for each of these groups, for each school and type of deception, are given in Chapter IX of

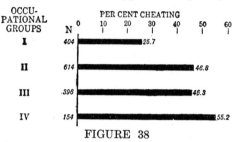

FIGURE 38

OCCUPATIONAL DIFFERENCES, IER SCHOOL CHEATING, POPULATIONS A, B, C, AND P

$r = -.450$

Book Two, on the basis of which the following figures have been drawn. The detailed tables deserve careful study, but their general significance can be well seen from the accompanying drawings, which summarize the facts for the several combinations of school populations that are indicated in connection with each figure. The coefficient of correlation which is printed with each diagram is a "biserial $r$," figured somewhat differently from the $r$'s discussed in Chapter VI but meaning much the same thing. In this case we take simply the fact of belonging or not belonging to one of the two top occupational groups — of being, that is, in the upper half or lower half of the occupational scale — and

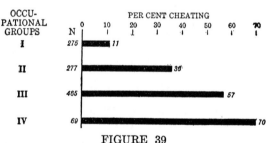

FIGURE 39

OCCUPATIONAL DIFFERENCES, SPEED TESTS, POPULATIONS C, L, M, P, AND F TO J

$r = -.549$

with this fact we associate the amount of deception. The resulting $r$ shows the extent to which belonging in one half or the other half of the occupational level is associated with deception.

In each one of these figures showing occupational differences, group I stands out as conspicuously the least deceptive.  In the Coördination test and the test taken home (Figures 40 and 41),

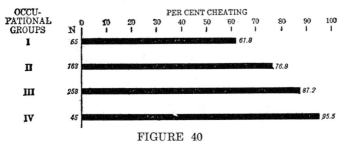

FIGURE 40

OCCUPATIONAL DIFFERENCES, COÖRDINATION TESTS, POPULATIONS
L, M, AND F TO J

$r = - .284$

groups II, III, and IV are much alike.  On the IER school test (Figure 38) groups II and III are about alike, standing between I and IV.  On the Speed test (Figure 39), there is a steady increase from I to IV, as there is also in the case of the CT ratio (Figure 42), which shows the number of times a pupil cheated in proportion to the opportunities offered.  As the CT ratio offers the best summary of the total situation, the means as well as medians are printed in Table XXVI together with the SD's * and SE's,* or standard errors of the means.

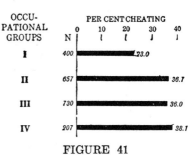

FIGURE 41

OCCUPATIONAL DIFFERENCES, IER
HOME CHEATING, POPULATIONS
A, B, C, P, AND F TO J

$r = - .089$

* Those unused to these terms may need to refer occasionally to Chapter VI.  The SD, or standard deviation, is the usual measure of variability.  The standard error is the usual measure of unreliability.  A mean may, in a large number of similar groups, vary *by chance* up to three times its SE in either direction.  Also the *difference between* two means must be three times the SE of the difference for one to feel certain that it is not a chance difference.

From this table it can readily be seen that most of the group differences are statistically significant, for it will be recalled from Chapter VI that the unreliability of the difference between two

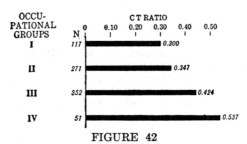

FIGURE 42

OCCUPATIONAL DIFFERENCES, CT RATIO, POPULATIONS
C, L, M, AND F TO J

$r = -.275$

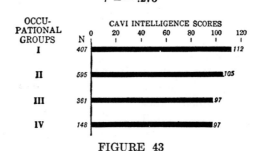

FIGURE 43

OCCUPATIONAL DIFFERENCES, INTELLIGENCE (CAVI),
POPULATIONS A, B, C, AND P

TABLE XXVI

OCCUPATIONAL DIFFERENCES IN CT RATIO, POPULATIONS C, L, M, AND F TO J

| GROUP | N | MEDIAN | MEAN | SD | SE |
|-------|-----|--------|------|------|------|
| I | 117 | .300 | .303 | .217 | .020 |
| II | 271 | .347 | .352 | .233 | .014 |
| III | 352 | .424 | .432 | .230 | .012 |
| IV | 51 | .537 | .530 | .258 | .036 |

means is shown by the formula $\sqrt{SE_1^2 + SE_2^2}$. The differences between proximate groups in multiples of their standard errors are as follows:

Group II minus group I    2.0
Group III minus group II    4.3
Group IV minus group III   2.6

As explained in Chapter VI, to be completely outside the limits of chance, these differences should be three times their standard errors; and this is the case not only between II and III, as shown by the table, where the difference is 4.3 times its SE, but by inference between I and III, I and IV, and II and IV. The chances are 977 in 1000 that the difference between II and I is a genuine difference and 995 in 1000 that the difference between IV and III is significant. The relationship of occupational level to deception is also shown by the $r$'s printed with each figure. These are all negative and significant.*

It is a curious thing that the *Word Knowledge* (home) test and *Coördination* (peeping) test show little difference between groups II, III, and IV, either in the median amount or the per cent taking advantage of the opportunity. Group I maintains its superiority, however, here as elsewhere. In the home test it may be that among the other occupational groups the children could get little help at home, anyway, perhaps because of greater use of foreign languages, or more illiteracy, or fewer dictionaries to which they might turn for help. Or there may be a difference in the degree to which children of different social levels are stimulated to make an effort to get a good mark by the word knowledge type of test, which was the one taken home.

In the Coördination test results, as shown in Figure 40, we see a discrepancy between the rise in amount of cheating and in percentage of cheaters. Apparently in this peeping test, as we go down the scale from II to IV there is a strong tendency for a larger proportion to open their eyes and get help but to make less and less use of the advantage which this gives them, perhaps because they are progressively less bold or less ambitious.

* The PE of none of them is over $\pm.03$.

The question will at once be raised as to whether the occupational differences in deception may not be due to differences in intelligence, in view of the correlation between deception and intelligence already shown in Chapter VII. Figure 43 gives weight to the suggestion that this may be the case, for level of intelligence certainly is associated with level of occupation. It is not possible to use the partial correlation technique to determine the matter; but since we have the correlation between CAVI intelligence scores * and the IER type of deception, we can tell, in the case of these school tests, whether the deception shown by each occupational group is greater or less than their median intelligence would lead one to expect. The facts are shown for the school Xi in Table XXVII, last column. This gives the median Xi score of all children in that population whose CAVI score is the same as the median of the occupational group concerned. The " expected " median is what one would expect the group concerned to exhibit, on the average, unless other factors than intelligence are at work to affect the amount of deception.

TABLE XXVII

COMPARISON OF OCCUPATIONAL DIFFERENCES IN SCHOOL DECEPTION ACTUALLY FOUND, WITH DIFFERENCES THAT MIGHT BE EXPECTED BECAUSE OF DIFFERENCES IN INTELLIGENCE, POPULATIONS A, B, C, AND P

| GROUP | N | ACTUAL MEDIAN Xi | EXPECTED MEDIAN Xi |
|-------|-----|-----|-----|
| I | 404 | 2.0 | 3.8 |
| II | 614 | 4.0 | 4.5 |
| III | 396 | 5.8 | 5.3 |
| IV | 154 | 6.0 | 5.3 |

Thus it may be seen from Table XXVII that, while groups III and IV cheat somewhat more than one might expect from children having their intelligence, groups I and II cheat less than would be expected — group I very much less. Furthermore, the *expected*

* See Chapter VII.

difference in amount of cheating between group I and group II is only .7 Xi (4.5 − 3.8), whereas the difference *actually found* is 2.0 Xi (4.0 − 2.0), or nearly three times as much as difference in intelligence alone would account for.

This comparison is made only for the school Xi, since on the home test there was little difference between the groups anyway and on the Speed and Coördination tests the *r* between cheating and intelligence is nearly zero in these particular school populations, so that intelligence could not be the determining factor in any case.

These indications all point to the conclusion that something more than difference in intelligence is needed to account for the occupational differences in the tendency to deceive.

## OCCUPATION AND GENERAL SOCIO–ECONOMIC LEVEL IN RELATION TO DECEPTION

In connection with our study of the relation of occupational level to deception we printed with Figures 38 to 42 a series of biserial *r*'s. It is of some interest to compare these *r*'s with those showing the relation of Sims scores to deception. For convenience both sets are gathered in Table XXVIII, with the *r*'s determined from populations on which both sets of data were at hand.

TABLE XXVIII

Sims Score and Occupational Level Compared as to the Association with Deception

| Test | Sims Score *r* | Occupation *r* |
| --- | --- | --- |
| Schools C and P, School IER Xi . . . . | − .490 | − .322 |
| Schools C and P, Home IER Xi . . . . | − .307 | − .426 |
| Schools C, P, L and M, F to J, Speed Xi . | − .293 | − .594 |
| Schools L, M, F to J, Coördination Xi . . | − .100 | − .284 |
| Schools C, L, M, J, CT ratio . . . . . | − .130 | − .275 |

In every case except the IER school Xi, the occupational level correlates higher than the Sims score with deception. This suggests that there is a difference among the factors which enter into the total socio-economic status and that the more significant factors are buried in the total score. This is only to be expected, as the Sims card was prepared for the purpose of measuring not deception, but home background.

## SIMS–BURDICK–OCCUPATION COMPOSITE

In view of the fact that the Sims and Burdick tests and the occupational rating involve different sets of home background factors,* it seemed wise to combine them in one score and find the correlation of this more comprehensive measure of home background with deception. These $r$'s for the IER school Xi and the Speed Xi are respectively $-.608$ and $-.507$.

## SUMMARY

The relation between economic and cultural factors and the tendency to deceive has now been indicated in a variety of ways, which need to be brought together for final comparison and evaluation. Table XXIX does this for us, ignoring differences in populations tested.

### TABLE XXIX

SUMMARY OF $r$'s BETWEEN CULTURAL FACTORS AND DECEPTION

| TYPE OF DECEIT | OCCUPA-TION LEVEL | SIMS SCORE | GOOD MANNERS | BURDICK SCORE | VISITOR'S RATING | SIMS-BURDICK | SIMS-BURDICK-OCCUPATION |
|---|---|---|---|---|---|---|---|
| IER school | − .322 | − .490 | − .376 | − .463 | − .400 | − .504 | − .608 |
| IER home | − .426 | − .307 | − .030 | − .037 | − .190 | − .243 | |
| Speed | − .594 | − .293 | | − .450 | | − .385 | − .507 |
| Coördination | − .284 | − .100 | | | | | |
| CT ratio | − .275 | − .130 | | | | | |
| Contest | | − .100 | | | | | |
| Party | | − .210 | | | | | |

* The inter-$r$'s are as follows: Sims-Burdick, .510; Sims-occupation, .759; Burdick-occupation, .475. For the $r$'s between occupation and deception tests we took Pearson product-moment $r$'s instead of the biserials already reported.

For the IER school cheating, the Sims-Burdick-occupation correlation is probably the best indication we have at present of the relation between this type of deception and the cultural aspect of the home background of the pupils, and with intelligence constant this $r$ would be approximately $-.40$.  We are not as yet in a position to make as satisfactory a prediction of the true relation between deceptiveness in general and the cultural background as we have made in the case of the relation between intelligence and deception, and it is hazardous to guess, since the data are insufficient.  Pending further information, however, we give as our present judgment the $r$ of $-.45$ as expressive of this relation and estimate that with intelligence constant this $r$ will be reduced to $-.30$.

# CHAPTER X

## THE BIOLOGICAL *VERSUS* THE CULTURAL INFLUENCE OF THE FAMILY *

We have had occasion to mention the complex character of much of our data. Nowhere is this better illustrated than in any study of the family, for here is the meeting ground of a host of cultural and biological factors the external manifestation of which may be a child's perfectly simple act, like shaking hands, or a highly complex act, like playing a Bach fugue. It has been one of the perennial interests of educational philosophy and research to try to unravel this web of social and biological factors into its components and estimate the extent to which the behavior of the children is the product of experience on the one hand and of heredity on the other.

Deceptive behavior is, of course, a case in point. While the direct and inciting occasion for a dishonest act may lie wholly outside the family, the predisposition to deceive rather than to be straightforward may arise from a variety of family experiences and inherited tendencies. The amount of these combined factors, so far as their source is within the family, is roughly indicated by the correlation† of siblings (children of the same parents) with respect to the tendency in question, inasmuch as individuals paired at random from the community would correlate zero. In order

* The substance and much of the form of this chapter appeared first in the *Twenty-Seventh Year Book* of the National Society for the Study of Education, 1928, and is used here with the permission of the Public School Publishing Company.

† If the two members of each pair of sibs were identical, the *r* would be +1.00. If each were the antithesis of the other in every pair, the *r* would be −1.00. If they resembled one another no more than they would by chance, the *r* would be zero.

to discriminate between the social and biological factors, it would be necessary to measure the resemblance of siblings who had been absented from the social influence of their homes from earliest infancy. Supplementary data could be secured from a study of foster children brought up in the same home and of " identical " * twins as compared with non-identical twins and ordinary siblings. Our own material is not so comprehensive as this and does not afford conclusive evidence regarding the relative significance of heredity and environment as predisposing factors in deceptive behavior, but some light is thrown on the problem by the resemblances that we have found between siblings, which seem to us to justify reporting the facts.

We shall first describe briefly the populations from which our sibling data are drawn and mention the tests to which the children had been subjected.

Population A. Suburban community with wide range of home environment, running from homes of comfort and affluence to those of abject poverty. The IER school and home tests and the Speed tests were used here.

Populations L and M. A smaller suburb in another state, containing only two schools. A narrower range of home background, lacking the lower end of the scale. The Speed and Coördination tests were used.

Populations F to J. Five schools in a congested city district, racially homogeneous and rather uniformly low on the economic-social scale. The Speed, Coördination, and IER home tests were used.

Population B. Several schools in a mid-western town of 200,000 inhabitants, representing a fairly wide range of home background. The IER school and home tests.

Population E. A suburban junior high school, homes above the average. The Coördination tests.

Populations K and D. Children from broken homes, those of

---

* By "identical" twins is meant twins who are in most respects almost exactly alike — a phenomenon which may result from the fact that they are produced from like gametes rather than unlike gametes.

K being orphans. In both cases these institutional children were from the same social background as populations F to J. The Speed and Coördination tests were given to D and the IER school tests to K.

## RESULTS

In order to make our discussion of the facts at all clear, it will be necessary to state them first in the form of a comprehensive table to which the reader may refer as the chapter proceeds. The basic facts appear in Table XXX, and certain important supplementary

TABLE XXX

STATISTICAL RESULTS OF SIBLING STUDY

| TEST | POPULATION | N PAIRS | $r$ | $\sigma$ |
|---|---|---|---|---|
| Speed | A | 76 | .220 | 3.27 |
| | L, M | 70 | .292 | 1.59 |
| | F to J | 224 | .208 | 3.42 |
| | A, L, M, F to J | 370 | .225 | 3.00 |
| | D | 43 | .300 | 2.65 |
| IER school | A | 108 | .445 | 1.46 |
| | B | 138 | .433 | 1.50 |
| | A, B | 246 | .440 | 1.38 |
| | K | 94 | .333 | 1.82 |
| | $+\frac{1}{2}$ } K * | 38 | .333 | 1.73 |
| | $-\frac{1}{2}$ | 46 | .333 | 2.03 |
| Coördination | F to J | 239 | .322 | 2.62 |
| | L, M | 74 | .271 | 3.02 |
| | E | 89 | .271 | 2.80 |
| | F to J, E, L, M | 402 | .400 | 2.86 |
| | D | 43 | .300 | 2.73 |
| IER home | A | 104 | .641 | 2.47 |
| | B | 88 | .472 | 2.25 |
| | F to J(1) | 94 | .695 | 2.13 |
| | F to J(2) | 55 | .832 | 2.73 |
| | A, F to J, B | 345 | .705 | 2.62 |

* $+\frac{1}{2}$ means those in the institution more than half their lives and $-\frac{1}{2}$ means those in the institution less than half their lives.

material will be found in Book Two, together with arguments which are too technical to be presented here.   Column 1 gives the population, referring by letter to the groups described.   Column 2 is the number of pairs of siblings in each case.   Column 3 gives the correlations * between pairs.   Column 4 gives the standard deviations of the scores of all the cases.

## INTERPRETATION

Before indicating the bearing of the facts of the table on various hypothetical explanations of sibling resemblance, certain features should be noted.   The important comparisons are between the different behaviors on the one hand and the different populations on the other.   First, as to behaviors.   The test taken home elicits the greatest resemblance between siblings, doubtless partly because of collusion.   The IER school test comes next, perhaps because the copying type of deception is more consciously dealt with by parents.   The Speed and Coördination tests come last, but still show genuine resemblance.

Second, as to populations.   The orphans, K and D, were not given the home test; but of the other populations, the congested population, F–J(1) and F–J(2), shows the greatest resemblance. In F–J(1) and F–J(2) two schools are combined, a better and a worse, in each case.   The average r for all of F–J is .763.   In the other behaviors little difference among the normal populations is found, but in the case of the IER school test there is considerable difference between the normal and the orphan groups.

We have now to account for these likenesses and differences among the populations and point out their significance for the interpretation of the sibling resemblance.   We shall discuss four possible explanations: collusion, common environment, intelligence, and heredity.

* In computing these correlations all combinations were inserted where there were more than two siblings in a family.   Also each pair was entered twice, each individual thus appearing on both the X and the Y axes of the scattergram, making the plot symmetrical, with N equal to the number of entries. For illustration, see Figure 44 on page 236.

## A. Collusion

This is possible only in the task done at home. Here we may expect that some children will either help one another or encourage each other in the use of forbidden aids. The size of the sibling $r$'s bears out this expectation. For all populations it is .705 and runs as high as .83 in one group containing fifty-five pairs. This is considerably higher than the reliability of this single test and indicates that there is greater likelihood that two siblings will cheat in equivalent amounts on a single occasion than that the same child will cheat in the same way on two occasions. If mere general home influence were the prepotent influence, this would not be the case. As a matter of fact, we saw in the previous chapter that there was only the slightest relation between cultural level and cheating at home, showing that whatever makes siblings resemble one another in deception on home work is not the kind of thing in which homes as such differ from one another, so far as we have measured them. The correlation between a pupil and those he names as his friends and companions and who do not, therefore, live in the same home is +.03.

Furthermore, if siblings helped each other on the home test or got help from a common source, one might expect the older to exert the greater influence. This cannot be shown from our data; but it is of interest that, although there is no great difference between the mean of the older and the mean of the younger, yet in a population of 119 pairs 9% were identical, in 61.5% of the pairs the younger cheated more than older, and in 29.5% of the pairs the older cheated more than the younger. The older and younger were nearly alike in variability.

## B. Common Environment

There are, of course, other home factors than collusion and direct assistance or example that make for honest rather than dishonest behavior, or *vice versa*, such as code, ideal, or general social stability, so that one might expect that two children reared in the same home would, by sharing certain common experiences, become more alike than if one were reared in one environment and the other in another. Of course the home is not really identical even for its own children, but certainly the range of social experience offered by a large number of homes is far wider than that offered by one. So far as deceptive behavior is built by experience in the family into habit systems and is not a mere matter of collusion or example in the home, it should appear in the correlation between siblings on tests taken *away* from home. We have already pointed out the existence of such correlations as are found in column 3 of our table, and it is our task in this section to determine, if possible, whether these correlations are to be wholly accounted for by this common experience of siblings in the family.

Reverting to the facts reported in the previous chapter, we might state the problem as follows : We noted there the existence of some sort of nexus between deception and cultural level. To the extent that this cultural level is a function of the home we should expect, therefore, to find a correlation between siblings brought up in the same home. That is, they should resemble one another more than they resemble children chosen at random from the community. The question then is, on the one hand, whether the sibling correlation is *merely* the natural consequence of such home influence or whether there are factors determining sibling resemblance other than the cultural unity of the home ; and, on the other, whether the correlation between deception and home background may not be in part biologically determined, the higher culture being associated with biological difference of some kind.

We have four ways of investigating this problem to which we shall now turn, *viz.*, (1) the relation of the size of the sibling r to the range of home background represented ; (2) the partial correlation technique, keeping home background constant ; (3) a similar procedure, comparing the r's from different narrow levels of home background with the r's from the entire range of home background ; and (4) the comparison of the actual sibling r's with those which might be statistically predicted if home background were the sole cause of the relation observed.

Method 1. The populations reported in the table offer about as wide divergence as is likely to be found in cities and suburbs. The inclusion of rural groups might have extended the range somewhat, but it is certainly wide enough to allow for variations in the size of the sibling correlations as longer or shorter sections of the entire range are taken for comparison. This may be illustrated by the scattergram of Figure 44, on which are plotted the sibling scores of populations B, C, F–J, P, and Q for the IER home test.

In this scattergram each dot represents the scores of a *pair* of siblings. The score for one member of the pair is placed opposite

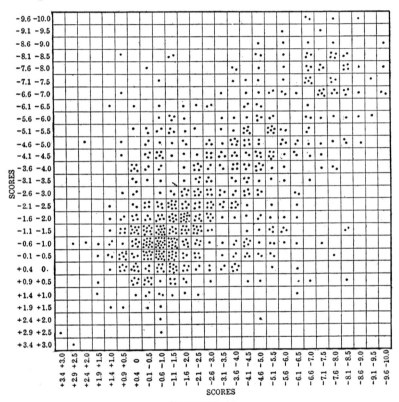

FIGURE 44

SCATTERGRAM OF SIBLING SCORES ON IER HOME TEST

the proper point on the left-hand scale, and the score for the other member of the pair is placed over the proper point on the scale at the bottom. Then another dot for this same pair is entered by putting the score for the first member over the proper point on the bottom scale and the score for the other member opposite the proper point on the scale at the left. If there are more than two siblings in the family, all combinations are entered in the same way ; thus for A, B, and C there would be A–B, A–C, and B–C, each entered twice by the method just now described.

If there were a correlation of +1.00 between home background scores and deception, by removing the cases with higher home background scores we would automatically shorten the range of deception scores. The scattergram that would be left would give an *r* much more like that of the scattergram of Figure 13, page 164, being reduced nearly to zero. On the other hand, if there is no relation at all between home background and deception, removing the cases with higher home background scores will not in the least affect the general appearance of the scattergram, for the cases that are removed will be removed at random rather than from one end. We know from the work already reported that home background does correlate somewhat with deception ; and we should therefore expect that, if the resemblance of siblings is due to these measured factors alone, the lower sibling *r*'s should be found in populations with narrower range of background. If it should turn out upon investigation that such were not the case, then this could properly be taken as evidence that the features of social background included in our measures are not the sole cause of the resemblance of the siblings.

In order to test the matter, it is necessary to indicate in some way the range of background represented in each of our populations. Partly by observation and common consent and partly by reference to the Sims scores already described, we have made these comparisons, with the results shown in Figure 45.

The range of background for the two orphan groups is really much narrower than indicated in the chart, for no matter what the range of background from which they came they had for some time been living in *one* environment, as though all were children in one big family.

In width of social range the populations rank roughly K–D, F–J, L–M, E, B, A.   To the extent that the social factors thus dis-

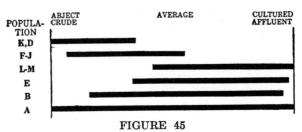

FIGURE 45

RANGE OF HOME BACKGROUND CHART

tributed are determinative of deception we should expect a corresponding variability in deception *r*'s.   Table XXX shows that this expectation is not realized.   For convenience the correlation ranks are gathered from Table XXX in Table XXXI, the columns of which are as follows:  Column 1 gives the rank order of the various populations in spread of home background as in the chart. Columns 2, 3, 4, and 5 give the rank order of these same populations in the size of correlation coefficients between siblings for the four behaviors.

TABLE XXXI

RANK ORDER OF POPULATIONS IN SOCIAL VARIABILITY AND SIBLING CORRELATION

| POPULATION | 1 | 2 | 3 | 4 | 5 |
|---|---|---|---|---|---|
| | RANGE OF BACKGROUND | SPEED | IER SCHOOL | COÖRDINATION | IER HOME |
| D | 1 | 2 | | 2 | |
| K | 1 | | 1 | | |
| F to J | 2 | 1 | | 3 | 5 |
| L to M | 3 | 2 | | 1 | |
| E | 4 | | | 1 | |
| B | 6 | | 3 | | 1 |
| A | 8 | 1 | 3 | | 3 |

From Table XXXI it can be seen that there is no *general* * correspondence between the size of the *r*'s and range of social background. Even the institutional population D, which is in a sense in one home, shows a larger sibling resemblance than populations F–J or A on the Speed test and a larger sibling resemblance than populations L–M or E on the Coördination test. Table XXX also shows that in orphan population K the children who had been living in the institution more than half their lives ("$+\frac{1}{2}$" of Table XXX) show the same sibling *r* as those who had been in the institution less than half their lives ("$-\frac{1}{2}$" of Table XXX) and only slightly less variability. If gross variation in environment is producing the sibling correlation, one would expect the *r* to be lower in the case of those who had been longer in the institution.

Method 2.  The second method of testing the environmental hypothesis involves securing some measure of the variability of home background with a view to determining its correlation with deception. If we can arrive at even an approximation of the correlation between variation in homes and deception, we can then use the partial correlation technique and hold the home variation constant in the sibling *r*'s.

In our preceding chapter we gave the results of our efforts to measure the economic-cultural level of the home and reported the *r*'s between the various scores received and different types of cheating. Since the socio-economic scores are available for most of our siblings, we can apply the partial correlation technique † to our observed *r*'s between siblings in respect to their deception scores. The results are given in Table XXXII on the following page.

These partial *r*'s, which are based on the assumption that the *r* between siblings in home background features is +1.00, indicate that brothers and sisters who come from the same general background will still resemble one another much more than will non-related children of the same general background.

Method 3.  As a check on this we took from populations L, M, and F–J all those who deviate more than about two sigma from the

---

* The rank difference *r*'s are given in Book Two, Chapter IX.

† For formulas see Book Two, Chapter IX.

## TABLE XXXII

### Sibling Resemblance, Sims Score Constant

| Test | Population | Observed r | Partial r |
|------|------------|-----------|-----------|
| Speed | A, L, M, F to J | .225 | + .237 |
| IER school | A, B | .440 | + .364 |
| Coördination | L, M, F to J, E | .400 | + .371 |
| All tests | | .470 | + .418 |

Sims socio-economic means. We found the r between the siblings for classroom deception beyond this extreme in the upper range to be .35 and beyond this extreme in the lower range .30. We then took a slice out of the middle, including all those between about +0.3 sigma and −0.3 sigma, and still got a correlation for classroom deception of about .35. These determinations check and verify the partials, suggesting quite definitely that the resemblance between siblings is not due merely to the influence of such factors in the home background as we have so far measured.

Method 4. The statistical procedures involved in the fourth method for testing the environmental hypothesis are set forth quite fully in Book Two and serve only to bear out what has already been stated.

**Association.** Another type of environmental influence is that of friendly association and classroom experience. As we shall show later, the latter tends to make children of the same class group resemble one another more than they would by chance; but as our siblings are almost invariably in different classrooms, this factor would not be operative. If the other type of association were wholly responsible for the sibling r's, then we should expect a child and his *closest friends* to be as much alike as brother and sister, for a child runs with his friends as much as he does with his older or younger brother or sister. Yet when we correlate a child with one of his friends *not in the same classroom*, the r for population A on the IER school test is .159; and for population B, where practically all the friends named by the children were in the same classroom, the $r$ between a child and one of his friends is .160, even with the classroom influence present to help in accounting for the resemblance. Our sibling $r$'s on this test are, as we have seen, from +.33 to +.44.

We may conclude our examination of the second general explanation of sibling correlations by saying that, while such environmental factors as we have been able to measure or observe are doubtless associated with deception and are in part influential in determining sibling resemblance in this regard, they do not account for all the resemblance found.

## C. Intelligence

The third possible explanation of the resemblance of siblings in deceptiveness is that it is due to their resemblance in intelligence. We are already familiar with the fact that there is a correlation of about .50 between intelligence and deception, which is higher than that between home background and deception. Furthermore, as we shall see presently, siblings correlate with each other about .50 in intelligence. It is to be presumed, therefore, that intelligence may have a good deal to do with the sibling $r$'s reported. But it should be recalled at once that the children of the same family have the *same* home background, not different homes which resemble each other only to the extent of an $r$ of .50. Hence we could hardly expect that intelligence could play so large a part in the determination of the sibling $r$'s as does the cultural factor in the environment.

TABLE XXXIII

SIBLING RESEMBLANCE, INTELLIGENCE CONSTANT

| Test | Population | $r$ | Partial $r$, Intelligence Constant |
|---|---|---|---|
| IER school Xi | A, B, C, P, Q | .440 | .433 |
| IER school Xi | K | .333 | .330 |
| Speed | E (F to J) | .225 | .215 |
| Speed | D | .300 | .300 |
| Coördination | E (F to J) | .400 | .396 |
| Coördination | D | .300 | .300 |

The method of keeping constant the intelligence of the sibs is reported in Book Two. Table XXXIII presents the essential facts.

It is quite apparent from Table XXXIII that we do not affect our $r$'s between siblings very greatly by partialing out variability in intelligence. We may turn then to our last proposed explanation of their resemblance in deception.

## D. HEREDITY

We have mentioned the probability that homes may differ widely in other respects than socio-economic or cultural levels. There may be wide variation among homes of the same socio-economic level in respect to attitudes toward children, general stability and adjustment, or even codes and ideals. These subtle factors may be correlated with deception to a much greater degree than those factors which are distributed in accordance with general socio-economic level. The existence of such factors, which is indicated by our sibling correlations, is forcibly illustrated by the fact that whatever makes for dishonesty is left behind as we go up in the social scale, but whatever makes for honesty is not dropped out as we go down in the social scale. On the lower social levels, therefore, the correlation between deception and home background is zero.

Had all possible environmental factors been kept constant in the partial $r$'s of Table XXXIII, we might claim that the remaining sibling resemblance in the matter of deception is due to biological factors. This statement of the hereditary factor is quite unsatisfactory, however, as nurture plays a rôle in the development of all measurable traits and is not " eliminated " in any true sense from any group of factors. Some elements in behavior, however, are usually regarded as less modifiable than others and more directly the result of biological growth than of interaction with the environment. General intelligence, for example, although its particular modes of exhibition are socially determined, is usually thought to change very little with training. Does the tendency to deceive belong in the same category, or is it due to particular environmental relations in which the prepotent factor or factors are subject to modification as are ideas or ideals or the ability to read or to translate Latin? The relatively innate factors * would be such as temperament, emotional stability, power of inhibition, response to persons as compared to things or ideas, and general intelligence.

It is commonly supposed that the correlation between the IQ's of siblings in a homogeneous age population of unrestricted range is around .50. Dr. Hildreth† summarizes work done up to 1925, showing that the actual results on over two thousand pairs run from .30 to .63. These yield an average of .48. Gordon's data on 219 pairs of orphans, when recalculated by Elderton by entering each pair twice in the scattergram, give a correlation of .467. Miss Hildreth reports .322 as the obtained *r* between 253 pairs of orphans. These two average .388.

The correlations between the IQ's of siblings in our own populations range from .118 to .350. How do these *r*'s compare with those we have reported for the resemblance of siblings in deception? To facilitate the comparison, we have extracted from Table XXX the *r*'s obtained on populations of widest and narrowest social range and placed them alongside the corresponding intelligence *r*'s in Table XXXIV. Both sets of *r*'s have also been corrected for chance errors.

If we now compare the corrected *r*'s for intelligence and deception, we can see at once that the correlation between siblings in deception is in each case except the first larger than the correlation between the same siblings in intelligence. Indeed, referring once more to Table XXXIII, the deception *r*'s, even when freed from the factor of intelligence, are still comparable to the intelli-

---

* It is of some importance that liars have been found to be " more suggestible, more imaginative, less steady in motor control involving an emotional disturbance." See the study in untruthfulness by Slaght, *University of Iowa Studies in Character Education*, No. 4, referred to by E. D. Starbuck, *Religious Education*, January, 1927.

† Hildreth, G. H., " The Resemblance of Siblings in Intelligence and Achievement," *Teachers College Contributions to Education*, No. 186, 1925.

TABLE XXXIV

COEFFICIENTS OF CORRELATION BETWEEN SIBLINGS IN DECEPTION
AND INTELLIGENCE, CORRECTED FOR ATTENUATION

| POPULATION | DECEPTION | | | INTELLIGENCE | |
|---|---|---|---|---|---|
| | Behavior | Raw $r$ | Corrected $r$ | Raw $r$ | Corrected $r$ |
| A, L, M, F to J<br>A, B<br>L, M, F to J, E | Speed<br>IER school<br>Coördination | .225<br>.440<br>.400 | .256<br>.510<br>.470 | .289<br>.350<br>.289 | .305<br>.369<br>.305 |
| Theoretical | All tests | .470 | .495 | | |
| Orphans D<br>Orphans K<br>Orphans D | Speed<br>IER school<br>Coördination | .300<br>.333<br>.300 | .341<br>.387<br>.353 | .118<br>.221<br>.118 | .125<br>.231<br>.125 |
| Theoretical | All tests | .370 | .390 | | |

gence $r$'s. Furthermore (comparing the top and bottom halves
of Table XXXIV), when the home background is restricted, as it
is in the case of the orphans, the deception $r$'s do not shrink any
more than do those for intelligence. These facts may be interpreted as meaning that the tendency to deceive is conditioned
by nature and nurture in about the same proportion as is general
intelligence.

## SUMMARY

Seven hundred thirty-four pairs of siblings scattered among
seven school populations were measured with four different types
of deception tests. The general socio-economic level of the homes
was measured in two populations by a scale made for this purpose
and by the careful estimates of a trained school visitor in one population. Two populations were orphans from one of the communities already measured. The range for the other two populations
was estimated.

These siblings were found to resemble one another in deception
whether the opportunity to cheat was offered at home or at school.

The resemblance in deception on the test taken at home was shown to be due chiefly to collusion. To account for the resemblance in deception on tests taken in school, when collusion was impossible, three theories were proposed, *viz.*, (1) the influence of environment, through which siblings develop the same standards and habits of school behavior; (2) resemblance in intelligence; and (3) the presence of a common hereditary factor or group of factors in children of the same parents showing itself in similar deceptive behavior. These theories are not mutually contradictory.

The data assembled show clearly that the coarser differences among homes in socio-economic status, although associated somewhat with differences in deception, do not fully account for likenesses between siblings. So far as the home training is responsible for the resemblances observed, it must be due to subtle factors not incorporated in our measures of cultural level. Furthermore, since orphan siblings show resemblances which cannot be attributed to present home background, what home influence, if any, is at work in their case must have been exercised in very early childhood.

Resemblance in intelligence is equally inadequate as an explanation of the correlation of siblings in deceptiveness.

A biological factor is thus suggested as a possibility which is made the more plausible in view of the fact that the resemblance of siblings in deception is about the same as their resemblance in intelligence, and shows as much stability amid home backgrounds of varying range as does resemblance in intelligence. Whatever arguments are adduced for or against the biological causation of sibling resemblance in intelligence are applicable also to the interpretation of sibling resemblance in deception.

# CHAPTER XI

## RACE, NATIONALITY, AND RELIGION IN RELATION TO DECEPTION

The cultural factors we have so far discussed have centered chiefly in the economic status, conditions of living, and cultural history of the home. Any causal association between these factors and the deceptiveness of children is presumably mediated by the members of the family. Whatever cultural influences may be tied up with the father's occupation, however, are in part at least an exception to this rule. There are, of course, economic limitations, and consequent cultural limitations, which are inevitable accompaniments of certain types of occupation; and to the extent that such factors are associated with the tendency to deceive, the children of fathers belonging to one level of occupation will resemble one another more than they resemble those whose fathers are differently situated. But in addition to these influences, which, though common, are nevertheless mediated by the parents, there are the traditions, codes, social contacts and outlook, standards of dress and of success, and general access to the community as a whole which are the direct consequence of being the son of a plumber rather than the son of a street cleaner, of a college professor rather than of a truck driver. Occupation impinges on the child, creating his attitudes and tastes and ideals not only by what the father says about it but, and perhaps chiefly, by what the father's friends of the same occupation say about it, what the neighbors who belong to the same general occupational level say about it, what the teacher, the employer or employee, the storekeeper, the bank teller, the newspaper, the motion pictures say about it, all of which come into direct touch with the children. It is not surprising that the children of one level of occupation are somewhat alike in their behavior.

In a similar way, the cultural influences associated with nationality, race, and religion operate directly upon the child as well as through the medium of the family. A homogeneous social milieu characteristic of some European country is transplanted along with the families who emigrate and establish communities elsewhere. The church, club, newspaper, books, neighborly gossip, and association of children all tend to keep alive the old codes and attitudes, and the new ways of meeting the strange social problems of the new country naturally grow up as community modes of adjustment. It is to be expected, therefore, that even over a wide range of social or occupational level the families of one race or nationality or religion would in certain modes of behavior resemble one another more than they resemble the families of other cultural groups.

In addition to the common cultural heritage of the homogeneous group, there is of course the possibility of biological differences which might be of such a nature as to influence either the strength of the tendency to deceive others or to inhibit the tendency once aroused. To separate such factors from the social experiences associated with the contact of one race, culture, or religion with another is not possible with the data available. Only three, or at most four, distinct racial groups are represented, and these are by no means unmixed, viz., a Nordic group, two Mediterranean groups, and a group of Negroes. In the case of the latter the fact of race is intermingled with a history of social oppression; with the Nordic groups, with a history of relative independence and freedom; with one Mediterranean group there is associated a long history of illiteracy and superstition; and with the other an equally long story of oppression and cultural pride. Nevertheless, certain differences are found which cannot be attributed to chance, whatever may be the real cause; and these we shall now report, dealing first with race and nationality and second with religion.

## RACE, NATIONALITY, AND DECEPTION

For a comparison of races and nationalities with respect to deceptiveness we have available the records of two populations, A, a suburban community of wide social range, and C, a city school in a relatively favored section. These groups had been given the IER school and home tests, which, as the reader will recall, furnish us with an excellent measure of intelligence as well as of deception.

It is the custom in many towns for the members of one racial group to form an almost segregated community, the members of which are all on about the same socio-economic level and are rather homogeneous with respect to intelligence and culture. In view of the fact, already discussed in detail, that both intelligence and cultural level are associated with degrees of honesty, it is apparent that no comparisons can give a correct picture of the relation between race or nationality and deceit unless they are based on truly representative groups or on groups from the same general level of intelligence and culture. If, for example, we compare the median deception scores of children of German parentage with the deception scores of a group of Italian parentage and find that the German group is far less deceptive than the Italian, this does not mean at all that the Italian nation is less honest than the German nation. A little investigation is likely to uncover the fact that in such an instance as we have used for illustration the Italians are all day laborers from the lower Italian classes with a low mean intelligence, whereas the Germans are well-to-do, middle-class people of relatively high intelligence.. Under such circumstances we could not expect any other results than those just hypothesized, and the evidence is by no means to be understood as indicating the true state of affairs in Italy and Germany.

Unfortunately, we are exactly in this position with much of our data on account of the fact that in population A the Italians, Negroes, Jews, and Slavs are in one section of the community, are selected from lower intelligence levels, and except for the Jews are largely in the fourth occupational group. This difficulty is somewhat corrected at school C, where all groups but the British move up in general intelligence and almost all move up in occupational level. We shall present first the facts concerning occupation and intelligence and then the facts relating to deception.

The occupational differences are shown in Table XXXV. The way in which national groups have been combined is of course debatable, but we intend no hard and fast classifications. The figures of the table are percentages of the total representation of each racial or national group, and the occupational score, given in the last column, is simply a rough summary of these percentages in terms of a score on an imaginary scale of 100. Thus the fathers of 72% of the Scandinavian group in population A, of whom there were 28 in all, were in small business or followed a trade, whereas in population C 94% (all but one of the 16) were on this occupational level. The Jews are the only group to show a radical change in status, rising from a score of 60 to one of 90.

TABLE XXXV

Occupational Status of Racial and National Groups in Populations A and C

| RACE OR NATIONALITY | NUMBER | | BIG BUSINESS, PROFESSIONAL | | SMALL BUSINESS, TRADES | | UNSKILLED LABOR | | OCCUPATIONAL SCORE | |
|---|---|---|---|---|---|---|---|---|---|---|
| | A | C | A* | C* | A* | C* | A* | C* | A | C |
| American | 228 | 121 | 30% | 40% | 63% | 59% | 7% | 1% | 70 | 80 |
| German | 51 | 63 | 12 | 29 | 74 | 68 | 14 | 3 | 60 | 70 |
| British | 47 | 50 | 11 | 16 | 72 | 74 | 17 | 10 | 60 | 60 |
| Jewish | 63 | 154 | 5 | 51 | 86 | 49 | 9 | 0 | 60 | 90 |
| Scandinavian | 28 | 16 | 3 | 6 | 72 | 94 | 25 | 0 | 50 | 60 |
| Italian | 90 | 16 | 1 | 0 | 53 | 75 | 46 | 25 | 30 | 40 |
| Negro | 109 | | 3 | | 44 | | 53 | | 20 | |
| French | | 12 | | 42 | | 58 | | 0 | | 80 |

* The figures are percentages of the total racial or national group falling at each occupational level.

The CAVI intelligence scores, which are given in Table XXXVI, show that most of the city groups have higher scores than the suburban groups, and that the most conspicuous differences are

TABLE XXXVI

Median CAVI Intelligence Scores of Racial and National Groups, Populations A and C

| RACE OR NATIONALITY | SCHOOL A | | SCHOOL C | |
|---|---|---|---|---|
| | N | CAVI | N | CAVI |
| American . . . . . . . . . | 250 | 105 | 113 | 105 |
| British . . . . . . . . . . | 49 | 104 | 51 | 99 |
| French . . . . . . . . . . | 10 | 102 | 12 | 115 |
| German and Austrian . . . . | 52 | 102 | 67 | 106 |
| Scandinavian . . . . . . . | 28 | 101 | 16 | 105 |
| Slavic . . . . . . . . . | 31 | 94 | | |
| Jewish . . . . . . . . . | 63 | 91 | 183 | 107 |
| Negro . . . . . . . . . . | 100 | 86 | | |
| Italian . . . . . . . . . | 79 | 84 | 18 | 93 |

found among the Jews and the small group of French. For the Jews, this change corresponds to the difference in occupational status.

The extent to which intelligence is likely to account for differences among racial and national groups is suggested by the correlation of −.72 between the median deception scores of eight of the groups of Table XXXV and their mean intelligence scores, showing definitely that the more honest groups are at the same time the more intelligent. We can make due allowance for such differences in intelligence by using the method by which we equalized occupational groups in Chapter IX. All that is required is that we first find the median intelligence score of each group and then find the median deception score of *all cases* having an intelligence score equal to this median of the racial or national group. Thus, for the American group of population A, we find a median Xi score of −1.9 and a median CAVI score of 105. We then examine the scattergram on which we have correlated the CAVI scores of population A with the Xi scores and find the Xi scores of those whose CAVI score is 105 or a little more or a little less. We find that the median Xi score of those whose CAVI scores are about 105 is −1.9. Hence we might

properly predict that any group having a median CAVI score of
105 in this population would, if other things were equal, have a
median Xi score of about −1.9.   The American group, whose
median CAVI score is 105, has a median Xi score of −1.9, which is
the same as would be expected from their intelligence median.
Similarly for the other groups we can figure how much more
or less honest they are than might be expected from their median intelligence.   Thus the factor of intelligence is in a sense equalized, and any difference above or below the expected Xi score
needs to be accounted for by reference to some other factor than
intelligence.*

Figure 46 sums up these comparative facts for our two populations, giving the amount in which each racial or national group
either exceeds or falls short of the deception score that might
have been expected from an unselected group having its median
intelligence.

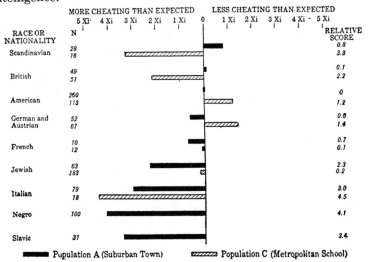

FIGURE  46

COMPARISON OF NATIONALITIES AND RACES IN RESPECT TO
INTELLIGENCE AND IER SCHOOL Xi

* Complete data appear in Book Two, Chapter IX, Table CXXVIII.

It is interesting to note the marked difference in the relative deceptiveness of the suburban and city groups which are of Scandinavian or British origin. In community A each of these national types cheats somewhat less than might be expected from its intelligence level, but in the city community each of them cheats far more than might be expected.

Other comparisons may be discovered by studying the occupational scores of Table XXXV. We note, for example, that the three groups showing the largest relative deceptiveness in population C, *viz.*, the British, Scandinavian, and Italian, are also most largely represented among the lower occupational levels at this school. The same is true of the Negroes and Italians of population A. One might conclude forthwith that these national and racial differences were simply a matter of cultural level, and that groups having the same intelligence and social status would exhibit about the same tendency to deceive in school, no matter what their race or national background — and this is no doubt largely true. But in two instances the facts in the case of school cheating do not bear out this generalization. The Jews, who have the highest occupational score in population C and higher than the average in population A, nevertheless appear more deceptive than one would expect from their level of intelligence. We saw in Chapter IX that in general the high socio-economic status goes with less tendency to cheat in school. The other instance is the Scandinavians in population A, who come from lower occupational groups than the Americans, Germans, British, or Jews, yet who cheat in that community far less than might be expected from their intelligence. In the case of these two groups in these particular communities it is evident that something in addition to either intelligence or general cultural level is influencing the children's conduct on the school tests.

Since Figure 46 contains facts drawn from only one type of deceptive behavior, it is important to present what data we have on a wider selection of tests. Part of the school-C population had from nine to fourteen classroom cheating tests, three party tests, four athletic contest tests, and a stealing test. We have computed the medians of the per cents which each child cheated in his total opportunities. These for the different nationalities are as follows : The Americans cheated on the average once in every three opportunities ; the British once in every three ; the Jewish once in every four ; the other nationalities once in about every three. Thus when all classroom cheating tests are combined, the Jewish children tend to cheat less than any other race. But at school C the median score of these same children on the Sims home background test is 14.0, whereas the score for the Americans is 12.00 and for the other races somewhat less.

Another bit of evidence showing that apparent race differences may be chiefly matters of socio-economic level, intelligence, etc., is the fact that the children of school D, with an average IQ of 96 and all coming from broken homes, cheat once in every two opportunities. These children are all Jewish. Thus on the Jewish race alone we have these facts : from school D, low IQ, broken homes, cheating once in every two times ; from school C, high IQ, good homes (four points above the Sims mean), cheating once in every four times ; from school P, still higher IQ, still better homes, cheating once in every five opportunities. It may be of some interest to know that in the case of ten boys who took money on the money tests at school C, two were Italian, two Greek, two German, two English, one American, and one Jewish.

With these somewhat indeterminate conclusions before us, let us turn now to the relation of religious differences to the tendency to deceive and see whether we may fare any better.

## RELIGIOUS AFFILIATION AND DECEPTION

One question on the Pupil Data Sheet reads, " What do you do on Sundays? " When this questionnaire was administered in schools A and B, the examiners requested the pupils who attended church or Sunday school to put down the name of the denomination or the name of the particular church. In this way we secured information concerning religious affiliations ; this was supplemented in population A by facts secured through the school system. What we have to say concerning the relation between religion and deception refers, therefore, only to these two communities, one of which, A, it will be remembered, is a small suburb, and the other, B, a mid-western city of some 200,000.   The tests on the basis of which comparison is made are the IER school tests.

Figure 47 is made in exactly the same way as was Figure 46 in the section on race and nationality.   There are in some cases wide differences between the denominations with respect to intelligence as well as social level, and it is necessary to equalize the intelligence factor as far as possible.   We have done this by predicting the median school Xi to be expected from groups having the median intelligence scores of the several religious groups.   The difference between this predicted Xi score and the median Xi score actually found is a measure of deceptiveness which is independent of the factor of intelligence.   Let us turn, then, to Figure 47.

The figures inserted after the names of the denominations are in this case not the number of children but their median CAVI intelligence score.   There is considerable difference between the two communities in general intelligence, but this is due chiefly to the fact that grades nine and ten are included in the scores of population B, but population A goes only through the eighth grade.

These differences between groups are allowed for in the chart, which shows the relation of the amount of cheating actually found to what might be expected from a group of unselected children all having an intelligence score equal to the median of the religious group.   The somewhat conspicuous groups are the Baptist, Episcopalian, Jewish, Methodist, and Roman Catholic.   Of these only the Baptists show more cheating than might be expected from their intelligence in *both* communities, and we know that in population A this is without doubt largely, if not wholly, a matter of social selection.*   We are unable, however, to account for the situation of the Baptists in population B, for there is not the same factor of social and racial selection at work there as in A.   The Jews, of course, are

* In A the Baptists all belong to one church, which ministers to a single racial group found almost exclusively in the congested quarter of the town and mostly attending one school.

the same group as has already been discussed in the section on race and nationality and offer no new problems here.

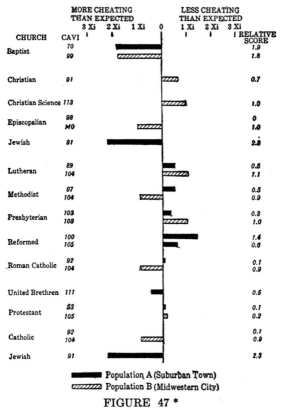

FIGURE 47 *

COMPARISON OF DENOMINATIONS WITH RESPECT TO INTELLIGENCE
AND IER SCHOOL Xi

## SUMMARY

Complete tables supporting the charts of this chapter will be found in Book Two, Chapter IX, and should be referred to for critical study.    The facts reported indicate that the differences among

* For actual figures, see Book Two, Chapter IX.

racial, national, and religious groups with regard to deceptive behavior in the classroom are not wholly accounted for by differences between these groups in either intelligence or general social status   We have no means of knowing whether the differences remaining after allowance has been made for intelligence and home background are attributable to biological differences or cultural differences of the sort mentioned at the beginning of the chapter, but we are inclined to believe that the essential factor is the interaction of fairly homogeneous social groups with the community in which they are gradually gaining a foothold — an interaction which is often colored by excessive ambition on the one side and by exclusiveness or oppression on the other.   Nor should one fail to consider the possibility of different ethical standards, particularly when the national and religious groupings are identical and thus reinforce one another.

## CHAPTER XII

## SCHOOL STATUS AND SCHOOL HONOR

It would be natural to presume that a child's status in the school system would have some relation to the development or loss of classroom honor. If his marks are low, does this influence him to take unfair advantage of an opportunity to raise them? If he has fallen behind in the race and is much older than his fellow pupils or if he is much duller than they or is younger and brighter, does such a displacement in grade increase the tendency to deceive? Are the children who are so well adjusted to what their teachers expect of them as to receive high marks in deportment also consistently honest in their dealings with the school authorities, or is their good behavior only a cloak for surreptitious forays on the teacher's credulity or good opinion? Do children get more honest or more dishonest as they advance from grade to grade? Our discussion of these questions is far less complete than their importance demands, but such data as we have will be of interest to those who are concerned with the relation of the schools to character and will open the way to our discussion in Part III of the relation between honor and morale, progressive methods, teacher influence, and definite efforts to teach honesty.

## SCHOOL GRADE AND DECEPTION

From our study of the relation of chronological age to deception it may properly be inferred that as pupils advance from grade to grade they do not, on the whole, show any corresponding change in their tendency to deceive. Since children of many ages, however, are to be found in any school grade and as they progress at different rates, it seemed wise to consider the problem of grade

257

independently. As our records cover only grades five to eight (in some cases reaching down to four and in some cases going as far as twelve), we are not in a position to say whether cheating begins to show itself in the kindergarten or in grade one, two, or three. Judging from what little work we have done in grade three, there is a process of experimentation going on there, similar to that of the still younger child in the home, in which the teacher and pupil are, so to speak, maneuvering for position and trying one another out. Practices which later come to be clearly defined as deceptive are appearing, partly because of misunderstanding of the teacher's directions and partly in a kind of struggle for existence; but it is probable that in most cases these acts, which seem to adults to be unfair, are not at first regarded in that light by the pupils but are rather taken for granted without moral reflection. There are some children, of course, who never cheat, either because it does not occur to them to do so or because the acts involved are distasteful to them for some reason, such as the fact that they are disapproved by their teacher or parents or because they are recognized by the children as unfair. On the other hand, there seem to be children who cheat whenever circumstances make it convenient, without giving the matter a second thought.

Whatever may be the origin of the behavior in any given case, by grade five the practice seems to be fairly well established and does not change materially through grade eight or, so far as our data go, through grade twelve. In Chapter VIII of Book Two will be found a complete table of correlation coefficients between grade and cheating for all kinds of deception tested and for all populations. These average approximately zero, ranging from $-.360$ to $+.272$. The larger $r$'s are gathered in Table XXXVII.*

The amount of these differences may be more graphically shown in Figure 48, which gives the median Xi's of successive grades in the case of the IER school test for populations A and P.

The contrast between the two populations is quite evident. In population A all the tests show a negative $r$ with grade, indicating that the higher-grade children are more honest than the lower.

* Descriptions of populations may be found in Chapter IV.

TABLE XXXVII

CORRELATIONS BETWEEN GRADE AND DECEPTION

| TEST | A | D | F TO J | K | P | S | R |
|---|---|---|---|---|---|---|---|
| IER school | − .329 | | | − .263 | + .272 | + .230 | |
| IER home | − .228 | | + .243 | | | | |
| Speed | − .338 | − .360 | + .239 | | | | |
| Puzzle | | + .256 | | | | | + .212 |
| Lying | − .310 | | | | | | |

But in this system, it will be recalled, we have a wide range of
social level, with the lower social and intelligence groups concen-
trated in a single elementary school.   Consequently, the lower

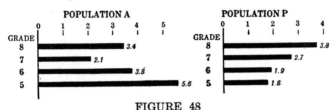

FIGURE 48

SCHOOL DIFFERENCES IN RELATION OF GRADE TO DECEPTION,
IER SCHOOL Xi

grades are overweighted with a selected population which has
larger cheating scores, grade for grade, than the rest of the system.
In P, on the other hand, although the Speed tests show no grade
differences (and are there-
fore not reported in Table
XXXVII), the IER test
scores get larger as we go
from the fifth to the eighth
grade.

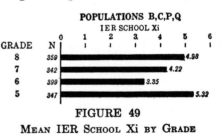

FIGURE 49

MEAN IER SCHOOL Xi BY GRADE

    Figures 49 and 50 depict
the grade norms on the
IER school tests and the
Speed tests for several populations.   The Speed test means rise

consistently and are accounted for, as previously explained, by a corresponding rise in the *ability* to cheat. But the IER tests show

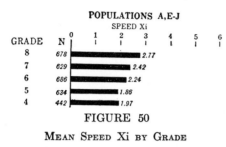

POPULATIONS A,E-J

FIGURE 50

MEAN SPEED Xi BY GRADE

genuine grade differences. Grade five is the most deceptive, but grade six is the least deceptive, and from these through grade eight there is a steady increase. There is only one chance in ten that these grade differences are accidental, and the difference between grade five and the other grades is far beyond the limits of chance.

We can only conclude that, with respect to some forms of deception, the school system as a whole does not produce any changes in the tendency to deceive, but that on other forms, particularly in the case of the IER school tests, schools such as B, C, P, and Q show a strong tendency for deception to increase above the fifth grade, with the fifth grade appearing more deceptive than the rest in some cases and about the same as the sixth in others.*

## RETARDATION AND DECEPTION

We have already called to mind the well-known fact that in any one grade there are children of widely different ages. The fifth-grade ages will range from eight to thirteen, the sixth grade from nine to fourteen, and so on. In some schools the range is wider and in others it is narrower. Theoretically the age for entering grade one is six, grade two seven, and so on up; but of course all children who enter grade one are not exactly six years old, and

* The influence of schooling as a whole should not be confused with the influence of a single school, as our transient populations move so frequently that in many schools there is a large turnover of pupils from year to year and hence less opportunity to influence any of them for good or for evil than if the children remained for many years in one place. This matter is taken up in Chapter XV, where we report that length of attendance at any one school is, so far as our data show, almost entirely unrelated to the tendency to deceive.

there are, furthermore, many delays in the general movement upward.  Consequently the actual norm is much higher than the theoretical norm.  McCall estimates the mean age of fifth-, sixth-, seventh-, and eighth-grade children to be, in the month of May,

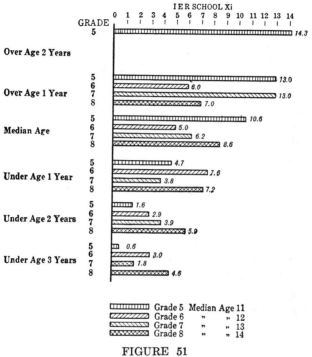

FIGURE  51

IER School Xi and Retardation, Population C

$r_{ac.g} = + .355$

respectively, 11 years and 9 months, 12 and 10, 13 and 11, and 15 years.*  Our own medians run about three months lower in general, so that we take the period from 11 years to 11 years and 11 months as normal for grade five.  If a child is in this year in the

* McCall, W. A., *How to Measure in Education*, p. 34, The Macmillan Company, 1922.

sixth grade, he is one year advanced or accelerated; but if he is anywhere from 11 years to 11 years and 11 months old when in grade four, he is one year retarded.

Child-guidance clinics frequently report poor grading, that is, acceleration or retardation, as a factor in the promotion of delin-

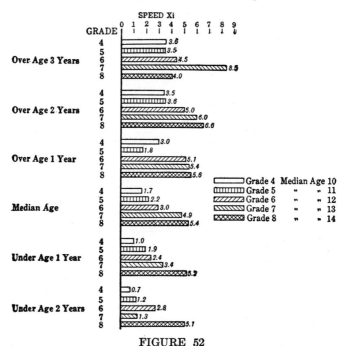

FIGURE 52

SPEED Xi AND RETARDATION, POPULATION F TO J

$$r_{ac.g} = + .328$$

quency. Is it also a factor in deceit? Before presenting the facts, let us keep in mind that the older children are, in any grade, those who have been kept back, and that the usual cause of retardation is incapacity or relatively less intelligence than the rest of the group of the same age. In view of the fact that the less intelligent tend to be the less honest, we might expect, therefore, that the over-age, who are also the less intelligent, would be in general less honest. We have determined the median deception scores in each type of test for each age level of each grade and each population and find results of which Figures 51, 52, 53, and 54 are typical illustrations. In each case the length of the band represents the

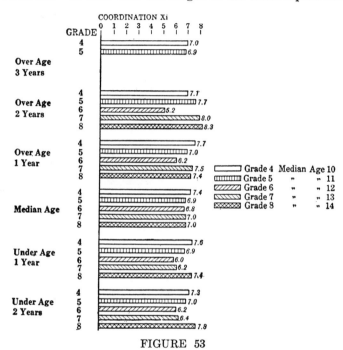

FIGURE 53

COÖRDINATION Xi AND RETARDATION, POPULATION F TO J

$r_{ac.g} = +.160$

median amount of cheating. The IER school and home tests and the Speed and Coördination tests are represented.

From these figures, which, as has been said, are typical of what is generally found, it may be seen that there is a tendency for the older pupils of each grade to cheat more on the IER school tests and Speed tests, but not on the Coördination and IER home tests.

In other words, if we take one grade at a time instead of putting all grades together as we did in our discussion of age and deception, we find that there is a positive correlation between age and deception in two types of test and a zero or sometimes even negative correlation in the other two. A more condensed way of express-

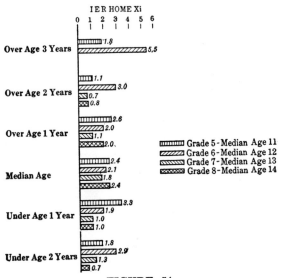

FIGURE 54

IER HOME Xi AND RETARDATION, POPULATION A

$$r_{ac.g} = -.111$$

ing this relation is the partial correlation coefficient between age and deception with grade kept constant ($r_{ca.g}$) — a figure which gives us approximately the *average* of all the *r*'s we would get if we correlated age and deception for each grade *separately*. This shows the effect of age within each grade. These partials are printed at the foot of each table.

## THE RELATION OF DECEPTION TO CLASSROOM DISPLACEMENT IN AGE AND INTELLIGENCE

The displacements with which we have been dealing so far in the discussion have been from the mean age of a large number of children in a great variety of classrooms, some of which were as a whole over-age and some of which were as a whole under-age. Consequently an individual child might deviate two years or more from the theoretical age norm for his grade and still be approximately at the age norm for his own classroom. As a matter of fact, in working out the deviations of over twelve hundred children from their own classroom norms in populations B and C we found only one child that deviated by more than a year from the median year of his own group. Such relatively small deviations could hardly be expected to affect the behavior of the over-age or under-age in comparison with their own groups as much as the far larger deviations from the general age norms which we have been discussing.

Dealing in months rather than years (since the deviations were small), we figured each child's deviation from the median age of his own class and then made a table for each room showing the number of those who did not cheat at all who fell in the median month, the number who were one month older than the median, the number two months older than the median, etc.; and then of those who cheated once we found the number whose age fell in the median month, in the next month, etc., working in both directions from the median. We did this for each room and then combined the results in one table for population B and another table for C. It is hardly worth while to print the tables, as no consistent relations between age displacement were discovered except that there was a noticeable tendency for a few individuals who were at either the over-age or under-age extreme to fall in the cheating rather than the non-cheating group. The facts are briefly summarized in Table XXXVIII.

Table XXXVIII reads as follows : 39% of those who were below the median age of their own classroom cheated on the school test and 61% did not. But approximately the same proportion, *viz.*,

TABLE XXXVIII

AGE DISPLACEMENT AND DECEPTION, SHOWING PER CENT CHEATING AND PER CENT NOT CHEATING AT SCHOOL AND AT SCHOOL AND HOME

| | School B | | | | School C | | | |
|---|---|---|---|---|---|---|---|---|
| | School | | School and Home | | School | | School and Home | |
| | C | H | C | H | C | H | C | H |
| Per cent below median | 39 | 61 | 62 | 38 | 60 | 40 | 76 | 24 |
| Per cent above median | 40 | 60 | 59 | 41 | 60 | 40 | 73 | 27 |

40% of those who were above their class median in age cheated on this test. In neither school does this coarse comparison show any general relation between cheating and over-age or under-age so far as the classroom is concerned. As the pupils are usually classified according to intelligence, the implication is that it is not just being over-age for one's grade that matters so much as being both older and duller and therefore with an older and duller group.

When we handle the deviations from the class median in CAVI score, we find that the facts correspond to those we have already reported for grade displacement. In Table XXXIX we have given the percentage cheating at each level of deviation.

From Table XXXIX one may read that in school B out of 110 children who deviated from 20 to 30 points on the CAVI test below the median score of their classroom, 52% cheated in school and 69% in either the school or home test, and so on. If the reader will run his eye up the columns of percentages, he will observe a tendency for the figures to increase as the eye ascends the columns. Since the intelligence deviations above the middle line are deviations in the direction of lower scores or lower intelligence, it can be seen that when one classroom at a time is considered there is in these two populations a *negative* correlation with CAVI score — the children whose mental ages are above the average for the class in which they do their work tend to cheat a little less frequently than those whose mental ages are lower than the average for their group.

TABLE XXXIX

INTELLIGENCE DISPLACEMENT AND DECEPTION, SHOWING PER CENT CHEAT-
ING ON THE SCHOOL TESTS AND ON SCHOOL AND HOME TESTS COMBINED

| | CAVI Deviations | SCHOOL B | | | SCHOOL C | | |
| | | School | | School and Home | School | | School and Home |
| | | N | Per Cent | Per Cent | N | Per Cent | Per Cent |
|---|---|---|---|---|---|---|---|
| Lower scores | 60 | 1 | 0 | 100 | | | |
| | 50 | 2 | 50 | 100 | | | |
| | 40 | 16 | 50 | 75 | 1 | 100 | 100 |
| | 30 | 49 | 67 | 80 }66% | 16 | 94 | 94 }79% |
| | 20 | 110 | 52 | 69 | 75 | 60 | 79 |
| | 10 | 144 | 51 | 74 | 110 | 66 | 79 |
| | 0 | 197 | 36 | 57 | 132 | 63 | 80 |
| Higher scores | 10 | 134 | 36 | 56 | 96 | 53 | 69 |
| | 20 | 75 | 25 | 45 | 57 | 54 | 70 |
| | 30 | 50 | 30 | 48 }54% | 30 | 50 | 63 }69% |
| | 40 | 21 | 24 | 43 | 10 | 30 | 40 |
| | 50 | 16 | 31 | 50 | 10 | 40 | 40 |
| | 60 | 6 | 33 | 33 | 1 | 0 | 0 |
| | 70 | 1 | 0 | 0 | | | |

As the two schools B and C are quite similar in the way displacement affects cheating, we may combine them in Table XL, which
shows the same facts in a somewhat different form. In this table
we give the per cent of all the honest children who are above the
median age and median intelligence score and the per cent who are
below in each case. We also show the average deviation of both
honest and dishonest cases above and below the median, and the
standard deviation, which of course includes variation in both
directions from the mean.

The standard deviations show the variability around the mean.
The dishonest children are more variable in age — that is, are less
well graded as to age — than the honest, but the honest children
show the greater variability in intelligence. This variability of
the honest children, however, is *less* than that of the dishonest

children *below* the median and greater only above it. Furthermore, the median intelligence of the honest is above that of the dishonest (43% of them lying below the median for their class as compared with 58% of the dishonest for the school test). Thus, when we compare the children class by class we still find that the cheaters tend to be a little older and duller than the non-cheaters.

TABLE XL

DISPLACEMENT IN AGE AND INTELLIGENCE IN RELATION TO DECEPTION — IER TESTS, SCHOOL AND HOME

| | CHRONOLOGICAL AGE | | | | | CAVI INTELLIGENCE | | | | |
| | Below Median | | Above Median | | SD* | Below Median | | Above Median | | SD |
| | Per Cent | AD* | Per Cent | AD* | | Per Cent | AD | Per Cent | AD | |
|---|---|---|---|---|---|---|---|---|---|---|
| **School** | | | | | | | | | | |
| Honest | 50 | 69 | 50 | 83 | 108 | 43 | 13.4 | 57 | 17.7 | 19.6 |
| Dishonest | 49 | 71 | 51 | 100 | 113 | 58 | 17.6 | 42 | 15.1 | 18.1 |
| **Home** | | | | | | | | | | |
| Honest | 46 | 67 | 54 | 99 | 113 | 47 | 13.3 | 53 | 17.6 | 19.3 |
| Dishonest | 55 | 74 | 45 | 89 | 126 | 56 | 15.6 | 44 | 14.8 | 18.3 |
| **Total** | | | | | | | | | | |
| Honest | 47 | 67 | 53 | 94 | 107 | 40 | 13.0 | 60 | 19.0 | 20.6 |
| Dishonest | 50 | 72 | 50 | 97 | 111 | 56 | 14.7 | 44 | 15.1 | 18.0 |

* The average and standard age deviations are expressed in days.

## ATTENDANCE AND DECEPTION

Under compulsory school laws one might not expect to find much, if any, relation between attendance and cheating except possibly in the case of truants, who might be deceptive because of other environmental influences. Nevertheless we tabulated the data from school C, finding the correlation between percentage of attendance for a half year and cheating to be zero. We also found the percentage of attendance of those who did not cheat at all and of those who cheated once, twice, three times, and four times on the IER school and home tests. These percentages are shown in Table XLI.

TABLE XLI

PERCENTAGE OF ATTENDANCE AND INSTANCES OF CHEATING, POPULATION C

| | CHEATING INSTANCES | | | | |
|---|---|---|---|---|---|
| | 0 | 1 | 2 | 3 | 4 |
| Percentage of attendance | 87 | 86 | 85 | 89 | 90 |
| Number of cases  .  .  . | 118 | 195 | 110 | 48 | 13 |

## SCHOOL ACHIEVEMENT AND DECEPTION

A child's status in school is a matter not only of grading and promotion but also of class standing and school marks. So far as our testing has gone, we have found evidence of a rather general school " drive " or eagerness to do well or at least to appear well in school work. We recognize of course that this drive varies greatly among schools and among pupils in the same school. Indeed, instances have been reported of boys being hazed for getting marks higher than they needed for passing. In many schools, however, there is not only keen competition among the pupils for academic recognition but also considerable pressure at home to maintain high marks.

Differences in incentive to do good work would, if other things were equal, constitute differences in incentive to cheat in order to secure higher grades. It is just here, however, that we might expect to find family differences or group differences, higher ambition being sometimes associated with higher standards of conduct and in other cases being dissociated from ethical considerations.

Furthermore, even when a strong school drive is operative it does not necessarily achieve its goal in high marks. While there is doubtless a positive correlation between drive and school achievement — possibly a higher correlation than between intelligence, apart from drive, and achievement — this association is not perfect by any means, and many a child who works hard is nevertheless disappointed in the results.   Again, we might expect this child to be more susceptible to opportunities to deceive than his more successful classmates.

In view of the existence of so many rather conflicting factors leading to school achievement, we might anticipate a low correlation between marks and deception, and this is just what we find. In two schools we have only the teachers' marks as evidence of achievement.   In one of these schools we have separated the scholastic from the non-scholastic grades, meaning by the latter music, drawing, and the manual arts.   In a third school we have achievement quotients and educational quotients based on standard school tests.   Since no relation between school achievement and deception is found, we will confine our report at this point to a table of correlation coefficients.

## TABLE XLII

### Correlation of Deception and School Achievement

|  | Population | | |
|---|---|---|---|
|  | A | B | C |
| Scholastic average and IER school Xi   .   .   . | − .200 | − .155 |  |
| Scholastic average and IER home Xi .   .   .   . | − .020 | + .180 |  |
| Non-scholastic average and school Xi   .   .   . |  | − .153 |  |
| Non-scholastic average and home Xi .   .   .   . |  | + .270 |  |
| AQ and school Xi   .   .   .   .   .   .   .   .   . |  |  | − .030 |
| AQ and home Xi   .   .   .   .   .   .   .   .   . |  |  | − .090 |
| AQ and CT ratio   .   .   .   .   .   .   .   .   . |  |  | + .004 |
| EQ and CT ratio   .   .   .   .   .   .   .   .   . |  |  | − .095 |

The achievement quotient is the ratio of educational age to mental age, and the educational quotient is the ratio of educational age to chronological age.   But no matter how measured, whether by teachers' rather subjective ratings or by standardized school tests, the $r$'s, though mostly negative, are so low that the slight association observed between higher marks and greater honesty might well be accounted for by the fact that those who get the higher marks are usually the more intelligent and, as we have seen, the less deceptive.    Apparently those who get higher marks cheat just about as much as those who get lower marks.    Are we to suppose that those with lower grades who also cheated did so to improve their standing, and that those with higher grades who also cheated did so to maintain it?    If high marks are made as much by those who cheat as by those who do not and if there is a tendency for those with less intelligence both to cheat more and, other things being equal, to get lower marks than those with higher intelligence, it might properly be asked whether the high grades of those who cheat would be secured if they did not cheat in the course of their school work.*

## SCHOOL DEPORTMENT AND DECEPTION

The final factor in school status with which we shall deal is the child's standing in the good opinion of his teachers, which is recorded by some kind of deportment mark.    If we were interested at this moment in validating our tests of deception in terms of their capacity to predict character or even only certain forms of general behavior, teachers' deportment grades would be valuable material for a criterion.    We have not considered our deception tests in this light, however, so that our interest in deportment grades takes another direction.    We are concerned here with the problem of whether such maladjustment between the pupil and the teacher or the school system in general as is reflected in deportment marks

* That correlations reported between intelligence and school marks are not higher than they are may be due partly to the fact that the marks result in part from deception, whereas the scores on an intelligence test may have no deceptive element in them.    Consequently, those whose grades have depended in part on deceit find themselves at a disadvantage when the practice of deception is entirely eliminated, and the two sets of scores, therefore, do not correspond as they theoretically should.

may also be associated with the tendency to get the better of the authorities whenever possible, as, for example, by putting something over on them during a test. Deception under such circumstances becomes a symptom of maladjustment.

We found deportment marks everywhere, but we secured data on three schools only as we found that in some schools the marks were almost all A's and hence quite useless as measures.* In Figure 55 we report the relation of deportment to IER school and home cheating and the Speed tests, in the two schools having usable deportment grades.

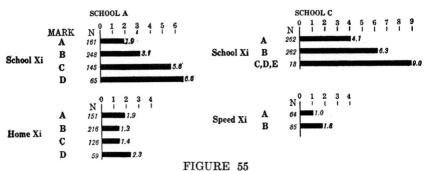

FIGURE 55

DEPORTMENT AND DECEPTION

Before discussing Figure 55 it would be well to supplement it with the correlations of Table XLIII.

TABLE XLIII

CORRELATION OF DEPORTMENT AND DECEPTION

| TEST | SCHOOL A | SCHOOL C |
|---|---|---|
| School Xi . . . . . . . . | − .376 ± .05 | − .287 ± .04 |
| Home Xi . . . . . . . . | − .04 | .00 |
| Arithmetic Xi . . . . . . . | | − .505 ± .05 |
| Speed Xi . . . . . . . . | | − .375 ± .07 |

* In Book Two, Chapter VII, we discuss the teacher's ability to rate accurately such types of behavior as honesty.

The $r$'s of Table XLIII are biserial $r$'s, the populations being divided either between those marked A and B or between those marked A and B on one side and those marked C and D on the other. Although thus subject to considerable error, they indicate, in conjunction with the charts of Figure 55, that there is a definitely negative relation between high deportment marks and deception when the test is a matter of school routine, but that when the cheating takes place outside the school those who get high deportment marks are no less inclined to make surreptitious use of the dictionary than those who are marked low.

As far as the school behavior goes, however, we can be sure that the tests reveal deceptive tendencies which are associated with the type of maladjustment registered in deportment marks. Nor is this association due to intelligence, for the correlation between deportment and intelligence is only $-.183$. Both in the deportment grades and in the deception scores we find evidence of disturbances in the pupil-teacher or pupil-school relation, and these disturbances, when they exist, tend to be in some way associated.

## SUMMARY

From our study of school status we may conclude that there is nothing in the general academic situation of grades four to eight which favors cheating *in general* more than it prevents or overcomes it. On some tests, however, such as the IER material, there is a strong tendency for cheating to become more prevalent in the upper grades. Retardation is associated with more cheating, but this seems to be because retardation is associated with less intelligence. There is no correlation between teachers' marks and the tendency to deceive, which indicates probably that the less intelligent, as a group, make up somewhat for their deficiencies by occasional cheating. Those who receive lower deportment ratings, partly because they tend to be the less intelligent, are more deceptive than those whom the teachers regard as well behaved.

# CHAPTER XIII

## MISCELLANEOUS FACTS ASSOCIATED WITH DECEPTION

Various matters on which we have information but which do not classify in the chapters that have preceded are brought together here to conclude our presentation of factors associated with deceit. These are: association among friends and in the classroom; sociability, as measured by the frequency with which one is named by others as a personal friend or companion; suggestibility, as measured by the Otis * test; and frequency of attendance at motion pictures.

### ASSOCIATION

Birds of a feather flock together. In human affairs, birds that flock together acquire similar plumage. On the Pupil Data Sheets which were used in populations A, B, and C we had the pupils name their best friends and those of their companions whom they liked best. There were few children who did not give at least three names and many gave five or six. In population A, about half of those named (who were in school at all) were in the same classroom and about half in different classrooms. In B almost all those named were in the same classroom. We were able to compare, therefore, the influence of class association with that of out-of-class association. In order that we might also compare the amount of sibling resemblance with resemblance between friends, we used for our comparisons only those who had at least one brother or sister among those we had tested. Taking these for our major cases,

* Otis, M., " A Study of Suggestibility in Children," Columbia University, *Archives of Psychology*, No. 70, 1924.

we correlated with the IER school Xi of each one of them the IER school Xi of each of his friends.    The resulting $r$'s * are given in Table XLIV–A.

### TABLE XLIV — A

RESEMBLANCE OF FRIENDS IN DECEPTION, IER SCHOOL Xi

|  |  | POPULATION A | POPULATION B |
|---|---|---|---|
| One friend with all friends . . . . . | (1) | .486 | .299 |
| One friend with all friends, all cases from one community . . . . . . . . | (2) | .654 | |
| One friend with all friends from his own classmates . . . . . . . . . | (3) | .662 | |
| One friend with all friends not in his class . . . . . . . . . . . | (4) | .225 | |
| One friend with one friend . . . . . | (5) | .418 | .160 |
| One friend with one friend in classroom | (6) | .727 | |
| One friend with one friend not in class-room . . . . . . . . . . . | (7) | .159 | |
| One friend with one classmate not a friend . . . . . . . . . . . | (8) | .598 | |
| One friend with several† classmates not friends . . . . . . . . . . . | (9) | .572 | |

† As many as he had named as friends.

These strong positive correlations show that classmates tend to resemble one another in deception.    A comparison of $r$'s (6) and (7) and (3) and (4) indicates that the significant factor in accounting for the resemblance of friends is classroom association, although there is a slight resemblance of friends who are not in the same room at school.    That this is in part at least due to the resemblance of friends in intelligence is shown by the correlations of Table XLIV–B.

### TABLE XLIV — B

RESEMBLANCE OF FRIENDS IN CAVI SCORE, POPULATION A

| | | |
|---|---|---|
| One friend with all friends . . . . . . . | (10) | + .349 |
| One friend with one friend . . . . . . . | (11) | + .318 |

* Corrected for errors of type 1.    See Book Two, Chapter VI.

A comparison of $r$ (11) with $r$ (5) and of (10) with (1) suggests the extent to which friends resemble one another in classroom deception more than in intelligence. Evidently intelligence plays a considerable part in the resemblance in deception.

Correlations (8) and (9) are interesting in view of the fact that one child is compared with one or more of his classmates not named by him as a friend but chosen at random from his class. These should be compared with $r$'s (3) and (6). This corroborates the statement just made that the mere fact of being in the same classroom is the significant cause of resemblance.

That the association of a child with other children who deceive is a large factor in accounting for his own deceptiveness seems to be clear, but this association apparently operates chiefly in connection with the classroom experience which the friends all share alike rather than in out-of-classroom relations. In Chapter XVII we shall return to this phenomenon of classroom resemblance.

## SOCIABILITY

In filling out the Pupil Data Sheets there were few children who did not name at least three friends or companions and many named five or six. For the purposes of this study we confine ourselves to population A, a suburban town. Although no limitation was placed on the term "friend" or "companion," about

### TABLE XLV

COMPARISON OF SOCIABLE AND UNSOCIABLE GROUPS OF ONE HUNDRED EACH, POPULATION A

|  | INTELLI-GENCE | SCHOOL Xi | | HOME Xi | |
|---|---|---|---|---|---|
|  | Mean | Median | Mean | Median | Mean |
| Sociable group . . . . | 95 | 3.1 | 3.5 | 1.7 | 2.6 |
| Unsociable group . . . | 97 | 3.8 | 3.3 | 1.8 | 2.7 |

three-fourths of the names were those of children in the grades tested. Some of these were mentioned many times by others and about two hundred were not named at all. We were able, therefore, to select two groups of a hundred each, one of which, the " sociable " group, received at least five mentions apiece, and the other of which, the " unsociable " group, received no mention at all. The comparative intelligence and deceptiveness of these two groups is shown in Table XLV.

The two groups are nearly alike; that is, the tendency to deceive has evidently no relation to the faculty of making friends.

## SUGGESTIBILITY

In any activity which takes place in the presence and with the knowledge of others there is always a large factor of suggestion. The individual may be influenced to do as the others do without regard to their opinion, or he may be influenced by their opinion even when their behavior is in doubt. In the case of our deception tests that involve the use of answer sheets, there is the further factor of the suggestive presence of the key. The degree to which it is used by a child in the face of caution, the sense of honor, and similar inhibiting forces may be in direct proportion to the child's susceptibility to suggestions which come to him in this sort of way. We had no means of measuring the child's responsiveness to the acts or opinions of other children, but in the Otis test of suggestibility we found an instrument well calculated to throw light on suggestibility of the more direct sort represented in the presence of answer sheets.

The Otis test presents a variety of situations to which the subject is to respond by expressing a judgment or stating a logical or factual relationship. In each case the correct response must be found in the face of a more obvious incorrect answer which is suggested by the way in which the situation is presented. The following are illustrations:

16. Now I shall show you another card. This will look like a boy knocking at the door. (Expose card No. 16 for 5 seconds.) If you saw the boy, draw a line under the word

*Yes* after No. 16 on your paper.   Indicate your answer in any case.

21.  Write the answer to this question : Do acorns come from pine trees or from maples?   (10 seconds)

25.  You see here the letters A, B, C, D, E, F, G, H, I, J.   If S comes before M in the alphabet, draw a line under the letter E.   (Pause)   When through with that, place a small dot under the letter A.

27–28.  You see again the words *True* and *False* printed eight times. I am going to read again eight sentences as I did before. If the sentence I read is true, draw a line under *True;* but if it is not true, draw a line under *False.*   Most of the sentences will be false.   Now ready!  Look at No. 1. Put your finger on No  1.

1.  Fish walk on land.

2.  The color of snow is black.

3.  There are eight days in a week.

4.  A desert has no rivers or lakes.

5.  Stones break more easily than glass.

6.  The automobile is a musical instrument.

7.  Doctors are useful because they are kind men.

8.  It is false that we can walk on water.

33.  Here are three squares.   Write a word in the middle square. If you cannot think of a word, you can write the word *tree* or *sun* or *pig.*   (10 seconds)

There are twenty questions in all, five of them similar to No. 16, which directly suggests the answer.   Inasmuch as a child might prefer agreeing with the teacher to giving his own opinion, these five may have in them a large factor of deception.   But there are two questions similar to No. 21, four similar to No. 25, and five similar to Nos. 27–28.   The latter acts by requiring a shift from a series of three like answers to an opposite answer on the theory that the more suggestible will fail to resist the tendency to keep on doing the same thing.   There are also four questions of doubtful significance, similar to No. 33, which directly suggest the answer; but probably these are not complicated with deception.

On the other hand, our copying tests are similar to these so-called suggestibility tests in offering the child an obvious thing to do and then telling him not to do it. The mere presence of the answer sheets may be highly suggestive too.

In population A we had the opportunity of administering this test to 303 fifth- and sixth-grade children. Whether the range of scores on the suggestibility test is for this reason restricted is not known. If it is, then the degree of association of suggestibility scores with deception scores which we found is the more remarkable. We shall show this relation first in the form of a chart, as usual. It should be noted that the test is scored in such a way as to measure resistance to suggestion; the higher the score, the greater the resistance. Thus we may group our cases in levels of suggestibility score and portray the amount of deception exhibited at each level. The deception tests are the IER school test and IER home test, with the results reported as median $Xi$'s and per cent cheating.

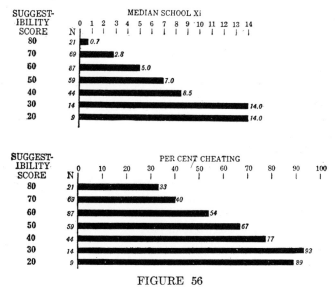

FIGURE 56

SUGGESTIBILITY AND DECEPTION, POPULATION A, GRADES FIVE AND SIX

The relation of scores on the suggestibility test to school cheating, home cheating, and other significant facts is shown in a series of coefficients of correlation reported in Table XLVI.

TABLE XLVI

CORRELATION BETWEEN RESISTANCE TO SUGGESTION AND SCHOOL CHEATING, HOME CHEATING, AGE, AND INTELLIGENCE

| | |
|---|---|
| $r$ with school cheating . . . . . . | − .60 |
| $r$ with cheating at home . . . . . | − .10 |
| $r$ with intelligence . . . . . . . | + .48 |
| $r$ with chronological age . . . . . | − .05 |

Partial $r$, intelligence constant, −.499; $r$, cheating and intelligence, −.42.

We may point out first that, although there is no relation between resistance to suggestion as measured by the Otis test and chronological age on our cases, her own records show an $r$ of .66 with age, over an age range of 7 to 21. The $r$ with intelligence, however, is +.48 on our cases. To some extent, therefore, the $r$ between the suggestibility test scores and deception, which, as with intelligence, is negative, is due to the common factor of intelligence; but even if all the children tested had been of the same intelligence, the $r$ between deception and the suggestibility scores would still have been as high as −.49. The picture of the facts in Figure 56 is consequently not far from the truth, even when intelligence is taken into consideration.

In view of the fact that the $r$ between suggestibility and home cheating, which was presumably done in solitude and with no obtruding suggestion of method, is small, it would seem apparent that the surreptitious use of answer sheets in order to gain a bigger score than one is entitled to is in part at least a function of sensitiveness to suggestions of this sort as measured by a test which probably involves only a slight factor of deception.

## ATTENDANCE AT MOTION PICTURES

We asked the pupils who had the Pupil Data Sheets several questions regarding motion pictures, such as the frequency with which they attended, the type of picture they liked best, and the names of pictures about which they had thought a good deal recently.   The facts for populations C and A in relation to frequency of attendance and school cheating are summarized in Figure 57.

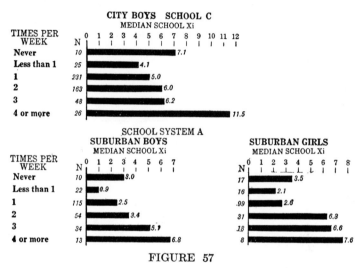

FIGURE 57

ATTENDANCE AT MOTION PICTURES AND CHEATING ON IER TESTS

A glance at Figure 57 indicates the fact that frequency of attendance and deception are correlated.   When A and C are combined, however, the $r$ between attendance and school Xi is only $+.167$.   There is great variability in the deceptiveness of each of the attendance groups.   Nevertheless, the fact that all three of the populations show the same regular increase in the tendency to deceive as attendance rises is probably significant of a closer relation between the two facts than the size of the $r$ would suggest.   Those who say they never attend are an apparent exception in each case. Whether these belong to an exceptionally poor home background or are inclined to falsify the facts regarding themselves is not known.

Whatever relation there is between attendance at pictures and deceit may possibly be due to differences in intelligence or general economic-social level, although neither of these factors correlates with attendance as highly as does deception. It is not asserted that the pictures cause the deception. All that is demonstrated is an association between frequency of attendance and deception, which is more likely to be due to some third factor or group of factors with which each of these is connected.

# CHAPTER XIV

# A COMPARISON OF HONEST AND DISHONEST CHILDREN

Up to this point in our discussion we have dealt almost entirely with whole communities or with cross sections of communities which range all the way up and down the scale of deceit. By taking the extremes of such a scale and comparing the most honest with the most dishonest cases, certain general facts already reported will be made more conspicuous, and at the same time it will be possible to give more attention to individuals than has so far been done.

In order to select our cases, we resorted to the Pupil Data Sheets, on which the children had been asked point-blank whether or not they had cheated on the IER tests. For our most dishonest group we took those who not only certainly cheated but who also lied about doing so afterwards. For our honest cases we took those whose Xi scores ranged around zero and whose Pupil Data Sheets gave no evidence of concealment or duplicity. In addition, we picked out the pupils who not only cheated but who admitted it afterwards. These we called the " confessors." In order to keep as many factors constant as possible, we selected our cases so that they would be proportionally distributed among the grades and schools and between the sexes. This selection yielded us, for population A, approximately eighty honest (H) cases, ninety dishonest (D) cases, and thirty-five confessors (C). Although no attention was paid to occupation or religion in picking out our cases, the resulting HDC group was fairly representative of the whole community in these particulars. The proportion of each occupational level and of Catholics, Jews, and Protestants was about the same in the total HDC group as it was in the entire school population. These proportions are shown in Table XLVII.

## TABLE XLVII

SOCIAL AND RELIGIOUS CONSTITUENCY OF THE HDC GROUP

| PER CENT IN EACH OCCUPATIONAL LEVEL | PER CENT IN EACH DENOMINATION |
|---|---|
| Professional (I) . . . . . 10 | Catholic . . . . . . . 30 |
| Trade (II and III) . . . . 71 | Jewish . . . . . . . 14 |
| Unskilled (IV) . . . . . 19 | Protestant . . . . . . 57 |

It was in school system A that our school visitor did her work, using the method of observation and report which is described in Chapter VIII. The cases assigned to her were the children of the HDC group. Of the HDC cases she was able to visit about one hundred and fifty, and the records of one hundred and twenty-eight of these are sufficiently complete for detailed comparison.

We shall report in the first place the pertinent available facts for each individual, classifying the cases in the three groups, most honest (Table XLVIII), most dishonest (Table XLIX), and confessors (Table L). Some explanation of the way in which the facts are reported in these tables will be necessary. The row of figures at the top consists of the identifying case numbers. Following the order of the tables, the other items are as follows:

I. Personal relations within the family

Parental example dishonest. Wherever evidence of such a fact appears, it is reported by a check mark under the case number.

Personality of father: (1) notoriously antisocial behavior; (2) occasional drinking sprees or sex irregularity; (3) lack of responsibility; (4) responsibility, exemplary character

Relations between parents: (1) complete antagonism, abuse, infidelity; (2) domination of one by the other; (3) occasional quarreling; (4) complete compatibility

Discipline. Four types of unsatisfactory treatment are listed, and wherever there is evidence of the presence of any of the four types the fact is indicated by a check mark.

Attitude of mother and of father toward the child : (1) grudging, antagonistic; (2) selfishly affectionate; (3) generous, sympathetic, but fostering infantilism, tending to repress; (4) generous but wise, developing child's affection and independence

Foreign language used. The fact is indicated by a check mark. " Presence of more favored child " means one who is brighter or more talented or otherwise superior.

Subject an only child. The fact is recorded.

Pressure on school work. Reference to overanxiety and nagging or urging on the part of parents or others in the family

II. Cultural status of family

Community rating. The town was geographically divided into sections and each section was rated according to the general physical conditions observed, such as congestion, size of houses, nearness to stores and amusements, play facilities, appearance of streets and grounds, probable rental value of the property. 12 is high and 1 is low.

Home background level. The visitor's records were grouped in fifteen classes or levels representing the general quality of the home. (See Chapter VIII.) 1 is high and 15 is low.

Burdick culture score. This is the score described in Chapter VIII, based on a test given in school several months after the children had been tested for deception, so that there are a good many records missing. The scores range from 12 to 109.

Nationality or race. The initials refer to race or to the country in which the parents were born, and have the following meanings :

A,  United States
E,  England
C,  Czechoslovakia
F,  Finland
Fr, France
G,  Germany
H,  Hebrew

Hu, Hungary
I,  Italy
L,  Lithuania
N,  Negro
No, Norway
P,  Poland
R,  Russia
S,  Sweden
Sc, Scotland

Economic or social level rising or falling.  Includes both the present generation and the previous generation where facts are available.

Ambition higher than attainment.  Important, but evidence slight

Religion: Catholic, C; Jewish, J; and Protestant, P

III. Personal data

Sex: Boy, B; girl, G

Intelligence.  The figure is the sigma deviation of the child's CAVI score from the mean of the children of his age, and is therefore above the mean (+) or below it (−).

Health.  Only the fact of poor health, with a history of diseases or accidents, is reported.

Age-grade displacement.  Assuming that the normal age for entering the first half of grade five is ten and allowing for the time when the tests were given, any deviation in age from the expected age is expressed in half-years, with a plus sign meaning over-age and a minus sign meaning under-age.  Thus, −4 means that the child is two years younger than the assumed normal age for his grade.  Less than a half-year deviation is ignored.  The median of the entire HDC group thus figured is zero, 38% deviating less than a half-year from the assumed norm.

School deportment.  The actual grade as reported by the school is given.

Cheating in classroom.  As the children are distributed in some twenty classrooms, it is important to know the relative deceptiveness of these rooms in relation to the child's own tendency to deceive. The facts are expressed as group ratings corresponding roughly to the per cent cheating in each class. Thus where the cheating was ten per cent or less, the rating is 1; where twenty to thirty per cent cheated, the rating is 2. In the classes cheating ninety per cent or over, there was a wide difference in mean $Xi$ scores, so that the groups which would have been rated 9 could be distributed from 9 to 14 by taking their mean $Xi$ scores also into consideration.

Maladjustment index. This is the figure described in Chapter VII, based on the Woodworth questions and certain other facts, such as frequency of punishment, fears, and number of teachers disliked. The larger the figure, the greater is the evidence of emotional maladjustment.

For convenience of study the facts are grouped in three classes: (I) personal relations within the family; (II) the general cultural position of the family; and (III) facts about the child, including the temptation to which he is exposed in the deceptive behavior of his classmates. The items were first selected for consideration before the results of our study were known to us, because it was thought that they might bear some relation to the tendency to deceive, either directly or in combination with other facts. It would be reasonable to suppose, for example, that a retarded child with relatively low intelligence might be persuaded to cheat in order to get better marks, particularly if pressure was put on him at home to do better work. As it turned out, none of our cases exactly fits this picture, but it may be of some interest that only one of the honest cases was under pressure at home whereas five of the dishonest cases were thus stimulated. Which of our items are associated with one group more than with another can thus be determined only by summarizing the facts and noting differences between the groups. This has been done in Table LI, which gives the percentage of cases in each of the three groups which " possess " the items of the detailed lists in Tables XLVIII–L.

# TABLE XLVIII
## HANDICAPS OF MOST HONEST CASES

| CASE NUMBER | 2 | 5 | 6 | 7 | 11 | 31 | 38 | 39 | 41 | 42 | 43 | 44 | 48 | 49 | 1 | 4 | 12 | 25 | 28 | 30 | 34 | 37 | 40 | 45 |
|---|---|---|---|---|---|---|---|---|---|---|---|---|---|---|---|---|---|---|---|---|---|---|---|---|
| **I. Personal relations with family** | | | | | | | | | | | | | | | | | | | | | | | | |
| Parental example dishonest * | 4 | 4 | 4 | 4 | 4 | – | 4 | 4 | 3 | 4 | 4 | 4 | 4 | 4 | 4 | – | – | 4 | 4 | 4 | 3 | 3 | 3 | 4 |
| Personality of father * | 3 | 3 | 3 | 4 | 4 | – | 3 | 4 | 3 | 4 | 4 | 3 | 3 | 4 | 3 | 3 | 3 | – | 3 | 4 | 3 | 3 | 3 | 4 |
| Relations between parents * | | | | | | | | | | | | | | | | | | | | | | | | |
| Discipline divided * | | | | | | | | | | | | | | | | | | | | | | | | |
| Discipline severe | √ | | | | | √ | | √ | | | | | | | | | | | | | √ | | √ | |
| Discipline spoiling | | | | | | | | | | | | | | | | | | | | | | | | |
| Lack of supervision * | 4 | 3 | 3 | 4 | 4 | 3 | 4 | 3 | 4 | 4 | 4 | 3 | 4 | 4 | 3 | 3 | 3 | 3 | 4 | 3 | 3 | 4 | 3 | 4 |
| Attitude of mother * | 3 | 3 | 3 | 4 | 4 | 3 | 3 | 3 | 3 | 4 | 4 | 3 | 4 | 4 | 3 | 3 | 3 | 3 | 4 | 4 | 3 | 3 | 3 | 3 |
| Attitude of father * | | | | | | – | | | | | | | | | | | | | | | | | | |
| Foreign language used * | | | | | √ | | √ | | √ | √ | | | | | | √ | √ | | | √ | √ | | √ | |
| Presence of more favored child | | | | | | | | | | | | | | | | | | | | | | | | |
| Subject an only child | | | | | | | | | | | | | | | | | | | | | | | | |
| Pressure on school work * | | | | | | | | | | | | | | | | | | | | | | | | |
| Handicap | 0 | 0 | 0 | 0 | 0 | 0 | 0 | 0 | 0 | 0 | 0 | 0 | 0 | 0 | 0 | 0 | 0 | 0 | 0 | 0 | 0 | 0 | 1 | 0 |
| **II. Cultural status of family** | | | | | | | | | | | | | | | | | | | | | | | | |
| Community rating * | 10 | 10 | 10 | 12 | 7 | 10 | 8 | 10 | 10 | 7 | 7 | 12 | 10 | 10 | 7 | 7 | 10 | 1 | 7 | 9 | – | 8 | 7 | 10 |
| Home background level * | 3 | 7 | 7 | 1 | 2 | 8 | 3 | 4 | 3 | 3 | 3 | 4 | 4 | 1 | 1 | 8 | 8 | 8 | 4 | 5 | 9 | 3 | 11 | 2 |
| Burdick culture score * | – | 90 | – | 92 | 66 | 74 | – | 75 | – | – | – | 68 | 68 | 109 | 41 | 48 | 49 | 67 | 60 | 60 | – | – | 58 | 91 |
| Nationality or race * | A | A | A | A | H | A | A | A | Sc | F | F | G/Sc | H | A | S | F | A | G | A | A | A | A | A | A |
| Economic or social level rising | √ | √ | √ | | √ | √ | | | √ | √ | | | √ | | | | | | √ | | | | | √ |
| Economic or social level falling * | | | | | | | | | | | | | | | | | | | | | | | | |
| Ambition higher than attainment | | | | | | | | | | | | | | | √ | | | | | | | | | |
| Religion | – | | | | | | | | | | | | | | | | | | | | | | | |
| Handicap | 0 | 0 | 0 | 0 | 0 | 0 | 0 | 0 | 0 | 0 | 0 | 0 | 0 | 0 | 0 | 0 | 0 | 0 | 0 | 0 | 0 | 0 | 1 | 0 |
| **III. The subject** | | | | | | | | | | | | | | | | | | | | | | | | |
| Sex | B | G | B | B | G | B | G | B | G | G | B | B | G | G | B | B | B | G | B | G | B | B | B | G |
| Intelligence * | +7 | +7 | +10 | +16 | –1 | –1 | –2 | +26 | +20 | +12 | +15 | +9 | – | +10 | +10 | –1 | +1 | +8 | +7 | –11 | +1 | +8 | +16 | +8 |
| Health poor | | √ | √ | | √ | | | | √ | √ | | | √ | | | | | √ | | √ | | | √ | |
| Age-grade displacement * | 0 | 0 | 0 | 0 | +2 | +1 | 0 | +2 | –3 | 0 | +2 | 0 | 0 | 0 | 0 | –1 | 0 | +2 | –5 | 0 | –5 | –1 | –1 | 0 |
| School deportment * | – | – | 85 | 0 | 95 | 99 | 88 | 85 | 95 | 95 | 95 | 85 | 94 | – | 95 | – | 95 | 95 | 85 | 95 | 75 | 85 | 85 | 95 |
| Cheating of classroom * | 4 | 1 | 4 | 1 | 3 | 2 | 2 | 3 | 2 | 3 | 4 | 3 | 5 | 4 | 3 | 4 | 3 | 2 | 3 | 3 | 3 | 4 | 4 | 4 |
| Maladjustment index * | 3 | 2 | 4 | 3 | 4 | 4 | 1 | 1 | 0 | 3 | 3 | 6 | 4 | 3 | 1 | 3 | 1 | 4 | 11 | 2 | 2 | 9 | 2 | 8 |
| Handicap | 0 | 0 | 0 | 0 | 0 | 0 | 0 | 0 | 0 | 0 | 0 | 0 | 0 | 0 | 0 | 0 | 0 | 0 | 1 | 1 | 1 | 1 | 0 | 1 |
| Total handicap score | 0 | 0 | 0 | 0 | 0 | 0 | 0 | 0 | 0 | 0 | 0 | 0 | 0 | 0 | 1 | 1 | 0 | 0 | 1 | 1 | 1 | 1 | 1 | 1 |

# TABLE XLVIII — Continued

| CASE NUMBER | 47 | 9 | 14 | 19 | 33 | 18 | 21 | 24 | 32 | 3 | 8 | 13 | 29 | 35 | 10 | 17 | 20 | 22 | 27 | 16 | 15 | 36 | 46 | 26 | 23 |
|---|---|---|---|---|---|---|---|---|---|---|---|---|---|---|---|---|---|---|---|---|---|---|---|---|---|
| **Personal relations with family** Parental example dishonest * | 4 | - |  | 4 |  |  |  |  |  |  |  |  | 4 |  |  | 4 |  |  |  |  |  |  |  | 2 | √ |
| Personality of father * | 4 | - | 3 | 4 | 2 | - | 3 | 3 | - | - | - | - | - | 2 | 3 | 3 | 3 | 3 | 1 | 2 | 3 | 3 | 3 | 1 | 1 |
| Relations between parents * |  |  | 1 | 3 | 8 | 3 | 3 | 3 |  |  |  |  | 1 | 1 | 2 | 3 | 3 | 3 |  | 1 |  | 3 | 3 | 1 | 1 |
| Discipline divided * | √ | √ |  | √ |  |  |  |  |  | √ | √ | √ |  |  | √ | √ | √ | √ | √ | √ | √ | √ | √ | √ | √ |
| Discipline severe |  |  |  |  |  |  |  |  |  | √ | √ | √ |  |  |  | √ |  |  |  |  |  | √ |  | √ | √ |
| Discipline spoiling |  |  |  | √ |  |  | √ | √ | √ | √ | √ | √ | √ |  | √ | √ | √ | √ |  | √ | √ | √ | √ |  |  |
| Lack of supervision * | 4 | 4 |  | 3 | 3 | 3 | 3 | 3 | 3 | 3 | 3 | 3 | D | 3 | 2 | 3 | 3 | 3 | 3 | 2 | 2 | 2 | 2 | 3 | 2 |
| **I,** Attitude of mother * | 4 | 4 | 3 | 3 | - | 3 | 3 | 3 | 2 | D | 3 | - | 4 | - | 3 | 3 | - | 3 | - | 3 | - | 2 | 2 | 2 | 1 |
| Attitude of father * | 4 | 4 | 1 | 3 | - |  | 3 | 3 |  | D |  |  |  |  | 3 | 3 |  |  |  | 3 |  |  |  |  |  |
| Foreign language used * |  |  |  |  |  |  |  | √ | √ | √ | √ | √ | √ | √ |  | √ |  |  |  | √ | √ | √ |  | √ | √ |
| Presence of more favored child |  |  |  |  |  |  |  |  |  |  |  |  |  |  |  |  |  |  |  |  |  |  |  |  |  |
| Subject an only child |  |  |  |  |  |  |  |  |  |  |  |  |  |  |  |  |  |  |  |  |  |  |  |  |  |
| Pressure on school work * | √ |  |  |  |  |  |  |  |  |  |  |  |  |  |  |  |  |  |  |  |  | √ |  |  |  |
| Handicap | 0 | 1 | 1 | 1 | 2 | 0 | 0 | 1 | 2 | 2 | 1 | 0 | 1 | 2 | 2 | 2 | 0 | 0 | 1 | 5 | 4 | 3 | 3 | 5 | 7 |
| **Cultural status of family** Community rating * | 10 | 12 | 12 | 10 | 8 | 7 | 14 | 8 | 8 | 10 | 10 | 11 | 5 | 11 | 11 | 11 | 11 | 12 | 13 | 7 | 12 | 1 | 7 | 4 | 1 |
| Home background level * | 10 | 5 | 13 | 10 | 8 | 10 | 14 | 8 | 8 | 11 | 10 | 11 | 5 | 11 | 11 | 11 | 11 | 12 | 13 | 15 | 12 | 11 | 12 | 11 | 14 |
| Burdick culture score * | - | - | - | 31 | 81 | - | 29 | - | - | 49 | 71 | 63 | 49 | 49 | - | - | 24 | 15 | 32 | 46 | 50 | 60 | 55 | - | 42 |
| **II** Nationality or race * | A | A | A | A | A | H | N | I | F | A | A | A | N | N | A | I | H | N | N | H | A | N | S | A | G/I |
| Economic or social level rising |  | √ |  | √ |  |  | √ |  |  |  |  | √ | √ | √ | √ |  | √ |  |  |  |  |  |  |  | √ |
| Economic or social level falling * |  |  |  |  |  | √ |  |  |  | √ | √ | √ |  |  |  | √ |  |  |  | √ | √ | √ | √ | √ | √ |
| Ambition higher than attainment |  |  |  |  |  |  |  |  |  |  |  |  |  |  |  |  |  |  |  |  |  |  |  |  |  |
| Religion | P | P | P | C | P | J | P | C | P | - | C | - | P | P | C | C | J | P | P | J | C | P | P | C | C |
| Handicap | 0 | 0 | 1 | 1 | 0 | 2 | 2 | 2 | 0 | 1 | 2 | 3 | 2 | 2 | 2 | 2 | 2 | 2 | 2 | 1 | 2 | 2 | 1 | 3 | 2 |
| **The subject** Sex | B | B | B | G | B | G | B | G | G | G | B | G | G | G | B | B | B | B | B | G | G | B | B | B | G |
| Intelligence * | +1 | +6 | -3 | -8 | +13 | - | -9 | -4 | +14 | +8 | -2 | 0 | +1 | +11 | +11 | -3 | -15 | -15 | -14 | -9 | +5 | +10 | -10 | +8 | -6 |
| Health poor |  |  |  |  |  |  |  |  |  |  |  |  |  |  |  |  | √ |  |  |  |  |  |  |  | -1 |
| **III** Age-grade displacement * | 0 | +2 | 0 | -4 | 0 | -1 | -2 | 0 | -2 | 0 | -3 | +1 | 0 | +2 | -4 | -4 | -8 | 0 | -3 | -2 | +1 | +1 | 0 | -6 | -1 |
| School deportment * | 85 | 80 | 85 | 93 | 92 | 95 | 89 | 89 | 95 | 95 | 95 | 99 | 82 | 89 | 85 | 75 | 65 | 75 | 95 | 92 | 95 | 72 | 80 | 80 | 76 |
| Cheating of classroom * | 5 | 5 | 3 | 3 | 2 | 14 | 14 | 2 | 2 | 4 | 1 | 2 | 6 | 2 | 3 | 2 | 12 | 10 | 10 | 3 | 3 | 2 | 5 | 6 | 6 |
| Maladjustment index * | 10 | 3 | 0 | 4 | 0 | 7 | 0 | 0 | 5 | 10 | 7 | 5 | 1 | 4 | 6 | 3 | 3 | 3 | 2 | 2 | 5 | 7 | 3 | 1 | 5 |
| Handicap | 1 | 1 | 0 | 0 | 0 | 0 | 0 | 0 | 0 | 0 | 0 | 0 | 0 | 0 | 0 | 0 | 0 | 0 | 0 | 0 | 0 | 0 | 0 | 2 | 3 |
| Total handicap score | 1 | 2 | 2 | 2 | 2 | 3 | 3 | 3 | 3 | 4 | 4 | 4 | 4 | 4 | 5 | 5 | 5 | 5 | 5 | 6 | 7 | 7 | 7 | 12 | 12 |

# TABLE XLIX

## Handicaps of Most Dishonest Cases

| | Case Number | 47 | 4 | 14 | 35 | 3½ | 6 | 11 | 12 | 13 | 19 | 20 | 40 | 42 | 50 | 52 | 1 | 5 | 10 | 22 | 39 | 43 | 48 | 51 | 15 | 16 | 24 |
|---|---|---|---|---|---|---|---|---|---|---|---|---|---|---|---|---|---|---|---|---|---|---|---|---|---|---|---|
| **I** Personal relations with family | Parental example dishonest * | — | √ | | | | | | | | | | | | | | | | | | √ | | √ | | | | — |
| | Personality of father * | — | 4 | 3 | 3 | 4 | 4 | 3 | 4 | 3 | 4 | 4 | 4 | 3 | 4 | — | 3 | 4 | 3 | — | 3 | 3 | — | 3 | — | 4 | 3 |
| | Relations between parents * | — | 3 | 3 | 3 | 4 | 3 | 2 | 3 | 3 | 3 | 3 | 3 | 3 | — | — | 3 | — | 3 | 3 | 4 | — | 3 | — | — | 3 | 3 |
| | Discipline divided * | √ | √ | √ | | | √ | | √ | √ | √ | | √ | | | | √ | | √ | | | | √ | | | √ | √ |
| | Discipline severe | | | | | | | | | | | | | | | | | | | | | | | | | | |
| | Discipline spoiling | | √ | √ | √ | | | | √ | | √ | √ | | | | | √ | | | √ | √ | √ | √ | | √ | √ | |
| | Lack of supervision * | 3 | 3 | 3 | 3 | 4 | 2 | 3 | 3 | 3 | 3 | 3 | 3 | 3 | 3 | 4 | 3 | 3 | 3 | 3 | 4 | D | 2 | 3 | 2 | 3 | 3 |
| | Attitude of mother * | 3 | 4 | 3 | 3 | 2 | 3 | 3 | 3 | 3 | 3 | 3 | 3 | 3 | 3 | D | 3 | 3 | 3 | 3 | 3 | 3 | 3 | 3 | 1 | 3 | 3 |
| | Attitude of father * | | | | | | | | | | | | | | | | | | | | | | | | | | |
| | Foreign language used * | √ | √ | | √ | √ | √ | √ | √ | | √ | √ | √ | √ | √ | √ | √ | √ | √ | √ | √ | | | √ | | √ | |
| | Presence of more favored child | | | | | | | | | | | | | | | | | | | | | | | | | | |
| | Subject an only child | | | | | | | | | | | | | | | | | | | | | | | | | | |
| | Pressure on school work * | | | | | | | | | | | | | | | | | | | | | | | | | | |
| | Handicap | 0 | 10 | 0 | 0 | 1 | 2 | 1 | 1 | 2 | 1 | 1 | 0 | 0 | 0 | 1 | 0 | 0 | 1 | 0 | 1 | 1 | 3 | 0 | 3 | 1 | 0 |
| **II** Cultural status of family | Community rating * | 8 | 7 | 7 | 10 | 10 | 10 | 7 | 10 | 7 | 7 | 10 | 10 | 10 | 10 | 10 | 10 | 4 | 7 | 7 | — | 1 | 10 | 4 | 7 | 10 | 1 |
| | Home background level * | 4 | 10 | 8 | 3 | 3 | 8 | 7 | 10 | 8 | 7 | 3 | 3 | 8 | 6 | 10 | 10 | 8 | 7 | 10 | 6 | 8 | 9 | 10 | 12 | 7 | 6 |
| | Burdick culture score * | 86 | 54 | 47 | 59 | 77 | 57 | 78 | 70 | 51 | 53 | 49 | 68 | 52 | 49 | 44 | 46 | 59 | 32 | 60 | 32 | 41 | 72 | — | — | 49 | 39 |
| | Nationality or race * | A | A | I | E | A | G | A | H | H | I | H | A | N | A | F | A | F | I | H | P | N | A | A | N | Fr | H |
| | Economic or social level rising | | √ | √ | √ | | √ | | √ | | √ | √ | √ | | | √ | √ | | | √ | √ | | √ | | | | √ |
| | Economic or social level falling* | | | | | | | | | | | | | | | | | | | | | | | | | | |
| | Ambition higher than attainment | | | | | | | | | | | | | | | | | | | | | | | | | | |
| | Religion | | | | | | | | | | | | | | | | | | | | | | | | | | |
| | Handicap | C | P | C | P | P | P | P | J | J | C | J | P | P | P | P | P | P | C | J | C | P | P | P | P | P | J |
| **III** The subject | Sex | G | B | G | B | B | B | G | G | B | G | G | G | G | G | G | G | B | B | B | G | B | G | G | B | B | B |
| | Intelligence * | −3 | −8 | −1 | +3 | −10 | +1 | +20 | +3 | +2 | −4 | −4 | 0 | −6 | +18 | −7 | −20 | −4 | −15 | +20 | −2 | +2 | +13 | +12 | −7 | +4 | −9 |
| | Health poor | √ | √ | √ | √ | | √ | √ | √ | | | | √ | √ | | | | | | | | | | | | √ | |
| | Age-grade displacement * | −3 | 0 | 0 | −1 | 0 | 0 | 0 | +4 | 0 | 0 | −1 | +3 | 0 | +4 | −1 | 0 | −4 | −1 | +3 | +4 | 0 | +2 | −3 | −2 | +4 | −2 |
| | School deportment * | 91 | 85 | 85 | 95 | 95 | — | 90 | 95 | 85 | 95 | 84 | 85 | 93 | 95 | 95 | — | — | 85 | 89 | 87 | 85 | 85 | 85 | 85 | 70 | 85 |
| | Cheating of classroom * | 2 | 3 | 3 | 2 | 4 | 5 | 5 | 3 | 3 | 3 | 2 | 4 | 5 | 4 | 5 | 4 | 7 | 3 | 2 | 5 | 6 | 2 | 7 | 3 | 6 | 8 |
| | Maladjustment Index * | 2 | 1 | 3 | 4 | 3 | 3 | 1 | 1 | 1 | 1 | 5 | 1 | 1 | 3 | 1 | 2 | 1 | 3 | 1 | 1 | 6 | 4 | 6 | 3 | 8 | 2 |
| | Handicap | 0 | 0 | 0 | 0 | 0 | 0 | 0 | 0 | 0 | 0 | 0 | 1 | 0 | 2 | 0 | 2 | 1 | 1 | 1 | 1 | 1 | 1 | 0 | 0 | 2 | 2 |
| | Total handicap score | 1 | 1 | 1 | 1 | 2 | 2 | 2 | 2 | 2 | 2 | 2 | 2 | 2 | 2 | 3 | 3 | 3 | 3 | 3 | 3 | 3 | 3 | 3 | 4 | 4 | 4 |

290

## TABLE XLIX — *Continued*

| CASE NUMBER | 25 | 28 | 44 | 46 | 49 | 2 | 7 | 21 | 27 | 34 | 9 | 17 | 26 | 30 | 45 | 8 | 18 | 38 | 29 | 41 | 31 | 36 | 23 | 37 | 32 | 33 |
|---|---|---|---|---|---|---|---|---|---|---|---|---|---|---|---|---|---|---|---|---|---|---|---|---|---|---|
| **I. Personal relations with family** | | | | | | | | | | | | | | | | | | | | | | | | | | |
| Parental example dishonest * | | √ | | | | | √ | | | | | | | | | | √ | | | | | | | | √ | √ |
| Personality of father * | | 1 | | 3 | | | 3 | 4 | 1 | 3 | 3 | 2 | 3 | 3 | 3 | 2 | 2 | 1 | 3 | 1 | 1 | 1 | 2 | 3 | 2 | 1 |
| Relations between parents * | 3 | 3 | 3 | 3 | 3 | | 3 | | 3 | 3 | 2 | 2 | 3 | 2 | | 3 | 2 | 2 | 3 | 1 | | 1 | 3 | | 2 | 1 |
| Discipline divided * | 2 | | 3 | | | √ | | √ | √ | | √ | √ | | | | | | √ | √ | √ | | √ | √ | √ | | √ |
| Discipline severe | | | √ | | | √ | | | | | | | | | | | √ | | | | | | | | | |
| Discipline spoiling | | √ | | √ | √ | √ | √ | | | √ | | | | | | | | | | | | | | | | √ |
| Lack of supervision * | | | | | | | | | | | | | √ | | √ | | | | | | | | | √ | | |
| Attitude of mother * | 3 | 3 | 2 | 2 | 3 | 2 | 3 | | 3 | 3 | 2 | 2 | D | 3 | 3 | 4 | 3 | 3 | 3 | 2 | 3 | 3 | 2 | 2 | 2 | 2 |
| Attitude of father * | 3 | 3 | 2 | 2 | 3 | | 3 | 3 | 3 | 3 | 3 | 2 | 4 | 3 | 3 | 2 | 3 | D | 3 | 2 | D | D | 2 | D | 1 | 1 |
| Foreign language used * | √ | √ | | | √ | √ | | | | √ | | | | | | | | | | √ | | | √ | √ | | |
| Presence of more favored child | | | | | | | | | | | | | | | | | | | | | | | | | | |
| Subject an only child | | | | √ | | | | | | | | | | | | | | √ | | | | | | | | |
| Pressure on school work * | | | √ | | √ | | | | | | | | | | | | | | | | | | | | | |
| Handicap | 2 | 3 | 3 | 8 | 3 | 2 | 2 | 3 | 3 | 1 | 2 | 5 | 2 | 2 | 2 | 2 | 3 | 3 | 2 | 6 | 4 | 5 | 6 | 4 | 6 | 7 |
| **II. Cultural status of family** | | | | | | | | | | | | | | | | | | | | | | | | | | |
| Community rating * | 1 | 12 | 10 | 8 | 10 | 4 | 7 | 12 | 12 | 1 | 7 | 7 | 9 | 1 | 1 | 4 | 7 | 1 | 10 | 7 | 1 | 1 | 1 | 1 | 1 | 1 |
| Home background level * | 1 | 12 | 10 | 8 | 7 | 4 | 7 | 12 | 12 | 1 | 7 | 11 | 9 | 13 | 9 | 12 | 14 | 15 | 10 | 12 | 14 | 13 | 11 | 12 | 14 | 14 |
| Burdick culture score * | 74 | 12 | 56 | | 52 | 12 | | 48 | | 33 | 35 | 49 | 33 | 49 | 42 | 44 | | 26 | 25 | | 23 | 22 | 46 | | | 38 |
| Nationality or race * | H | I | A | Hu | Fr | A | H | Sc | I | H | A | A | N | H | N | A | A | N | I | C | P,L | H | L | L | I | L,G |
| Economic or social level rising | √ | √ | √ | | | | | | | √ | | | | | √ | | | | | | | √ | | | | √ |
| Economic or social level falling * | | √ | | √ | | | √ | √ | √ | | √ | √ | | | | | | | | √ | √ | | √ | √ | √ | |
| Ambition higher than attainment | | | | | | √ | √ | | | | √ | | | | | | | | | | | | | | | |
| Religion | J | C | C | C | C | P | P | P | C | J | C | G | P | J | P | P | C | C | P | C | C | C | C | C | P | C |
| Handicap | 1 | 2 | 1 | 1 | 1 | 2 | 1 | 1 | 1 | 2 | 2 | 1 | 2 | 2 | 2 | 2 | 2 | 2 | 2 | 2 | 2 | 2 | 2 | 3 | 2 | 2 |
| **III. The subject** | | | | | | | | | | | | | | | | | | | | | | | | | | |
| Sex | G | B | B | G | B | G | B | B | B | B | G | G | B | G | G | B | B | G | B | G | B | G | B | B | G | G |
| Intelligence * | +3 | -8 | -2 | +9 | +16 | -15 | +29 | -10 | -10 | -6 | -14 | +1 | -6 | -11 | -21 | -10 | +3 | -5 | -12 | +2 | -14 | -11 | +4 | -9 | -23 | -18 |
| Health poor | | | | | | | | | | | | | | | | | | | | | | | | | | |
| Age-grade displacement * | 0 | 0 | +1 | -1 | +2 | -2 | +2 | 0 | -2 | 0 | -4 | +1 | -2 | 0 | -6 | -4 | +1 | 0 | -4 | 0 | 0 | 0 | -4 | -6 | -7 | -1 |
| School deportment * | 85 | 85 | 95 | 95 | 97 | 95 | 85 | 75 | 85 | 76 | 84 | 95 | 82 | 97 | 85 | 70 | 80 | 75 | 73 | 85 | 78 | 95 | 65 | 75 | 73 | 85 |
| Cheating of classroom * | 2 | 2 | 2 | 2 | 2 | 3 | 7 | 3 | 4 | 12 | 5 | 3 | 14 | 14 | 8 | 6 | 5 | 10 | 10 | 3 | 3 | 10 | 8 | 10 | 14 | 10 |
| Maladjustment index * | 6 | 2 | 2 | 2 | 2 | 1 | 2 | 9 | 3 | 3 | 7 | 3 | 6 | 0 | 8 | 3 | 11 | 8 | 7 | 3 | 3 | 2 | 5 | 6 | 3 | 3 |
| Handicap | 1 | 2 | 0 | 0 | 0 | 5 | 5 | 5 | 5 | 5 | 6 | 6 | 6 | 6 | 6 | 7 | 7 | 7 | 4 | 0 | 3 | 2 | 2 | 3 | 3 | 2 |
| Total handicap score | 4 | 4 | 4 | 4 | 4 | 5 | 5 | 5 | 5 | 5 | 6 | 6 | 6 | 6 | 6 | 7 | 7 | 7 | 8 | 8 | 9 | 9 | 10 | 10 | 11 | 11 |

# TABLE L

## HANDICAPS OF CONFESSORS

| | | Case Number | 2 | 22 | 4 | 24 | 1 | 3 | 15 | 26 | 11 | 13 | 25 | 6 | 14 | 16 | 27 | 7 | 8 | 21 | 10 | 20 | 5 | 9 | 19 | 12 | 18 | 23 | 17 |
|---|---|---|---|---|---|---|---|---|---|---|---|---|---|---|---|---|---|---|---|---|---|---|---|---|---|---|---|---|---|
| **I** | Personal relations with family | Parental example dishonest * | — | — | | | | | | | | | | | | | | | | | | | | | | | | | |
| | | Personality of father * | — | — | | ✓ | | | | | | | | ✓ | | | | | | | | | | | | | | ✓ | ✓ |
| | | Relations between parents * | — | | | | | | ✓ | ✓ | | | ✓ | | | | | | | | | | | | | | | ✓ | ✓ |
| | | Discipline divided * | ✓ | ✓ | ✓ | ✓ | ✓ | ✓ | ✓ | ✓ | | | | ✓ | | ✓ | | | ✓ | ✓ | ✓ | | ✓ | ✓ | | ✓ | ✓ | ✓ | ✓ |
| | | Discipline severe | | | | | | | | | | | | | | | | | | | | | | | | | | | |
| | | Discipline spoiling | ✓ | ✓ | ✓ | ✓ | ✓ | ✓ | ✓ | ✓ | | | ✓ | ✓ | | | | | ✓ | ✓ | ✓ | ✓ | ✓ | ✓ | | | ✓ | ✓ | |
| | | Lack of supervision * | 3 | 3 | 3 | 4 | 3 | 3 | 3 | 2 | 3 | 3 | 3 | 2 | ✓ | 3 | 4 | ✓ | 2 | 3 | 2 | ✓ | 2 | 2 | 2 | 2 | D | 2 | 2 |
| | | Attitude of mother * | 3 | 3 | 3 | 4 | 3 | 3 | 3 | 2 | 3 | 3 | 3 | 2 | D | 3 | 4 | D | 2 | 3 | 2 | 3 | 2 | 2 | 2 | 2 | D | 2 | 2 |
| | | Attitude of father * | — | — | 3 | 4 | 3 | 2 | 3 | 2 | 3 | 3 | — | 2 | 4 | 3 | 3 | 2 | 3 | 3 | 2 | 3 | 2 | 2 | 1 | 2 | 1 | 1 | 2 |
| | | Foreign language used * | | | | | ✓ | ✓ | | ✓ | ✓ | | | ✓ | ✓ | ✓ | ✓ | | | ✓ | | | | | ✓ | ✓ | | ✓ | ✓ |
| | | Presence of more favored child | | | | | | | | | | | | | | | | | | | | | | | | | | | |
| | | Subject an only child | | | | | | | | | | | | | | | | | | | | | | | | | | | |
| | | Pressure on school work * | | | | | | ✓ | ✓ | ✓ | | ✓ | ✓ | | | | ✓ | ✓ | ✓ | | | ✓ | ✓ | | | | | | |
| | | Handicap | 0 | 0 | 1 | 0 | 1 | 1 | 1 | 3 | 1 | 0 | 2 | 3 | 2 | 1 | 1 | 5 | 5 | 1 | 4 | 2 | 6 | 4 | 3 | 3 | 4 | 7 | 7 |
| **II** | Cultural status of family | Community rating * | 7 | 7 | 7 | 1 | 1 | 7 | 1 | 8 | 1 | 0 | 2 | 3 | 2 | 1 | 4 | 5 | 10 | 1 | 4 | 2 | 1 | 1 | 3 | 1 | 4 | 7 | 1 |
| | | Home background level * | 10 | 11 | 6 | 1 | 1 | 8 | 10 | 5 | 7 | 9 | 5 | 5 | 9 | 10 | 9 | 10 | 12 | 13 | 12 | 10 | 15 | 12 | 11 | 12 | 14 | 15 | 12 |
| | | Burdick culture score * | 63 | — | 45 | 76 | 36 | 35 | — | 61 | 40 | 25 | 61 | 45 | 33 | 38 | 50 | 29 | 42 | — | 32 | — | 48 | — | 37 | 28 | — | 33 | 33 |
| | | Nationality or race * | Sc | H | G | H | No | A F | I | Hu | I | I | A | A | N | I | H | A | A | I | H | N | I | H | N | I | N | A | N |
| | | Economic or social level rising | | | | | | | | | | | | | | | | | | | | | | | | | | | |
| | | Economic or social level falling * | ✓ | | | | | | ✓ | ✓ | ✓ | ✓ | ✓ | ✓ | ✓ | ✓ | ✓ | ✓ | ✓ | ✓ | | | | | ✓ | ✓ | ✓ | ✓ | ✓ |
| | | Ambition higher than attainment | | | | | | | | | | | | | | | | ✓ | | | | | | | | | | | |
| | | Religion | C | J | P | J | P | P | C | C | C | C | P | P | P | C | J | J | P | C | J | P | C | J | P | C | P | — | P |
| | | Handicap | 1 | 1 | 1 | 1 | 2 | 1 | 2 | 2 | 2 | 2 | 1 | 1 | 2 | 3 | 2 | 1 | 1 | 1 | 2 | 2 | 2 | 2 | 2 | 3 | 2 | 2 | 3 |
| **III** | The subject | Sex | G | G | P | J | B | B | C | B | B | G | B | B | B | B | B | B | B | B | G | B | B | B | G | C | B | B | B |
| | | Intelligence * | +16 | +6 | -1 | +23 | -7 | +1 | +10 | -9 | -3 | -15 | +3 | -2 | -9 | -17 | +6 | -7 | +2 | -10 | -12 | -34 | -2 | -13 | -15 | -13 | -11 | -4 | +7 |
| | | Health poor | | | | | ✓ | ✓ | | ✓ | | | | | | | | ✓ | ✓ | | | | | | | | | | |
| | | Age-grade displacement * | 0 | +2 | 0 | +2 | -3 | +1 | 0 | -2 | 0 | 0 | 0 | +2 | 0 | +1 | +1 | -2 | -1 | -4 | 0 | -4 | -2 | -6 | 0 | -1 | -3 | -1 | +1 |
| | | School deportment * | 90 | 95 | 83 | 88 | 75 | 76 | 83 | 100 | 88 | 82 | 75 | 70 | 65 | 64 | 71 | 85 | 60 | 83 | 83 | 75 | 75 | 83 | 75 | 79 | 57 | 77 | 73 |
| | | Cheating of classroom * | 5 | 4 | 5 | 12 | 3 | 5 | 6 | 2 | 12 | 14 | 2 | 5 | 6 | 3 | 6 | 3 | 6 | 6 | 6 | 10 | 3 | 6 | 14 | 6 | 12 | 2 | 2 |
| | | Maladjustment Index * | 3 | 8 | 6 | 10 | 11 | 11 | 1 | 4 | 2 | 5 | 7 | 4 | 3 | 11 | 10 | 10 | 7 | 10 | 3 | 5 | 1 | 8 | 9 | 14 | 7 | 9 | 9 |
| | | Handicap | 0 | 1 | 1 | 2 | 1 | 2 | 1 | 0 | 2 | 3 | 2 | 2 | 2 | 2 | 3 | 1 | 1 | 4 | 2 | 4 | 1 | 3 | 4 | 4 | 4 | 2 | 2 |
| | | Total handicap score | 1 | 2 | 3 | 3 | 4 | 4 | 4 | 4 | 5 | 5 | 5 | 6 | 6 | 6 | 6 | 7 | 7 | 7 | 8 | 8 | 9 | 9 | 9 | 10 | 10 | 11 | 12 |

292

" Possession " requires no interpretation in the case of the check marks. In translating the *ratings* into percentages of possession, we called a rating of either 1 or 2, that is, below average, " possession " of the less desirable type of personality or relationship, such as " notoriously antisocial," for the father's personality; " grudging, antagonistic," for the attitude toward the child; or " complete antagonism, abuse, infidelity," in the case of the relations between parents.   The nationality figures represent percentages of cases outside the following national or racial groups, which are selected for preference because of the facts reported in Chapter XI: A, E, F, Fr, G, S, Sc.   The figure for the religious groups is not a handicap score and will be explained presently, as will also the figure for sex differences.   " Possession " of age-grade displacement is indicated when the displacement is more than one year in either direction.   The items which are given in terms of scores are translated into percentages of possession by dividing the scores at the mean or median, those falling on the unfavorable side, such as lower home background level, being counted as " possessing " the item.   In the case of the Burdick scores, however, the limit is placed a little lower than the mean, *viz.*, at 45; and the same is true of the classroom cheating score, the limit of possession in this case being placed at 6 instead of at the mean.   The means are given in Table LIV.

With Table LI before us we can now compare the prevalence of the items listed among the three groups.   The items on which there is a considerable difference can readily be seen by glancing across the table.   A difference of double the percentage between the honest group and either of the others is regarded as an indication that the item concerned represents what we may call a " handicap." These items are starred, and the starred items are combined in a handicap percentage for each section of the table and for the table as a whole.

Having determined in this way which of the items seem to differentiate the honest from the dishonest or confessing group, we are now in a position to give each individual a handicap score, consisting of the number of handicaps he labors under.   These indi-

TABLE LI

PERCENTAGE OF PREVALENCE OF HANDICAPS AMONG THE H, D, AND C GROUPS

|  | HONEST | DISHONEST | CONFESSORS |
|---|---|---|---|
| TOTAL HANDICAPS | 18% | 31% | 43% |
| I. PERSONAL RELATIONS WITHIN FAMILY | 11 | 22 | 29 |
| Parental example dishonest * . . . | 2 | 15 | 11 |
| Personality of father * . . . . . | 15 | 27 | 26 |
| Relations between parents * . . . | 18 | 29 | 35 |
| Discipline of child . . . . . . . | 18 | 25 | 31 |
| Divided * . . . . . . . . . | 22 | 29 | 44 |
| Severe . . . . . . . . . | 22 | 31 | 41 |
| Spoiling . . . . . . . . . | 22 | 27 | 19 |
| Lacking supervision * . . . . . | 4 | 13 | 19 |
| Attitude of mother * . . . . . . | 13 | 27 | 42 |
| Attitude of father * . . . . . . | 13 | 22 | 50 |
| Foreign language used * . . . . . | 12 | 29 | 26 |
| Presence of more favored child . . | 8 | 10 | 11 |
| Subject an only child . . . . . | 16 | 15 | 15 |
| Pressure on school work * . . . . | 2 | 10 | 11 |
| II. CULTURAL STATUS OF FAMILY . . . | 28 | 43 | 58 |
| Community rating * . . . . . . | 29 | 44 | 63 |
| Home background level * . . . . | 43 | 60 | 70 |
| Burdick culture scores * . . . . . | 27 | 38 | 70 |
| Nationality or race * . . . . . . | 29 | 58 | 67 |
| Economic or social level changing . . | 37 | 53 | 26 |
| Rising . . . . . . . . . . | 27 | 38 | 4 |
| Falling * . . . . . . . . . | 10 | 15 | 22 |
| Ambition higher than attainment . . | 10 | 17 | 7 |
| Catholic . . . . . . . . . . | 29 | 35 | 37 |
| Jewish . . . . . . . . . . | 27 | 35 | 38 |
| Protestant . . . . . . . . . | 44 | 30 | 25 |
| III. PERSONAL HANDICAPS . . . . . . | 20 | 33 | 52 |
| Boys . . . . . . . . . . . | 51 | 42 | 63 |
| Girls . . . . . . . . . . . | 49 | 58 | 37 |
| Intelligence * . . . . . . . . . | 36 | 62 | 63 |
| Health . . . . . . . . . . . | 18 | 17 | 22 |
| Age-grade displacement . . . . . | 20 | 31 | 19 |
| More than 1 year over-age * . . | 0 | 12 | 0 |
| More than 1 year under-age . . . | 20 | 19 | 19 |
| School deportment * . . . . . . | 23 | 30 | 77 |
| Cheating of classroom * . . . . . | 15 | 24 | 48 |
| Maladjustment index * . . . . . | 29 | 39 | 70 |

vidual handicap scores are entered in Tables XLVIII to L, being figured for each section of the table separately as well as for all the items combined. All the items starred in Table LI have been used in computing the individual scores except the fact of race or nationality, which has been ignored ;* and with some exceptions,† " possession " means the same thing as in Table LI. Before attempting to interpret the meaning of these handicaps, let us digress long enough to get clearly in mind certain fundamental differences between the honest, dishonest, and confessing groups which are in themselves significant in relation to the tendency to deceive.

## DIGRESSION FOR THE PRESENTATION OF FUNDAMENTAL DIFFERENCES BETWEEN THE H, D, AND C GROUPS

The first class of differences to be reported consists of facts concerning occupational level, religion, and race or nationality. The first two are shown roughly in Table XLVII, but in the case of the religious differences the reduction in the number of cases from two hundred or more to one hundred twenty-eight entailed certain changes in the proportionate representation of the different religious groups. The facts are therefore given in Table LII for the cases actually used in our study.

The religious groups are indicated at the left of the table, and the adjoining column shows the approximate way in which these three communions are distributed in the school system. Column 1 then gives the number of cases of the combined HDC group that belongs to each denomination. Column 2 shows the per cent which each of these figures is to the total number of HDC cases, and may

* Where the Burdick score is lacking, the fact of race or nationality is taken into consideration.

† The exceptions are as follows: home background limit at 10 instead of 9; Burdick score limit, 50 instead of 45; intelligence deviation, −10 instead of 0; school deportment, 80 instead of 85. The handicap for section II is based on three items: community rating, falling economic status, and *either* the home background level or the Burdick score, whichever is lower.

STUDIES IN DECEIT

be compared with the proportional representation of the school community. Thus, whereas 60% of the school population taken as a whole are Protestant, in our HDC groups 53% are Protestant.

TABLE LII

DENOMINATIONAL PROPORTIONS IN H, D, AND C GROUPS

| DENOMINATION | POPULATION PROPORTION | HDC | | HONEST | | | | DISHONEST | | | | CONFESSING | | | |
|---|---|---|---|---|---|---|---|---|---|---|---|---|---|---|---|
| | | 1 | 2 | 3 | 4 | 5 | 6 | 7 | 8 | 9 | 10 | 11 | 12 | 13 | 14 |
| | | Number | Per Cent | Number | Per Cent | Per Cent | Per Cent | Number | Per Cent | Per Cent | Per Cent | Number | Per Cent | Per Cent | Per Cent |
| Catholics | 29 | 36 | 31 | 10 | 24 | 28 | 29 | 17 | 33 | 47 | 35 | 9 | 36 | 25 | 37 |
| Jews | 11 | 19 | 16 | 5 | 12 | 26 | 27 | 9 | 18 | 47 | 35 | 5 | 20 | 26 | 38 |
| Protestants | 60 | 63 | 53 | 27 | 64 | 43 | 44 | 25 | 49 | 40 | 30 | 11 | 44 | 17 | 25 |

Columns 3, 7, and 11 give the number of children of each denomination who are classified respectively in the H, D, or C group; and the adjoining columns, 4, 8, and 12, show the per cent of the honest group who are Catholic, Jewish, and Protestant, the per cent of the dishonest group who are divided in the same way, and likewise for the confessing group. Thus columns 4, 8, and 12 give what might be called the "denominational structure" of the three contrasting groups. It is essential that differences between the H, D, and C groups taken each as a whole, in intelligence, home background, and other factors be interpreted in the light of the preponderance of certain social factors in each of the three deception groups, and this is shown in columns 4, 8, and 12.

These percentages, however, do not give us a fair picture of the association of deception *with each denomination*, since the representation of the different denominations in the total HDC group is uneven. It is to be expected that there will be more Protestants than Jews in the honest group as there are more than three times as many Protestants as Jews in the total HDC group. Hence we give in columns 5, 9, and 13 the per cent of each religious group falling respectively in the H, D, and C groups. Thus 43% of the Protestants of the total HDC group are in the honest group, 40% of them are in the dishonest group, and 17% among the confessors. Columns 5, 9, and 13, therefore, show the number of honest, dishonest, and confessing cases that would have been found in each of the three religious groups if there had been one hundred of each religious group to start with.

We can now indicate what the structure of the H, D, and C groups *would have been* if there had been one hundred of each instead of the number indicated in column 1. This we do by showing in columns 6, 10, and 14 the per cent which each figure in columns 5, 9, and 13 is of the total of its column. Centering attention on these three columns, we now read the table as follows: If there had been one hundred Catholics, one hundred Jews, and one hundred Protestants in the entire HDC group, then 29% of the H group would have been Catholic, 27% Jewish, and 44% Protestant; also (column 10) 35% of the D group would have been Catholic, 35% Jewish, and 30% Protestant; while, finally, we see by column 14 that of the confessors 37% would have been Catholic, 38% Jewish, and 25% Protestant. This is the fairest comparison we can make of the constituency of the H, D, and C groups, and it is this figure which is used in Table LI to show the denominational representation. The differences are not large enough to warrant our regarding membership in one or another religious group as a handicap in the matter of honest behavior.

Table LIII analyzes the racial and national differences in the way used for Table LII.

As far as race and nationality are concerned we see from column 2 of Table LIII that the proportions for our HDC group are about the same as for the whole population the percentages of which are given at the left side of the table. As before, columns 5, 9, and 13 show the proportion of each racial and national group.falling in the H, D, or C group; and columns 6, 10, and 14 show what per cent of the H, D, and C groups respectively would have belonged to national groups I, II, III, and IV if there had been one hundred

TABLE LIII

RACIAL AND NATIONAL PROPORTIONS IN THE H, D, AND C GROUPS

| RACIAL AND NATIONAL GROUPS | POPULATION PROPORTION | HDC | | HONEST | | | | DISHONEST | | | | CONFESSING | | | |
|---|---|---|---|---|---|---|---|---|---|---|---|---|---|---|---|
| | | 1 | 2 | 3 | 4 | 5 | 6 | 7 | 8 | 9 | 10 | 11 | 12 | 13 | 14 |
| | | Number | Per Cent | Number | Per Cent | Per Cent | Per Cent | Number | Per Cent | Per Cent | Per Cent | Number | Per Cent | Per Cent | Per Cent |
| I. A, E, F, Fr, G, No, S, Sc . . . . | 58 | 65 | 51 | 34 | 69 | 52 | 41 | 22 | 42 | 34 | 20 | 0 | 33 | 14 | 14 |
| II. I, Hu, L, P . . . | 16 | 26 | 20 | 4 | 8 | 15 | 12 | 14 | 27 | 54 | 31 | 8 | 30 | 31 | 31 |
| III. J . . . . . . | 11 | 20 | 16 | 5 | 10 | 25 | 20 | 10 | 19 | 50 | 29 | 5 | 19 | 25 | 25 |
| IV. N . . . . . . | 15 | 17 | 13 | 6 | 12 | 35 | 28 | 6 | 12 | 35 | 20 | 5 | 19 | 30 | 30 |
| II, III, and IV . | 42 | 63 | 49 | 15 | 31 | 24 | | 30 | 58 | 48 | | 18 | 67 | 29 | |

of each of these four groups. The marked tendency for the American-born and North Europeans to be better represented among the H group is in conformity with the findings of Chapter XI and warrants our taking the fact of nationality and race into consideration, so far as this community is concerned, in making up the handicap scores of Table LI.

The figures for sex differences shown in Table LI are made in the same way as for religious differences, and need hardly be reported in detail. There were in all 69 boys and 59 girls, the percentage of each being respectively 54 and 46. Had there been one hundred of each, then, as may be seen by referring to Table LI, 51% of the honest group would have been boys and 49% girls. The figures for the dishonest group, however, are for boys 42% and for girls 58%.

We may now present certain facts concerning the intelligence, home background, deportment, maladjustment index, and classroom deception ratings of the three deception groups; but in studying these facts the reader should keep in mind the structural differences reported in columns 3, 7, and 11 of Tables LII and LIII.

Since we are dealing with fundamental group differences which we have shown to have some relation to the tendency to deceive, we should evaluate in some way the differences reported in Table LIV in order that we may see which factors seem to be most

## TABLE LIV

### CERTAIN HANDICAP SCORES OF THE H, D, AND C GROUPS

| GROUP | INTELLIGENCE | | | | HOME BACKGROUND | | | |
|---|---|---|---|---|---|---|---|---|
| | Median | Mean | SD | Number | Median | Mean | SD | Number |
| HDC | − .09 | − .02 | 1.12 | 124 | 9.2 | 8.8 | 3.5 | 128 |
| H | + .63 | + .40 | .99 | 45 | 8.0 | 7.6 | 4.0 | 49 |
| D | − .35 | − .21 | 1.10 | 52 | 9.3 | 9.3 | 2.8 | 52 |
| C | − .65 | − .38 | 1.11 | 27 | 10.1 | 9.9 | 2.8 | 27 |

| | DEPORTMENT | | | | MALADJUSTMENT INDEX | | | |
|---|---|---|---|---|---|---|---|---|
| | Median | Mean | SD | Number | Median | Mean | SD | Number |
| HDC | 84.2 | 83.9 | 9.1 | 115 | 3.8 | 4.6 | 2.9 | 127 |
| H | 89.1 | 87.0 | 7.8 | 43 | 3.4 | 3.6 | 2.8 | 48 |
| D | 84.1 | 84.4 | 7.8 | 46 | 3.4 | 4.3 | 2.5 | 52 |
| C | 77.7 | 77.8 | 10.0 | 26 | 6.9 | 6.8 | 3.1 | 27 |

| | COMMUNITY RATING | | | | BURDICK CULTURE SCORES | | | |
|---|---|---|---|---|---|---|---|---|
| | Median | Mean | SD | Number | Median | Mean | SD | Number |
| HDC | 6.9 | 5.9 | 3.9 | 125 | 53.1 | 45.8 | 18.7 | 92 |
| H | 7.4 | 7.2 | 3.5 | 48 | 60.0 | 54.0 | 21.9 | 30 |
| D | 6.8 | 5.7 | 4.0 | 50 | 46.9 | 43.3 | 15.7 | 42 |
| C | 1.3 | 3.8 | 3.6 | 27 | 40.0 | 38.5 | 14.3 | 20 |

### CLASSROOM DECEPTION RATING OF THE CLASSES REPRESENTED AMONG THE THREE GROUPS

| GROUP | MEDIAN | MEAN | SD | NUMBER |
|---|---|---|---|---|
| HDC | 3.6 | 4.9 | 3.5 | 126 |
| H | 3.2 | 3.9 | 2.6 | 48 |
| D | 4.2 | 5.1 | 3.8 | 51 |
| C | 5.4 | 6.2 | 3.9 | 27 |

responsible for them. This we do by expressing the differences between the means in terms of their standard error. In our discussion of how to interpret differences between group means we pointed out in Chapter VI that to be beyond the limits of chance such a difference would need to be at least three times its standard error. Consequently, the relative significance of the factors under discussion may be roughly shown in comparing the size of the figures in Table LV. Wherever these figures are over 3.0, we may be sure that the difference indicated by the symbol H–D, H–C, or D–C, that is, the honest group mean minus the dishonest group mean, or the honest group mean minus the confessing group mean, or the dishonest group mean minus the confessing group mean, is genuinely significant, and that ratios of less than 3.0 lose their significance as they approach zero. For convenience in tabulating, the differences are always expressed in the forms H–D, H–C, and D–C, no matter which mean happens to be the larger. Consequently a + sign means that the first mean of the pair is larger, and a − sign indicates that the second member of the pair is the larger.

TABLE LV

Statistical Significance of Mean Differences Reported in
Table LIV

|  | H–D | H–C | D–C |
|---|---|---|---|
| Intelligence . . . . . . . | + 2.9 | + 3.0 | + 0.7 |
| Home background . . . . | + 2.4 | + 2.9 | + 0.9 |
| Deportment . . . . . . | + 1.6 | + 4.1 | + 2.9 |
| Maladjustment index . . . | − 1.2 | − 4.3 | − 3.6 |
| Community rating . . . . | + 2.0 | + 4.0 | + 2.1 |
| Burdick culture score . . . | + 2.3 | + 3.0 | + 1.2 |
| Classroom deception . . . | − 1.8 | − 2.7 | − 1.2 |

Having now presented our major group differences, we return to the consideration of the problem of what essentially distinguishes the honest, dishonest, and confessing children from one another.

## RELATIVE SIGNIFICANCE OF BASIC GROUP DIFFERENCES FOR THE DIFFERENTIATION OF THE H, D, AND C GROUPS

We have already noted that religious differences do not seem to account for the contrasting behavior of our three groups of cases. Whatever may be the biological and cultural factors associated with race and nationality, however, these seem to have some influence on the relative deceptiveness of the H, D, and C children. Let us turn then to Table LV and see whether the three groups differ from one another in any other significant way. Taking the ratios in order of size, we see that the maladjustment index heads the list, with a difference between the honest and confessing groups of 4.3 times its unreliability, and a still further difference between the dishonest and confessing groups of 3.6 times its unreliability. But this item fails to discriminate between the honest and dishonest groups, those who cheated and lied about it having about the same index as those who did not cheat at all. The next largest difference is in the matter of deportment, and here again it is between the honest and confessing groups, which differ from each other by 4.1 times the unreliability of the difference. Also, the ratio is 2.9 between the dishonest and confessing groups. That those who cheat and own up to it should receive so much worse deportment marks than either the honest children or those who cheat and don't own up to it raises an interesting question regarding the way teachers give their deportment grades. It would seem as though the effort to " get away " with certain forms of disapproved behavior was in some cases quite successful, and that those who tended to confess their faults were penalized for their pains.

Next comes the general character of the community in which the children live. In terms of probability the chances are 98 in 100 that the honest and dishonest are significantly different in this respect, and the difference between the honest and the confessors places the latter without doubt in the less desirable section of the town. This fact, coupled with the fact that with respect to intelligence, level of home background, and cultural level as measured by the Burdick test the confessors are also significantly lower on the scale than the honest while the dishonest are less so, assists us in classifying the confessors as a distinct group, ill adjusted to its circumstances, rather badly behaved on the whole, and lacking opportunities afforded by a good neighborhood and a comfortable home. Regarding the stimulus toward deception to which the children are subjected in the classroom (the last row of Table LV), the honest, dishonest, and confessors seem to be similarly exposed, but there is strong probability that the confessors as a group are subject to greater temptation than the honest.

From all this it should be apparent that no one factor accounts for a pupil being found in the H group rather than in the D or C group. The causes leading to honorable as against deceptive behavior are seen to be complex, as we suggested they would be earlier in this report. Our next thought is, therefore, that, while no single handicap is sufficient to explain deceit in any case, or even in any group, the cumulative effect of several handicaps operating at once may be adequate to discriminate between them. In order to pursue this suggestion, it is necessary to revert to the handicap scores which we assigned to each child in Tables XLVIII to L. Each score is the sum of handicaps faced by the pupil, no one of which seems to explain his conduct but all of which taken together may do so. Let us first compare the three groups with reference to their total handicap scores. Figure 58 shows the complete distribution in terms of the per cent of each group having the number of handicaps indicated at the left of the chart.

As we shall presently show, there is a very great difference in total handicap scores between the honest group and *both* the dishonest and confessing groups, and the difference between the dishonest and the confessors is probably a genuine difference and not due to chance. Even so, there is considerable overlapping, 5 out of the 49 honest children having a higher handicap score than the mean of the confessors and 14 of them having a higher handicap score than the mean of the dishonest children. However, only 2 of the 27 confessors have fewer handicaps than the mean handicap score of the honest, and similarly only 9 of the 52 dishonest are better off than the average of the honest in the matter of total handicaps.   Furthermore, 29% of the honest have no handi-

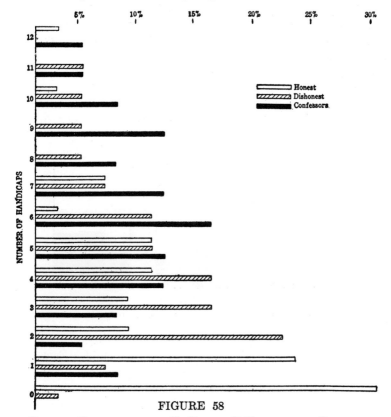

FIGURE 58

GRAPHIC DISTRIBUTION OF H, D, AND C GROUPS WITH REGARD
TO HANDICAP SCORES

Each bar represents the per cent of the group having the number of handicaps shown at the left.

cap at all, whereas the same thing is true of only 2% of the dishonest and of none at all of the confessors.

Early in our discussion we explained that we had classified the
handicaps in three types of items, (I) those referring to family

relations, (II) those referring to the cultural status of the family, its cultural level, neighborhood rating, and socio-economic acceleration, and (III) those of a personal nature.   It might prove illuminating to find the way in which our three deception groups compare with respect to each of these three classes of handicaps. This we do in Tables LVI, LVII, and LVIII.

Before turning to these tables let us examine briefly a graphic translation of the essentials in Figure 59.   Each of the three rectangles of this chart represents the total number of handicaps to which the children of each group *might have been* exposed, there

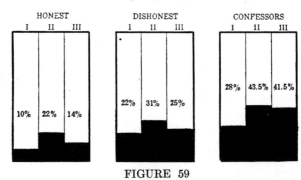

FIGURE 59

COMPARATIVE HANDICAPS OF H, D, AND C GROUPS

being in our list 9 handicaps of type I, 3 of type II, and 5 of type III, making a possible maximum of 17 for each child.   Each of the columns I, II, and III represents one of the three classes of handicaps, and the proportion of possible handicaps actually suffered by each of the three deception groups is shown by the height of the black in each of the columns.   One can thus see at a glance that the second group of factors shows a larger percentage of handicaps than either of the other two in the case of all three deception groups.   This group of items consists chiefly of the home background score and neighborhood rating.   The relative significance of the three classes of items can best be seen, however, by studying the tables, to which we may now turn.

It is from the per cents at the extreme right of Table LVI that

the chart of Figure 59 is drawn.    The rest of the table gives exactly
the same facts in terms of the average or mean number of handicaps
of each type manifested by the H, D, and C groups respectively.

### TABLE LVI

DIFFERENTIATED HANDICAP SCORES OF THE H, D, AND C GROUPS

| HANDICAP | MAXIMUM SCORE | MEAN | | | SD | | | PER CENT OF HANDICAP | | |
|---|---|---|---|---|---|---|---|---|---|---|
| | | H | D | C | H | D | C | H | D | C |
| I. Family relations  . | 9 | .94 | 1.98 | 2.52 | 1.49 | 1.82 | 2.08 | 10.4 | 22.0 | 28.0 |
| II. Cultural status . . | 3 | .88 | 1.25 | 1.74 | .96 | .78 | .65 | 21.9 | 31.2 | 43.5 |
| III. Personal status . . | 5 | .71 | 1.25 | 2.07 | .90 | 1.07 | 1.19 | 14.3 | 25.0 | 41.5 |
| Total    . . . . | 17 | 2.55 | 4.48 | 6.22 | 2.75 | 2.73 | 2.68 | 15.0 | 26.4 | 36.6 |

### TABLE LVII

RELATIVE SIGNIFICANCE OF HANDICAPS

The means of Table LVI are here weighted (each is divided by the SD of
its distribution) so as to show what their relative size would have been if there
had been the same number of handicaps in each section of items.

| HANDICAP | HONEST | DISHONEST | CONFESSORS |
|---|---|---|---|
| I. Family relations . . . . . | .63 | 1.09 | 1.21 |
| II. Cultural status   . . . . . | .91 | 1.60 | 2.69 |
| III. Personal status   . . . . . | .78 | 1.17 | 1.74 |

### TABLE LVIII

SIGNIFICANCE OF THE DIFFERENCES BETWEEN THE H, D, AND C GROUPS
EXPRESSED AS MULTIPLES OF THE STANDARD ERRORS OF THE DIFFERENCES

| | I. FAMILY RELATIONS | II. CULTURAL STATUS | III. PERSONAL HANDICAPS | TOTAL HANDICAPS |
|---|---|---|---|---|
| D–H | 3.16 | 2.14 | 2.73 | 3.54 |
| C–H | 3.50 | 4.65 | 5.15 | 5.66 |
| D–C | 1.14 | 2.97 | 2.95 | 2.72 |

Thus the honest children had an average of .94 handicap in the matter of family relations, whereas the dishonest had 1.98 handicaps of this type on the average, and the confessors 2.52, or two and a half times as many as the honest. Of 17 possible handicaps, the honest children had on the average two and a half apiece, the dishonest four and a half, and the confessors six and a quarter.

Turning now to Table LVII, we may compare the relative contribution to the total handicap made by the three groups of items. The home background and neighborhood factors are seen to be the largest for each of the three groups, H, D, and C, being half as large again as the family-relations items in the case of the honest and dishonest children and twice as great for the confessors. Personal handicaps have about the same importance as family-relations handicaps for the several groups.

Finally, then, Table LVIII shows us the extent to which the H, D, and C groups are genuinely differentiated by these three sets of factors as well as by the total handicap score, the distributions of which are shown in Figure 58. As already pointed out, the difference between the total number of handicaps suffered by the children is genuinely significant of their relative deceptiveness, for the ratios in the last column of the table are, for the dishonest minus the honest and for the confessors minus the honest, considerably more than 3.0. The largest difference noted is between the honest and the confessors in the matter of personal handicaps, such as intelligence, maladjustment index, and deportment (see the list in Table LI). Here the mean difference is over five times its unreliability. Next comes the cultural and neighborhood difference between the same two groups, with a ratio of over four and a half. The honest and dishonest groups, though genuinely differing in the total handicap score, show an absolutely certain difference for the separate types of handicap in the case of family relations, with personal handicaps a close second in importance. And interestingly enough, the dishonest and confessing groups are practically distinct in the matter of both background and personal handicaps.

It is quite clear that we can differentiate our groups by reference to the total number of handicaps suffered and, at some points, in the matter of the type of handicap. But the distributions of Figure 58 show us at once that we have not accounted for the behavior of all of our *individuals*. Considering the fact that we are dealing in all our cases with only two kinds of cheating, school and home, and these measured by only three tests all together, it may be claimed that we have gone about as far as could be expected in tracing the causes of this special form of dishonesty. We will do what we can, however, to account for our individual differences, and for this purpose we shall consider not the total *number* of handicaps under which the pupil suffers, but particular *combinations* of handicaps. We should do this, however, in the light of the total picture that we are now able to draw of the general characteristics of each of our three groups. A study of Tables LI, LVII, and LVIII, in which their differences are set forth, leads to the following descriptions.

### DESCRIPTION OF H, D, AND C GROUPS

1. **The Confessing Group.** Here are the children with an unusually large number of personal handicaps. They have low intelligence and their maladjustment scores show them to be badly adjusted to their general environment. That they do not get along well with their teachers is evidenced by the fact that their deportment average is only 78 as compared with 87 for the honest children. About two-thirds of them are boys, or almost twice as many as we might expect from the distribution of the sexes in the HDC group as a whole, 54% of whom are boys.

The homes from which these children come are situated in the worst districts of the town and exhibit a level of cultural and social status considerably below the average. The details of the home background do not stand out clearly save by way of contrast with the other two groups; in almost every respect that one could think of we find among the confessors a far larger amount of unwholesome influence than among the honest children, and in most matters their homes are less favored than those even of the dishonest group.

**2. The Dishonest Group.** These children suffer from fewer handicaps than the confessors, being particularly weak, however, in the matter of family relations. On the whole they are somewhat less intelligent than the honest group. But in deportment they are about average and show no great sign of general maladjustment. It is rather in the total family situation that the dishonest children are inferior, for not only do they live in a somewhat less desirable section of the community, but the evidences of culture and social achievement are fewer. The most conspicuous differences between the honest and dishonest are to be found in parental example, attitude, and supervision, although in almost every respect there are more cases of unwholesome influence among them than among the honest.

**3. The Honest Group.** In comparison with the other groups the honest children stand out clearly from the confessing group, with higher intelligence, no sign of maladjustment, and excellent school deportment. They live in better neighborhoods and their families are on a far higher social level, showing few examples of parental inferiority. Boys and girls are divided about as one might properly expect from their proportion in the entire group. Their differentiation from the children who cheated and also lied about it, however, is not quite so distinct, although it is apparent that with respect to all the advantages which set them off from the confessing group they are also almost invariably superior to the dishonest group. The picture is somewhat blurred, however, and for this reason it is necessary to study our cases individually rather than merely *en bloc*. To this more difficult task let us now proceed.

## INDIVIDUAL DIFFERENCES BETWEEN HONEST AND DISHONEST CHILDREN

In undertaking to explain why some children are honest and some are dishonest in terms of particular combinations of handicaps they may possess, we may as well admit at once that we are doomed to failure. We can, to be sure, reach a better " understanding " of a given child by gathering all the facts about him into one place and letting them coalesce, as it were, into a complete picture; but such a process does not " account for " the child in a scientific sense: it does not subsume his behavior under a law. There are some who feel that the idea of " law " is hardly applicable to human behavior in the concrete, and that all we may properly expect is a sort of insight into a man's total character which recognizes at once his entire uniqueness.  And no one is apt to question the thought that we are not likely to come upon two children who have precisely the same combination of handicaps and advantages, which makes the discovery of a typical combination or law of combination out of the question.  This is one of the weaknesses of the case method.  We think we have found in some particular concatenation of circumstances the real explanation of a refractory child's conduct.  But scientific confidence in our explanation rests upon the probability of the recurrence of the precise group of causes we have listed in association with the precise social defect we are studying.*  And this is just what does not happen.  No two cases are alike or, if several are much alike, they are too few in number to establish a law.

With this precaution in mind, let us examine a few of our own cases.  Here, for example, is a girl from an exceedingly poor home. The father is dishonest and of a rather vicious personality.  The parental relations are unhappy.  The parents' attitude toward the child is unsympathetic or hostile, and their discipline does everything to her except spoil her.  They live in the worst part of the community, and the general level of the home background is almost as low as there is.  One parent is German and the other Italian, and they report themselves as Catholic.  The child herself is of less than average intelligence but is somewhat ahead in her school grade, and her teachers evidently regard her as a nuisance, for her deportment trend is 76.  Furthermore, 60% or more of her classmates cheated on the test taken in school.  The child's neurotic index, however, is only a point higher than the average.  This would seem to be an almost perfect picture of a child who has the

* It should be remembered that we are dealing here with scores on our IER school and home tests.

handicaps leading most frequently to deception. Yet this child did not cheat at all. We are tempted to resort to the expression, "She's not that kind of girl," which illustrates the case method type of conclusion.

Here are two children of the same family. One is in the honest group and one is in the dishonest group. They have the same general home background and are treated by their parents in much the same way. These background factors yield a general handicap of 5 in each case. Whatever differences there are between them must be personal. Are we on the track of a genuine explanation when we note that the honest child is a boy of superior intelligence, that the dishonest child is a girl of inferior intelligence, and that both of them are far younger than their classmates, which puts an added pressure on the girl, particularly as she has a record of poor health? The girl's case might indeed seem to be explained by this combination of circumstances — a superior brother, and attempting to do school work which is not only in advance of her age but for which she is doubly disqualified by low intelligence and poor health. But this exact combination does not recur again, and furthermore, we find that honest cases Nos. 16 and 27 are similarly handicapped, both being girls accelerated in school but backward in intelligence, one a Negro and one a Jew. However, as noted, these girls were *honest*, whereas the girl we have been discussing was dishonest.

As for the boy of superior intelligence, it is of interest that there are only two such cases among the dishonest group (Nos. 7 and 49). One of these has an example of dishonesty in his parents, and the other is an only child, whose parents speak a foreign language at home, tend to spoil him, and at the same time nag him about his school work. Yet the confessors have among them a boy of superior intelligence (No. 24), and it would seem as though he had almost every advantage except that he is in a classroom which cheated nearly one hundred per cent. But the *honest* children from three rooms of like character were in every case considerably *below* average in intelligence.

And so we might go on. We have printed the individual cases in the order of their handicaps so that anyone who chooses to do so may pursue this elusive quest still farther.   The critical cases are those of the honest who have high handicap scores, and those of the dishonest who have low handicap scores.   These need to be accounted for in some such way as we have just now illustrated.

## SUMMARY

Our study of the three groups of cases confirms our findings regarding the facts associated with deceit and illustrates them rather forcibly.   It is clear that there are significant differences between the extremely honest and the extremely dishonest in respect to intelligence, home background, and school deportment, and possibly in the matter of race or nationality and sex.   It is not clear, however, that such facts, whether taken separately, added together, or considered in certain combinations, can account for deceit in individual cases, although, as illustrated, a close scrutiny of the details may lead to a better understanding of the subject and, as in the case of the sister who cheated while her brother was honest, may suggest very definite ways of correcting the conditions that may possibly be leading to the practice of deceit.

# PART III

## Moral Values in Contemporary Education

### CHAPTER XV

## PROGRESSIVE METHODS AND SCHOOL MORALE

As was indicated in Chapter IV, we have used one or another of our techniques to measure the deceptive tendencies of some ten thousand children, all of whom were in school and nearly all of whom had been exposed to school influences for from four to seven years. As we reported in Chapter XII, we find that in many schools the tendency to cheat when opportunity is offered is somewhat more prevalent in the higher grades than in the lower, while in other schools the reverse is the case. Since, however, the membership of grade eight, say, in any one school is by no means the same as was the membership of grade five three years previously or even of grade seven the year before, the influence of the school as a whole can be measured only by its cumulative effect on individuals and not by the relative standing of the ascending grades. If the school is tending to make its children less and less deceptive the longer they remain in it, this fact will show in a negative correlation between deception and length of attendance at this school; but if it tends to allow children to become more and more deceptive the longer they stay, then this fact will be shown by a positive correlation between deception and length of attendance.

We have figured such correlations for four school populations, and the results are given in Table LIX for several types of deceptive behavior.

313

TABLE LIX

THE CORRELATION BETWEEN LENGTH OF ATTENDANCE AT A GIVEN SCHOOL
AND DECEPTION IN SCHOOLS C, D, F TO J, AND P

|  | C | D | F TO J | P |
|---|---|---|---|---|
| IER school Xi . . . . . . | − .142 | − .041 |  | + .100 |
| IER home Xi . . . . . . | + .148 |  |  | − .076 |
| CT ratio . . . . . . . |  | − .103 | + .081 |  |
| Out-of-class tests . . . . |  | − .015 |  |  |
| Stealing test . . . . . . |  | − .161 |  |  |

In public school C and its affiliated school at institution D we find that most of the *r*'s are negative but very small. Whatever influence exists is in the direction of less cheating, not more. In private school P, however, whatever influence exists is in the direction of more cheating, not less, even though the school as a whole is far less deceptive than the public schools which we have tested. But these *r*'s contain the influence of age, slight as it is, since the longer children are in school, the older they grow. If we eliminate this factor by keeping age constant or by taking what amounts to the average of a series of *r*'s each of which shows the relation between deception and length of attendance for just one age group at a time, we get the true influence of the school. For the IER cheating at school in population C this *r* changes from − .142 to − .24, showing that apart from change due to age the school has an influence in the direction of greater honesty the longer the children stay in it. For school D the corresponding partial is + .003 and for school P − .001, which means that in these places cheating is almost totally unrelated to the length of time spent in school.

We have not made any general statements concerning the prevalence of the tendency to deceive since no one technique has been given to a large enough number of properly selected cases to make any generalization valid. Some idea of what has been found, however, may be gained from Figure 60, which shows the per cent of all the children taking certain kinds of tests who cheated at least once.

In Figure 60, the school populations have been lumped together. When school populations are dealt with separately, however, extreme differences between schools are noted, particularly between private and public schools.  On one of the classroom tests, for example, we found that 40% of 1200 public school children cheated, whereas on this same test only 11% of 850 private school children cheated.   The same difference was found in the case of a test done at home.   These public school children were in good city schools in two cities, and the private school children were in six schools in various localities.   On the other hand, we noted that some public school classrooms were as free from the tendency to cheat as the most honest of the private school classrooms.

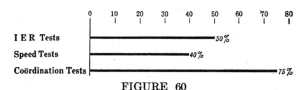

FIGURE 60

Per Cent of Cases Cheating on Three Kinds of Tests

The existence of these contrasts between classrooms seemed to us to open up some fundamental problems concerning the moral values inherent in contemporary educational situations.  How is this difference to be accounted for?   Is it due to difference in educational method?   Or to the background of the home?   How much effect does the teacher have through her personality, her convictions, her way of treating the pupils?   Is there a general school morale, or a classroom morale, perhaps, or a group code which favors or hinders the development of classroom honor?   These factors and others undoubtedly are operative, separately and in combination.   Let us analyze them and weigh as well as we can their relative importance.   In this chapter we shall concern ourselves with three: selected home background, progressive *versus* conventional school methods, and general school morale.

## HOME BACKGROUND *VERSUS* PROGRESSIVE METHODS

If the superiority of the private schools tested is due to superiority in home background, then children in public schools coming from homes of the same economic and social condition as those from which the private school children come should show no more tendency to deceive than the private school children do.  To test this argument, we selected thirty-three children from a public school who matched an equal number from a neighboring private school in age, intelligence, and home background as measured by the Sims Score Card.*  Instead of exhibiting about the same amount of deception, as our argument requires, these two groups showed a significant difference in favor of the private school group. These facts are presented graphically in Figure 61, which gives the mean Xi scores of both groups for the IER school test and the Speed test.

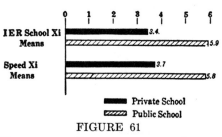

FIGURE 61

Comparative Deceptiveness of Public and Private School Children from the Same Socio-economic Level and of the Same Intelligence

In spite of the economic-social equivalence of the backgrounds of these two groups, there might still be subtle differences not measured by the Sims card which would influence one set of parents to send their children to a good private school charging tuition rather than to a free public school, and these subtle differences in homes might well be associated with different ethical codes.  It seemed best to test the hypothesis under consideration still further, therefore, by taking two public schools drawing from the same population, but with one using progressive methods and the other using traditional methods.  In this way the contrast in method between the two schools would be retained, but the two schools would be alike as to tuition, social prestige, and the like.

* Described in Chapter VIII.

Ideally what we need is a community in which there are two public schools, one progressive and one traditional, which are attended by equal numbers of children of the same ages, the same intelligence, and the same home background, and in which the children are assigned to one school or the other by chance. Naturally such an ideal situation could not be found, but we discovered one approximating it in a small town having two schools of which one (M) is a distinctly good but conventional school and the other (L) an experimental school conducted in connection with a normal school and with the reputation of being one of the best examples of progressive method in the East. Both schools are public and free, and, so far as could be determined, each school draws its pupils from its immediate neighborhood. The local school people, furthermore, felt that there was no difference between the two groups as to home background.

The details of this comparison are presented fully in Book Two and will be merely summarized here. We gave ten deception tests in all, the six Speed tests, the three Coördination tests, and the Arithmetic test from the IER battery. The fourth-grade children omitted the Arithmetic test and one of the Speed tests. Grades five to seven also had the Sims Score Card, and for all the children scores from the McCall Multi-mental Test were available.

Inasmuch as the fourth grade had only eight chances to cheat as against ten for the rest, we translated the cheating scores into cheating ratios, dividing the number of c's each child scored by the number of chances he had to cheat. The mean of this cheating or CT ratio for each grade and each test is graphically portrayed in Figure 62.

These differences in deceptiveness are significant and are in favor of the experimental school. Grade for grade, the progressive school children are less deceptive than those attending the more conventional school. As is explained in Book Two, the contrast between the two schools cannot be accounted for by the differences in the age, mental age, or IQ of the two groups. In spite of local opinion, there was a significant difference between the schools in the Sims home background score, the experimental school rating one point higher. But when the cases with lower socio-economic scores were eliminated from the conventional group and the means thus equalized, the deception differences remained as they were. Furthermore, in this particular population, the Sims score correlated *positively* with deception, instead of negatively, as is the case with a large unselected population, so that if factors measured by the Sims card were the cause of the difference, the traditional school should have proved *less* deceptive rather than more.

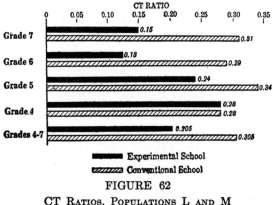

FIGURE 62

CT Ratios, Populations L and M

Another check on home background factors is found in the occupational level of the groups. As reported in Chapter IX, the higher occupational levels are associated with less cheating than are the lower, generally speaking. There is a distinct tendency for the children of the conventional village school to represent occupations of lower economic-social rating than the children of the progressive school. But when the two populations are classified by occupational level, the progressive school shows less deception at *each* level. The facts are shown graphically in Figure 63, which is based on Table CXXXIV of Book Two.

One final bit of evidence on the matter of home background remains to be brought forward. In the experimental school we found twelve children who were brought to the school from a neighboring city. Since they were not residents, we have not included them in any of the figures reported. Evidently their parents selected this school voluntarily, placing themselves thus in the same general category as parents who select a private school to which to send their children. It is a matter of some interest that these children were just about halfway between the experimental group and the conventional school population. The cases are too few to afford a basis for generalization, but such as they are they lend support to the judgment that home background makes a real

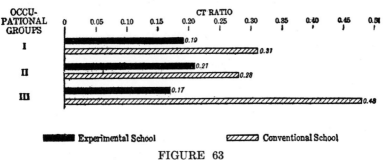

FIGURE 63

MEAN CT RATIO OF EACH OCCUPATIONAL LEVEL FOR SCHOOLS
L AND M

difference in the behavior of the children, but is in any given school situation less significant than the influence of the school itself.

So much for external evidence regarding the effect of home background. Let us now turn to the internal evidence. Figure 62 shows differences in CT ratio from grade to grade in the two schools. In the fourth grade the two schools are seen to be alike, a wide difference appears in grade five, and the gap is still greater in grades six and seven. Whether or not the children in the higher grades have been in the school longer than those in the lower grades we do not know, but the experimental school has been under its present management long enough for the seventh-grade pupils who have been living in this community to have had the benefit of progressive methods through the greater part of their school life. If, however, the change from grade to grade is not to be accounted for by the accumulation of moral values, it may be that the similarity of the fourth grades is due to similarity of the fourth-grade teachers and that greater differences in method appear in grades six and seven. In either case the widening gap between the two schools is to be explained only by reference to their respective methods.

We here conclude the discussion of the relative significance of home background and progressive methods in accounting for school differences in deception. Whatever influence home background may have on behavior, there still remains sound evidence for believing that progressive school experiences are not as likely to be associated with the tendency to deceive as are conventional school experiences. Without dropping out of mind either of these two factors, let us now introduce a third, which we shall call school morale.

## SCHOOL MORALE

This third factor is suggested by the fact that private schools are much alike as to the honesty of their pupils, even while varying widely in method from most progressive to very traditional. Also public schools are found which vary greatly in deceptiveness even while much alike in general method. Let us see, then, whether a third factor, such as school morale, can be isolated from general method and home background.

Unfortunately, we do not have clear cases of all three variables operating in known amounts, but in the following schools a rough estimate may be made of the status of each variable.

| School | Technique | Morale | Home Background | |
|--------|-----------|--------|-----------------|---|
| a. Public | Experimental | ? | Outlying | High |
| b. Public | Conventional | ? | Village | High |
| c. Public | Conventional | Good | Outlying | Medium |
| d. Public | Conventional | Good | Outlying | Medium |
| e. Public | Conventional | Poor | Village | Medium |
| f. Private | Experimental | Good | City | High |
| g. Private | Experimental | Good | City | High |
| h. Private | Conventional | Good | Mixed | High |

We shall report in Table LX the comparable facts we have for these schools in the matter of deception and then discuss their significance.*

TABLE LX

DECEPTION SCORES IN GRADES 5 AND 6

| SCHOOL | TEST A † | | | IER SCHOOL TEST | | | HOME TEST | | |
|---|---|---|---|---|---|---|---|---|---|
| | Number | Mean | Per Cent | Number | Mean | Per Cent | Number | Mean | Per Cent |
| a | 34 | 1.00 | 14.7 | | | | | | |
| b | 103 | 3.80 | 54.4 | | | | | | |
| c | 70 | 1.36 | 21.5 | 71 | 3.10 | 20.6 | 70 | 2.70 | 40.2 |
| d | 22 | 2.23 | 45.4 | 22 | 2.53 | 22.7 | 21 | 4.65 | 40.9 |
| c and d | 92 | 1.57 | 27.2 | 93 | 2.06 | 21.1 | 91 | 3.15 | 40.4 |
| e | 62 | 2.87 | 23.9 | 62 | 4.09 | 29.2 | 47 | 3.88 | 44.7 |
| f | 146 | 1.44 | 13. | | | | 146 | 1.63 | 15.8 |
| g | 80 | 1.39 | 12.5 | | | | 79 | 1.39 | 10.1 |
| h | 27 | 1.45 | 7.4 | | | | | | |

† One of the IER tests, though not always the same one.   Had identical tests been used, the scores reported for (c), (d), and (e) might have been slightly larger.   All mean scores are Xi's and represent amounts of deception.

Schools (a) and (b) are the ones we have just been discussing, (a) being the one connected with the normal school, situated some little distance from the village, and (b) being the school in the center of the village.   It will be recalled that our Sims scores did show some difference in socio-economic and occupational level between the children attending (a) and those attending (b), and it was recognized that subtle factors not measured by the Sims card might be influencing the two sets of children in diverse ways.   One group, for example, lives near the center of the town and the other on the outskirts.   The parents of the latter group may have chosen this place of residence partly because the school here was known to be better or partly because the family was less dependent on the

*In Book Two, Chapter X, the unreliability of differences such as those given in Table LX is reported.

village for amusements and service. Such discrimination on the part of the parents might well be associated with differences in the behavior of the children.

Schools (c) and (d), however, are also on the outskirts of the village in which school (e) is located; and although the village school, just as in the case of (a) and (b), is much more deceptive than (c) or (d), there is no difference in the amount of deception practiced at home. From this it may be inferred (1) that the fact of living on the outskirts is not in itself evidence of such differences in homes as would account for differences in deceptiveness, and (2) that differences in deceptiveness between (a) and (b), (c) and (e), and (d) and (e) are due not to home background, but to teaching method or school morale or both. We have no evidence concerning the morale of schools (a) and (b), so that both general morale and general technique may be working to increase deception in the case of (b) and decrease it in the case of (a). But with (c) and (d), there is no contrast in teaching method. All three schools are conventional suburban schools under one supervision. There is, however, a distinct difference in the *atmosphere* of schools (c) and (d) as compared with (e). School (e) is in the same building with older grades which draw from all social levels in the community. There is a feeling of "tension" here and a certain arbitrariness of discipline not noticeable in schools (c) and (d). Whatever may be true of (a) as compared with (b), it is probable that the difference between (c) or (d) and (e) in the matter of deceit is due not to teaching technique, but to some such factor as school morale.

Now let us consider schools (f), (g), and (h). These are all private schools, drawing from a selected home background. Schools (f) and (g) are experimental and progressive and consist almost entirely of city children. School (h), though a school with fine morale, does not pretend to use the methods found in (f) and (g), yet in school (h) we find as little deception as in (f) and (g). Clearly, then, difference in technique is not in this case the significant factor. We must therefore attribute the likeness of (h), (f), and (g) in honesty either to likeness in home background or to likeness in morale. But we have already demonstrated in the case of (a) *versus* (b) and (c)–(d) *versus* (e) that likeness in home background does not inevitably produce likeness in deception, but may be associated with *difference* in deception if morale, or morale in combination with technique, is sufficiently diverse. Hence there is left only morale as the predominant source of differences and likenesses exhibited in these schools.

Finally it is rather extraordinary that schools (c) and (d) should compare favorably with (f), (g), and (h), showing about the same amount of deceptive behavior, for (c) and (d) are public schools using traditional methods, whereas (f) and (g) are private schools using progressive methods and (h) is a private school using traditional methods. This likeness, therefore, cannot be due to progressive teaching methods nor to highly selected home background. Again morale is left as the only common variable by which to explain the facts.

In thus emphasizing morale we do not reject our previous conclusion that progressive methods are more likely to be associated with classroom honor than are conventional methods. Rather are we trying to point out how the evidence at hand seems to require that we discriminate between the more formal and technical aspects of progressive method and the type of school morale or spirit with which it is likely to be (and may inherently be) associated. It is the latter rather than the former which the progressive schools under consideration share with the more conventional schools of the same level of school honor, and which we conclude must give the progressive school its advantage. It remains now to consider certain components of morale and their relations to the deceptiveness of children. This we shall do in the next chapter.

# CHAPTER XVI

## TEACHER INFLUENCE

" School morale," as has been suggested, is rather a vague term and its sources are not clearly known. We have been thinking of it as the product of the general administrative policy of the school system, the character of the supervision, the relation of teacher and pupils. It is with the particular aspect of morale that expresses itself in the attitude of the teacher toward the pupils and the attitude of the pupils toward the teacher and the school that we wish now to deal. In this chapter we shall discuss the influence of the teacher.

It is not possible, with the data at hand, to distinguish between the influence of the teacher's personality and that of her method. The personality factors could be objectively studied if time permitted and would doubtless resolve themselves into particular manners and skills, most of which could be controlled. Some of these manners and skills would be found to be included in the general theory underlying the more advanced schools, such as respect for the pupil's personality. Many teachers, quite untouched by modern movements in educational practice, show genuine respect for their pupils in their contacts with them, so that even formal classroom procedures have, under their guidance, a quite different moral effect from what is found when such respect is lacking.

We do not know which of the teachers whose pupils have been tested possess this attitude toward their children, and it is mentioned only as a possible illustration of real differences among teachers who are working along traditional lines. Certainly we find extreme differences in the deceptiveness of classrooms that may be accounted for in part, at least, by reference to some such difference among teachers in personality and attitude. Typical illustrations from three different schools are given in Figure 64.*

Case I is a school in which cheating was almost universal in three classrooms. In the 6A group, however, there was significantly less. This class differs from any of the other three by more than four times the standard error † of the difference. Yet there was no difference among the rooms in the way the pupils were selected. This is true also of cases II and III.

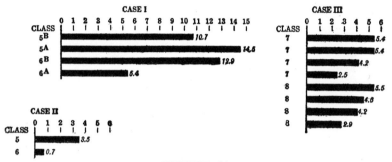

FIGURE 64

MEAN Xi CHEATING SCORES OF ADJOINING ROOMS OF THREE SCHOOLS

Case II is a school in which there was relatively little cheating. Yet even here the two rooms differ by more than three times the standard error of the difference.

Case III is from a junior high school in a mid-western city. Each group has its home room and a certain amount of class organization. In both the seventh and eighth grades there is a significant difference between the bottom group and the top group.

The mere fact that differences between classes occur may not be important. But if such differences are repeated when the same pupils are subjected to other tests, they point more certainly to the existence of some constant factor or factors in the situation. We do not, as a matter of fact, find that all classrooms show such constancy in behavior, but a large number do. This is illustrated

* The figures are given in full in Book Two, Table X.
† For explanation of terms, see Chapter VI.

in Table LXI, which ranks certain classes in grades four, five, and six of four schools according to their honesty in either two or three tests. The teachers and pupils are the same for each test reported. Each school may be expected to possess considerable homogeneity in general method, type of teacher, and pupil background.

TABLE LXI

RANK ORDER OF CERTAIN CLASSROOM DECEPTION MEANS

| SCHOOL I | | | SCHOOL II | |
|---|---|---|---|---|
| Speed | Puzzles | IER | Speed | Puzzles |
| 1 | 1 | 6 | 1 | 1 |
| 2 | 2 | 3 | 2 | 2 |
| 3 | 3 | 1 | 3 | 3 |
| 4 | 4 | 2 | 4 | 5 |
| 5 | 6 | 4 | 5 | 4 |
| 6 | 5 | 5 | 6 | 6 |

| SCHOOL III | | | SCHOOL IV | |
|---|---|---|---|---|
| Speed | Puzzles | IER | Speed | IER |
| 1 | 2 | 2 | 1 | 1 |
| 2 | 1 | 3 | 2 | 2 |
| 3 | 3 | 4 | 3 | 3 |
| 4 | 4 | 1 | 4 | 4 |
| 5 | 3 | | | |

In each case the classes are arranged in order from the most honest to the most dishonest according to mean scores, the first column giving the ranking for the first test and the second and third columns giving the ranking for the other two tests. Comparison of the Speed and Puzzle test ranks shows only two displacements of one step each among twelve classrooms, and in school IV the Speed and IER ranks are identical. In none of these instances did the same examiner appear twice in the same room, so that we may feel sure that whatever is responsible for the relative constancy of these groups is a function of the classroom itself. We naturally think of the teacher as the effective influence.

In our preceding chapter we called attention to the existence of extreme differences between schools in the matter of deception. In this chapter we have noted similar differences between classrooms within the *same school* and have attributed this fact to teacher influence or perhaps a classroom morale. We have based our argument, however, on very few cases. We should strengthen it considerably if we could include not only selected rooms but all the rooms tested. This we did, using a statistical method which is too complicated to describe here but which is reported in full in Book Two, Chapter X. By this method we were able to include in our survey of class differences seventy-one rooms in eight schools.

The result of this procedure confirms us in our conclusion that genuine classroom differences are the rule rather than the exception and that these differences are not to be accounted for by such facts as differences in age, intelligence, or home background. Yet they are much too large to be accounted for by chance. In the experimental schools, the differences among classrooms, though smaller than those observed in public schools, are nevertheless genuine. The fact that such differences occur even in schools where conscious effort is made to employ more modern methods lends support to the suggestion that the significant factor is the personal relation of teacher and pupils rather than other elements of technique.

At the beginning of this chapter we drew attention to certain classrooms which were conspicuously more *honest* than their neighbors. So far in our discussion we have not been able to say that such differences have been caused by this or that particular teacher, but only that the teacher-pupil relation has seemed to be of significance. But in testing one of the experimental schools we came upon certain groups which were conspicuous in being more *dishonest*, and it seemed worth while to test this school again after the lapse of one year to see whether these differences could be traced to individual teachers.

The data involved in this last experiment are too extensive and complex to justify more than a brief summary here, but will be found elaborately set forth in Book Two, Chapter X. The two sets of tests enable us to compare five teachers in a progressive school, whom we shall call A, B, C, D, and F. A and B are fifth-grade teachers, C and D are sixth-grade, and F seventh. Pupils pass each year from A to C, from B to D, and the girls of C and D pass to F. From the tables in Book Two it may be seen that teacher B in October, 1925, had in her class about twice as much cheating as any other teacher. There were of course some differences among the other teachers, but none so large as this. But a year later, i.e., in October, 1926, the pupils B then had did not show this exaggerated tendency. This fact led us to question whether the differences found were to be laid at the door of the teacher with whom the pupils were when tested or to the influence of their preceding teacher, especially since in October, when the tests were given, the pupils had been with their teachers less than a month as compared with nine months under the influence of the preceding teachers.

We therefore made another comparison, considering only the pupils for whom we had records for both years. When we tested them the following year (under another teacher), we found that the pupils B had had from October to June, who were so much less honest than the others in 1925, were, in 1926, only half as deceptive as before and were, moreover, the least deceptive of the five groups. In the course of one year, from being the most dishonest group they had become the most honest. Furthermore, in March, 1926, nearly one academic year after the first test, which consisted of the IER material, we happened to give our Speed tests in this school. B's pupils, although they began that academic year by being the most deceptive, had by then become the least deceptive of any.

By all these observed facts we felt confirmed in our assumption that the critical influence had been exerted by the teacher who had had the pupils the previous year and that B's influence was unusually large.

The hypothesis may be entertained, then, that a subtle difference between teachers exists, even when all are working consciously and skillfully along progressive lines, and that this difference is occasionally large enough to account for wide differences in deceptive behavior.  In further investigations it should be borne in mind, however, that even here variations in home background and in the character of particular children may account for a particular teacher's success or failure in any given year by introducing thus into any brief record a large element of chance.

# CHAPTER XVII

# GROUP MORALE

It is reasonable to suppose that the influence of the school and teacher, whether for good or ill, is reflected not only in the immediate acts of the children but also in their growing stock of attitudes and habits. In Chapter XIII we showed how similar children are, merely through classroom association. It is even conceivable that these attitudes and habits, becoming more fixed each year, may in the course of a few school sessions prove stronger than the influence of any but the most able teacher. Furthermore, since each group of pupils passes through experiences which are peculiar to itself, each group may be expected to develop its own characteristic code of conduct. One can see, therefore, the necessity of considering, along with the factor of teacher influence, the accumulated results of the influence of a series of teachers as these are registered in the group code or group morale.

The evidence underlying this phase of our discussion consists of five sets of correlations and their statistical relations. The facts correlated are, for each of the five correlations, two sets of mean deception scores for a number of classrooms. For two correlations we have the mean scores of the same pupils tested twice under the same teacher, in one case with the same test repeated and in the other case with another test. In two correlations we have to do with the same teachers for each set of mean scores, but one set of means is for the pupils these teachers have in one term and the other set of means is for the pupils these same teachers have the next term. As before, the same test is repeated in one case and in the other case a different test is used. The last correlation involves the mean scores of the same groups of pupils when tested under two sets of teachers. For this we have available only the same test repeated. The following scheme will aid in keeping these various relations in mind. After each pair of facts is placed the corresponding coefficient with its probable error.*

TABLE LXII

CORRELATION OF MEAN DECEPTION SCORES

| | | | | | r | PE |
|---|---|---|---|---|---|---|
| Same teacher | Same pupils | Same test (Speed repeated) | | (1) | .761 | .049 |
| | | Different test (Speed and Puzzles) | | (2) | .257 | .104 |
| | Different pupils | Same test (IER repeated) | | (3) | .69 | .067 |
| | | Different test (Arithmetic and Speed) | | (4) | .81 | .042 |
| Same pupils | Same teacher | Same test | | (1) | .761 | .049 |
| | | Different test | | (2) | .257 | .104 |
| | Different teacher | Same test (Arithmetic repeated) | | (5) | .90 | .032 |
| | | Different test † | | | | |
| | Self-correlation of Speed test ‡ | | | (6) | .78 | .018 |
| | Self-correlation of IER test ‡ | | | (7) | .75 | .024 |
| | r, Speed and Puzzle test | | | (8) | .31 | .027 |

† Data not available.

‡ By " self-correlation " is meant the correlation between two sets of scores from the same test given to the same pupils on separate occasions, *i.e.*, its reliability.

We shall discuss, first, correlations (1) and (2), where the teachers and groups remain the same for each set of paired facts; second, correlation (5), where the groups remain the same but have one set of teachers for one test and another set for the other; and third, correlations (3) and (4), where the teachers remain the

* Readers who feel a little at a loss by the frequent use of statistical terms are urged to stop at this point and review briefly the explanations given in Chapter VI in order that the purport of this and of subsequent discussions may be apparent.

same but have one set of pupils for one test and another set for the other test.

First, correlation (1) is about the same as (6) and correlation (2) is about the same as (8). This is what we should expect if the groups did not differ from one another any more than they would just by chance. But we have already shown that they do differ materially from one another, and have suggested that this difference might be due to the distinctive influence of each teacher on her classroom. Let us examine the implications of this likeness between (1) and (6) and between (2) and (8) and see whether we can account for the facts by reference to such teacher influence.

First, it should be borne in mind that any relatively permanent differences among the rooms which tend to make them differ in deceptiveness more than can be attributed to chance would operate to raise the correlation of the group means above that of the self-correlation of the test (or the $r$ between two different tests). Second, any *temporary* influences affecting the rooms unequally, either at the moment of testing or between the tests, would tend to lower the correlation of the means below the self-correlation of the test (or the $r$ between two different tests). Now, inasmuch as the two Speed tests of correlation (1) were given only a week apart and the Speed and Puzzle tests of correlation (2) were given the same day, we can hardly hold the teachers responsible for any group fluctuations which occurred, since they were not in the room at the time of the test and were unaware of its purpose. Hence, since the $r$'s are neither raised nor lowered, we may conclude that there were probably slight differences in the conditions under which the two tests were administered, such as difference in time of day or in the personality of the two examiners, which tended to *lower* the $r$ of the means, but *these influences were apparently offset by some more permanent influence, such as the group morale* (possibly due to the teacher), which tended to *raise* the $r$ of the means.

Correlation (5). Here we have the same test given to the same groups of children on two different occasions, with a change of teachers in the interval. This $r$ should be compared with (7). The fact that (5) greatly exceeds (7) indicates that between the two test occasions nothing happened to the pupils to make any radical changes in their relative deceptiveness. The interval between tests was a year in some cases and a half year in others, which ought to be time enough for the varying influence of the first set of teachers, if it exists, to show itself in the changed behavior of the pupils. We must conclude, then, that so far as these eleven classes compared in correlation (5) are concerned, the teachers all exerted about the same influence, or else that in the year or half-year during which they were in charge of their classes their influence was negligible. This corresponds to what we found in the experimental school, in which one teacher stood out as exceptionally influential. Viewed from another direction, this same fact may be taken as evidence of the existence of a group code or custom which persists as the group advances from room to room.

Correlations (3) and (4). These r's are between the mean scores of *successive* groups of children taught by the *same* teacher. It is the teacher who seems to show a constant influence here. The pupils are quite different in each case, yet in the one case where the same test was repeated, and in the other case where a different test was used, the surprising correlations of .69 and .81 are observed. This would seem to be a contradiction. The situations were as follows. In the case of the smaller r of .69 the IER tests were given first in October, 1925, and repeated a year later, giving the teachers only a month with each set of pupils. In the case of the larger r of .81, the IER tests were given some in November, 1924, and some in February, 1925, while the Speed tests were given respectively in March, 1926, and January, 1926. Thus in the second case the teachers had one set of pupils not less than a half-year and the other set about a month. As a month is rather a short time for the building of stable habits, we must infer that such influence as the teacher has may be exerted at the very beginning of her contact with a class, although the higher r in the second case also suggests that this influence is greater when there is time for it to develop more permanent habits and attitudes in the pupils. So much is fairly clear and reasonable. Our main problem lies in the paradox of having at the same time a high correlation between two testings of the *same* groups when the *teachers* are changed and two testings under the *same* teacher when the *groups* are changed. The first suggests that the dominant fact is the morale or code of the group. The second suggests that after all the teacher is the determining factor, for how otherwise are we to account for the fact that the relative deceptiveness of sixteen classrooms remained so nearly unchanged (*r*, .81) although one of two tests was given to the children who were in these rooms during one term and the other test to the children who happened to be in the same rooms another term? We have more than once brought forward evidence for believing that only in exceptional cases does any one teacher greatly influence a class. If this evidence and the reasoning based on it are sound, to what are we to attribute these correlations between the means of different groups in the same classroom when the classroom is tested twice? The discussion of this last problem concludes what we have to say concerning a possible group code or morale.

In the ordinary school system, a group of children once brought together in a first grade keeps together for a period of years, except for such changes as are due to removals, newcomers, and shifts in grading. Assuming a substantial nucleus moving on from year to year, together, the code or morale of the group may easily become the dominant factor in the behavior of all the children. The facts summarized in correlation (5) point to the existence of some such factor carried on from grade to grade.

A second characteristic of the ordinary school system is that the teachers of grade one, of grade two, of grade three, etc. are arranged rather permanently in vertical sequent groups as illustrated by the following table, in which the teachers are lettered A, B, C, D, etc. and the grades numbered I, II, III, IV, etc.

The scheme is simplified by assuming that each teacher keeps her pupils for a year, when they are advanced to the next grade. Thus the group of children who begin with teacher A go on to teacher B, not to teacher L or T, and those that begin with teacher K move on to teacher L, not to teacher B or T. Each eighth-grade class or seventh-grade class, therefore, can be called not only H's

| GROUP 1 | | GROUP 2 | | GROUP 3 | |
|---|---|---|---|---|---|
| Teacher | Grade | Teacher | Grade | Teacher | Grade |
| H | $VIII_1$ * | R | $VIII_2$ | Z | $VIII_3$ |
| G | $VII_1$ | Q | $VII_2$ | Y | $VII_3$ |
| F | $VI_1$ | P | $VI_2$ | X | $VI_3$ |
| E | $V_1$ | O | $V_2$ | W | $V_3$ |
| D | $IV_1$ | N | $IV_2$ | V | $IV_3$ |
| C | $III_1$ | M | $III_2$ | U | $III_3$ |
| B | $II_1$ | L | $II_2$ | T | $II_3$ |
| A | $I_1$ | K | $I_2$ | S | $I_3$ |

* The arabic figures refer to grade group or section. Thus $I_1$ is grade I, class 1; $I_2$ is grade I, class 2; etc. In many schools the different grade groups represent different intelligence levels.

pupils, or R's pupils, but, with equal accuracy, pupils of A, B, C, D, E, F, G, and H or of K, L, M, N, O, P, Q, and R. It is not unreasonable to suppose that each sequent group of teachers has a differential influence on particular classes of children which results, other things being equal, in a characteristic deception tendency for each class at each grade level, through the sequence, and in a characteristic deception tendency for the whole series of classes in the sequent group. Consequently, when the whole school population shifts from one classroom to another at the time of promotion, the relation among the sequent groups is not changed. This is particularly true if the grade groups represent intelligence levels. Of course some children do change from one sequent group to another, but there are not enough such changes to affect the group morale.

Now when we come to correlate the mean scores of the pupils taught by the teachers of, say, grades five and six one year with the mean scores of the pupils taught by these same teachers another year, what we have done (referring to the table) is to compare F's pupils with the pupils taught by E the year before, P's pupils with the pupils taught by O the year before, and W's pupils with the pupils taught by V the year before. We have not compared

E's pupils with the pupils taught by N the year before, nor P's
pupils with the pupils taught by W the year before. We have
taken each pair of facts to be correlated from within one sequent
group. Back of the pupils of teacher E in sequent group 1 are
several years of experience which tend to make her classes more
like one another than they are like the pupils of sequent group 2,
the classes of which have their own differentiating experience.
Hence if E's pupils are more honest than O's one year, they are
likely to be so the next, not merely because of what influence E
exerts in distinction from the influence of O, but also, and perhaps
more, because of the accumulated influence of teachers A, B, C, and
D, all of whom have taught the two groups whose means are being
compared. This resemblance of the members of the several
sequent groups is reflected in the correlations of .69 and .81 which
are now under discussion. The more sequent groups there are in
proportion to the number of grades from which the classes to be
compared are drawn, the higher will be the correlation. The
twelve classes whose two sets of children are compared for correlation (3), which is .69, are taken from three sequent groups. The
sixteen classes represented in correlation (4), which is .81, are
drawn from five sequent groups.

The correlation is further augmented by whatever permanent
differences there may be among the teachers of any sequence. We
have already pointed out that these are occasionally significant.
The general progress of the classes in a sequence is arrested or
accelerated by these divergent teachers in the same way each year
or half-year; but, as we have indicated, this cannot account for
the whole of correlations (3) and (4) since, except in extreme cases,
these divergences do not measurably affect the behavior of the
class.

The sequent group arrangement we have described is of course
only schematic and is only approximated in any given case. This
only tends to drop the r's between group means below what they
might be if the facts corresponded exactly to the table. Such
approximations are found where there are several separate school
buildings in any system in each of which there is one class to each

grade. Under such conditions, there is just one succession of teachers through which the pupils attending each school can pass. It is not surprising, therefore, that schools develop characteristic distinguishing tendencies in honesty as well as in other matters, like the schools described in the previous chapter where we attributed differences in the matter of deception to school morale. Doubtless in such a situation other factors in the school enter into the picture, such as the personality of the principal or the appearance and utility of the building and grounds.

Another type of approximation to the scheme is found in large schools and is illustrated in the table on page 335, where there are several classes to each grade and the pupils are divided into VA1, VA2, VA3, etc., the ones, twos, and threes representing in each case some definite mode of selection. When this selection is by level of intelligence, the children of similar intellectual capacity are kept together year after year and the teachers of VA1, VIB2, IVA3, and all the other groups tend always to teach the " one " group or the " two " group or " three " group respectively each year. Thus we have the equivalent of the sequences found in the separate school buildings. The correlation between intelligence and deception is too low for such differences in intelligence as distinguish the ones, twos, and threes of a system to account for similarity within each such sequent group in the matter of deception. But even if it were possible to account for correlations such as (3) and (4) by means of likenesses and differences in intelligence, the deceptive tendencies would nevertheless be specific, concrete, and separately measurable, constituting a part of the habit system of the members of the class.

So far this habit system characteristic of the group, which we now picture as accumulating from year to year, has been indiscriminately referred to as the group code, custom, or morale. If by " code " is meant a standard consciously adhered to, then the term is probably not appropriate, as there is some evidence * that the

* See " Testing the Knowledge of Right and Wrong," sixth article, *Religious Education*, May; 1927, reprinted in " Monograph No. 1 " of the Religious Education Association.

average child behaves and thinks as the group does without much awareness of his own consistency or inconsistency. The term " group morale " is therefore less ambiguous.

## SUMMARY

Chapters XV, XVI, and XVII may now be summarized as follows:

1. Schools that we have measured differ in deception from one another in ways that are to be accounted for rather by school atmosphere or morale than by technique or selection of population, although the latter is doubtless in many cases a significant factor.

2. The teachers we have compared differ from one another only slightly in any one school system so far as influence on deception is concerned and only slightly modify the deceptive behavior of their pupils.   They are rather part of a system of sequent groups, each such group of classes accumulating its characteristic habits. Occasionally, and in some schools more than in others, teachers diverge enough from their fellows in any sequent system to induce marked changes in their children, which persist into the next room. But this is the exception and not the rule.

3. Class groups differ from one another in deception and tend to maintain these differences from year to year, each class building up a habit system which, without much consciousness on the part of the individual members, operates to differentiate it from other groups.

# CHAPTER XVIII

# SAMPLE STUDIES OF THE EFFECTS OF MORAL AND RELIGIOUS EDUCATION

The three educational agencies dealt with in this chapter and the next were selected by accident rather than by design. We happened on them in the course of our examination of school children. It is farthest from our thought that the facts reported here should be regarded as in any sense a complete survey of the moral values of these organizations. We dealt in each case with groups too restricted for wide generalization, and even here we limited ourselves to a study of the comparative honesty of the children, ignoring other and doubtless equally important effects. We hold no brief for or against the organizations of which the pupils tested were members. The methods they employ, however, should be a matter of concern to all educators as they are typical of methods used by many agencies which hold themselves responsible for the moral education of children and of many plans which find vogue in our public schools. Yet the negative tenor of the results of this study should make us neither cynical nor pessimistic, but rather cautious and inquisitive. The one thing that stands out is the need for more extensive investigations, by means of objective and standardized techniques, into the social significance of contemporary education.

## SYSTEM X

The organization we shall call system X is a device for interesting school children in the achievement of virtues through practice. When we encountered this scheme, each child was expected to keep a daily record of certain good deeds (among which was truth telling) ; and, to stimulate him in his effort and so make sure that each virtue was properly practiced, he was rewarded for a good record by being advanced in the organization from rank to rank. Obviously a premium was placed on making a good showing. Since the date of our study certain changes have been made which mitigate the evident dangers of this procedure, but it is followed in principle in a variety of moral education plans.

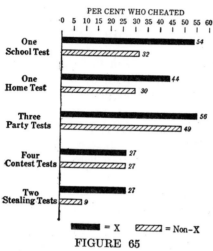

PER CENT WHO CHEATED

FIGURE 65

CHEATING OF X AND NON-X BOYS IN SCHOOL C

This figure reads: 54% of the X boys and 32% of the non-X boys cheated on one of the IER school tests; etc.

In trying out certain of our deception tests in school C we discovered that we had tested certain boys who had had this training. It happened that, in this school, membership in the organization was optional, so that there were several classrooms in which about half the boys had joined and half had not. This gave us an excellent opportunity to compare boys in the same classroom, under the same teacher, with the same intelligence and home background. There were 143 X boys and 126 non-X boys. The results, which are printed fully in Book Two, Chapter XI, are summarized in Figures 65 and 66.

The rather startling contrasts between the X boys and non-X boys pictured in Figures 65 and 66 give one pause. The members of the organization cheated more on every test than the non-members except in the case of the athletic contest, in which there was no difference between the two groups. Furthermore, the higher the rank achieved, the greater the deception. It would seem necessary to conclude either that the organization automatically selected for membership the less honest members of the rooms concerned or else made them less honest after they had joined. And concerning the members, what is there to say except either that the satisfactory reports were handed in by the less honest or that the practice of reporting their good deeds made them less honest?

Although these results seemed unfavorable to the method under consideration, the number of cases was too small to warrant the forming of any final conclusions. The principal of this school, moreover, was not in sympathy with the plan and some of the teachers did not enter into it whole-heartedly. Also, the pupils were all boys. Accordingly, at the suggestion of our advisers, we decided to make a more complete study and settle the issues at stake. In doing so it seemed wise to broaden somewhat the scope of the problem.

The procedure under consideration is typical of much formal moral education used to supplement the usual public school curriculum. Some principals lay great stress on these extra-curricular methods, taking advantage of every opportunity to instill moral ideals, point out delinquencies and duties, and reward virtuous behavior. This interest in the characters of their children is often accompanied by warm personal affection for individual pupils and the development of lasting attachments.

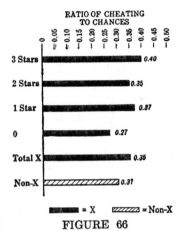

FIGURE 66

RELATION OF RANK IN X TO DECEPTION RATIO OF BOYS IN SCHOOL C

This figure reads: X boys having won three stars cheated 4 times in ten chances; those having won two stars cheated 3.5 times in ten chances; etc.

We were interested in comparing schools which depended upon these extraneous methods for results in character with schools where such added devices were regarded as out of place and which depended on the discipline of the usual school routine for the moral effects expected from the school system.

In a congested metropolitan district we found these conditions rather well realized in schools F, G, H, I, and J of our list in Chapter IV. Although H and I are two schools, each with its own principal, we shall handle them in this study as though they were one. We may therefore reletter our populations as follows:

A. Mixed, through grade six; girls, seven and eight
B. Boys, through six; girls, through eight
C. Girls, through eight
D. Mixed, through six

In school A we found great emphasis on character education. System X, beginning with grade four, had been in use here from its inception three and a half years previously. Pageants by the children were presented from time to time portraying and idealizing certain virtues on which system X laid stress. There were also the Junior Red Cross and the regular opening exercises, the one offering opportunities to engage in acts of usefulness and the other to hear talks that occasionally were directed to the inculcation of ideals. The principal was profoundly interested in her children, who were in turn devoted to her.

In school B not all the pupils above grade three had had system X, and these two groups, the one which had had it and the one which had not, are called respectively Bx and B. The two principals were not so certain of the value of all the extraneous activities used in school A, nor did they maintain the same type of personal intimacy with the pupils characteristic of the principal of A.

Schools C and D did not believe in extra-curricular activities and in particular were not in sympathy with system X.

The children in these four groups were practically all of the same race, the same religion, the same general intelligence, and the same type of home background, as our records quite clearly demonstrate.

The tests used in making our comparisons consisted of the Word Knowledge test, taken at home and indicating the amount of surreptitious use made of a dictionary or other assistance, the Speed tests, and the Coördination tests.  As usual, the fourth grade omitted one Speed test and the test done at home.  This made eight deception tests for those in the fourth grade and ten for all above the fourth grade.  In addition, the Department of Psychology at Teachers College, with our financial assistance, administered the Pintner non-language intelligence test to all our groups, and we gave all above the fourth grade the Sims Score Card* for measuring socio-economic level.  The Pintner non-language test was used partly because no one intelligence test had been used with all the schools and partly because many of the children were not very familiar with the English language.

A complete record of the results of this testing for each classroom will be found in Book Two, Chapter XI, together with a number of summary tables, from which we shall quote here and on which we shall base certain figures and conclusions now to be presented.

## SUMMARY OF DATA CONCERNING THE RELATIVE DECEPTIVENESS OF SCHOOLS A, B, C, AND D WITH AND WITHOUT SYSTEM X

Our first comparison is between the groups having system X, *viz.*, A and part of B, and the groups which had not had X, *viz.*, part of B and all of C and D.  But the variation in ages among the groups suggested the need of matching them in this particular and for home background and intelligence as well.  Table LXIII gives the mean scores in these respects for the populations concerned.

The slight correlation between age and deception is cared for by matching the groups for age.  Even if they were not also matched for intelligence and home background, it would not affect our comparisons, as no correlation was found between the intelligence scores or home background scores and deception.  Any differences found in deception are therefore due to other factors than age, IQ, or home background.  These deception differences are summarized

* See Chapter VIII for a description of this instrument.

TABLE LXIII

MEAN AGES, SIMS SCORES, AND IQ'S OF X AND NON-X GROUPS
MATCHED IN AGE

|  | Ax | Bx | B | C–D |
|---|---|---|---|---|
| Number of cases . . . . . . . | 570 | 327 | 95 | 465 |
| Chronological age . . . . . . . | 12/5 | 12/3 | 12/5 | 12/6 |
| Home background . . . . . . . | 8.95 | 9.18 | 8.97 | 9.07 |
| IQ . . . . . . . . . . . . | 102 | * | * | 100 |

\* The intelligence scores for B were not available when the schools were matched for age. However, the comparison of groups indicates that there would be no significant variation from the other schools, and in any case the low correlations would make variation of no consequence.

in Table LXIV. The deception ratio was found, as previously described, by dividing the number of c's by the number of chances to deceive and stating the result as a percentage of cheating to opportunity. The cheating on the home test is shown by the per cent of the group taking advantage of the opportunity this offered.

TABLE LXIV

DECEPTION SCORES OF X AND NON-X GROUPS

|  | Ax | Bx | B | C–D |
|---|---|---|---|---|
| Number of cases . . . . . . . | 570 | 327 | 95 | 465 |
| Mean deception ratio . . . . . . | .46 | .52 | .59 | .70 |
| Per cent cheating on home test . . | 37 | 46 | 51 | 51 |

At first sight the X groups seem to have the advantage over the non-X groups, for their deception scores on both the school tests and the home test are lower than those of the non-X children.

When groups are matched for age, however, certain essential influences are confused owing to the varying grade groupings in the schools and the necessary omission of a large number of cases. A detailed comparison, grade for grade, is therefore more illuminating.   From the tables of Book Two, which give these comparisons, the charts which follow have been made.

From the tables of Book Two and these charts we may observe the following facts concerning the 2300 pupils whose records were usable :

1. On the test taken home there are no significant differences between X and non-X pupils.   School Ax is slightly better than the others, however.   See Figure 67.

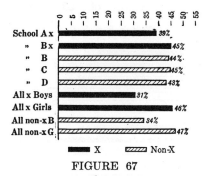

FIGURE 67

PER CENT OF X AND NON-X CHILDREN CHEATING ON HOME TEST

2. In the classroom, the X boys and non-X boys are alike in deception, each group cheating on the average 4.74 times in ten chances.   But the X girls have a deception ratio of .442 as against a ratio of .590 for the non-X girls.   See Figure 68.

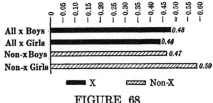

FIGURE 68

CT RATIOS OF X AND NON-X CHILDREN, BY SEX

So much for the X and non-X groups as a whole.   Certain grade comparisons are also instructive.

3. In all the schools, the seventh and eighth grades, which contain only girls, are more deceptive than the girls of the lower grades. See Figure 69.
4. In school B, the Bx boys of grades five and six are more deceptive than the non-X boys of the same grades, having a mean score of .627 as against .530. But in the seventh- and eighth-grade girls' classes, the X girls prove far less deceptive than the non-X, having a mean score of .494 as against a non-X score of .629. See Figure 70.

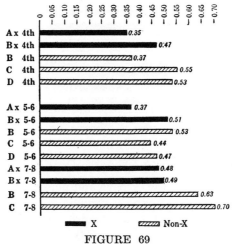

FIGURE 69

CT RATIOS OF X AND NON-X CHILDREN, BY GRADE

The conclusions so far outlined concern the contrasts between the pupils of system X and those who are not members of this organization. The element of time during which pupils have been under the influence of the organization may be an important item, as is suggested by the following facts:

5. In schools Ax, Bx, and B, the fifth and sixth grades are *more* deceptive than the fourth; but in schools C and D, where system X has not been in force, the fifth and sixth grades are *less* deceptive than the fourth. See Figure 69. Fur-

thermore, in schools Ax and Bx the lower fourth-grade, or 4A, children, who had been in the system less than six weeks when the tests were given, show up better than the

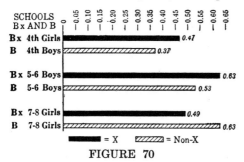

FIGURE 70

CT RATIOS OF X AND NON-X CHILDREN, BY GRADE AND SEX

upper half, or 4B, pupils, who had had the training for over a term.  This fact must be taken with caution, however, for it is also true of grades 4A and 4B of school C, though not of school D.  See Figure 71.

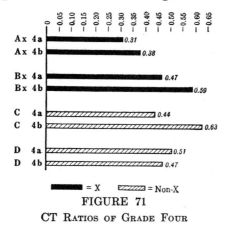

FIGURE 71

CT RATIOS OF GRADE FOUR

6.  In school Ax and Bx those pupils entering above the fourth grade in September, 1926, a month before the tests were given, are less deceptive on the home test than those who

have been in the school several terms, and the per cent cheating increases with the number of terms. When *all* tests are considered, this is true only of school Bx, however. See Figures 72, 73, and 74.

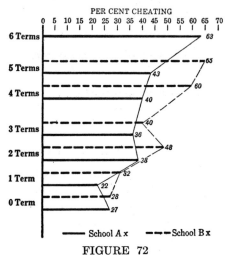

FIGURE 72

RELATION OF CHEATING ON HOME TEST TO LENGTH OF MEMBERSHIP IN X

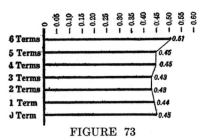

FIGURE 73

RELATION OF CHEATING ON ALL TESTS (CT RATIO) TO LENGTH OF MEMBERSHIP IN X, SCHOOL AX

7. Even when grades five to six and seven to eight are handled independently, there is a positive correlation between length of time in the organization and amount of deception.

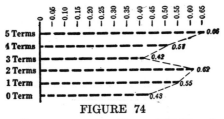

FIGURE 74

RELATION OF CHEATING ON ALL TESTS (CT RATIO) TO LENGTH
OF MEMBERSHIP IN X, SCHOOL Bx

Greater deception, however, is associated not only with longer
experience of the organization but also with rise in rank and rate of
progress, as the following statements testify:

8. In agreement with the results reported on the first school
tested, there is a positive correlation between the rank
attained and the tendency to deceive on our tests. The
higher the pupils of schools Ax and Bx go in the system,
the more they cheat, up to a certain rank, beyond which
there is improvement in school Ax. This is true, on the
whole, even when grade level is kept constant. See
Figures 75 to 77.

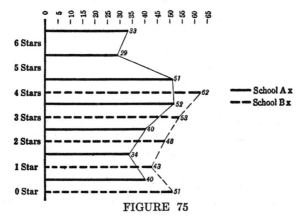

FIGURE 75

RELATION OF PER CENT CHEATING ON HOME TEST TO RANK
ACHIEVED IN X

9.  In schools Ax and Bx there is also a definite relation between
    rate of progress and deception.   The average progress is
    one button or rank a term.   Those that move along at

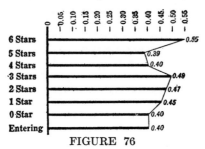

FIGURE 76

RELATION OF CHEATING ON ALL TESTS (CT RATIO) TO RANK
ACHIEVED IN X, SCHOOL AX

this rate cheat the least.   Those who move up more
rapidly and get more than one button a term and those
who move slowly and get less than a button a term cheat

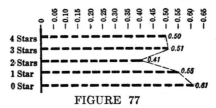

FIGURE 77

RELATION OF CHEATING (CT RATIO) TO RANK ACHIEVED IN X,
SCHOOL BX

the most.   This is true not only of the school tests but
also of the test taken home.   See Figures 78 and 79.

10.  Those who have been in the system a term or more and yet
    have achieved no buttons are more deceptive than those
    who have obtained one rank.   Presumably they are not
    interested.   But those who have obtained three or four
    ranks are quite as deceptive as those who have done
    nothing.   This is hardly lack of interest.   See Figures 78
    and 79.

There remain certain comparisons between the schools that are of interest.

11. When both sexes are included, school Ax stands best, with an average cheating score of 4.17 times in ten chances.

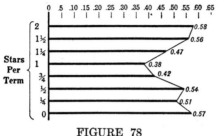

FIGURE 78

RELATION OF CHEATING ON ALL TESTS (CT RATIO) TO RATE OF ADVANCEMENT IN X, SCHOOLS AX AND BX COMBINED

School D is next, with a CT ratio of .491, Bx next, with .501, and schools B (those of B not members of X) and C follow with scores of .551 and .608 respectively. See Figure 80.

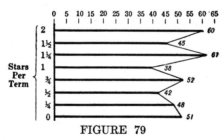

FIGURE 79

RELATION OF PER CENT CHEATING ON HOME TEST TO RATE OF ADVANCEMENT IN X

12. In all the schools, including Ax, the correlation between length of time in school and cheating is zero.

13. Taking the records class by class, there is considerable overlapping among the schools, though schools Ax and Bx

show a wider range in deceptiveness from class to class than do schools C and D.

Schools B and C are inferior to Ax and Bx primarily in grades seven and eight, not in grades four, five, and six, which in all schools are less deceptive than seven and eight, as noted in No. 3.

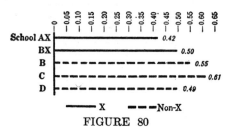

FIGURE 80

MEAN CT RATIOS OF SCHOOLS AX, BX, B, C, AND D

## INTERPRETATION OF FACTS REPORTED FOR SCHOOLS A, B, C, AND D AND SYSTEM X

Let us first state the essential facts in order.

1. On the test taken home there is no difference between the X and non-X children. This is the test which most nearly corresponds to the situation of the organization itself, which requires the checking of good deeds done at home.
2. On the school tests, the boys of X are no less deceptive than the boys not in X, but the X girls are less deceptive than the non-X girls.
3. School A, with system X, is less deceptive than the others on all the tests, including the one taken home; and the girls of school Bx are less deceptive than those of B, C, or D on the school tests, but not on the test taken home.

The facts to be accounted for are the relative honesty of all of school A and of the girls of school Bx. Is system X responsible for this state of affairs? Certainly it does not work in that way with boys. If the causal factor in the case of the girls is system X, then how account for the contradictory facts that the longer they are in the organization, the higher their rank, and the more rapidly they advance, the more they cheat? We can only conclude that it is not the system which is responsible for this greater degree of honesty among the X girls.

The contrary is not necessarily true, however, as was suggested in our discussion of the results of the first school in which the X and non-X pupils were compared. We stated there that it was not clear whether the organization merely selects for advancement those most proficient in subterfuge or makes them more facile liars.

Let us call these two proposals the " selection " hypothesis and the " influence " hypothesis and state the arguments pro and con.

*Pro.* It is true, says the selection theory, that the more successful pretenders are advanced in rank irregularly, but those who advance normally, at the rate of a rank a term, are among the most honest of the whole population.

*Con.* True, but of the " rate of progress " groups shown in Figure 78, five out of seven of those which are advancing either too fast or too slowly are more deceptive than school D, which has had no X, and these five groups contain 77% of all the X pupils.

*Pro.* It will have to be admitted that a large majority of the X pupils are more deceptive than they would have been if they had gone to school D, but in comparison with school C they are much *less* deceptive, for none of these " rate of progress " groups has a mean score as large as that of school C.

*Con.* But school C is all girls and contains the seventh- and eighth-grade classes who were the most deceptive groups we found. It may be admitted that the X pupils are not as deceptive as they would have been if they had all been girls in the seventh and eighth grades of school C, yet it remains true that only a few are better than other non-X groups and the bulk of them grow more deceptive the longer they are in the organization. Consequently, even if it is admitted that for the 23% who advance normally the organization is of value (though it may quite properly be claimed that these children were honest to start with and followed the plan conscientiously), nevertheless for the remaining 77% it looks bad.

*Pro.* But if the organization is not improving its members, how account for the fact that those just entering it in school Bx are so much less honest than those who have been in it some time?

*Con.* There seems to be no obvious explanation of this fact, but over against it should be set the still more startling one that, in the school which is claimed to be the outstanding representative of the system, those just entering above the fourth grade who have had the system for less than six weeks are *less* deceptive than those who have been in it for several terms. And also, when the cases of X are lumped together, as has been noted, there is a positive correlation between length of membership and cheating. . . .

While the case is not settled, the arguments seem to favor the " influence " hypothesis. It is quite likely that both selection and training are at work to produce the results observed.

Another fact of interest concerns the superiority of school A. We have mentioned the interest of this school in moral education and the character of the principal. It is rather remarkable that the children in this school do not become more honest the longer they stay. But they do not. Yet they show up more favorably than the members of the other schools. Also, as we have seen, those just entering are less deceptive than those who have been there a few terms. Apparently what influence for good the school exerts makes itself felt when the pupils first enter the school, for they come from the very same neighborhood and the same type of homes as do those who belong to the other schools tested. There is, furthermore, small difference in the matter of deception at home. But in school the pupils apparently meet at the very beginning of their career a type of attitude and interest which makes deception less attractive. This influence is not universal, however, and doubtless the principal has not been able to surround herself with teachers all of whom show the same interest in the moral welfare of the children as she does herself. Actually, the fact that the pupils do not become increasingly honest under this favorable régime may possibly be due to the hampering influence of system X, through which a premium is put on a certain kind of falsification. If it had not been for that particular feature of X, now happily discarded, which made advancement depend on the pupil's own unchecked report as to his daily conduct, school A might well have shown even less deception than it did.

In other respects than honesty system X may of course have been making genuinely helpful contributions to the character of the pupils.    The moral of the tale is that these other presumed effects should also be measured.

# CHAPTER XIX

## SAMPLE STUDIES OF THE EFFECTS OF MORAL AND RELIGIOUS EDUCATION (*Continued*)

The organization which engaged our attention in the preceding chapter is confined to public schools. It is almost exclusively concerned with the conscious acquisition of good traits. The names and descriptions of traits are learned, historic and legendary characters possessing the traits are talked about, and the members are supposed to perform daily a series of specified acts in order that the traits may become habits.

There are several organizations or schemes similarly devoted to the direct and conscious development of traits, which have found their way into the schools of this or that city or state. In general procedure they are not unlike the average Sunday school except that the latter has for the most part confined itself to such illustrations of traits as could be drawn from Biblical heroes and heroines and Biblical situations. This is particularly true of Protestant Christian schools. In view of the large numbers of children in attendance at these schools and the serious interest of their leaders in the effects of the teaching on character, the relation of Sunday schools to deception may be of interest.

In system X, the tests for deception were given in the same rooms where the ethical instruction took place. In the case of the Sunday schools, however, the ethical instruction was in one place with one group of children and the deception tests were given in another place (the day school) with the children in quite different groups. We could hardly expect, therefore, that the results of the teaching in Sunday schools would have an effect on the deception scores at all comparable to that of system X. The facts are as follows.

## SUNDAY-SCHOOL TEACHING AND DAY-SCHOOL CONDUCT

In school system A we found Sunday-school records for the children attending four out of the six public schools in the community. One of these two missing schools is near the town limit and only one of its pupils apparently was enrolled in any of the town Sunday schools. In the other, only a dozen pupils attended Sunday schools from which we could secure a record, and these were therefore left out of the computations which follow.

The population of the remaining four schools was distributed among the various religious groups as follows:

| CHURCH | NUMBER | | PER CENT | |
|---|---|---|---|---|
| Protestant (enrolled) . . . . . | 217 | | 38.5 | |
| Protestant (not enrolled). . . . | 76 | | 13.5 | |
| Total Protestant. . . . . . | | 293 | | 52 |
| Catholic . . . . . . . . . | 140 | | 25 | |
| Jewish . . . . . . . . . . | 48 | | 8.5 | |
| No church . . . . . . . . | 82 | | 14.5 | |
| Total non-Protestant . . . . | | 270 | | 48 |
| Total not enrolled in Protestant schools . . . . . . . . | | 346 | | 61.5 |
| Total cases . . . . . . . | | 563 | | 100 |

Nearly a fourth of those who said that they went to a Protestant Sunday school were not found on any Sunday-school roll. Some of these may, of course, have gone to schools outside the town, particularly if they lived on the outskirts. But there are 217 whose deceptive behavior may be compared with that of Protestants not enrolled in Sunday school and with the remainder of the community. Table LXV gives these comparisons in terms of the per cent cheating at least once in school and the per cent cheating on the test taken home.

It is of interest that the Protestants not enrolled are slightly less deceptive than the Protestants enrolled, though the difference is too small to be reliable in view of the number of cases. The difference of nine per cent, however, in favor of the Protestants enrolled as compared with *all* not enrolled in the Protestant schools is 2.2 times its unreliability in the case of the school tests. In the case of the home test those not enrolled have an insignificant advantage over those enrolled.

### TABLE LXV

RELATIVE DECEPTIVENESS OF SUNDAY-SCHOOL CHILDREN, GRADES FIVE TO EIGHT, SCHOOL SYSTEM A

|  | PER CENT CHEATING AT SCHOOL | PER CENT CHEATING AT HOME |
|---|---|---|
| All the children of the four public schools . . . . . . . . . . | 36 | 28 |
| Protestant children enrolled in Sunday school . . . . . . | 31 | 29 |
| Protestant children not enrolled in Sunday school . . . . . . | 29 | 18 |
| All not enrolled in Protestant Sunday schools . . . . . . . | 40 | 27 |

In school system B the school population is nominally about 90% Protestant, but the names of only 417 out of 945 were found on Sunday-school rolls. The comparative deceptiveness of those enrolled and those not enrolled in Sunday schools for this system is shown in Table LXVI.

### TABLE LXVI

RELATIVE DECEPTIVENESS OF SUNDAY-SCHOOL CHILDREN, GRADES FIVE TO TEN, SCHOOL SYSTEM B

|  | PER CENT CHEATING IN SCHOOL | PER CENT CHEATING AT HOME |
|---|---|---|
| Whole population . . . . . . | 41 | 36 |
| Sunday-school population . . . | 38 | 38 |
| Non-Sunday-school population . | 43 | 34 |

The percentages are again closely alike, with the Sunday-school children having slightly the advantage in school and slightly the disadvantage at home.

Apparently, then, the tendency to deceive is about as prevalent among those enrolled in Sunday school as it is among those who are not in one community, and in another those enrolled are less deceptive than those not enrolled.  This does not mean, however, that Sunday-school children are all alike.  On the contrary there are wide differences among them.  It is important to know whether such differences are at all attributable to the length of time the children have been associated with Sunday school or to the regularity of their attendance.

Unfortunately we were able to secure a record of attendance for a period of years for only one school, and here for only 52 pupils who were tested for deception in school and only 46 who took the home test.  These children range in length of membership in this school from one to twelve years.  The correlation between years of attendance and both school cheating and cheating on the test taken home is zero.

For the year 1924 to 1925 we have more adequate records, giving the number of absences for 204 children in several schools of Protestant denominations.  The correlation between deception and regularity of attendance expressed in per cent of Sundays attended during 1924–25 is zero.  This fact is more graphically portrayed by dividing the Sunday-school population into three groups — (1) those who attended regularly; (2) those who attended from 75% to 99% of the time; and (3) those who attended less than 75% of the time — and noting the median amount of cheating at school and on the test taken home for each of these three groups. These comparisons are made in Table LXVII.

Furthermore, the mean per cent of attendance of those who cheated once was exactly the same as the mean attendance of those who did not cheat at all.

Too much weight should not be attached to these facts, however, not only because of the small number of cases included, but also for two other reasons.  In the first place, the forty Sunday-

TABLE LXVII

MEDIAN CHEATING SCORES OF 204 PROTESTANT SUNDAY-SCHOOL CHILDREN

|  | SCHOOL Xi | HOME Xi |
|---|---|---|
| Perfect attendance . . . . . . | − 1.2 | − 1.0 |
| 75% to 99% . . . . . . . . . | − 1.8 | − 1.0 |
| 0 to 74% . . . . . . . . . . | − 1.2 | − 1.3 |

school periods represented cover a great deal of ground, in the course of which the problem of honesty is touched very little if at all.  In the second place, the average attendance of these 204 children was 90%, which allowed for too little variation in attendance to bring out such differences in the effect of Sunday-school teaching as might have been present.  Yet so far as the facts go, we may say that neither the length of time that children are associated with Sunday school nor the regularity of their attendance seems to be at all associated with their tendency to deceive either at school or on work taken home.

## HEBREW–SCHOOL TEACHING AND DAY–SCHOOL CONDUCT *

What we have just been saying refers only to Protestant Sunday schools.  In certain centers the Jews maintain religious schools which meet during the week as well as on Sunday and which are therefore a little closer to the day school both in the amount of time given to instruction and in the way this time is distributed through the week.  In five of our schools we asked the pupils, practically all of whom were Jews, whether they attended religious school and if so to give the name of the school.  In case they had religious instruction at home, the name of the instructor was asked. In this way we secured the religious school record of 1871 children,

* We are indebted to Dr. J. Maller, a graduate student at Teachers College, Columbia University, for the assembling of the data on Hebrew schools.

of whom 714, or 38%, were receiving some sort of religious instruction. These pupils were in grades five to eight; 56% of them were girls and 44% boys.

We had given from eight to ten deception tests here and had computed the CT ratios showing the number of times each child cheated out of ten chances. Table LXVIII gives the essential comparisons.

TABLE LXVIII

RELATIVE DECEPTIVENESS OF HEBREW-SCHOOL CHILDREN, GRADES FIVE TO EIGHT

|  | MEAN | SD |
|---|---|---|
| All children . . . . . . . . . . . | .499 | .112 |
| Children receiving religious instruction . | .485 | .145 |
| Children receiving no religious instruction . . . . . . . . . . . . . | .502 | |

Although such difference as appears is in favor of the religious group, the chances are about even that as great a difference would be found between two groups chosen at random from the same population. It should be noted, however, that a similar slight difference in favor of the children receiving religious instruction occurs in *each of four* schools, two of these being for girls only. In the fifth school, for boys only, the difference favors the non-religious group.

From the children reporting attendance upon religious instruction, 151 cases who gave the name of their religious school were selected and followed up to determine the length of their association with religious schools. The correlation between length of attendance and CT ratio is $+.128 \pm .05$. With chronological age kept constant, the partial $r$ between attendance and deception is $+.074$, *i.e.*, there is no relation between the two.*

---

* In *Shebile Hachinuch* for February, 1928, Dr. Maller reports further that the 151 children attended four different Hebrew schools. The length of attendance of each child from the day of admission to the day of the honesty

The results of this study of Hebrew schools are thus in general accord with what we have already reported for Protestant Sunday schools.

## SYSTEM Y

In quite distinct contrast with the type of theory and practice represented in system X and in the average religious school is the typical recreational organization which attempts to occupy a boy's or girl's leisure time in ways which are interesting, wholesome, and of significance for the formation of character. Camp craft and

test was established. The following table shows the mean CT ratio for the children of each of the four groups, the mean length of attendance of each of the four groups, and the correlation between length of attendance and the CT ratio for the children of each group.

| Schools: | JC N = 28 | DT N = 44 | ZT N = 44 | OT N = 35 |
|---|---|---|---|---|
| CT ratio, mean  .    .    .    . | .56 | .46 | .43 | .39 |
| Length of attendance, mean | 17 | 24 | 31 | 34 |
| $r_{CA}$  .   .   .   .   .   .   .   . | − .20 | +.19 | + .24 | −.27 |

It is noteworthy that there is a perfect negative relationship between means of length of attendance and means of CT, that is, the group which has a record of longest attendance in religious school shows the lowest CT ratio and the group having the record of shortest length of attendance has the highest CT ratio. Thus, while within a given group the relationship between religious training and honesty is quite indefinite, still when means of groups are compared such relationship becomes overt. It indicates that length of attendance generally tends to increase *honest* behavior.

A comparison of the four correlations shows that schools *differ* radically with regard to the relation between length of attendance and honesty, the difference being from a correlation of − .27 to a correlation of + .24. While a longer stay in one school tends to make the children less deceptive (− .27), in another school prolonged attendance results in greater deceptiveness. The mean CT ratio for all the 723 children who reported receiving religious training was .485. The mean CT of these 151 children who reported the names of the religious school is .460. The mean of the rest of the religious groups (those who received religious training outside of any religious school) is .493.

civic activities make up the bulk of the program of these organizations, which differ widely in the type of symbolism employed in the formulation of ideals and the planning of ceremonies.   The lore of the Indian, the pioneer, and the knight is variously used, now and then with emotional power and literary beauty.   In the following characteristics, the organization we shall now discuss, which we shall call system Y, is much like many others.

1. It has a high standard of leadership, but is obliged to depend on local volunteers, who naturally differ widely among themselves in ability and training.
2. It publishes a manual and sundry books and pamphlets.
3. It reaches chiefly middle-class children.
4. It defines quite specifically what it expects of members and requires that before joining the organization they shall promise to obey certain rules and observe certain principles of behavior, among which honesty is quite prominent.
5. Good standing depends on good behavior, and progress depends on the achievement of specific skills and information.   The fact of good behavior is determined partly by observation and partly by the member's own unverified report of himself.   The other skills and information are treated more objectively, so that it is easier to maintain standards of success here than in that part of the program which has for its purpose the development of character.

As in the case of system X we came on the work of this organization in the course of our testing and found it interesting to compare members with non-members, and as before the results were so important as to justify further investigation.

In the material which follows only boys are included.   In school C, which consisted mostly of boys in the grades we worked with, we found that many of the pupils belonged to system Y; so we were able to compare their tendency to deceive with that of the whole school.   This comparison is shown in two respects in Figure 81.

From this we see that the 92 Y's cheated somewhat more than the average on the tests done at home, but somewhat less on the tests done in school.

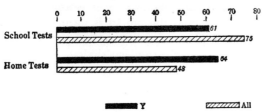

FIGURE 81

PER CENT OF Y'S CHEATING ON SCHOOL AND HOME TESTS, AS COMPARED WITH WHOLE POPULATION OF SCHOOL C

In a suburban community (A) we found the facts presented in Figure 82.

In spite of the fact that these 72 Y's in population A had higher IQ's and a better home background than the average, they nevertheless cheated more than the average both in school and at home.

It was these initial findings which led us to seek more cases. These we found in a much larger suburb than the previous one. They were members of school E, a junior high school consisting mostly of girls, but with 150 boys who were members of Y and 180 who did not belong to any similar organization. We first selected from these two groups such cases as would match in age and IQ. The cheating scores of Y's and non-Y's are shown in Figure 83.

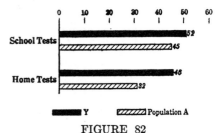

FIGURE 82

PER CENT OF Y'S CHEATING ON SCHOOL AND HOME TESTS, AS COMPARED WITH WHOLE OF POPULATION A

The cheating means of the Y's turn out to be lower than those of the non-Y's, but in the case of the Speed tests the difference would have to be twice as great as it is to be statistically reliable, that is, to be certainly more than a chance difference; and in the case of the Coördination tests the difference would have to be seven times as great as it is for one to be sure that it was not due to chance.

Figures 84, 85, 86, and 87 show the same and other facts about the Y's, those belonging to other organizations than Y, and those belonging to no organization at all, when no effort is made to match the groups for age or IQ. Tables CLX to CLXIV, Book Two, give the basic data.

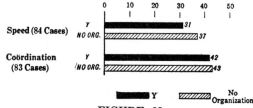

FIGURE 83

RAW DECEPTION SCORES OF BOYS BELONGING TO Y AND TO NO ORGANIZATION

The results displayed in Figures 84, 85, 86, and 87 may be summarized as follows: Comparing all Y's (150) with members of other organizations

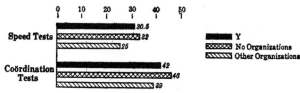

FIGURE 84

DECEPTION SCORES OF Y'S, MEMBERS OF NO ORGANIZATION, AND MEMBERS OF ORGANIZATIONS OTHER THAN Y (MEANS OF RAW SCORES)

(22) and with all not belonging to any (180), we find no significant differences in IQ, CA, or deception. There is a tendency for the Y's to be older and more intelligent than those not belonging to any organizations, but the differences could be accounted for by chance.

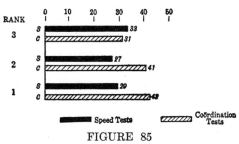

FIGURE 85

DECEPTION AND RANK IN Y (MEANS OF RAW SCORES)

The small group of 22 who belong to various organizations not Y's are not significantly less deceptive than the average of all the boys taken together, but their difference from the average of all boys is, in terms of the standard error of the differences, ten times as great as in the case of the Y's (.16 for Y's and 1.65 for other organizations).

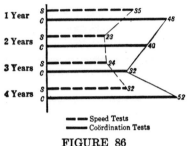

**FIGURE 86**

DECEPTION AND LENGTH OF MEMBERSHIP IN Y (MEANS OF RAW SCORES)

There are twelve groups containing enough Y's to make some comparison with those not belonging to any organization. The median number of times the Y's and non-Y's cheated is the same in seven of these twelve groups. In three the median for the Y's is higher (more cheating) than the non-Y's, and in two groups the median for the Y's is lower (less cheating) than for the non-Y's.

Apparently in this particular situation the Y's show only the slightest difference from the group as a whole, standing midway between those not belonging to any organization and those belonging to other organizations.

In this school there are no statistically reliable differences between those who have achieved different ranks or who have been members of the organization for different lengths of time. Yet such differences as are found are of interest. In one test those of higher rank are less deceptive, and in another test those of lower rank are less deceptive.

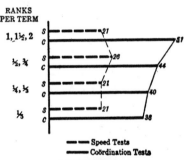

**FIGURE 87**

DECEPTION AND RATE OF ADVANCEMENT IN Y (MEDIANS OF RAW SCORES)

Those who move up faster in rank cheat more than those who progress slowly. In two types of tests those just entering the organization and those who have been members for four years or more are more deceptive than those who have been members for two or three years. As the four-year groups are over age (this being a junior high school) they may be expected to be more deceptive than the others. Omitting this group, the rest show, on the average, an increase in honesty with length of attendance.

The numbers on which these three studies of system Y have been based are of course too small to warrant broad generalizations concerning the organization as a whole; and its sponsors, moreover, say that it is not at its best in the communities from which our cases come. We can only conclude that in these places this widely used agency for moral education, whatever its effect may be elsewhere, is either neutral or deleterious with regard to one of its major aims, the teaching of honesty. This conclusion must be at once supplemented, however, for system Y as for system X and the religious schools, by the caution that in other ways it may be having a vast influence for good. But with Y as with X and the rest, these other objectives also must some day pass through the refining fire of scientific measurement.

# CHAPTER XX

## EXPERIMENTAL EFFORTS TO TEACH HONESTY

We have not as yet undertaken any experiment in the teaching of honesty. In several instances, however, we have coöperated with others who wished to do so by furnishing tests in order that they might be able to measure their results. Two such experiments have been reported to us which, though too brief and incomplete to be conclusive, are nevertheless of considerable interest.

For the first experiment and its measurement Professor W. C. Trow of the University of Michigan is responsible. He very kindly offered to coöperate with us in the conduct of an experiment and to administer and score the tests. Neither the teaching nor the testing, however, was done under his own supervision.

The six junior high school groups used for the experiment were selected with a view to equivalence in sex, age, and intelligence. A ninth-grade civics class consisting of both boys and girls, a seventh-grade home room of boys, and an eighth-grade home room of girls were each given fifteen minutes of daily instruction for three weeks in *The Honesty Book*.* The lessons consist of interesting stories of honest and dishonest behavior and discussions of the problem of honesty as it appears in various life situations. For such direct teaching the material offered seemed the best available.† The other three classes, which served as " controls," were another ninth-grade civics class of boys and girls, a seventh-grade class of girls, and an eighth-grade class of boys. To each of these six classes

* W. B. Forbush, published by the National Honesty Bureau, 115 Broadway, New York City.

† The book contains also some helpful suggestions about using ordinary school situations for gaining experience in the practice of honesty.

were given the Sims Score Card and the Speed and Coördination tests. The deception tests were given just before the three weeks of intensive teaching began and again just after it was completed. It was expected that the effectiveness of the teaching would be shown by comparing the change that had taken place by the end of the three weeks in the experimental groups (those subjected to the teaching) with the change that had taken place in the control groups (those which had *not* had the teaching).

Intelligence scores (Terman group test) and of course chronological ages were available. There was no significant difference between the experimental and control groups in age or Sims score (socio-economic level). The difference in IQ, however, was two and a half times its unreliability, the experimental groups being as a whole more intelligent than the control groups.

The results of the experiment may be summarized* as follows:

On the Speed tests both the experimental and control groups were very honest as compared with populations previously tested, so that there was little room for improvement in any case. The Coördination tests, however, showed mean deception scores of about $-2.0$ Xi, which, though smaller than we found in even the more honest groups in other places, was nevertheless large enough to allow for considerable change in the direction of honesty. Figures 88 and 89 show what change there actually was.

Figure 88 shows that in the case of the Coördination tests all groups except the first experimental group were slightly more deceptive after the training than before. The first experimental group changed insignificantly for the better. When combined, the three experimental groups show a slight loss in honesty, and the control groups a somewhat greater loss in honesty.

The facts for the Speed test are somewhat different. Here all experimental groups were less deceptive after the three weeks of training. But so also were two of the *control* groups, and the one that was more deceptive at the end of the period was only insignificantly so. We might be inclined to attribute to the effects of the teaching the change shown by the three groups that had the train-

* See tables in Chapter XI of Book Two.

ing were it not for the fact that the second control group changed almost as significantly as its experimental counterpart and the third control group changed even more than the third experimental group in the direction of honest performance.   Certainly it was not the teaching that made these two control groups improve, *for they had had none.*   Consequently it is hardly reasonable to attribute

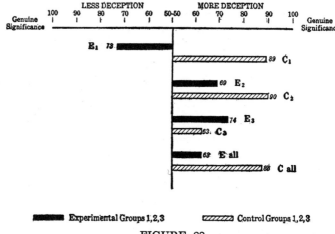

FIGURE 88

Changes in Coördination Test Scores during Three Weeks' Intensive Teaching of Honesty, Population N

The length of the bars as compared with the long lines at the top shows the probability that the differences are reliable.   The center represents an even or fifty-fifty chance.

the change in the experimental groups to the influence of the course on honesty.*

So far as our results go, the particular method of teaching honesty employed in this experiment for fifteen consecutive school periods of fifteen minutes each did not make the pupils concerned less inclined than they already were to falsify their records in order

* As a matter of fact, the mean changes represented for the groups rather a loss of interest than an increase of honesty as they occurred within the limits of honest variability.

to improve their scores. This does not mean that individual pupils may not have been benefited by the teaching, but that such benefits, if any, were confined to very few or were so restricted in character as to make no difference in the classroom behavior of most of the children.*

The second experiment we shall report was conducted by Dr. J. Maller, a graduate student at Teachers College, Columbia University. His purpose was to find what effect the mention of God in

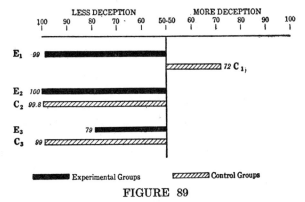

FIGURE 89

CHANGES IN SPEED TEST SCORES DURING THREE WEEKS' INTENSIVE TEACHING OF HONESTY, POPULATION N

The length of the bars as compared with the long lines at the top shows the probability that the differences are reliable. The center represents an even or fifty-fifty chance.

connection with a test would have on the honesty of children. The idea of God was introduced by the statement: God loves an honest man. But the ideas of God and honesty are here used in

* These same children were also given a test of moral knowledge both before and after the period of training. There was no change in the mean score in the case of either the three experimental groups or the three control groups. The tests are described in a monograph by the authors called "Testing the Knowledge of Right and Wrong," published by the Religious Education Association, 308 N. Michigan Ave., Chicago, Ill. As the items range over a wide territory of social situations, it is not surprising that the teaching in regard to honesty had no effect on the scores.

conjunction, so that it was necessary to determine the effect of the idea of honesty when the idea of God was not associated with it. This was accomplished by using first the statement: Honesty is the best policy.

The Speed tests were used for measuring deceptiveness. As there are six of these, they could be treated in three groups of two each. First of all, the entire six were administered as usual for the two practice trials, which were then collected. Then when the last trial was given, which the pupils were to score, the procedure was as follows:

1. Tests 1 and 2 were given and scored without comment, so that whatever deception occurred was without reference to the two ideas to be introduced.

2. Before beginning test 3 the examiner wrote on the board, " Honesty is the best policy," and then administered tests 3 and 4, after which he erased the words and left the room.

3. Before the fifth test he wrote, " God loves an honest man," and then, having given tests 5 and 6, he erased the phrase and left the room. There was thus introduced into the situation not only the stimulus of the words which theoretically would operate to lessen cheating, but also the additional time and the factor of having the examiner leave the room for a moment, which theoretically would operate to increase cheating.

This plan was followed with three groups of children, two of them being classes in Hebrew schools and one being a public school class consisting in part of children attending religious school during the week and in part of children without such training. The facts are summarized in Table LXIX, which gives the mean deception score for each of the three pairs of tests, the SD of the distribution and the SD or unreliability of the mean, and the number of cases.

The first row, R, is the record for the public school children who have religious instruction. The second row, NR, is for those in the same class who do not. The third row, H1, is for the Hebrew school giving mild religious instruction, and the last row, H2, for the school giving more careful instruction.

TABLE LXIX

EFFECT ON DECEPTION OF THE MENTION OF DEITY

| GROUP | NUMBER | TESTS 1 AND 2 | | | TESTS 3 AND 4 | | | TESTS 5 AND 6 | | |
|---|---|---|---|---|---|---|---|---|---|---|
| | | M | SD | σM | M | SD | σM | M | SD | σM |
| R | 25 | 8.9 | 5.3 | 1.06 | 6.4 | 4.2 | .84 | 5.5 | 3.8 | .76 |
| NR | 15 | 3.8 | 1.4 | .36 | 7.8 | 3.5 | .90 | 10.0 | 4.6 | 1.19 |
| H1 | 29 | 5.2 | 4.8 | .89 | 6.1 | 3.9 | .72 | 6.3 | 2.4 | .45 |
| H2 | 26 | 7.8 | 2.8 | .55 | 6.3 | 4.3 | .84 | 1.1 | 4.9 | .96 |

Of the public school class, the children who have religious teaching get progressively more honest as the idea of honesty and then the idea of God in association with the idea of honesty are introduced, whereas the children of the same classroom who do not attend religious school get progressively less honest under the same circumstances. Of the two Hebrew classes, one is not changed by either phrase; and the other, while not responding to the first phrase, is apparently greatly affected when the idea of God is mentioned.

This experiment was only preliminary to a more adequate study, and the number of cases is too small for reliable conclusions. It is reported, however, as suggestive of the kind of experiment that might be easily conducted to discover the values for conduct that inhere in various customary forms of control. The differences between the groups and between the behavior of the same group under the described conditions are large enough to warrant the feeling that in certain forms of religious training there are potential values for the control of conduct that are far from being realized in the ordinary life of the children concerned. The differences between the groups, put into terms of the probability that differences equally large would not recur by chance and translated into graphic diagrams, are presented in Figure 90. Each filled-in section of the long rectangles indicates the " significance " of the difference it represents. The longer the shaded portion, the greater the probability that it shows a genuine difference between the groups under the influence of the experimental conditions. The total rectangle stands for one thousand comparisons of like nature, and the shaded portion is the proportion of one thousand group differences that are likely to be due to the influence described, the unfilled portion being, conversely, the number of chances in a thousand that the difference obtained would occur between the groups by chance alone.

The top bar in the case of each comparison given in Figure 90 shows the public school group not attending religious school (NR) as far more honest than the religious school group in the same classroom or either of the two groups in the Hebrew schools. When honesty is mentioned, however, as the middle bar shows, all the religious groups now become less deceptive than the NR group, though not significantly so. But when the idea of God is brought in, all the religious groups become significantly more honest than those who have no religious instruction. This difference, it should be noted, is due more to the fact that the non-religious group gets progressively more dishonest, in spite of what is written on the board, whereas H1 remains about the same throughout. H2 gets strangely honest after the idea of God is brought in, though on the first two tests it was far more deceptive than the non-religious group.

What motives operated to change the behavior of the H2 group and the R group are not known, but whatever they were they did not do more than serve as a brake to prevent the H1 from getting worse and had no effect whatever on the NR group. It seems to be a fair conclusion to draw that the behavior of children in respect to the mode of deceit involved is in part at least a function either of the teaching they have received in religious schools or of miscellaneous factors associated with the fact that they are sent to such schools by their parents. That the former hypothesis is not entirely without foundation is suggested by the behavior of H2, which showed very little change for the better when honesty alone was brought into the situation but very marked change when the idea of God was mentioned.

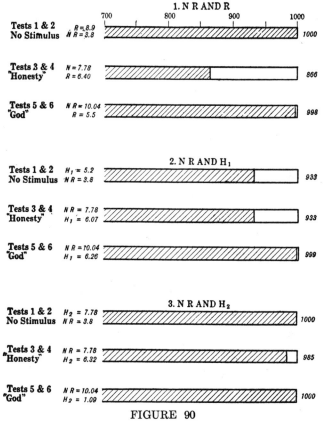

FIGURE 90

PROBABLE SIGNIFICANCE OF THE DIFFERENCES IN DECEIT BETWEEN MALLER'S GROUPS ON TESTS 1 AND 2, 3 AND 4, AND 5 AND 6

NR = the portion of the public school class not attending religious school
R = the portion of the same class attending religious school
H1 = the Hebrew school giving mild religious instruction
H2 = the Hebrew school giving more careful religious instruction

The length of the filled-in portion of the rectangle shows the probability that the difference given at the left is significant. The left end represents a chance of 700 in 1000.

# PART IV

## General Conclusions and Problems

### CHAPTER XXI

## THE SPECIFIC NATURE OF CONDUCT AND ATTITUDE

In the first chapter of this volume we set forth the general characteristics of the modes of behavior which we have classified under the term " deceit " and pointed out their significance for the individual and society. We have dealt with the matter psychologically rather than in terms of ethics, concerning ourselves with objective concomitants and consequences rather than with the moral struggles of the individual or with social approvals and disapprovals, important as these may be. We have held that a person may deceive another in all good conscience, if his training has been of a certain kind, but that what he does is no less deceptive. The essence of the act is its pretense. Hence it can be described and understood only in terms of the human elements in the situation. It is not the act that constitutes the deception, nor the particular intention of the actor, but the *relation* of his act to his intentions and to the intentions of his associates. This relation can be defined in psychological terms. The typical deceptive act implies a conflict of wills with regard to either means or ends or both and the concealment of either the act or its intention or both in order to gain the end or utilize the means concerning which the conflict has arisen. The term applies to the cat that watches her chance to help herself from the kitchen table as well as to the citizen who gives pious reasons for robbing the state of its natural resources. If the intentions or methods of either were known to those whose

377

rights were being infringed, the act of the deceiver would be frustrated. Success requires that the wolf appear in sheep's clothing.

Conversely, honest behavior is behavior which does not resort to subterfuge to gain its ends. But there are degrees of subterfuge. A person may be dishonestly honest. He may be honest in little things in order to gain the reputation of being honest in all things. This is his sheep's clothing under which his more subtle acts of aggression are concealed. Or one may be honest because it pays in a business way, but may publish as his reason for honesty that it is the only mode of conduct that appeals to an honorable man. He wins thus for himself a degree of confidence quite unwarranted by his true character.

Honesty in greater or less degree has for centuries been regarded as a virtue even though in the practical conduct of life its practice is in constant conflict with other equally admired ideals. The " honesty " of an employee is relative to the " loyalty " of the employee to the purposes and methods of the firm. National " honor " and national " honesty " are often in opposition. Truth which would inflict a fatal shock may be withheld from a sick patient in the interest of his recovery. The futility of the attempt to build character by accumulating virtues which in the nature of the case are frequently inconsistent with one another was long since forcibly portrayed by Coe in his address on " Virtue and the Virtues" at the meeting of the National Education Association in San Francisco.* A man may possess all the virtues without being virtuous. It is not the quality of the isolated act which distinguishes the good man from the bad, but the quality of the *man* as an organized and socially functioning self. We may add up his characteristics, whether these be virtues or vices, but the algebraical sum is not his character.

To this attack on the concept of virtues as elements of character has been added in more recent years the attack on the virtues as unified traits. Not only does character not consist of a sum of virtues, but the virtues themselves are not psychological entities

* Printed in the *Proceedings* of the National Education Association for 1911 and in *Religious Education*, Vol. VI, 1912, pp. 485–492.

with any real existence.  They are not acts.  They are classifications of acts.  To attribute to a man who acts honestly a faculty or trait of honesty is like explaining the act of remembering by referring it to some faculty of memory, which our popular systems of mnemonics are supposed to develop as one would train a muscle. Of course some people remember better than others, but to refer this difference to some mysterious and specialized power of memory is to stuff our ignorance with words.  Similarly, to say that an honest act is caused by a man's honesty is like saying that it is cold because the temperature has fallen.  Some men, it may be, can learn to be honest more easily than others because of real mental differences of the nature of which we are not as yet aware ; but whatever honesty a man possesses resides not in a secret reservoir of honest virtue nor in the ideal of honesty which he may hold before himself as worthy of his best effort, but in the quality of the particular acts he performs.

We propose to bring together in this chapter and in the accompanying chapter of Book Two the data and arguments supporting the position taken in the last paragraph, which we may briefly characterize as the doctrine of specificity.  According to this view a trait such as honesty or dishonesty is an achievement like ability in arithmetic, depending of course on native capacities of various kinds, but *consisting in* the achieved skills and attitudes of more or less successful and uniform performance.

As an introduction to the statement of the case, let us take the ability to add and the correlative ability to subtract.  If a class had been faithfully taught how to add but not a word about how to subtract, no inherent faculty of figuring would come to their rescue if they were given a test which included problems in subtraction. Much alike as these two related processes may seem to an adult, they have to be learned ;  and the correlation between the two seemingly similar abilities will depend on (1) the actual elements which they have in common, (2) the amount of experience which the pupils have had with both, and (3) the extent to which the two processes are comprehended under a single more inclusive picture in terms of which they can be related to one another.

Honest and dishonest acts are specialized in the same way. Even after the principle of honesty is understood, the deceptive aspect of certain acts may not be noticed until one's attention is drawn to them. One may be meticulously honorable in his relations with his neighbors but steal a ride on the street car without thinking himself a thief. Acts are not accurately labeled because they are not completely analyzed. Consequently, an otherwise entirely honest man may be shocked and insulted when his sharp business practices are called stealing or his purchase of votes, political corruption.

Our conclusion, then, is that an individual's honesty or dishonesty consists of a series of acts and attitudes to which these descriptive terms apply. The consistency with which he is honest or dishonest is a function of the situations in which he is placed in so far as (1) these situations have common elements, (2) he has learned to be honest or dishonest in them, and (3) he has become aware of their honest or dishonest implications or consequences.

In support of the foregoing conclusion let us examine two types of evidence, the first relating to the specific nature of conduct and the second to the specificity of attitude associated with conduct.

## THE SPECIFIC NATURE OF CONDUCT

We have to consider, first, the probability that an individual will behave in the same way when a given situation is repeated; second, the probability that an individual will behave in the same way on different tests in the same situation when only the material of the test is changed; and third, the probability that an individual will behave in the same way when the nature of the situation is markedly altered. We may assume that changes in behavior between the two test occasions may be regarded as functions of changes in the situation, particularly if these changes are proportional to the differences in the situations.

We have repeated only the IER home and school tests and the Speed and Coördination tests. Omitting the first, for which there was only one test, Table LXX gives the self-correlations of each test of each of these techniques and the average for each technique.

### TABLE LXX

SELF-CORRELATION OF IER, SPEED, AND COÖRDINATION TESTS

| IER School | | SPEED | | COÖRDINATION | |
|---|---|---|---|---|---|
| Arithmetic . . . | .530 | Test 1 . . . . | .632 | Squares . . . . | .587 |
| Completion . . . | .790 | " 2 . . . . | .605 | Circles . . . . | .571 |
| Information . . | .710 | " 3 . . . . | .582 | Mazes . . . . | .548 |
| | | " 4 . . . . | .473 | | |
| | | " 5 . . . . | .600 | | |
| | | " 6 . . . . | .525 | | |
| Average | .676 | | .569 | | .566 |

In the case of the IER school tests, six months elapsed between the two occasions, and there was a change of classroom for all pupils.   Furthermore, on the second occasion there was considerable confusion as the children had expected to have a half-day off.   The mean deception scores for the two tests were therefore quite different.   But for the other two techniques, which were repeated after a few days, the means for the two tests were almost identical.   Thus we can predict with considerable accuracy what a group will do on a second occasion if the situation is unchanged and if we know what it does on the first occasion.   But even slight changes in the situation affect individual behavior in unpredictable ways, so that the $r$'s are lower than would be required for accurate prediction of individual behavior.

In the above illustration we kept the material constant but changed the general situation as to the day, the examiner, time of day (for the Coördination tests), and classroom (for the IER tests). In order to measure the likelihood that an individual will behave in the same way when the only change is in the material of the test, we correlate one test with another and find the average of these intercorrelations.   Thus there are three IER school tests, and the average intercorrelation of these three with one another is .696. Table LXXI gives similar $r$'s for several types of deception.

## TABLE LXXI

### INTERCORRELATIONS AMONG DECEPTION TESTS OF THE SAME TYPE

| | |
|---|---|
| IER school . . . . . | .696 |
| Speed . . . . . . . | .440 |
| Coördination . . . . . | .462 |
| Puzzles . . . . . . . | .500 |
| Contest . . . . . . . | .458 |
| Lying . . . . . . . | .836 |

The first three $r$'s are similar to those we found when the gross situation was altered. In the case of the Speed and Coördination tests these gross changes make less difference than changing the *material* of the test while employing the same technique. For the IER test, the gross changes, to which we referred, are large enough to affect a greater change in behavior than changing the material from arithmetic to completions, etc., while keeping gross factors constant.*

This tendency for the behavior to change with the material is still more forcibly portrayed in Figures 91 and 92, which show the average amount of cheating of several populations on the three Coördination and the six Speed tests.

Xi SCORES

4.1 4.2 4.3 4.4 4.5 4.6 4.7 4.8 4.9 5.0 5.1 5.2 5.3 5.4

Squares

Circles

Mazes

### FIGURE 91

AMOUNT OF CHEATING ON COÖRDINATION TESTS, POPULATIONS F TO J

N = 2379

The children cheated significantly more on the mazes than on the circles or squares, and all the Speed differences except between test 2 and test 3 are significant.

We interpret these differences to mean that even such slight changes in the situation as between crossing out A's and putting dots in squares are sufficient to alter the amount of deception both in individuals and in groups.

* There was also a slight change in the technique, the answer sheets being passed out *with* the Arithmetic test, but not passed for Completions or Information until the tests had been in each case completed.

Our third comparison concerns the probability that an individual will behave the same way when the situation is radically altered, as when he cheats by adding more scores to his paper instead of by copying answers from a sheet or by faking the solution of a puzzle rather than falsifying his score in an athletic contest. We may present these facts in terms of the correlations between different types of test in Table LXXII.

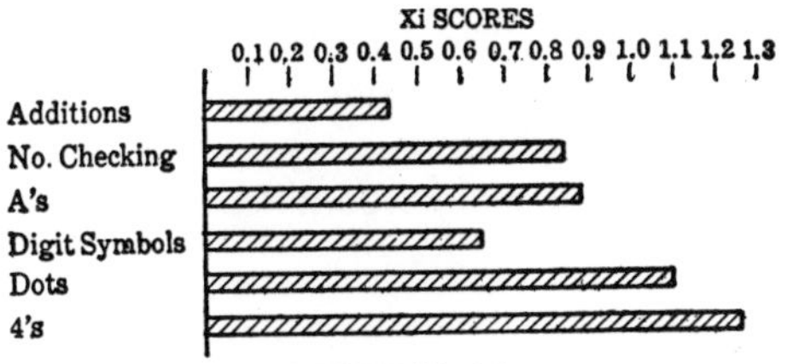

FIGURE 92

AMOUNT OF CHEATING ON SPEED TESTS, POPULATIONS A, C, D, E, P, R, AND U

TABLE LXXII

AVERAGE CORRELATIONS BETWEEN SINGLE TESTS OF DIFFERENT TECHNIQUES

|  | SPEED | COÖRDINA-TION | PUZZLES | CONTESTS | STEALING | LYING |
|---|---|---|---|---|---|---|
| IER | .292 | .285 | .291 | .198 | .127 | .312 |
| Speed |  | .219 | .255 | .194 | .128 | .254 |
| Coördination |  |  | .196 | .062 | .160 | .161 |
| Puzzles |  |  |  | .184 | .283 | .208 |
| Contests |  |  |  |  | .162 | −.003 |
| Stealing |  |  |  |  |  | .132 |

This table reads: One IER test will correlate on the average .292 with one Speed test, .285 with one Coördination test, etc.

From Table LXXI we see that copying from a key on one test will correlate .696 with copying from a key on another test; adding on scores on a speed test will correlate .440 with adding on scores on another speed test; but copying from a key on one test will correlate only .292 with adding on scores. Indeed the average of the six intercorrelations of the four classroom tests reported in Table LXXII is only .256. Reference to Table LXXI again will show that the different single tests in any one technique are more highly correlated than any one of those tests is with one of another technique. Changing the situation lowers the $r$'s.

The eight $r$'s between the four classroom tests and the two out-of-classroom tests, contests and stealing, average only .167 — still lower than .256, which is the average of the classroom $r$'s. The lying test, which was also given in the classroom, averages .234 with the other classroom tests and .064 with the two out-of-class-

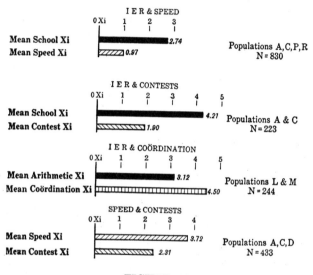

FIGURE 93

AMOUNT OF CHEATING ON DIFFERENT DECEPTION TESTS

room tests. Thus as we progressively change the situation we progressively lower the correlations between the tests.

As before, we interpret these facts to mean that the consistency of the individual is a function of the situation.

That the situation is a real factor in determining the amount of deception can best be shown by comparing the mean Xi scores of large groups on different types of test. If the constant tendency to cheat or be honest were the sole or chief cause of specific amounts of deception, these Xi scores ought to be alike, but as Figure 93 shows, they are vastly different.

These differences are anywhere from 4 to 25 times the standard error of the difference and are far larger than those of Figures 91 and 92, which give the differences in amounts of cheating on different tests of the same technique.*

These are differences among large groups of children, it must be remembered, and therefore reveal a constant tendency for certain types of opportunity and material to induce more cheating than certain other opportunities and types of material.

We have shown how correlations between tests fluctuate downward as the situations become increasingly different. Our theory requires that, if we had a sufficient number of varying techniques, these $r$'s would run from $+1.00$ to zero, that is, from the point where there was a sufficient number of identical elements, a sufficient amount of common experience, and a sufficient comprehension of the situation for the two situations to function in exactly the same way, to the point where there was so little resemblance between the two situations, so little common experience, and so little comprehension of their significance that deceptive behavior in the two situations would be totally unrelated.

It may be contended of course that as a matter of fact we rarely reach a zero correlation, no matter how different may be our techniques, and that this implies some such common factor in the individual as might properly be called a trait. We would not wish to quarrel over the use of a term and are quite ready to recognize the existence of some common factors which tend to make individuals differ from one another on any one test or on any group of tests. Our contention, however, is that this common factor is not an inner entity operating independently of the situations in which the individuals are placed but is a function of the situation in the sense that an individual behaves similarly in different situations in proportion as these situations are alike, have been experienced as common occasions for honest or dishonest behavior, and are comprehended as opportunities for deception or honesty.

We have just referred to the fact that individuals differ on any one test or group of tests. In selected populations and with tests

* The scale for Figures 91 and 92 is five times as coarse as that for Figure 93.

which are relatively unmotivated we find a large proportion of children who do not cheat, with the rest distributed somewhat after the fashion of the normal probability curve. But in large populations the proportion of honest cases is reduced and the total curve closely approximates the normal. In Figure 94, for example, is the distribution of the CT ratio for 2443 children of populations C, D, F–J, L, and M, in which each pupil had at least ten tests.

As the fact of cheating used in making up the CT ratio represents only the extreme probability of 999 cases in 1000, it is clear that a good many of those who are marked as cheating once, twice, or three times and also of those who have zeros are probably misplaced. The shifting of all cases toward the upper end of the scale would tend to straighten up the curve to approximate the shape of the normal probability curve, in the form of which most facts about human nature are distributed. At first thought this might be interpreted to mean that these individuals differed from one another with respect to a unified trait varying all the way from just not any honesty to complete honesty.

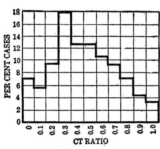

FIGURE 94

DISTRIBUTION OF CT RATIOS, POPULATIONS C, D, F TO J, L, AND M

N = 2443

But in order for this to be true, it would be necessary for the CT ratio to represent a *scale* with equal steps, whereas, as we saw above, cheating on the IER tests is by no means equivalent to cheating on the Speed tests, etc. Inasmuch, therefore, as the units of the ratio mean cheating once in a hundred times on *any test*, twice in a hundred times *on any two tests*, etc., the shape of the curve can be explained only in terms of the unique relation which each individual bears to each situation — a relation which makes it more likely that, if the same tests were repeated, he would cheat on just the same ones than that he would cheat on any others. This likelihood is expressed by the relative size of the self-correlation of the tests and the intercorrelation of the tests of different techniques.*

## THE SPECIFIC NATURE OF ATTITUDES

Strictly speaking, what we measure by our techniques is not conduct but tendency or attitude, for we remove the external barriers which ordinarily prevent the full expression of the tendency and permit the individual to go as far as he wishes to in the direction of dishonest performance. In an experiment† reported in 1926 and printed in full in Book Two, we came upon evidence for believing that the attitudes constituting the driving power of the act are as specialized as the act itself. The tendency to copy answers from answer sheets and substitute them for one's own work, for example, exists in a measurable quantity peculiar to the individual. Whatever may be the motives which combine to make him use the answer sheet, they operate to overcome just so much resistance and no more, and this resistance can be arranged to begin with just no resistance at all and move up by measured steps to the point where no one will overcome it in order to cheat. The scheme used was roughly as follows:

We first arranged a test so that it would be very troublesome and risky to cheat on it. The answers to the questions were made by drawing a line in ink around the correct answer. In order to cheat, a pupil had to erase this mark made in ink and draw another. At the other end of the scale was a spelling test the answers to which were made by entering a check mark in lead pencil against a misspelled word. To cheat, all one had to do was to add more check marks or erase and change those already made. In between were procedures requiring varying amounts of time and trouble in

* As may be seen from the tables of Chapter XII, Book Two, none of these inter-*r*'s when corrected for attenuation exceeds .60, so that no matter how many times any one type of test were repeated it would not be possible to predict from it whether an individual would cheat or not on any other technique.

† "First Steps toward a Scale for Measuring Attitudes," *Journal of Educational Psychology*, March, 1926.

order to make one's paper appear like the answer sheet. In order to be absolutely sure of every change made, we gave the test in school and then took it to the office and had an exact copy made of each paper. Then we returned to the school and asked the pupils to score their own papers by referring to the keys we provided. We then compared their papers as they now appeared with what they were before the scoring had been done. In this way every bit of deception was recorded.

By figuring the percentage of cases that cheated at each level of difficulty we were able to give a numerical value to the amount of resistance that had to be overcome at each level of difficulty. We found that practically all who cheated at any one level cheated also at each lower level, and that all the one-cheaters cheated at the lowest level, the two-cheaters at the two lowest levels, etc. In other words, we had a scale for measuring the amount of the tendency to cheat. The extent to which this scale actually worked is shown in Figure 95. The steps on the scale are represented by the darkness of the shaded bands, each one of which stands for one of the tests. The length of a band represents the number of cases cheating at that level. If the scale had been perfect, there would have been no gaps in it. As it is, 89% of the gaps are filled; *i.e.*, the scale is 89% perfect.

An illustration from another field may help to make clear the meaning of the chart. Suppose we have seven makes of cartridges and wish to measure the relative velocity with which each will project its bullet. As a rough measure we might take a series of substances of varying density, such as a steel plate one inch thick, a block of hard wood two feet thick, a block of hard wood one foot thick, a block of soft wood a foot thick, a piece of asphalt three inches thick, a piece of plate glass, and a heavy piece of cardboard. We might then proceed to shoot cartridges of each make into these various substances, keeping a careful record of each shot to see which bullet pierced which substance and at what point in the series of increasing densities a certain type of bullet was stopped from any further progress. Bullets with practically no velocity would strike the cardboard and fall to the ground; but some would

FIGURE 95

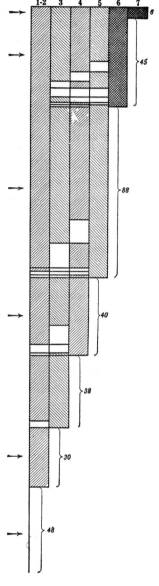

THE SCALING OF ATTITUDES ASSOCIATED
WITH ONE FORM OF DECEPTION

The numbers at the top refer to the following tests, which are described in Book Two:

> 1–2 Arithmetic and Spelling
> 3 Word Knowledge
> 4 Completions
> 5 Reading
> 6 Disarranged Sentences
> 7 Information (ink)

doubtless pierce the steel plate, and these would also pierce all the substances offering less resistance.

In the case of cartridges of uniform quality, there would be few exceptions to the rule that any make or style which passed through a given resistance would also pass through any less resistance. Also the different styles could be identified as "steel-piercing" or "softwood" cartridges, meaning that they possessed just whatever force was needed to pierce the object named.

So with the velocity or force or drive of a particular type of deception such as using an answer sheet for answers. Apparently the habit or act is associated with a tendency or attitude of a specific *amount*, which carries the individual just so far and no farther. Those who overcome the greatest resistance in order to cheat will overcome also all weaker resistances, and those that can overcome only the least resistance will be found cheating only on the test which requires the adding of a check mark, but not on the test which requires the writing of sentences or words in order to deceive.

On the chart, the arrows represent the direction in which the cheating drive is operating, and, as was suggested before, the darkness of the shaded blocks represents the varying resistances to be overcome if cheating is to be accomplished.  Forty-eight cases, like the bullets without velocity, did not overcome even the least resistance, but six overcame even the heaviest resistance and all six also cheated on all the tests with less resistance.

The significance of this for our present discussion is that, although other types of cheating may probably each be scaled in the same way, when the types are intermingled the results *do not* scale. That is, if we put together a series of speed tests, those cheating on the one requiring the most trouble to cheat will also cheat on the rest.  But if we attempt to combine all techniques in one scale, as we might by using the CT ratio or a ratio representing all tests whether in classroom or out, the results do not scale, *i.e.*, the drives are specific and are a function of the situation and the mode of deception for which the situation calls.

# CHAPTER XXII

# THE MOTIVATION OF DECEIT

At the very beginning of this report we stated as our opinion that the study of character must include the objective determination of the facts concerning conduct : What does the child actually do? What are the circumstances under which he does it? With what other facts is the act associated? This volume has reported what we have been able to discover concerning one type of conduct the essential features of which are (1) a conflict of wills and (2) either the concealment of the act by which one party to the conflict surreptitiously gains his ends, or the misrepresentation of his motive. Variation in the ends sought, the acts resorted to, and the motives in operation does not affect the essential nature of an act of deception, psychologically conceived, but differences in ends sought and motives operating as well as particular ways used to deceive others do have a great deal to do with our understanding and control of the tendency ; and since control as well as prediction is an important objective of educational research, our report would be incomplete without the inclusion of such facts as we have been able to gather concerning this aspect of our problem.

The reader will recognize at once, however, how difficult it is to deal *experimentally* with motives when studying deception. One might easily invent a situation in which the subject would be tempted to fake the answer to a puzzle, say, by a gradually ascending series of bribes until the point was reached where he could no longer resist. We have carefully avoided doing anything of the sort, but have depended altogether on the operation of normal school motives even when attempting to control them. How these normal motives operate we shall point out presently. So far as any other type of motivation is concerned, we shall have to discover it either by direct questioning of the pupils or by inference from other facts. Both of these methods have also been utilized.

## THE CONTROL OF SCHOOL MOTIVES

We attempted to control the operation of ordinary school motives in two ways: first, by stating the purpose of the test when it was being administered and, second, by showing the pupils the norms for pupils of their grade and the score which would be equivalent to the usual school marks, A, B, C, etc.

### A. STATING THE PURPOSE OF THE TEST

In Chapter IV we described our first use of the IER tests and our effort to standardize the motives under which the pupils should work. It will be recalled that we had five batteries of directions. In one set, no motive was stated for giving the tests. In each of the other four a phrase intended to arouse a specific motive was frequently repeated. These phrases represented respectively (1) personal achievement, (2) individual competition with other members of the class, (3) group competition, and (4) helpfulness to the examiner with no individual or group recognition. The detailed results flowing from the use of these phrases are given in Book Two, Chapter IV. We found that it made almost no difference in the amount of cheating whether appeal was made to the competitive tendencies, where cheating would profit the individual or the group, or to the desire to be of service, where cheating could be of no advantage to anybody in the class. There was, furthermore, as much cheating when nothing at all was said about the purpose of the tests as when any one of the four phrases was used.

Three conclusions are possible from this experiment. We may conclude that the children paid no attention whatever to what was said about the purpose of the tests, or that they heard what was said but did not believe it, or, finally, that the general school drive or desire for good marks together with the habits to which it was attached was too powerful to be deflected by a mere statement by the examiner.

## B. Stating Test Norms

In the experiment referred to in the previous chapter and described in Chapter XII of Book Two, we presented each pupil with a sheet of paper * giving the scores that might be expected from pupils of his grade and the equivalent school marks for these grades, thus providing a standard toward which to work. In one instance we said nothing about the use that might be made of the pupils' scores and in the other instance we stated that the grades would count on the pupils' monthly report. Although these same pupils were not tested with the same material without the presence of the norms, they had material which was quite similar; and it is apparently the case that the mere presence of the norms tends to increase the amount of cheating, and that the knowledge that the scores will count toward the monthly standing increases it still further.

Such facts do not in the least justify the cheating or lend support to the contention that all school reports have a bad influence on the pupils. They merely indicate that, unless there is some change in the resistance to the tendency to deceive, an increase in the profits from deception will increase the amount of deception.

## THE QUESTIONING OF PUPILS

In our discussion of lying we quoted certain questions which appeared on our Pupil Data Sheet bearing on pupils' conduct during the examinations in which we had measured their tendency to deceive. One of these questions was:

" If you did copy on any of these tests that you took a little while ago or received any help you should not have received, just why did you do so? "

Only a small percentage of the cheaters were willing to answer the question, the rest either saying nothing or insisting that they did not copy or get unfair help. We have tabulated the answers of those who replied, classifying them as shown in Table LXXIII.

* Or used the blackboard.

## TABLE LXXIII

### Motives Given by Children for Cheating

|  | A | B | C | Total | Per Cent |
|---|---|---|---|---|---|
| Test too hard . . . | 30 | 53 | 29 | 112 | 45.7 |
| To stand high . . . | 17 | 10 | 23 | 50 | 20.3 |
| Misunderstood . . . | 7 | 13 | 3 | 23 | 9.4 |
| Others cheated . . . | 7 | 6 | 3 | 16 | 6.5 |
| Don't know . . . . | 4 | 7 | 4 | 15 | 6.1 |
| Lazy or felt like it . . | 2 | 6 | 6 | 14 | 5.7 |
| Too many chances . . | 2 | 4 | 0 | 6 | 2.4 |
| Test unfair . . . . | 2 | 3 | 0 | 5 | 2.3 |
| So class would win . | 4 | 0 | 0 | 4 | 1.6 |
|  |  |  |  | 245 |  |

Almost half of those who answered the questions at all said that they cheated because the test was too hard. The next most frequent reason given is " to stand high," which is similar to the first. Putting these two together, we have two thirds of these cases admitting that they cheated in order to do well on the test. This confirms the suggestion gained from the two experiments we have described, *viz.*, that the " school drive " or " success motive " operates very strongly and is particularly likely to result in deceptive practices when the situation is difficult and deception is possible. But here again we must not conclude that school tests " cause " children to cheat or that the desire for high grades is in itself an adequate motive, for many children who find tests difficult and who want good marks do not resort to subterfuge in order to appear well. We must qualify any such general statement by saying that, when a child's resistance to cheating is low, the presence of the desire for good marks may tempt him to use unfair methods to gain them, particularly when he feels that he is in a tight place or that the task required is unfair to him.

## INFERENTIAL DATA

### A. Relation between Deception and Ability

If it be true, as stated by certain of those who cheated, that the difficulty of a test is a primary cause of deception, then we might properly expect that those with less ability would cheat more than those with greater ability. In the double-testing technique we have, as will be remembered, two scores for each child, one secured under " honesty " conditions, and representing his ability, and one secured under conditions which permitted cheating. We are able, therefore, to determine the different amounts of cheating at different levels of test ability. Chapter XII of Book Two reports the results of this study for the IER tests with three populations.

It is found that there is always a negative correlation between the ability to do the test and the amount of cheating exhibited on the test. That is, those who are better able to do the test cheat less than those who find it more difficult. These $r$'s range from $-.045$ to $-.513$. As ability to do tests like these is in part a function of intelligence, it is necessary to show what the relation between ability and deception is when intelligence is kept constant. The partial $r$'s are therefore also given in Book Two, and these range from $+.049$ to $-.338$, showing that in most cases cheating is in part due to lack of ability to do the test. This fact is quite conspicuous in the case of the Completions test, which correlates $-.513$ with the amount of deception shown on this test. The facts are presented graphically in Figure 96, which gives the difference between the gain or loss when no answer sheets were available on either of the two test occasions, and the gain or loss when on one occasion the children had access to the answer sheets. Each bar represents a different level of honest ability, the honest score being indicated at the left, in terms of the actual number of correct answers on the test. The length of the bar represents the amount of deception shown, on the average, by pupils having the test ability given at the left. Thus, those who scored 16 or 17 points on the Completion test when there was no chance to cheat gained, when they had the answer sheets available, 8.15 points more than they could have been expected to. But those who scored 30 or 31 on the test had an excess gain or cheating score of only 1.38 points. Obviously the cheating was proportional to the lack of ability.

The less able did not cheat more because they had more room on the test to cheat, as might be at first imagined, for on this test there were 55 items, and even when the answer sheets were available the largest score shown was 40.

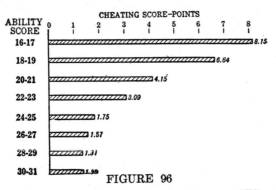

CHEATING SCORE—POINTS

FIGURE 96

RELATION OF CHEATING TO TEST ABILITY, IER COMPLETION TEST, POPULATION C

When we turn to the results of the Speed tests, we find a quite different picture. Here cheating is accomplished not by copying answers from a sheet but by *doing more of the very thing that constitutes the test*, only doing it surreptitiously. As shown in Book Two, Table CLXXVIII, the correlations between honest ability and deception scores are all *positive*, ranging from +.036 to +.434 in four populations. That is, those with greater facility in performing rapid mechanical operations actually make more use of the opportunity to cheat than those with less facility. This is quite the opposite of the case just reported for the IER tests, where those with less ability proved to be the greater cheaters.

Two reasons for this difference are suggested. In the IER tests there was a rapid rise in difficulty as the tests proceeded, so that those with less ability soon found out their limits and were confronted with the certainty of what seemed to them to be a low score unless the answer sheets were used. As the use of these sheets did not require the same ability that was needed for doing the tests, the more able had no advantage over the less able when it came to copying answers. Consequently the less able cheated the more.

On the other hand, the Speed tests were mechanical in nature, not graded in difficulty, and the material was so unfamiliar that there was no way of knowing what constituted a good score. Furthermore, cheating depended on the use of the function being tested, so that those with greater ability did have an advantage over those with less ability in the use that could be made of the time set aside for the self-scoring of the papers. Therefore, with no special incentive to stimulate the less able more than the more able, and with the more able having the advantage in the speed with which answers could be added, naturally the more able did the more cheating.

All this goes to show that the motives leading to deceptive behavior are determined not only by the relation of the pupil to the school in general, or to the teacher, or to his parents' zeal for his success, or to his own ambition, but also to the specific nature of the test material itself and his ability to master it.*

* As evidence of the effect of the situation on motivation, Dr. J. Maller offers the following brief summary of one phase of a study he is conducting in coöperation with the Inquiry:

A test of coöperativeness was given which required the children to work at times for their class on a class project, while at other times the same task was performed by each child in a personal enterprise. An opportunity to be deceptive was introduced and the amount of deception of each child at each opportunity was measured. It was then possible to compare the amount of deception when the motive was to work for the class with the amount of deception when the motive was to work for self. A consistent tendency on the part of the boys tested was to cheat considerably more when working for self than when working for the class. The difference in terms of the standard deviation was 2.26. (That is, in 989 cases out of 1000, the boys will be more deceptive when the motive is a personal enterprise than when it is a class project.)

The deception of children when working for themselves and when working on a class project was measured. The means (of scores of deception) for the boys and girls of each class were compared. A definite relationship was observed between the difference in deception of the boys and of the girls within each class and the difference in number between the two sexes within the same class. A positive correlation of .51 showed that, where the boys were

## B. Miscellaneous Concomitants of Deception

From what has been said, the desire for good marks seems to be the most common motive leading to deceit in tests given in school. It is obvious, however, that this same motive leads also to honest achievement. Indeed there is probably no single motive exclusively attached to deception except in certain rare cases where the individual has cheated so much that he enjoys doing so for its own sake or for the excitement he gets from his secret conflict with the teacher. The *motivation* of deceit is to be found rather in particular combinations of incentive, opportunity, standards, and attitude, which, as was suggested in Chapter XIV, are so numerous as to defy organization in the form of a law of motivation save in the most general terms. Let us attempt, however, some such general formulation.

The child brings to school as part of his own inner equipment three sets of interrelated factors bearing on his practice of school honor: first, his ambition for school achievement, no matter how aroused, how large or how small, or how influenced by the school itself; second, his standards, code, or ideals regarding the methods by which he shall get what he wants, whether by genuine achievement or by hook or crook; third, his responsiveness to such standards, including his ability to obey them, to resist temptations to ignore them, to keep them in mind, etc.

In school, the child faces a complex situation many aspects of which are involved in any single act of deception. There are the general school standards, which he becomes aware of through

in a majority, their deception score for class tended to be greater than the deception score of the girls, and where the girls were more in number, their deception for class tended to be greater than that of the boys. The majority group of a class thus having a stronger motivation to work for the class (it involved the winning of a prize for the class) expressed that motivation in a definite attempt to increase the score of the class even through deception. Considering the deception means of the boys when working for class separately and correlating those means with the ratio of their number to the number of girls, we find an $r$ of .44. That is, there was a positive correlation between the size of the majority and the amount of deception.

hearsay or direct statement by the authorities; the code of the classroom, which he learns in like manner; the example of the other pupils, to which by nature he may be more or less susceptible; the relation of the teacher to the pupils, whether friendly and coöperative or hostile; the personality, prestige, and statements of the examiner and the extent to which he allows opportunity to use deceptive methods; and the particular stimulus of the test itself, which, as we have seen, makes considerable difference in the nature of the deceptive act. Whether or not a child deceives on a test depends, then, upon the way in which these various factors are combined in his particular case. Some children do not take advantage of the opportunity to cheat under ordinary school motives. Presumably these are cases in which the standards brought to school or achieved in school are against dishonest practices and in which also there is the ability to adhere to such standards in the face of temptation. Under ordinary conditions these constitute a group by themselves, but there is no apparent reason for supposing that they would continue to constitute such a group if the incentives to deceive were raised. But as was shown in the previous chapter, with the incentives left as they are those who do yield to the temptation to deceive differ among themselves in the amount that they deceive, much as they differ in any other physical or social fact which is caused by a great variety of unrelated factors.

Those who yield to the opportunity to deceive do not do so in any wholesale way, however, but in a rather specialized way according to the particular situation in which they are placed. Just what the factors are in any situation which tempt one child to cheat but leave another untouched it is very difficult to say. We have drawn attention in our preceding chapters to various aspects of the situation that are associated with deception, such as the fact of being over-age and at the same time dull, or the fact of belonging to a racial or national group that occupies a socially inferior position in the community, or the fact of being in a class with a friendly and coöperative atmosphere or whose pupils have developed a group morale that does not favor deception. Once cheating is admitted as a possibility, however, none of these things seems to be as significant as the actual test situation itself in determining differences among the children, for none of the correlations we secure with any of these factors equals, for the individual, the self-correlations of the tests. That is, if a child tends to use an answer sheet at all, he tends to use it again when this kind of opportunity comes around, the reason for doing so being presumably his feeling that he has to in order to get a good mark, and that there is nothing to prevent it. But when this same child is placed in another situation, which requires for deception that he cheat a classmate rather than his teacher, or that he add on answers instead of copying them from a key, or that he take money out of a puzzle box, the fact that he copied answers from the key has almost no bearing on the question of his honesty in these other situations. He may cheat with the key and be honest in all the rest. In other words, his deception is as much a function of the particular situation in which he is placed as it is of his own inner experience and training, his general ideas and ideals, his fears, ambitions, and purposes. All these operate not in general but in relation to specific situations which, as far as their power to stimulate deception goes, must be interpreted in terms of their relation to the abilities of the individual and his comprehension of their significance both to his ambition and his standards.

As long as there is conflict between the teacher and the school authorities generally on the one side, and the pupils on the other, there will be deception. Some pupils, because of the out-of-school environment in which they live or because for some reason they do not feel the conflict, will not deceive. Others will be afraid to. Others will have too little ambition to take the trouble to cheat. Others, although responsive to the ideal of honor, will be unable to resist temptations to cheat particularly when urged to do better work than their ability warrants. If there is anything in school procedure which puts a premium on subterfuge, it would be folly to imagine that any teaching of honesty, whether in school or out, would greatly alter the actual practice of the children. Hand in hand with the development of codes must go the types of experience in which honor is the natural and rewarded behavior, to be learned by practice in those situations where the child finds himself ethically at home.   Only when thus learned, is it to be expected that, as his experience enlarges to include areas of life which have not yet been brought under the dominance of ethical ideals, the child will possess the insight and self-mastery to challenge an imperfect world with a high ideal.

# CHAPTER XXIII

# PROBLEMS AND CONCLUSIONS

From the outset we have insisted that these studies in deceit are of necessity fragmentary and incomplete, for the number of situations in which deception may be practiced and the number of ways of deceiving others are truly legion. A correct scientific procedure would be to collect from actual life a large number of such situations, tabulate them, note the frequency of their occurrence, and then build test situations around the most frequent. In this manner are vocabulary tests and spelling tests made. But the case of conduct is not so simple as that of vocabulary or spelling. A word is a word and is always the same, but no recurring situation is ever an exact duplicate of its former occurrence. The best that could be done, then, would be to judge by external appearances and classify situations according to their major features. But even this would be an enormous undertaking.

Another approach to the problem may be made by analyzing deceptive situations, and this procedure we shall illustrate. In the following study we have assumed that all deceptive situations have in common certain elements. These elements we have classified under five headings and then further analyzed each group.

## PRELIMINARY ANALYSIS OF DECEPTION

A complete act of deception involves at least the following factors: (1) the person, persons, or institution deceived, (2) the motive for doing it, (3) the thing about which the deceiver deceives, (4) the way in which it is done, (5) the consequences to the deceiver, the deceived, and others.

I. Persons or institutions deceived
   A. Persons to whom the deceiver is or pretends to be loyal, such as members of the immediate family and friends
   B. Institutions or organizations to which the deceiver is or pretends to be loyal, such as his church (if he is a member), his school, his clubs, his teams
   C. Persons to whom the deceiver owes no special allegiance, such as acquaintances, strangers, merchants, plumbers
   D. Institutions or organizations to which he owes no special allegiance, such as the railroad company, the gas company
   E. Enemies of the deceiver
II. General motives for deceiving
The number of specific motives for deception is very great, and no detailed analysis is here attempted, but most of them may be classified as follows:
   A. The desire to do positive harm to the deceived and cause suffering and hardships (Motive: *e.g.*, revenge)
   B. The desire to cause inconvenience or embarrassment or perhaps dishonor to the deceived (Motive: *e.g.*, jealousy or envy)
   C. The desire to gain something in the way of money, objects, property, or advantage, prestige, applause, approval, etc. (Motive: *e.g.*, aggressive greed)
   D. The desire to protect or defend oneself against reproof, embarrassment, physical pain, punishment, dishonor, loss of property, etc. (Motive: defense tendencies)
   E. The desire to compensate oneself for some loss or some handicap (Motive: compensatory tendencies)
   F. The desire to promote or defend the interests and welfare of a person or persons to whom the deceiver owes allegiance (A of section I above) (Motive: loyalty to friends)
   G. The desire to promote or defend the welfare and interests of B of section I above (Motive: loyalty to a cause)

H. The desire to promote or defend the welfare and happiness of C of section I above (Motive: social justice)

I. The desire to promote or defend the welfare of D of section I above (Motive: community welfare)

J. The desire to promote or defend the welfare of E of section I above (Motive: coöperative respect)

III. The things about which the deceiver deceives

A. Social values, such as the importance of events

B. Economic values, the worth of goods

C. Acts of conduct, his own or others'

D. Motives for conduct, his own or others'

E. Inventions

F. Knowledge or information, possessed by himself or others

G. Skills and abilities

H. Physical events, such as storms, or facts of time and place

I. Beliefs, his own or others'

J. Feelings, his own or others'

IV. How the deception is accomplished

A. By giving the deceived actual false information either oral or written but communicated by language, such things as fabrications, invention of stories, reporting events that never happened

B. By distorting true information so that the deceived will be misled as to conclusions. This is done by overstatements, exaggerations, etc. or by understatements or by otherwise twisting the truth.

C. By concealing information, by silence, evasions, denials, etc.

D. By *acting* in such a way as to mislead the deceived concerning the true intentions, motives, beliefs, or feelings of the deceiver or others

E. By supplying the deceived with inadequate sensory data, so that a total situation will appear different from what it really is. Sleight-of-hand tricks, fake advertisements, etc. are illustrations.

V. Possible undesirable consequences to the deceiver, if caught,
   or to the deceived or others
   A. Severe punishment or suffering
   B. Imprisonment and deprivations
   C. Loss of all social standing, social ostracism
   D. Loss of membership in some organization
   E. Loss of friends
   F. Loss of confidence of others
   G. Loss of property, fines
   H. Severe reprimand
   I. Mild rebuke or reproval
   J. Temporary embarrassment

Some notion of the number of possible situations involving deception may be had by merely figuring the permutations and combinations of the items in this outline. If persons or institutions deceived are kept in five classes, and motives in ten, and things about which deception takes place in ten, etc., and if each situation is composed of five elements, one from each general heading, there are 25,000 possible combinations. As a matter of fact, the different kinds of persons or institutions deceived are more than five, the motives many more than ten, and so on for the other elements, so that the total number of situations will run into the millions. But there are probably no more than a thousand that are frequent enough to justify inclusion in a test.

In Chapter III it is pointed out that we selected our test situations more with reference to convenience than to frequency, but tried to choose those which are important in child life. They do not nearly cover, therefore, the field charted in the outline given. The persons intended to be deceived by those who cheat in our test situations are usually the teacher, the examiner, the classmate or fellow contestant, and probably the parents or friends. The general motives,* as far as we have detected them, are for the most part the desire to do well and to compensate for the difficulty of the test. The things deceived about are mainly abilities or

* See Chapter XXII.

skills, and the deception usually takes place by distorting true information so that facts will appear to be different from what they really are.

In Chapter V we predicted how many more situations similar to those we have would be needed to measure deception adequately in certain typical situations. These predictions were made on the assumption that the average intercorrelations among all situations would remain the same as among those measured. In other words, the number of tests required depends on the extent to which the situations measured are random samples of the total number. Of course they were not intended as random samples, although they might turn out to be so. Most of them are school situations. Even the parties, in one population, were given at school. The home test is the only strictly non-school situation in the list, and even here the work done at home is for school credit.

To complete the picture, more situations are needed that center about the home, the store, the playground, or the club. The persons intended to be deceived should be parents, brothers or sisters, the merchant, the gas company, the employer, the club, and the like. The motive should be controlled as far as possible to include certain altruistic motives listed as F to J in the outline presented. The situations should be so arranged that the deceiver deceives about such things as economic values, his own motives, intentions, feelings or beliefs, or his own conduct. Such situations are easy enough to arrange but difficult to administer in actual tests. Children are available in groups mainly in school, and this is the reason why most of our tests are school situations. It would be necessary to do a great deal of individual testing before the whole range of deceptive conduct could be adequately sampled, and individual testing of this sort is slow and expensive. The first major problem, therefore, for a complete study of deceit is that of adequately sampling life situations in which deceit is practiced.

Another major problem ahead is to determine the significance of deceit in the total complex of character. This necessitates some measure or estimate of character as a whole, which would enable us to correlate with it either the total deception score or parts of it.

It may be, for instance, that some types of deception are more frequently associated with less developed character than others or than a total deception score. But satisfactory measures or estimates of character are not at present available and so we have not so far been able to undertake this important inquiry. Indeed, one of the aims of the research, of which this volume reports only one phase, is to build a series of tests that will " measure " character. Until such a " character test " is made by someone, the relation of deceptive tendencies to character as a whole must remain a matter of speculation rather than of empirical investigation.

## GENERAL CONCLUSIONS FROM THE STUDIES IN DECEIT

### A. RESULTS OF PRIMARY STUDIES

The primary studies are concerned with devising tests and techniques for measuring deceptive behavior. The general procedure has been to place the child in a situation in which deceit may be practiced and record his conduct. Three types of deceptive conduct have been tested : cheating, lying, and stealing. The situations in which deceit has been measured are : (1) certain classroom situations in which the pupils may or may not cheat on a test, examination, or class exercise, (2) certain situations in connection with athletic contests in which the contestants may or may not deceive concerning their achievements, (3) certain situations arising in party games in which contestants may or may not cheat, (4) a situation involving school work done at home. Lying has been tested (1) by asking the child whether he did or did not cheat in some of the above tests, (2) by asking questions about those items of conduct which are generally approved but which are not often practiced. Stealing has been tested by placing the subject in a situation (1) in which there is an opportunity to take money and (2) in which there is an opportunity to take small articles.

The whole battery of deception tests contains 22 opportunities to cheat in classroom work, 4 opportunities in athletic contests, 2 in party games, and 1 in school work done at home. The lying tests consist of 36 questions in one case and 10 in the other which may be answered falsely; and the stealing tests offer 2 chances to steal money and 1 to steal small articles.

Granted that these situations, as we have shown, are not an adequate sampling of the whole range of possibilities, since we specifically limited our research to certain types of situations; yet, as far as they go, they are reliable and valid. That is, we do not claim to have measured deception in general but only in the types of situations studied.

## B. RESULTS OF SECONDARY STUDIES

Some eleven thousand children of ages 8 to 16 have been subjected to parts (and in a few cases to nearly all) of our test situations. The results have been related to the following factors: age, sex, intelligence, physical and emotional condition, socioeconomic level of the home, the cultural level of the home, the race, nationality, and religion of parents, school grade, attendance, achievement, retardation, deportment, association with friends and classmates, sociability, suggestibility, attendance at motion pictures, progressive *versus* conventional school methods, teacher influence, school and class morale, membership in clubs or organizations purporting to develop character, Sunday-school attendance, and certain efforts to teach or affect honesty. The more outstanding results of the studies follow.

**1. The Relation of Deceit to Age.** The older pupils in any given school group are slightly more deceptive than the younger children. The differences vary with the test situation and the group tested.

**2. Sex Differences.** Sex seems to make no difference. On some tests and in some groups, the boys are more deceptive; on other tests and in other groups the girls are more deceptive. In the home situation the girls usually cheat more than the boys, but the cause is presumably a difference in interest rather than in honor.

**3. Relation of Deception to Intelligence.** Honesty is positively related to intelligence. In almost any group of children of approximately the same age, those of higher levels of intelligence deceive definitely less than those of lower levels. The child who scores above the average for his age in intelligence will, other things being equal, score below the average for his age in deception.

**4. Emotional Instability.** Children who show symptoms of emotional instability or maladjustment (as measured by one standard test) are more likely to deceive than those with fewer such symptoms.

**5. Physical Condition.** This, as measured by our tests, is unassociated with deceit even in athletic contests.

**6. Socio-economic Background.** Deceit is definitely associated with the economic level of the home. Children whose fathers are engaged in occupations yielding the higher incomes are less deceptive than children of day laborers. When the occupations of fathers are classified in four levels, the children from the higher levels deceive the least, those from the second higher next, and so on to those of the lowest level, who cheat the most. When more detailed studies of the economic and social conditions of the home are made, the results show again that children from the higher socio-economic levels deceive less than children from lower socio-economic levels.

**7. Cultural Background.** Children who have better manners, who are better acquainted with art and music and the influences that indicate culture and refinement, and whose parents treat them decently are less deceptive than others who do not show these refinements.

**8. Other Home Conditions.\*** Deceit is associated with such factors as parental discord, parental example, bad discipline, unsocial attitude toward the children, impoverished type of community, and changing social or economic situation; and certain combinations of these " handicaps " with personal handicaps tend to distinguish the group of most dishonest from the group of most honest children.

**9. Nationality of Parents.** Children of parents who were born in North Europe or America are less deceptive in classroom cheat-

* Based on our study of 150 homes in one community.

ing situations than children of parents born in South Europe. Colored children cheat more than most of the white groups. Certain racial and national differences persist even when allowance is made for differences in intelligence and socio-economic level.

**10. Religious Affiliations.** Between children reporting affiliation with the three main religious groups, Catholics, Jews, and Protestants, and between various Protestant groups, there are no *general* differences which are not attributable to differences in intelligence and social level; but on certain tests the particular groups measured show real differences not thus entirely accounted for.

**11. Kinship.** Deception runs in families to about the same extent as eye color, length of forearm, and other inherited structures. This does not prove that it is inherited. But the general drift of the evidence inclines one to believe that, if all children received identical nurture, they would still vary in deception.

**12. Grade.** In most tests there are no grade differences. In the IER school tests, there is a steady increase in deception from grades six to eight, but grade five is the most deceptive.

**13. Grade Retardation.** Children who are over-age for their grade tend to cheat more than those who are under the average age for their grade. The more intelligent in the grade or in the class group cheat less, and the less intelligent cheat more. It is probably not the fact of being over-age for one's grade that matters, but of being both older and also less intelligent.

**14. School Achievement.** Those who get high marks cheat slightly less than those who get low marks; but where their achievement is stated in terms of their mental age, there is no evidence of any relation between their academic status and their tendency to deceive.

**15. Deportment.** Deportment marks vary with the school and teacher, but on the whole high deportment marks are associated with less cheating in school and low marks with more cheating in school. Pupils who receive A in deportment cheat definitely less than those who receive C.

**16. Associates.** There is considerable resemblance in amount of cheating between classmates. That is, a pupil's cheating score on certain of the classroom tests is very much like that of his associates. There is a slight resemblance between friends even when they are not in the same class.

**17. Suggestibility.** Greater resistance to the sort of suggestion found in the Otis suggestibility tests is associated with less cheating.

**18. Movie Attendance.** Children who attend the movies more than once a week tend to cheat slightly more than children who attend occasionally but less than once a week.

**19. Teacher Influence.** The general relations that exist between the teacher and the class influence cheating. On the whole, there is less cheating when these relations are free and cordial and there is a spirit of good will and coöperation.

**20. Progressive Method and Morale.** The progressive schools tested do not cheat as much as most of the conventional schools tested. This seems to be due to the factor of school or classroom morale, for which the teacher is largely responsible but which also characterizes the whole school or class group from year to year.

**21. Sunday-School Enrollment and Attendance.** Those enrolled in Protestant Sunday schools cheat less than those not enrolled. There is no relation, however, between Sunday-school attendance and deception. Children who attend regularly cheat in day school about the same as those who rarely or never attend.

**22. Membership in Organizations Purporting to Teach Honesty.\*** Children who belong to certain organizations purporting to teach honesty deceive about the same as (and in one case more than) children who do not belong. Furthermore, in one organization length of membership and rank achieved were positively correlated with deceptiveness.

**23. Deceit Not a Unified Trait.** The results of these studies show that neither deceit nor its opposite, "honesty," are unified character traits, but rather specific functions of life situations. Most children will deceive in certain situations and not in others. Lying, cheating, and stealing as measured by the test situations used in these studies are only very loosely related. Even cheating in the classroom is rather highly specific, for a child may cheat on

---

\* Based on our study of systems X and Y.

an arithmetic test and not on a spelling test, etc. Whether a child will practice deceit in any given situation depends in part on his intelligence, age, home background, and the like and in part on the nature of the situation itself and his particular relation to it.

**24. The Motivation of Deceit.** The motives for cheating, lying, or stealing are complex and inhere for the most part in the general situations themselves. The most common motive for cheating on classroom exercises is the desire to do well.

**Summary.** The concomitants of deceit are, in order of their importance, (1) classroom association; (2) general personal handicaps, such as relatively low IQ, poor resistance to suggestion, and emotional instability; (3) cultural and social limitations in the home background; and (4) such other miscellaneous facts as are loosely correlated with deception.

## IMPLICATIONS

Any implications for moral education that arise from these studies of deceptive tendencies are obviously tentative and incomplete. We have not reported the relation of this type of social failure to its opposite, coöperative helpfulness, nor to the intellectual habits, the ideas, and information which are involved in any response that can be regarded as having moral significance. No conclusive experiments have yet been undertaken by which education in the particular forms of behavior under discussion, much less in character as a whole, has been successfully demonstrated.

Nevertheless, there are a few results that have a direct bearing on the evaluation of current practices and which are suggestive for the setting up of controlled experiments for the further study of problems of character growth. We shall state our interpretation of these results in the form of propositions.

1. No one is honest or dishonest by " nature." Where conflict arises between a child and his environment, deception is a natural mode of adjustment, having in itself no " moral " significance. If indirect ways of gaining his ends are successful, they will be continued unless definite training is undertaken through which direct and honest methods may also become successful.

2. Apart from the actual practice of direct or honest methods of gaining ends where a conflict of wills is actually involved, the mere urging of honest behavior by teachers or the discussion of standards and ideals of honesty, no matter how much such general ideas may be " emotionalized," has no necessary relation to the control of conduct. The extent to which individuals may be affected, either for better or for worse, is not known, but there seems to be evidence that such effects as may result are not generally good and are sometimes unwholesome.

3. This does not imply that the teaching of general ideas, standards, and ideals is not desirable and necessary, but only that the prevailing ways of inculcating ideals probably do little good and may do some harm.

4. The large place occupied by the " situation" in the suggestion and control of conduct, not only in its larger aspects, such as the example of other pupils, the personality of the teacher, etc., but also in its more subtle aspects, such as the nature of the opportunity to deceive, the kind of material or test on which it is possible, the relation of the child to this material, and so on, points to the need of a careful educational analysis of all such situations for the purpose of making explicit the nature of the direct or honest mode of response *in detail*, so that when a child is placed in these situations there may be a genuine opportunity for him to practice direct methods of adjustment.

5. Along with such practice of direct or honest responses there should go a careful study of them in terms of the personal relations involved, so that in the child's imagination the honest mode of procedure may be clearly distinguished from the dishonest mode as a way of *social* interaction, and the consequences of either method may be observed and used in evaluating the relative desirability of direct *versus* indirect procedures. Such analyses would provide the foundation for the understanding of social ideals and laws and the basis for an intelligent allegiance to such ideals as proved consonant with social welfare.

6. The association of deceit with sundry handicaps in social background, home condition, companions, personal limitations,

and so on indicates the need for *understanding* particular examples of dishonest practice before undertaking to " judge " the blameworthiness of the individual.   As far as possible, such social and personal limitations should be removed, not only for the sake of getting more honest behavior, but for the sake of the child's whole development.   But obviously the widespread practice of deceit makes the application of radical environmental changes an absurdity.   There is no evidence for supposing that children who are more likely to resort to deceptive methods than others would not use honorable methods with equal satisfaction if the situation in which dishonesty is practiced were sufficiently controlled by those who are responsible for their behavior.   That is, the main attention of educators should be placed not so much on devices for teaching honesty or any other " trait " as on the reconstruction of school practices in such a way as to provide not occasional but consistent and regular opportunities for the successful use by both teachers and pupils of such forms of conduct as make for the common good.

# $C$lassics In
# $C$hild $D$evelopment

*An Arno Press Collection*

Baldwin, James Mark. **Thought and Things.** Four vols. in two. 1906-1915

Blatz, W[illiam] E[met], et al. **Collected Studies on the Dionne Quintuplets.** 1937

Bühler, Charlotte. **The First Year of Life.** 1930

Bühler, Karl. **The Mental Development of the Child.** 1930

Claparède, Ed[ouard]. **Experimental Pedagogy and the Psychology of the Child.** 1911

**Factors Determining Intellectual Attainment.** 1975

**First Notes by Observant Parents.** 1975

Freud, Anna. **Introduction to the Technic of Child Analysis.** 1928

Gesell, Arnold, et al. **Biographies of Child Development.** 1939

Goodenough, Florence L. **Measurement of Intelligence By Drawings.** 1926

Griffiths, Ruth. **A Study of Imagination in Early Childhood and Its Function in Mental Development.** 1918

Hall, G. Stanley and Some of His Pupils. **Aspects of Child Life and Education.** 1907

Hartshorne, Hugh and Mark May. **Studies in the Nature of Character. Vol. I: Studies in Deceit; Book One, General Methods and Results.** 1928

Hogan, Louise E. **A Study of a Child.** 1898

Hollingworth, Leta S. **Children Above 180 IQ, Stanford Binet:** Origins and Development. 1942

Kluver, Heinrich. **An Experimental Study of the Eidetic Type.** 1926

Lamson, Mary Swift. **Life and Education of Laura Dewey Bridgman, the Deaf, Dumb and Blind Girl.** 1881

Lewis, M[orris] M[ichael]. **Infant Speech:** A Study of the Beginnings of Language. 1936

McGraw, Myrtle B. **Growth: A Study of Johnny and Jimmy.** 1935

**Monographs on Infancy.** 1975

O'Shea, M. V., editor. **The Child: His Nature and His Needs.** 1925

Perez, Bernard. **The First Three Years of Childhood.** 1888

Romanes, George John. **Mental Evolution in Man:** Origin of Human Faculty. 1889

Shinn, Milicent Washburn. **The Biography of a Baby.** 1900

Stern, William. **Psychology of Early Childhood Up to the Sixth Year of Age.** 1924

**Studies of Play.** 1975

Terman, Lewis M. **Genius and Stupidity:** A Study of Some of the Intellectual Processes of Seven "Bright" and Seven "Stupid" Boys. 1906

Terman, Lewis M. **The Measurement of Intelligence.** 1916

Thorndike, Edward Lee. **Notes on Child Study.** 1901

Wilson, Louis N., compiler. **Bibliography of Child Study.** 1898-1912

[Witte, Karl Heinrich Gottfried]. **The Education of Karl Witte,** Or the Training of the Child. 1914